# BEYOND PATRIARCHY

## ESSAYS BY MEN ON PLEASURE, POWER, AND CHANGE

Edited by MICHAEL KAUFMAN

Toronto   New York
OXFORD UNIVERSITY PRESS

Oxford University Press
70 Wynford Drive, Don Mills, Ontario M3C 1J9

Toronto   Oxford   New York
Delhi   Bombay   Calcutta   Madras   Karachi
Petaling Jaya   Singapore   Hong Kong   Tokyo
Nairobi   Dar es Salaam   Cape Town
Melbourne   Auckland

and associated companies in
Berlin   Ibadan

CANADIAN CATALOGUING IN PUBLICATION DATA
Main entry under title:
Beyond patriarchy

Bibliography: p.
Includes index.
ISBN 0-19-540534-X

1. Men. 2. Masculinity (Psychology). 3. Patriarchy.
4. Power (Social sciences).    I. Kaufman, Michael,
1951-

HQ1090.B49 1987      305.3'1      C87-093543-7

*To our fathers, brothers, and sons*

# Contents

## II. MEN, WORK, AND CULTURAL LIFE

# Acknowledgments

T. Carrigan, B. Connell, and J. Lee. 'Hard and Heavy: Toward a New Sociology of Masculinity' from *Theory and Society* (14) September 1985, Elsevier, Amsterdam, by permission of Martinus Nijhoff Publishers, Dordrecht, The Netherlands.

Stan Gray. An earlier version of 'Sharing the Shop Floor' appeared in *Canadian Dimension,* vol. 18, no. 3 (June 1984). Reprinted by permission.

Seymour Kleinberg. 'The New Masculinity of Gay Men, and Beyond' from *Alienated Affections* by Seymour Kleinberg, copyright © 1980 by Seymour Kleinberg, reprinted by permission of St. Martin's Press, Inc., New York. 'Life After Death' reprinted by permission of *The New Republic* © 1986, The New Republic, Inc.

E. Anthony Rotundo. 'Patriarchs and Participants: A Historical Perspective on Fatherhood'. An earlier version of this article appeared under the title 'American Fatherhood' from *American Behavioral Scientist,* Vol. 29, No. 1 (Sept/Oct. 1985). Reprinted by permission of Sage Publications, Inc.

Robin Wood. 'Raging Bull: The Homosexual Subtext in Film' is extracted from *Hollywood from Vietnam to Reagan.* Copyright © 1986 Columbia University Press. Reprinted by permission.

# Preface

Many people have contributed to this book, but the biggest debt is to the intellectual and political climate generated by the modern feminist movement. Feminism has redrawn the boundaries of critical inquiry and everyday life. As men we have been challenged to rethink our lives, our relationships, and our assumptions about the world. This book is a response to that challenge and an attempt by various men, sympathetic to feminism, to add our own voices to this process of inquiry and reflection.

It is a pleasure to recall the help of many people in the development of this book. A number of people participated in a day-long workshop several years ago to discuss drafts of various articles; others participated in smaller discussions or provided comments, suggestions, and support. These friends and colleagues include, in addition to those who made comments to the individual authors, Jonathan Barker, Wally Brant, Howard Buchbinder, Bembo Davies, Sue Findlay, Debbie Field, Richard Fung, Bob Gallagher, Mac Girvan, Cecilia Green, Ron Labonte, Ian Lumsden, Meg Luxton, Ned Lyttleton, Donald MacPherson, Heather Jon Maroney, Earl Miller, Eric Mills, Leon Muszynski, Mary O'Brien, David Rayside, Maureen Simpkins, Dorothy Smith, Michael Smith, Sandy Steinecker, Ken Theobault, Mariana Valverde, Peter Warrian, Shelagh Wilkinson, and Alex Wilson. A critical source of support, ideas, and insight were the participants in various men's groups, men's conferences, and university classes.

Richard Teleky, Managing Editor of Oxford Canada, provided valuable guidance and direction, Phyllis Wilson assisted in the editorial process, and Freya Godard did an outstanding job editing the manuscript.

# Introduction

Halfway through the movie *Casablanca* a distressed Ingrid Bergman asks Humphrey Bogart about the character of the lecherous police chief from whom she must obtain emigration papers: "What kind of man is Captain Renault?" Bogart replies with his characteristic blend of cynicism and compassion: "Just like any other man, only more so."

It is a surprising line for a movie from the 1940s. Although it seems to suggest a natural order of things, the action of the movie and in particular the sympathetic evolution of Bogart's character, speak to a different reality. That reality is of men who attempt to balance—at tremendous cost to women, children, the world, and themselves—individual and social structures of domination and control with the personal tug of human needs and compassion. As we know, in all societies since tribal and communal ones, the social regimes of gender, class, and other forms of domination have won out over individual men's compassion. Indeed men have consciously and unconsciously perpetuated the structures of men's power.

Understanding these structures of power is, to say the least, complex and challenging. The difficulty is to understand the constantly changing patterns of domination and to grasp the interplay between oppression at the individual level and the grand social, political, economic, and ideological structures based on hierarchy and privilege. The difficulty is compounded because we take into our personalities—we internalize—the social structures of oppression and power. This internalization not only affects our vision of reality, but in a sense it *is* our vision of reality. Each of us is part of the world we are seeking to comprehend; our understanding is not detached and neutral. To put it simply, we all have something to gain or lose by the conclusions we reach and the actions that follow. At first glance this would seem to be a matter only of women gaining and men losing, but the challenge of feminism speaks to us all in complex ways. One of the common themes of the articles in this book is that while men have something to lose in the feminist challenge to our relative power and privileges, we also have much to gain. To give up something might mean to gain much more. In that spirit we can imagine a different ending to *Casablanca:* not the sentimental ending with another job done, another situation under control, a sad parting, and the need for

Bogart to lie low for a while before fighting the next good fight, but with him stepping into the plane and flying off into a world of promise yet uncertainty.

The problem for men is not merely the fear of an uncertain future in a nonsexist, nonpatriarchal world—after all, one of the traits we value so highly is courage. The problem is that our current world of certainties reaffirms our self-definition of what it means to be a man. What makes feminism a threat for so many men, or at least a source of confusion and struggle, is not only that we have privileges to lose, but that it appears—or at least feels—as if our very manhood is at stake.

What is actually at stake, as is argued in this book, at times analytically and at times with passion, is not our biological manhood, our sex, but our historically specific, socially constructed, and personally embodied notions of masculinity. We confuse maleness (biological sex) with masculinity (gender) at our peril. But this confusion is not surprising since the difference is systematically obscured by culture, science, dominant beliefs, religion, and education, not to mention our own experiences, which are limited to societies dominated by men. Many of the articles in the book look at the institutions that perpetuate the ideology and the regimen of men's domination—the nuclear family, the organization of working life, our conceptions of science, the prohibitions on homosexuality, sports, advertising, films, and political structures.

The oppression of women is not simply a matter of the behavior of men and women. Centuries-old patriarchal orders will not be overturned by good public relations, boys playing with dolls, and women having access to bank directorships and military training. Domination by men is based on, and perpetuated by, a wide range of social structures, from the most intimate of sexual relations to the organization of economic and political life. A common theme of the articles in this book is that we must address the issues of power and domination at the level of society as a whole. But at the same time, because we carry these relations within ourselves, it is not really possible to separate the "personal" from the "social." This is one meaning of "the personal is political," a key theme of the women's liberation movement. This book addresses the relations of oppression and power at both levels and seeks to analyze the social meaning of the individual personalities and behavior of men and the social institutions upon which patriarchies, that is, societies dominated by men, are based. Although each article necessarily has a particular focus and often draws from a particular discipline, such as anthropology, psychology, history, the natural sciences, political science, or sociology, most articles tend to be interdisciplinary. Certainly the book forms an interdisciplinary whole, notwithstanding differences of emphasis and interpretation from author to author.

One common conclusion arising from this analysis is that the struggle to crack the structures of patriarchy is not secondary to other economic and political changes that will make the world a better place to live. Indeed, the very possibility of creating new social orders is predicated, at least in part, on challenging the oppression of women. This is because patriarchy forms part of the cement of societies based on the domination of some humans over others and of humans over nature—forms of social organization that have led to the coexistence of abundance and poverty, to the possibility of global nuclear destruction or ecological catastrophe, and to countless forms of oppression based on physical, national, religious, and sexual differences. Patriarchy is one of the bases of the current organization of the world's societies; its demise is a precondition for fundamental social, economic, and political change.

Cracking the structures of patriarchy includes in part cracking the individual armor that men acquire within these societies. The way in which individual men acquire this armor of masculinity is addressed by a number of the articles in this book. Along with many other men, each contributor is attempting to crack his own armor and challenge his oppressive relations with women and other men. In other words, the purpose of this book is not only intellectual but practical, for it relates to the daily lives and the political activities of the contributors. Needless to say, the title, *Beyond Patriarchy,* does not suggest that any of us is naive enough to think he has transcended sexism and the society in which he lives. It only suggests the need for analysis and understanding, and for activities at the personal and social levels that will enable men to make a strong contribution to the struggle against patriarchy.

And here we arrive at the central theme of the book. Much of the literature by men on male-female relations tends to be at one extreme or another: many look at how men are scarred and deformed by our roles but do not examine men's privileges and power over women. Furthermore, many such books and articles play down or ignore the social structures of men's power and the power relations among men, in particular the oppression of homosexual men and class and racial domination among men. At the other end of the spectrum is the approach that recognizes men's privileges and power, but does not acknowledge that men are also losers in this process. The general approach of this book is to combine a number of different elements:

an analysis of the oppression of women and of gay men, an analysis of the social structures of domination and the individual expression of these structures, and, finally, an appreciation of how men are scarred and brutalized by the very system that we perpetuate and that gives us our privileges and power.

The book is critical but hopeful. It not only condemns patriarchy and men's domination, but affirms and celebrates the constructive powers of men. While we are very critical of the overall shape of masculinity in today's societies, we want to affirm the many qualities associated with masculinity that are within every human being's range of possibilities: our sexual desire, our physical and emotional strength, our ability to operate under pressure, our courage, our creativity and intellect, our dedication to a task, self-sacrifice, and so on. Of course these abilities are often distorted (operating under pressure becomes workaholism) and exaggerated (maintaining an image of courage requires suppressing our fears), but this should not obscure their merits. Nor should we be fooled by the dominant definitions of manhood and ignore the care and attention that many men give to nurturing and love, although patriarchal societies devalue these roles and although so many of us clearly deemphasize them.

## THE AUTHORS AND THE ARTICLES

What is considered masculine differs from society to society, class to class, age to age, sexual orientation to sexual orientation, and so forth. This book is written by men from a variety of backgrounds. Although over half are living in Canada, three-quarters of the contributors grew up, were educated, or now live in the United States, England, or Australia. Also, several of us have lived in, or have devoted years of study, to other developed countries or to countries in the Third World. As might be expected in such a book, most contributors are academics, but we come from a range of class backgrounds as well as different ethnic and religious backgrounds. Some of us define ourselves as heterosexual, some as homosexual, some as bisexual; at least one stubbornly resists such terms altogether. Perhaps the greatest lack of diversity that should be acknowledged is that all of us are whites, although some of us have been subjected to extreme forms of religious, ethnic, sexual, or class oppression. Although the book is more analytical than experiential, many of our personal experiences are referred to or, where unspoken, inform the analysis of each article in terms of both strengths and possible blind spots.

The articles in the book cover a diverse and rich body of exploration and analysis.

Part One, "Masculinity, Sexuality, and Society," begins with my article on the individual construction of masculinity, that is, the manner in which patriarchy is developed and expressed within individual men and, more generally, within social structures. It extends this analysis by looking at the self-reinforcing triad of men's violence: against women, against other men, and against ourselves.

Anthropologists Richard Lee and Richard Daly enter the controversy on the origins of men's domination. They suggest that, although some tribal societies had elements of male privilege, only with the rise of state societies did patriarchy emerge as a coherent and dominant system.

Sociobiology is the latest of various theories that exaggerate the importance of physical differences and provide biological explanations of social differences. Carmen Schifellite not only challenges the conclusions of sociobiologists, but he questions the whole theoretical basis of biodeterminist arguments.

Tony Rotundo looks at the continuing evolution of the institution of fatherhood in the United States, concluding with some thoughts on the tentative emergence of new forms of fatherhood and the social changes that will be necessary to strengthen them.

Political scientists Gad Horowitz and I use a somewhat reconstructed interpretation of psychoanalytic theory to present a theory of male sexuality—that is, its individual development and expression within societies of male domination—and to examine the nature of sexual liberation. We apply this analysis to pornography and the objectification of women.

Gary Kinsman argues that although same-sex love is a universal possibility, homosexuality, along with heterosexuality, as such is a rather recent creation. He looks at the evolution of gay male identity and raises thought-provoking questions about the implications of gay liberation for all men.

Starting in the world of bathhouses and clubs, Seymour Kleinberg looks at the new masculinity of gay men, analyzing what is desirable and undesirable about the prevalent images of North American gay men from the mid-1970s. Jumping ahead a decade, he then looks at the constraints to gay male identity and expression resulting from the AIDS epidemic.

The final article of Part One is a comprehensive analysis of the literature of the 1970s by men on men and masculinity. This review by Tim Carrigan, Bob Connell, and John Lee sets a standard for rigorous yet constructive criticism of the "men's" literature. They conclude with suggestions about the future direction of analyses by and about men.

Part Two, "Men, Work, and Cultural Life," explores the world of men at work, in sports, films, science, literature, advertising, and political life. It begins with an article in which the physicist Brian Easlea studies the fascinating history of the evolution of the modern sciences, in particular the patriarchal assumptions and images intrinsic to nuclear physics. His article ranges from a look at some of the roots of nuclear madness to the prospects for a science integrated with the natural environment.

Stan Gray's article is based on his personal experiences while supporting the struggles of women at a Westinghouse plant. Unlike the articles by the many academic contributors, this is a view from the shop floor. His conclusion is a provocative exploration of the connections between the class oppression of male workers and their own oppressive behavior towards women.

Former Olympic runner Bruce Kidd traces the evolution of the modern activities and ideology of sport and, in doing so, demonstrates the links between sports and patriarchy. But just as these links are a product of history, so too is the possibility for a world of sports and physical play and excellence that steps beyond its current boundaries.

The film "Raging Bull," which portrays the life of the boxer Jake La Motta, provides film critic Robin Wood with a chance to explore what he terms the homosexual subtext in Hollywood movies and, indeed, in so much of our daily lives, and to explore the horrible consequences of repressing part of our sexuality.

Michael Kimmel studies what he calls the cult of masculinity in politics and society in the United States, from the cowboys to the Contras. His article offers clues to the interaction of patriarchy, individual personality, and state politics, and uses gender as a lens through which to view social and political events, in particular, U.S. foreign policy.

Through an analysis of the changing images of men in advertising, Andrew Wernick demonstrates the flexibility of the dominant conceptions and portrayals of masculinity. Not only is it an original look at one of the most manipulative institutions of our society, but it helps us realize the limitations to the changes in mainstream society since the rise of the women's liberation movement.

And finally, Peter Fitting looks at the images of men and women in the feminist utopian literature since the 1960s. In doing so he gives us an opportunity to explore a world freed of exploitation and oppression and to ask what such a world might look like for ourselves.

The book ends with a list of bibliographies on men and women, and notes on the contributors.

Michael Kaufman
Toronto

# PART I

# Masculinity, Sexuality, and Society

# The Construction of Masculinity and the Triad of Men's Violence

## MICHAEL KAUFMAN

The all too familiar story: a woman raped, a wife battered, a lover abused. With a sense of immediacy and anger, the women's liberation movement has pushed the many forms of men's violence against women—from the most overt to the most subtle in form—into popular consciousness and public debate. These forms of violence are one aspect of our society's domination by men that, in outcome, if not always in design, reinforce that domination. The act of violence is many things at once. At the same instant it is the individual man acting out relations of sexual power; it is the violence of a society—a hierarchical, authoritarian, sexist, class-divided, militarist, racist, impersonal, crazy society—being focused through an individual man onto an individual woman. In the psyche of the individual man it might be his denial of social powerlessness through an act of aggression. In total these acts of violence are like a ritualized acting out of our social relations of power: the dominant and the weaker, the powerful and the powerless, the active and the passive . . . the masculine and the feminine.

For men, listening to the experience of women as the objects of men's violence is to shatter any complacency about the sex-based status quo. The power and anger of women's responses force us to rethink the things we discovered when we were very young. When I was eleven or twelve years old a friend told me the difference between fucking and raping. It was simple: with rape you tied the woman to a tree. At the time the anatomical details were still a little vague, but in either case it was something "we" supposedly did. This knowledge was just one part of an education, started years before, about the relative power and privileges of men and women. I remember laughing when my friend explained all that to me. Now I shudder. The difference in my responses is partially that, at twelve, it was part of the posturing and pretense that accompanied my passage into adolescence. Now, of course, I have a different vantage point on the issue. It is the vantage point of an adult, but more importantly my view of the world is being reconstructed by the intervention of that majority whose voice has been suppressed: the women.

This relearning of the reality of men's violence against women evokes many deep feelings and memories for men. As memories are recalled and recast, a new connection becomes clear: violence by men against women is only one corner of a triad of men's violence. The other two corners are violence against other men and violence against oneself.

On a psychological level the pervasiveness of violence is the result of what Herbert Marcuse called the "surplus repression" of our sexual and emotional desires.[1] The substitution of violence for desire (more precisely, the transmutation of violence into a form of emotionally gratifying activity) happens unequally in men and women. The construction of masculinity involves the construction of "surplus aggressiveness." The social context of this triad of violence is the institutionalization of violence in the operation of most aspects of social, economic, and political life.

The three corners of the triad reinforce one another. The first corner—violence against women—cannot be confronted successfully without simultaneously challenging the other two corners of the triad. And all this requires a dismantling of the social feeding ground of violence: patriarchal, heterosexist, authoritarian, class societies. These three corners and the societies in which they blossom feed on each other. And together, we surmise, they will fall.

THE SOCIAL AND INDIVIDUAL NATURE OF VIOLENCE AND AGGRESSION

*Origins of Violence*

The most vexing question in the matter of men's violence is, of course, its biological roots. It would be very useful to know whether men in particular, or humans in general, are biologically (for example, genetically or hormonally) predisposed to acts of violence against other humans.

From the outset, feminism has been careful to draw a distinction between sex and gender. The strictly biological differences between the sexes form only the substrate for a society's construction of people with gender. Indeed, the appeal of feminism to many men, in addition to the desire to ally ourselves with the struggle of our sisters against oppression, has been to try to dissociate "male" from "masculine." While many of the characteristics associated with masculinity are valuable human traits—strength, daring, courage, rationality, intellect, sexual desire—the distortion of these traits in the masculine norm and the exclusion of other traits (associated with femininity) are oppressive and destructive. The process of stuffing oneself into the tight pants of masculinity is a difficult one for all men, even if it is not consciously experienced as such.

But the actual relation of sex and gender is problematic. For one thing, what might be called the "gender craft" of a society does its work on biological entities—entities whose ultimate source of pleasure and pain is their bodies.[2] What makes the relationship between sex and gender even more difficult to understand is that the production of gender is itself an incredibly complex and opaque process. As Michele Barrett and Mary McIntosh point out, although stereotypical roles do exist, each individual is not "the passive victim of a monolithically imposed system."[3]

In recent years there has been a major attempt to reclaim for biology the social behaviour of human beings. Sociobiology aims at nothing less than the reduction of human social interaction to our genetic inheritance. The study of apes, aardvarks, and tapeworms as a means of discerning the true nature of humans is almost surprising in its naivete, but at times it is socially dangerous in its conception and execution. As many critics have pointed out, it ignores what is unique about human beings: our construction of ever-changing social orders.[4]

Indeed, humans are animals—physical creatures subject to the requirements of genes, cells, organs, and hormones of every description. Yet we do not have a comprehensive understanding of how these things shape behavior and, even if we did, behavior is just a small, fragmented moment to be understood within the larger realm of human desire and motivation. Even if we did have a more comprehensive knowledge, what is important is that humans, unlike apes or even the glorious ant, live in constantly evolving and widely differing societies. Since the era when humans came into existence, our history has been a movement *away* from an unmediated, "natural," animal existence.

Even if we could ascertain that humans in general, or men in particular, are predisposed to building neutron bombs, this does not help us answer the much more important question of how each society shapes, limits, or accentuates this tendency. To take only the question of violence, why, as societies develop, does violence seem to move from something isolated and often ritualistic in its expression to a pervasive feature of everyday life? And why are some forms of physical violence so widely accepted (corporal punishment of children, for example) while others are not (such as physical attacks on pharoahs, presidents, and pontiffs)?

That much said let us also say this: there is no psychological, biological, or social evidence to suggest that humans are *not* predisposed to aggression and even violence. On the other hand, a predisposition to cooperation and peacefulness is also entirely possible. It is even possible that men—for reasons of hormones—are biologically more aggressive and prone to violence than women. We do not know the answer for the simple reason that the men we examine do not exist outside societies.[5]

But in any case, the important question is what societies do with the violence. What forms of violence are socially sanctioned or socially tolerated? What forms of violence seem built into the very structure of our societies? The process of human social development has been one of restraining, repressing, forming, informing, channeling, and transforming various biological tendencies. Could it not be that this process of repression has been a very selective one? Perhaps the repression of certain impulses and the denial of certain needs aggravate other impulses. I think of the man who feels he has no human connections in his life and who goes out and rapes a woman.

In spite of a general feminist rejection of sociobiology, this pseudo-science receives a strange form of support among some feminists. In her book, *Against Our Will. Men, Women and Rape,* Susan Brownmiller argues, not only that violent, male aggression is psychologically innate, but that it is grounded in male anatomy. And conversely, the view of female sexuality appears to be one of victimization and powerlessness. She argues, "By anatomical fiat—the inescapable construction of their genital organs—the human male was a natural predator and the human female served as his natural prey."[6] Alice Echols suggests that many cultural feminists also tend to repeat many traditional, stereotypical images of men and women.[7]

The essential question for us is not whether men are predisposed to violence, but what society does with this violence. Why has the linchpin of so many societies been the manifold expression of violence perpetrated disproportionately by men? Why are so many forms of violence sanctioned or even encouraged? Exactly what is the nature of violence? And how are patterns of violence and the quest for domination built up and reinforced?

## The Social Context

For every apparently individual act of violence there is a social context. This is not to say there are no pathological acts of violence, but even in that case the "language" of the violent act, the way the violence manifests itself, can only be understood within a certain social experience. We are interested here in the manifestations of violence that are accepted as more or less normal, even if reprehensible: fighting, war, rape, assault, psychological abuse, and so forth. What is the context of men's violence in the prevalent social orders of today?

Violence has long been institutionalized as an acceptable means of solving conflicts. But now the vast apparati of policing and war making maintained by countries the world over pose a threat to the future of life itself.

"Civilized" societies have been built and shaped through the decimation, containment, and exploitation of other peoples: extermination of native populations, colonialism, and slavery. "I am talking," writes Aimé Césaire, "about societies drained of their essence, cultures trampled underfoot, institutions undermined, lands confiscated, religions smashed, magnificent artistic creations destroyed, extraordinary possibilities wiped out. . . . I am talking about millions . . . sacrificed."[8]

Our relationship with the natural environment has often been described with the metaphor of rape. An attitude of conquering nature, of mastering an environment waiting to be exploited for profit, has great consequences when we possess a technology capable of permanently disrupting an ecological balance shaped over hundreds of millions of years.

The daily work life of industrial, class societies is one of violence. Violence poses as economic rationality as some of us are turned into extensions of machines, while others become brains detached from bodies. Our industrial process becomes the modern-day rack of torture where we are stretched out of shape and ripped limb from limb. It is violence that exposes workers to the danger of chemicals, radiation, machinery, speedup, and muscle strain. It is violence that condemns the majority to work to exhaustion for forty or fifty years and then to be thrown into society's garbage bin for the old and used-up.

The racism, sexism, and heterosexism that have been institutionalized in our societies are socially regulated acts of violence.

Our cities themselves are a violation, not only of nature, but of human community and the human relationship with nature. As the architect Frank Lloyd Wright said, "To look at the plan of a great City is to look at something like the cross-section of a fibrous tumor."[9]

Our cities, our social structure, our work life, our relation with nature, our history, are more than a backdrop to the prevalence of violence. They are violence; violence in an institutionalized form encoded into physical structures and socioeconomic relations. Much of the sociological analysis of violence in our societies implies simply that violence is learned by witnessing and experiencing social violence: man kicks boy, boy kicks dog.[10] Such experiences of transmitted violence are a reality, as the analysis of wife battering indicates, for many batterers were themselves abused as children. But more essential is that our personalities and sexuality, our needs and fears, our strengths and weaknesses, our selves are created—not simply learned—through our lived reality. The violence of our social order nurtures a psychology of violence, which in turn reinforces the social, economic and political structures of violence. The ever-increasing demands of civilization and the constant building upon inherited structures of violence suggest that the development of civilization has been inseparable from a continuous increase in violence against humans and our natural environment.

It would be easy, yet ultimately not very useful, to slip into a use of the term "violence" as a metaphor for all our society's antagonisms, contradictions, and ills. For now, let us leave aside the social terrain and begin to unravel the nature of so-called individual violence.

THE TRIAD OF MEN'S VIOLENCE

> *The longevity of the oppression of women must be based on something more than conspiracy, something more complicated than biological handicap and more durable than economic exploitation (although in differing degrees all these may feature.)*
>
> *Juliet Mitchell[11]*

> *It seems impossible to believe that mere greed could hold men to such a steadfastness of purpose.*
>
> *Joseph Conrad[12]*

The field in which the triad of men's violence is situated is a society, or societies, grounded in structures of domination and control. Although at times this control is symbolized and embodied in the individual father—patriarchy, by definition—it is more important to emphasize that patriarchal structures of authority, domination, and control are diffused throughout social, economic, political, and ideological activities and in our relations to the natural environment. Perhaps more than in any previous time during the long epoch of patriarchy, authority does *not* rest with the father, at least in much of the advanced capitalist and noncapitalist world. This has led more than one author to question the applicability of the term patriarchy.[13] But I think it still remains useful as a broad, descriptive category. In this sense Jessica Benjamin speaks of the current reign of patriarchy without the father. "The form of domination peculiar to this epoch expresses itself not directly as authority but indirectly as the transformation of all relationships and activity into objective, instrumental, depersonalized forms."[14]

The structures of domination and control form not simply the background to the triad of violence, but generate, and in turn are nurtured by, this violence. These structures refer both to our social relations and to our interaction with our natural environment. The relation between these two levels is obviously extremely complex. It appears that violence against nature—that is, the impossible and disastrous drive to dominate and conquer the natural world—is integrally connected with domination among humans. Some of these connections are quite obvious. One thinks of the bulldozing of the planet for profit in capitalist societies, societies characterized by the dominance of one class over others. But the link between the domination of nature and structures of domination of humans go beyond this. Various writers make provocative suggestions about the nature of this link.

Max Horkheimer and T.W. Adorno argue that the domination of humans by other humans creates the preconditions for the domination of nature.[15] An important subtheme of Mary O'Brien's book *The Politics of Reproduction* is that men "have understood their separation from nature and their need to mediate this separation ever since that moment in dark prehistory when the idea of paternity took hold in the human mind. Patriarchy is the power to transcend natural realities with historical, man-made realities. This is the potency principle in its primordial form."[16] Simone de Beauvoir says that the ambivalent feelings of men toward nature are carried over onto their feelings toward women, who are seen as embodying nature. "Now ally, now enemy, she appears as the dark chaos from whence life wells up, as this life itself, and as the over-yonder toward which life tends."[17] Violence against nature, like violence against women, violence against other men, and violence against oneself, is in part related to what Sidney Jourard calls the lethal aspects of masculinity.[18]

## The Individual Reproduction of Male Domination

> No man is born a butcher.
>
> Bertolt Brecht[19]

In a male-dominated society men have a number of privileges. Compared to women we are free to walk the streets at night, we have traditionally escaped domestic labor, and on average we have higher wages, better jobs, and more power. But these advantages in themselves cannot explain the individual reproduction of the relations of male domination, that is, why the individual male from a very early age embraces masculinity. The embracing of masculinity is not only a "socialization" into a certain gender role, as if there is a pre-formed human being who learns a role that he then plays for the rest of his life. Rather, through his psychological development he embraces and takes into himself a set of gender-based social relations: the person that is created through the process of maturation becomes the personal embodiment of those relations. By the time the child is five or six years old, the basis for lifelong masculinity has already been established.

Two factors, intrinsic to humans and human development, form the basis for the individual acquisition of gender. These conditions do not explain the existence of gender: they are simply preconditions for its individual acquisition.

The first factor is the malleability of human desires. For the infant all bodily activities—touch, sight, smell, sound, taste, thought—are potential sources of sexual pleasure. Or rather, they *are* sexual pleasure in the sense of our ability to obtain pleasure from our bodies. But this original polysexuality is limited, shaped, and repressed through the maturation process that is necessary to meet the demands of the natural and social world. Unlike other animals our sexuality is not simply instinct: it is individually and socially constructed. It is because of this, and because of the human's capacity to think and construct societies and ideologies, that gender can exist in differentiation from biological sex.

As Herbert Marcuse and, following him, Gad Horowitz have pointed out, the demands of societies of domination—of "surplus-repressive" societies—progressively narrow down sexuality into genital contact, with a heterosexual norm. (Marcuse argues that a certain "basic repression"—a damming up or deflection—of human desires is necessary for any conceivable human association. But in addition to this, hierarchical and authoritarian societies require a "surplus repression" to maintain structures of domination.)[20]

This narrowing down onto genital contact is not simply a natural genital preference but is the blocking of energy from a whole range of forms of pleasure (including "mental" activities). And for reasons discussed elsewhere in this volume by Horowitz and Kaufman, the acquisition of the dominant form of masculinity is an enhancement of forms of pleasure associated with activity and the surplus repression of our ability to experience pleasure passively.

We try to compensate for this surplus repression with the pleasures and preoccupations of work, play, sports, and culture. But these are not sufficient to offset the severe limits placed on love and desire. To put this crudely, a two-day weekend cannot emotionally compensate for five days of a deadening job. And what is more, these social activities are themselves sources of struggle and tension.

The second factor that forms the basis for the individual's acquisition of gender is that the prolonged period of human childhood results in powerful attachments to parental figures. The passionate bonding of the young child to the primary parental figures obtains its particular power and salience for our personal development in societies where isolated women have the primary responsibility for nurturing infants and children, where the child's relation with the world is mediated most strongly through a small family rather than through a small community as a whole, and in which traits associated with the "opposite" sex are suppressed.

This prolonged period of human childhood is a prolonged period of powerlessness. The intense love for one or two parents is combined with intense feelings of deprivation and frustration. This natural ambivalence is greatly aggravated in societies where the attention parents are able to provide the young is limited, where social demands place additional frustrations on top of the inevitable ones experienced by a tiny person, and where one or two isolated parents relive and repeat the patterns of their own childhood. As will be seen, part of the boy's acquisition of masculinity is a response to this experience of powerlessness.

By the time children are sufficiently developed physically, emotionally, and intellectually at five or six to have clearly defined themselves separately from their parents, these parental figures have already been internalized within them. In the early years, as in later ones, we identify with (or react against) the apparent characteristics of our love objects and incorporate them into our own personalities. This is largely an unconscious process. This incorporation and internalization, or rejection, of the characteristics of our love objects is part of the process of constructing our ego, our self.

This internalization of the objects of love is a selective one, and it is a process that takes place in specific social environments. The immediate environment is the family, which is a "vigorous agency of class placement and an efficient mechanism for the creation and transmission of gender inequality."[21] Within itself, to a greater or lesser extent, the family reflects, reproduces, and recreates the hierarchical gender system of society as a whole.[22]

As noted above, the child has ambivalent feelings toward his or her primary caring figures. Love combines with feelings of powerlessness, tension, and frustration. The child's experience of anxiety and powerlessness results not only from the prohibitions of harsh parents but also from the inability of even the most loving parents who cannot exist solely for their young, because of the demands of society, demands of natural reality, and demands of their own needs.

Both girls and boys have these ambivalent feelings and experiences of powerlessness. But the feelings toward the parents and the matter of power are almost immediately impregnated with social meaning. Years before the child can put words to it, she or he begins to understand that the mother is inferior to the father and that woman is inferior to man. That this inferiority is not natural but is socially imposed is beyond the understanding of the child and even beyond the understanding of sociobiologists, presidents, and popes. (Size itself might also feed into this perception of inferiority, or perhaps it is simply that in hierarchical, sexist society, size becomes a symbol of superiority.) In the end the biological fact of "otherness" becomes overlaced with a socially imposed otherness. The child is presented with two categories of humans: males, who embody the full grandeur and power of humanity, and females, who in Simone de Beauvoir's words, are defined as "other" in a phallocentric society.[23]

The human's answer to this powerlessness and to the desire to find pleasure is to develop an ego and a superego, that is, a distinct self and an internal mechanism of authority. An important part of the process of ego development is the identification with the objects of love. Progressively both sexes discover and are taught who the appropriate figures of identification are. But the figures of identification are not equal.

Society presents the young boy with a great escape. He may feel powerless as a child, but there is hope, for as an adult male he will have privilege and (at least in the child's imagination) he will have power. A strong identification—that is, an incorporation into his own developing self—of his image of his father in particular and male figures in general is his compensation for his own sense of powerlessness and insecurity. It is his compensation for distancing himself from his first love, his mother.

In this process the boy not only claims for himself the activity represented by men and father. At the same time he steps beyond the passivity of his infantile relationship to the mother and beyond his overall sense of passivity (passivity,that is, in the sense of feeling overwhelmed by desires and a frustrating world). He embraces the project of controlling himself and controlling the world. He comes to personify activity. Masculinity is a reaction against passivity and powerlessness and, with it comes a repression of all the desires and traits that a given society defines as negatively passive or as resonant of passive experiences. The girl, on the other hand, discovers she will never possess men's power, and henceforth the most she can aspire to is to be loved by a man—that is, to actively pursue a passive aim.

Thus the achievement of what is considered the biologically normal male character (but which is really socially created masculinity) is one outcome of the splitting of human desire and human *being* into mutually exclusive spheres of activity and passivity. The monopoly of activity by males is not a timeless psychological or social necessity. Rather, the internalization of the norms of masculinity require the surplus repression of passive aims—the desire to be nurtured. The repression of passivity and the accentuation of activity constitute the development of a "surplus-aggressive" character type. Unfortunately, such a character type is the norm in patriarchal societies, although the degree of aggressiveness varies from person to person and society to society.

Part of the reason for this process is a response to the fear of rejection and of punishment. What does one fear? Loss of love and self-esteem. Why, in the child's mind, would it lose love and self-esteem? Because it does what is prohibited or degraded. In order to not do what is prohibited or degraded, during this process of identification the child internalizes the values and prohibitions of society. This is the shaping of the superego, our conscience, sense of guilt, and standards of self-worth. Through the internalization of social authority, aggressiveness is directed against oneself.[24]

This whole process of ego development is the shaping of a psychic realm that mediates between our unconscious desires, the world, and a punishing superego. But as should now be clear, the development of the ego is the development of masculine or feminine ego. In this sense, the ego is a definition of oneself formed within a given social and psychological environment and within what Gayle Rubin calls a specific sex-gender system.[25]

The boy is not simply *learning* a gender role but is becoming *part* of that gender. His whole self, to a greater or lesser extent, with greater or lesser conflict, will be masculine. Ken Kesey magnificently captured this in his description of Hank, a central character in *Sometimes a Great Notion:* "Did it take that much muscle just to walk, or was Hank showing off his manly development? Every movement constituted open aggression against the very air through which Hank passed."[26]

## The Reinforcement of Masculinity

Masculinity is unconsciously rooted before the age of six, is reinforced as the child develops, and then positively explodes at adolescence. Beauvoir's comment about girls is no less true for boys: "With puberty, the future not only approaches; it takes residence in her body; it assumes the most concrete reality."[27]

It is particularly in adolescence that masculinity obtains its definitive shape for the individual. The masculine norm has its own particular nuances and traits dependent on class, nation, race, religion, and ethnicity. And within each group it has its own personal expression. Adolescence is important because it is the time when the body reawakens, when that long-awaited entrance into adulthood finally takes place, and when our culture makes the final socio-educational preparations for adult work life. In adolescence the pain and fear involved in repressing "femininity" and passivity start to become evident. For most of us, the response to this inner pain is to reinforce the bulwarks of masculinity. The emotional pain created by obsessive masculinity is stifled by reinforcing masculinity itself.

The family, school, sports, friends, church, clubs, scouts, jobs, and the media all play a role as the adolescent struggles to put the final touches on himself as a real man. The expression of male power will be radically different from class to class. For the middle class adolescent, with a future in a profession or business, his own personal and social power will be expressed through a direct mastering of the world. Workaholism or at least a measuring of his value through status and the paycheck might well be the outcome. Fantasies of power are often expressed in terms of fame and success.

For a working class boy, the avenue of mastering the world of business, politics, the professions, and wealth is all but denied. For him male power is often defined in the form of working class machismo. The power to dominate is expressed in a direct physical form. Domination of the factors of production or of another person is achieved through sheer bravado and muscle power. In an excellent examination of the development of white male, working class identity in Britain, Paul Willis demonstrates that the acquisition of a positive working class identity is coterminous with the development of a particular gender identity. Though stigmatized by society as a whole, manual labor becomes the embodiment of masculine power. "Manual labor is suffused with masculine qualities and given certain sensual overtones for 'the lads.' The toughness and awkwardnes of physical work and effort . . . takes on masculine lights and depths and assumes a significance beyond itself."[28]

Adolscence is also the time of our first intense courtships. Although so much of pre- and early-adolescent sexual experience is homosexual, those experiences tend to be devalued and ignored. Relations with young women are the real thing. This interaction furthers the acquisition of masculinity for boys because they are interacting with girls who are busy acquiring the complementary femininity. Each moment of interaction reinforces the gender acquisition of each sex.

## The Fragility of Masculinity

Masculinity is power. But masculinity is terrifyingly fragile because it does not really exist in the sense we are led to think it exists, that is, as a biological reality—something real that we have inside ourselves. It exists as ideology; it exists as scripted behavior; it exists within "gendered" relationships. But in the end it is just a social institution with a tenuous relationship to that with which it is supposed to be synonymous: our maleness, our biological sex. The young child does not know that sex does not equal gender. For him to be male is to be what he perceives as being masculine. The child is father to the man. Therefore, to be unmasculine is to be desexed—"castrated."

The tension between maleness and masculinity is intense because masculinity requires a suppression of a whole range of human needs, aims, feelings, and forms of expression. Masculinity is one half of the narrow, surplus-repressive shape of the adult human psyche. Even when we are intellectually aware of the difference between biological maleness and masculinity, the masculine ideal is so embedded within ourselves that it is hard to untangle the person we might want to become (more "fully human," less sexist, less surplus-repressed, and so on) from the person we actually are.

But as children and adolescents (and often as adults), we are not aware of the difference between maleness and masculinity. With the exception of a tiny proportion of the population born as her-maphrodites, there can be no biological struggle to be male. The presence of a penis and testicles is all it takes. Yet boys and men harbor great insecurity about their male credentials. This insecurity exists because maleness is equated with masculinity; but the latter is a figment of our collective, patriarchal, surplus-repressive imaginations.

In a patriarchal society being male is highly valued, and men value their masculinity. But everywhere there are ambivalent feelings. That the initial internalization of masculinity is at the father's knee has lasting significance. Andrew Tolson states that "to the boy, mas-culinity is both mysterious and attractive (in its promise of a world of work and power), and yet, at the same time, threatening (in its strangeness, and emotional distance). . . . It works both ways; attracts and repels in dynamic contradiction. This simultaneous distance and attraction is internalized as a permanent emotional tension that the individual must, in some way, strive to overcome."[29]

Although maleness and masculinity are highly valued, men are everywhere unsure of their own masculinity and maleness, whether consciously or not. When men are encouraged to be open, as in men's support and counselling groups, it becomes apparent that there exists, often under the surface, an internal dialogue of doubt about one's male and masculine credentials.

One need think only of anxieties about the penis, that incompara-ble scepter, that symbol of patriarchy and male power. Even as a child the boy experiences, more or less consciously, fearful fantasies of "castration." The child observes that the people who do not have penises are also those with less power. In the mind of a four- or five-year-old child who doesn't know about the power of advertising, the state, education, interactive psychological patterns, unequal pay, sexual harassment, and rape, what else can he think bestows the rewards of masculinity than that little visible difference between men and women, boys and girls?

Of course at this early age the little penis and testicles are not much defense against the world. Nor can they measure against the impossi-bly huge genitals of one's father or other men. I remember standing in the shower when I was five or six years old, staring up in awe at my father. Years later I realized a full circle had turned when I was showering with my five-year-old son and saw the same crick in his neck and the same look in his eyes. This internalized image of the

small, boyish self retains a nagging presence in each man's unconscious. This is so much so that, as adults, men go to war to prove
themselves potent, they risk their lives to show they have balls.
Expressions such as these, and the double meaning of the word
impotent, are no accident.

Just the presence of that wonderfully sensitive bit of flesh, as highly
valued as it is in patriarchal culture, is not enough to guarantee
maleness and masculinity. But if there are indeed such great doubts in
adolescence and beyond about one's masculine credentials, how is it
that we combat these doubts? One way is by violence.

### Men's Violence Against Women

> In spite of the inferior role which men assign to them, women are the
> privileged objects of their aggression.
>
> Simone de Beauvoir[30]

Men's violence against women is the most common form of direct,
personalized violence in the lives of most adults. From sexual harassment to rape, from incest to wife battering to the sight of violent
pornographic images, few women escape some form of male
aggression.

My purpose here is not to list and evaluate the various forms of
violence against women, nor to try to assess what can be classed as
violence per se.[31] It is to understand this violence as an expression of
the fragility of masculinity and its place in the perpetuation of masculinity and male domination.

In the first place, men's violence against women is probably the
clearest, most straightforward expression of relative male and female
power. That the relative social, economic, and political power can be
expressed in this manner is, to a large part, because of differences in
physical strength and in a lifelong training (or lack of training) in
fighting. But it is also expressed this way because of the active/passive
split. Activity as aggression is part of the masculine gender definition.
That is not to say this definition always includes rape or battering, but
it is one of the possibilities within a definition of activity that is
ultimately grounded in the body.

Rape is a good example of the acting out of these relations of power
and of the outcome of fragile masculinity in a surplus-repressive
society. In the testimonies of rapists one hears over and over again
expressions of inferiority, powerlessness, anger. But who can these
men feel superior to? Rape is a crime that not only demonstrates
physical power, but that does so in the language of male-female sex-

gender relations. The testimonies of convicted rapists collected by Douglas Jackson in the late 1970s are chilling and revealing.[32] Hal: "I felt very inferior to others. . . . I felt rotten about myself and by committing rape I took this out on someone I thought was weaker than me, someone I could control." Carl: "I think that I was feeling so rotten, so low, and such a creep . . ." Len: "I feel a lot of what rape is isn't so much sexual desire as a person's feelings about themselves and how that relates to sex. My fear of relating to people turned to sex because . . . it just happens to be the fullest area to let your anger out on, to let your feelings out on."

Sometimes this anger and pain are experienced in relation to women but just as often not. In either case they are addressed to women who, as the Other in a phallocentric society, are objects of mystification to men, the objects to whom men from birth have learned to express and vent their feelings, or simply objects with less social power and weaker muscles. It is the crime against women par excellence because, through it, the full weight of a sexually based differentiation among humans is played out.

This anger and pain are sometimes overlayed with the effects of a class hierarchy. John: "I didn't feel too good about women. I felt that I couldn't pick them up on my own. I took the lower-class woman and tried to make her look even lower than she really was, you know. 'Cause what I really wanted was a higher-class woman but I didn't have the finesse to actually pick these women up."

Within relationships, forms of male violence such as rape, battering, and what Meg Luxton calls the "petty tyranny" of male domination in the household[33] must be understood both "in terms of violence directed against women as women and against women as wives."[34] The family provides an arena for the expression of needs and emotions not considered legitimate elsewhere.[35] It is the one of the only places where men feel safe enough to express emotions. As the dams break, the flood pours out on women and children.[36] The family also becomes the place where the violence suffered by individuals in their work lives is discharged. "At work men are powerless, so in their leisure time they want to have a feeling that they control their lives."[37]

While this violence can be discussed in terms of men's aggression, it operates within the dualism of activity and passivity, masculinity and feminity. Neither can exist without the other. This is not to blame women for being beaten, nor to excuse men who beat. It is but an indication that the various forms of men's violence against women are a dynamic affirmation of a masculinity that can only exist as distinguished from femininity. It is my argument that masculinity needs constant nurturing and affirmation. This affirmation takes many different forms. The majority of men are not rapists or batterers, although it is possible that the majority of men have used superior physical strength or physical coercion or the threat of force against a woman at least once as a teenager or an adult. But in those who harbor great personal doubts or strongly negative self-images, or who cannot cope with a daily feeling of powerlessness, violence against women can become a means of trying to affirm their personal power in the language of our sex-gender system. That these forms of violence only reconfirm the negative self-image and the feeling of powerlessness shows the fragility, artificiality, and precariousness of masculinity.

## Violence Against Other Men

At a behavioral level, men's violence against other men is visible throughout society. Some forms, such as fighting, the ritualized display violence of teenagers and some groups of adult men, institutionalized rape in prisons, and attacks on gays or racial minorities are very direct expressions of this violence. In many sports, violence is incorporated into exercise and entertainment. More subtle forms are the verbal putdown or, combined with economic and other factors, the competition in the business, political, or academic world. In its most frightening form, violence has long been an acceptable and even preferred method of addressing differences and conflicts among different groups and states. In the case of war, as in many other manifestations of violence, violence against other men (and civilian women) combines with autonomous economic, ideological, and political factors.

But men's violence against other men is more than the sum of various activities and types of behavior. In this form of violence a number of things are happening at once, in addition to the autonomous factors involved. Sometimes mutual, sometimes one-sided, there is a discharge of aggression and hostility. But at the same time as discharging aggression, these acts of violence and the ever-present potential for men's violence against other men reinforce the reality that relations between men, whether at the individual or state level, are relations of power.[38]

Most men feel the presence of violence in their lives. Some of us had fathers who were domineering, rough, or even brutal. Some of us had fathers who simply were not there enough; most of us had fathers who either consciously or unconsciously were repelled by our need for touch and affection once we had passed a certain age. All of us had experiences of being beaten up or picked on when we were young. We learned to fight, or we learned to run; we learned to pick on others, or we learned how to talk or joke our way out of a confrontation. But either way these early experiences of violence caused an incredible amount of anxiety and required a huge expenditure of energy to resolve. That anxiety is crystallized in an unspoken fear (particularly among heterosexual men): all other men are my potential humiliators, my enemies, my competitors.

But this mutual hostility is not always expressed. Men have formed elaborate institutions of male bonding and buddying: clubs, gangs, teams, fishing trips, card games, bars, and gyms, not to mention that great fraternity of Man. Certainly, as many feminists have pointed out, straight male clubs are a subculture of male privilege. But they are also havens where men, by common consent, can find safety and security among other men. They are safe houses where our love and affection for other men can be expressed.

Freud suggested that great amounts of passivity are required for the establishment of social relations among men but also that this very passivity arouses a fear of losing one's power. (This fear takes the form, in a phallocentric, male-dominated society, of what Freud called "castration anxiety.") There is a constant tension of activity and passivity. Among their many functions and reasons for existence, male institutions mediate this tension between activity and passivity among men.

My thoughts take me back to grade six and the constant acting out of this drama. There was the challenge to fight and a punch in the stomach that knocked my wind out. There was our customary greeting with a slug in the shoulder. Before school, after school, during class change, at recess, whenever you saw another one of the boys whom you hadn't hit or been with in the past few minutes, you'd punch each other on the shoulder. I remember walking from class to class in terror of meeting Ed Skagle in the hall. Ed, a hefty young football player a grade ahead of me, would leave a big bruise with one of his friendly hellos. And this was the interesting thing about the whole business; most of the time it was friendly and affectionate. Long after the bruises have faded, I remember Ed's smile and the protective way he had of saying hello to me. But we couldn't express this affection without maintaining the active/passive equilibrium. More precisely, within the masculine psychology of surplus aggression, expressions of affection and of the need for other boys had to be balanced by an active assault.

But the traditional definition of masculinity is not only surplus aggression. It is also exclusive heterosexuality, for the maintenance of masculinity requires the repression of homosexuality.[39] Repression of homosexuality is one thing, but how do we explain the intense fear of homosexuality, the homophobia, that pervades so much male interaction? It isn't simply that many men may choose not to have sexual relations with other men; it is rather that they will find this possibility frightening or abhorrent.

Freud showed that the boy's renunciation of the father—and thus men—as an object of sexual love is a renunciation of what are felt to be passive sexual desires. Our embrace of future manhood is part of an equation:

male = penis = power = active = masculine.

The other half of the equation, in the language of the unconscious in patriarchal society, is

female = castrated = passive = feminine.

These unconscious equations might be absurd, but they are part of a socially shared hallucination of our patriarchal society. For the boy to deviate from this norm is to experience severe anxiety, for what appears to be at stake is his ability to be active. Erotic attraction to other men is sacrificed because there is no model central to our society of active, erotic love for other males. The emotionally charged physical attachments of childhood with father and friends eventually breed feelings of passivity and danger and are sacrificed. Horowitz notes that the anxiety caused by the threat of losing power and activity is "the motive power behind the 'normal' boy's social learning of his sex and gender roles." Boys internalize "our culture's definition of 'normal' or 'real' man: the possessor of a penis, therefore loving only females and that actively; the possessor of a penis, therefore 'strong' and 'hard,' not 'soft,' 'weak,' 'yielding,' 'sentimental,' 'effeminate,' passive. To deviate from this definition is not to be a real man. To deviate is to arouse [what Freud called] castration anxiety."[40]

Putting this in different terms, the young boy learns of the sexual hierarchy of society. This learning process is partly conscious and partly unconscious. For a boy, being a girl is a threat because it raises anxiety by representing a loss of power. Until real power is attained, the young boy courts power in the world of the imagination (with superheroes, guns, magic, and pretending to be grown-up). But the continued pull of passive aims, the attraction to girls and to mother,

the fascination with the origin of babies ensure that a tension continues to exist. In this world, the only thing that is as bad as being a girl is
being a sissy, that is, being like a girl.[41] Although the boy doesn't
consciously equate being a girl or sissy with homosexual genital
activity, at the time of puberty these feelings, thoughts, and anxieties
are transferred onto homosexuality per se.

For the majority of men, the establishment of the masculine norm
and the strong social prohibitions against homosexuality are enough
to bury the erotic desire for other men. The repression of our bisexuality is not adequate, however, to keep this desire at bay. Some of the
energy is transformed into derivative pleasures—muscle building,
male comradeship, hero worship, religious rituals, war, sports—
where our enjoyment of being with other men or admiring other men
can be expressed. These forms of activity are not enough to neutralize
our constitutional bisexuality, our organic fusion of passivity and
activity, and our love for our fathers and our friends. The great
majority of men, in addition to those men whose sexual preference is
clearly homosexual, have, at some time in their childhood, adolescence, or adult life, had sexual or quasi-sexual relations with other
males, or have fantasized or dreamed about such relationships.
Those who don't (or don't recall that they have), invest a lot of energy
in repressing and denying these thoughts and feelings. And to make
things worse, all those highly charged male activities in the sports-
field, the meeting room, or the locker room do not dispel eroticized
relations with other men. They can only reawaken those feelings. It is,
as Freud would have said, the return of the repressed.

Nowhere has this been more stunningly captured than in the wres-
tling scene in the perhaps mistitled book, *Women in Love,* by D.H.
Lawrence. It was late at night. Birkin had just come to Gerald's house
after being put off following a marriage proprosal. They talked of
working, of loving, and fighting, and in the end stripped off their
clothes and began to wrestle in front of the burning fire. As they
wrestled, "they seemed to drive their white flesh deeper and deeper
against each other, as if they would break into a oneness." They
entwined, they wrestled, they pressed nearer and nearer. "A tense
white knot of flesh [was] gripped in silence." The thin Birkin "seemed
to penetrate into Gerald's more solid, more diffuse bulk, to interfuse
his body through the body of the other, as if to bring it subtly into
subjection, always seizing with some rapid necromantic fore-
knowledge every motion of the other flesh, converting and coun-
teracting it, playing upon the limbs and trunk of Gerald like some
hard wind. . . . Now and again came a sharp gasp of breath, or a sound

like a sigh, then the rapid thudding of movement on the thickly-carpeted floor, then the strange sound of flesh escaping under flesh."[42]

The very institutions of male bonding and patriarchal power force men to constantly reexperience their closeness and attraction to other men, that is, the very thing so many men are afraid of. Our very attraction to ourselves, ambivalent as it may be, can only be generalized as an attraction to men in general.

A phobia is one means by which the ego tries to cope with anxiety. Homophobia is a means of trying to cope, not simply with our unsuccessfully repressed, eroticized attraction to other men, but with our whole anxiety over the unsuccessfully repressed passive sexual aims, whether directed toward males or females. But often, Otto Fenichel writes, "individuals with phobias cannot succeed in avoiding the feared situations. Again and again they are forced to experience the very things they are afraid of. Often the conclusion is unavoidable that this is due to an unconscious arrangement of theirs. It seems that unconsciously they are striving for the very thing of which they are consciously afraid. This is understandable because the feared situations originally were instinctual aims. It is a kind of 'return of the repressed.' "[43]

In the case of homophobia, it is not merely a matter of an individual phobia, although the strength of homophobia varies from individual to individual. It is a socially constructed phobia that is essential for the imposition and maintenance of masculinity. A key expression of homophobia is the obsessive denial of homosexual attraction; this denial is expressed as violence against other men. Or to put it differently, men's violence against other men is one of the chief means through which patriarchal society simultaneously expresses and discharges the attraction of men to other men.[44]

The specific ways that homophobia and men's violence toward other men are acted out varies from man to man, society to society, and class to class. The great amount of *directly expressed* violence and violent homophobia among some groups of working class youth would be well worth analyzing to give clues to the relation of class and gender.

This corner of the triad of men's violence interacts with and reinforces violence against women. This corner contains part of the logic of surplus aggression. Here we begin to explain the tendency of many men to use force as a means of simultaneously hiding and expressing their feelings. At the same time the fear of other men, in particular the fear of weakness and passivity in relation to other men, helps create our strong dependence on women for meeting our emotional needs and for emotional discharge. In a surplus-repressive patriarchal and class society, large amounts of anxiety and hostility are built up, ready to be discharged. But the fear of one's emotions and the fear of losing control mean that discharge only takes place in a safe situation. For many men that safety is provided by a relationship with a woman where the commitment of one's friend or lover creates the sense of security. What is more, because it is a relationship with a woman, it unconsciously resonates with that first great passive relation of the boy with his mother. But in this situation and in other acts of men's violence against women, there is also the security of interaction with someone who does not represent a psychic threat, who is less socially powerful, probably less physically powerful, and who is herself operating within a pattern of surplus passivity. And finally, given the fragility of masculine identity and the inner tension of what it means to be masculine, the ultimate acknowledgement of one's masculinity is in our power over women. This power can be expressed in many ways. Violence is one of them.

## Violence Against Oneself

When I speak of a man's violence against himself I am thinking of the very structure of the masculine ego. The formation of an ego on an edifice of surplus repression and surplus aggression is the building of a precarious structure of internalized violence. The continual conscious and unconscious blocking and denial of passivity and all the emotions and feelings men associate with passivity—fear, pain, sadness, embarrassment—is a denial of part of what we are. The constant psychological and behavioral vigilance against passivity and its derivatives is a perpetual act of violence against oneself.

The denial and blocking of a whole range of human emotions and capacities are compounded by the blocking of avenues of discharge. The discharge of fear, hurt, and sadness, for example (through crying or trembling), is necessary because these painful emotions linger on even if they are not consciously felt. Men become pressure cookers. The failure to find safe avenues of emotional expression and discharge means that a whole range of emotions are transformed into anger and hostility. Part of the anger is directed at oneself in the form of guilt, self-hate, and various physiological and psychological symptoms. Part is directed at other men. Part of it is directed at women.

By the end of this process, our distance from ourselves is so great that the very symbol of maleness is turned into an object, a thing. Men's preoccupation with genital power and pleasure combines with a desensitization of the penis. As best he can, writes Emmanuel Reynaud, a man gives it "the coldness and the hardness of metal." It becomes his tool, his weapon, his thing. "What he loses in enjoyment he hopes to compensate for in power; but if he gains an undeniable power symbol, what pleasure can he really feel with a weapon between his legs?"[45]

## BEYOND MEN'S VIOLENCE

Throughout Gabriel Garcia Marquez's *Autumn of the Patriarch,* the ageless dictator stalked his palace, his elephantine feet dragging forever on endless corridors that reeked of corruption. There was no escape from the world of terror, misery, and decay that he himself had created. His tragedy was that he was "condemned forever to live breathing the same air which asphyxiated him."[46] As men, are we similarly condemned, or is there a road of escape from the triad of men's violence and the precarious structures of masculinity that we ourselves recreate at our peril and that of women, children, and the world?

Prescribing a set of behavioral or legal changes to combat men's violence against women is obviously not enough. Even as more and more men are convinced there is a problem, this realization does not touch the unconscious structures of masculinity. Any man who is sympathetic to feminism is aware of the painful contradiction between his conscious views and his deeper emotions and feelings.

The analysis in this article suggests that men and women must address each corner of the triad of men's violence and the socioeconomic, psycho-sexual orders on which they stand. Or to put it more strongly, it is impossible to deal successfully with any one corner of this triad in isolation from the others.

The social context that nurtures men's violence and the relation between socioeconomic transformation and the end of patriarchy have been major themes of socialist feminist thought. This framework, though it is not without controversy and unresolved problems, is one I accept. Patriarchy and systems of authoritarianism and class domination feed on each other. Speaking of the relation of capitalism and the oppression of women, Michele Barrett says that male-female divisions

> are systematically embedded in the structure and texture of capitalist social relations . . . and they play an important part in the political and ideological stability of this society. They are constitutive of our subjectivity as well as, in part, of capitalist political and cultural hegemony. They are interwoven

into a fundamental relationship between the wage-labour system and the organization of domestic life and it is impossible to imagine that they could be extracted from the relations of production and reproduction of capitalism without a massive transformation of those relations taking place.[47]

Radical socioeconomic and political change is a requirement for the end of men's violence. But organizing for macrosocial change is not enough to solve the problem of men's violence, not only because the problem is so pressing here and now, but because the continued existence of masculinity and surplus aggressiveness works against the fundamental macrosocial change we desire.

The many manifestations of violence against women have been an important focus of feminists. Women's campaigns and public education against rape, battering, sexual harassment, and more generally for control by women of their bodies are a key to challenging men's violence. Support by men, not only for the struggles waged by women, but in our own workplaces and among our friends is an important part of the struggle. There are many possible avenues for work by men among men. These include: forming counselling groups and support services for battering men (as in now happening in different cities in North America); championing the inclusion of clauses on sexual harassment in collective agreements and in the constitutions or by-laws of our trade unions, associations, schools, and political parties; raising money, campaigning for government funding, and finding other means of support for rape crisis centers and shelters for battered women; speaking out against violent and sexist pornography; building neighborhood campaigns on wife and child abuse; and personally refusing to collude with the sexism of our workmates, colleagues, and friends. The latter is perhaps the most difficult of all and requires patience, humor, and support from other men who are challenging sexism.

But because men's violence against women is inseparable from the other two corners of the triad of men's violence, solutions are very complex and difficult. Ideological changes and an awareness of problems are important but insufficient. While we can envisage changes in our child-rearing arrangements (which in turn would require radical economic changes) lasting solutions have to go far deeper. Only the development of non–surplus-repressive societies (whatever these might look like) will allow for the greater expression of human needs and, along with attacks on patriarchy per se, will reduce the split between active and passive psychological aims.[48]

The process of achieving these long-term goals contains many elements of economic, social, political, and psychological change each of which requires a fundamental transformation of society. Such a transformation will not be created by an amalgam of changed individuals; but there *is* a relationship between personal change and our ability to construct organizational, political, and economic alternatives that will be able to mount a successful challenge to the status quo.

One avenue of personal struggle that is being engaged in by an increasing number of men has been the formation of men's support groups. Some groups focus on consciousness raising, but most groups stress the importance of men talking about their feelings, their relations with other men and with women, and any number of problems in their lives. At times these groups have been criticized by some antisexist men as yet another place for men to collude against women. The alternatives put forward are groups whose primary focus is either support for struggles led by women or the organization of direct, antisexist campaigns among men. These activities are very important, but so too is the development of new support structures among men. And these structures must go beyond the traditional form of consciousness raising.

Consciousness raising usually focuses on manifestations of the oppression of women and on the oppressive behavior of men. But as we have seen, masculinity is more than the sum total of oppressive forms of behavior. It is deeply and unconsciously embedded in the structure of our egos and superegos; it is what we have become. An awareness of oppressive behavior is important, but too often it only leads to guilt about being a man. Guilt is a profoundly conservative emotion and as such is not particularly useful for bringing about change. From a position of insecurity and guilt, people do not change or inspire others to change. After all, insecurity about one's male credentials played an important part in the individual acquisition of masculinity and men's violence in the first place.

There is a need to promote the personal strength and security necessary to allow men to make more fundamental personal changes and to confront sexism and heterosexism in society at large. Support groups usually allow men to talk about our feelings, how we too have been hurt growing up in a surplus-repressive society, and how we, in turn, act at times in an oppressive manner. We begin to see the connections between painful and frustrating experiences in our own lives and related forms of oppressive behavior. As Sheila Rowbotham notes, "the exploration of the internal areas of consciousness is a political necessity for us."[49]

Talking among men is a major step, but it is still operating within the acceptable limits of what men like to think of as rational behavior. Deep barriers and fears remain even when we can begin to recognize them. As well as talking, men need to encourage direct expression of emotions—grief, anger, rage, hurt, love—within these groups and the physical closeness that has been blocked by the repression of passive aims, by social prohibition, and by our own superegos and sense of what is right. This discharge of emotions has many functions and outcomes: like all forms of emotional and physical discharge it lowers the tension within the human system and reduces the likelihood of a spontaneous discharge of emotions through outer- or inner-directed violence.

But the expression of emotions is not an end in itself; in this context it is a means to an end. Stifling the emotions connected with feelings of hurt and pain acts as a sort of glue that allows the original repression to remain. Emotional discharge, in a situation of support and encouragement, helps unglue the ego structures that require us to operate in patterned, phobic, oppressive, and surplus-aggressive forms. In a sense it loosens up the repressive structures and allows us fresh insight into ourselves and our past. But if this emotional discharge happens in isolation or against an unwitting victim, it only reinforces the feelings of being powerless, out of control, or a person who must obsessively control others. Only in situations that contradict these feelings—that is, with the support, affection, encouragement, and backing of other men who experience similar feelings—does the basis for change exist.[50]

The encouragement of emotional discharge and open dialogue among men also enhances the safety we begin to feel among each other and in turn helps us to tackle obsessive, even if unconscious, fear of other men. This unconscious fear and lack of safety are the experience of most heterosexual men throughout their lives. The pattern for homosexual men differs, but growing up and living in a heterosexist, patriarchal culture implants similar fears, even if one's adult reality is different.

Receiving emotional support and attention from a group of men is a major contradiction to experiences of distance, caution, fear, and neglect from other men. This contradiction is the mechanism that allows further discharge, emotional change, and more safety. Safety among even a small group of our brothers gives us greater safety and strength among men as a whole. This gives us the confidence and sense of personal power to confront sexism and homophobia in all its various manifestations. In a sense, this allows us each to be a model of a strong, powerful man who does not need to operate in an oppressive and violent fashion in relation to women, to other men, or to himself. And that, I hope, will play some small part in the challenge to the oppressive reality of patriarchal, authoritarian, class societies. It will be changes in our own lives inseparably intertwined with changes in society as a whole that will sever the links in the triad of men's violence.

## NOTES

My thanks to those who have given me comments on earlier drafts of this paper, in particular my father, Nathan Kaufman, and to Gad Horowitz. As well I extend my appreciation to the men I have worked with in various counselling situations who have helped me develop insights into the individual acquisition of violence and masculinity.

[1]Herbert Marcuse, *Eros and Civilization* (Boston: Beacon Press, 1975; New York: Vintage, 1962); Gad Horowitz, *Repression* (Toronto: University of Toronto Press, 1977).

[2]Part of Freud's wisdom was to recognize that, although the engendered psychology of the individual was the product of the maturation of the individual within an evolving social environment, the body was in the last analysis the subject and the object of our desires

[3]Michele Barrett and Mary McIntosh, *The Anti-Social Family* (London: Verso/New Left Books, 1982), 107.

[4]See the critical remarks on biological determinism by Carmen Schifellite elsewhere in this volumn.

[5]On the range of societies, see the article by Richard Lee and Richard Daly in this volume.

[6]Susan Brownmiller, *Against Our Will: Men, Women and Rape* (New York: Bantam Books, 1976), 6.

[7]Alice Echols, "The New Feminism of Yin and Yang" in Ann Snitow *et al.*, eds., *Powers of Desire* (New York: Monthly Review Press, 1983) 439-59; and Alice Echols, "The Taming of the Id;: Feminist Sexual Politics, 1968-83," in Carol Vance, ed., *Pleasure and Danger* (London: Routledge and Kegan Paul, 1984), 50-72. The two articles are essentially the same.

[8]Aimé Césaire, *Discourse on Colonialism* (New York: Monthly Review Press, 1972), 21-2; first published in 1955 by Éditions Présence Africaine.

[9]C. Tunnard, *The City of Man* (New York: Scribner, 1953), 43. Quoted in N.O. Brown, *Life Against Death* (Middletown: Wesleyan University Press, 1959), 283.

[10]This is the approach, for example, of Suzanne Steinmetz. She says that macrolevel social and economic conditions (such as poverty, unemployment, inadequate housing, and the glorification and acceptance of violence) lead to high crime rates and a tolerance of violence that in turn leads to family aggresion. See her *Cycle of Violence* (New York: Praeger, 1977), 30.

[11]Juliet Mitchell, *Psychoanalysis and Feminism* (New York: Vintage, 1975), 362.

[12]Joseph Conrad, *Lord Jim,* (New York: Bantam Books, 1981), 146; first published 1900.

[13]See for example Michele Barrett's thought-provoking book, *Women's Oppression Today* (London: Verso/New Left Books, 1980), 10-19, 250-1.

[14]Jessica Benjamin, "Authority and the Family Revisited: or, A World Without Fathers?", *New German Critique* (Winter 1978), 35.

[15]See *ibid.*, 40, for a short discussion of Adorno's and Horkheimer's *Dialectic of Enlightenment.*

[16]Mary O'Brien, *The Politics of Reproduction* (London: Routledge and Kegan Paul, 1981), 54–5.

[17]Simone de Beauvoir, *The Second Sex* (New York: Vintage, 1974), 162; first published 1949. Dorothy Dinnerstein pursues a similar line of argument but, in line with the thesis of her book, points to mother-raised-children as the source of these ambivalent feelings toward women. See Dinnerstein, *op. cit.*, especially, 109-10.

[18]Sidney Jourard, "Some Lethal Aspects of the Male Role" in Joseph H. Pleck and Jack Sawyer, eds., *Men and Masculinity* (Englewood Cliffs: Prentice-Hall, 1974), 21-9.

[19]Bertolt Brecht, *Threepenny Novel,* trans. Desmond I. Vesey (Harmondsworth: Penguin, 1965), 282.

[20]Marcuse, *op. cit.,* and Horowitz, *op. cit.*

[21]Barrett and MacIntosh, *op. cit.,* p. 29.

[22]This is true not only because each socioeconomic system appears to create corresponding family forms, but because in turn, that family structure plays a large role in shaping the society's ideology. In Barrett's and McIntosh's words, in our society a family perspective and family ideology have an "utterly hegemonic status" within society as a whole. And there is a dialectical interaction between family form and the organization of production and paid work (*ibid.,* 78, 130).

[23]De Beauvoir, *op. cit., passim.*

[24]Sigmund Freud, *Civilization and Its Discontents* (New York: W.W. Norton, 1962), 70, 72.

[25]Gayle Rubin, "The Traffic in Women: Notes on the 'Political Economy' of Sex" in Rayna R. Reiter, ed., *Toward an Anthropology of Women* (New York: Monthly Review Press, 1975), 157-210.

[26]Ken Kesey, *Sometimes a Great Notion* (New York: Bantam, 1965), 115. (One is eerily reminded of St. Augustine's statement, "Every breath I draw in is a sin." Quoted in Horowitz, *op. cit.,* 211.)

[27]De Beauvoir, *op. cit.,* 367.

[28]Paul Willis, *Learning to Labor* (New York: Columbia University Press, 1981), 150. And see Stan Gray's article elsewhere in this volumn.

[29]Andrew Tolson, *The Limits of Masculinity* (London: Tavistock, 1977), 25.

[30]Simone de Beauvoir, in the *Nouvel Observateur,* Mar. 1, 1976. Quoted in Diana E.H. Russell and Nicole Van de Ven, eds., *Crimes Against Women* (Millbrae, Calif.: Les Femmes, 1976), xiv.

[31]Among the sources on male violence that are useful, even if sometimes problematic, see Leonore E. Walker, *The Battered Woman* (New York: Harper Colophon, 1980); Russell and Van de Ven, *op. cit.;* Judith Lewis Herman, *Father-Daughter Incest* (Cambridge, Mass.: Harvard University Press, 1981); Suzanne K. Steinmetz, *The Cycle of Violence* (New York: Praeger, 1977); Sylvia Levine and Joseph Koenig, *Why Men Rape* (Toronto: MacMillan, 1980); Susan Brownmiller, *op. cit.,* and Connie Guberman and Margie Wolfe, eds., *No Safe Place* (Toronto: Women's Press, 1985).

[32]Levine and Koenig, *op. cit.,* pp. 28, 42, 56, 72.

[33]Meg Luxton, *More Than a Labour of Love* (Toronto: Women's Press, 1980), 66.

[34]Margaret M. Killoran, "The Sound of Silence Breaking: Toward a Metatheory of Wife Abuse" (M.A. thesis, McMaster University, 1981), 148.

[35]Barrett and MacIntosh, *op. cit.,* 23.

[36]Of course, household violence is not monopolized by men. In the United States roughly the same number of domestic homicides are committed by each sex. In 1975, 8.0% of homicides were committed by husbands against wives and 7.8% by wives against husbands. These figures, however, do not indicate the chain of violence, that is, the fact that most of these women were reacting to battering by their husbands. (See Steinmetz, *op. cit.,* p. 90.) Similarly, verbal and physical abuse of children appears to be committed by men and women equally. Only in the case of incest is there a near monopoly by men. Estimates vary greatly, but between one-fifth and one-third of all girls experience some sort of sexual contact with an adult male, in most cases with a father, stepfather, other relative, or teacher. (See Herman, *op. cit.,* 12 and *passim.*)

[37]Luxton, *op. cit.,* p. 65.

[38]This was pointed out by I.F. Stone in a 1972 article on the Vietnam war. At a briefing about the U.S. escalation of bombing in the North, the Pentagon official described U.S. strategy as two boys fighting: "If one boy gets the other in an arm lock, he can probably get his adversary to say 'uncle' if he increases the pressure in sharp, painful jolts and gives every indication of willingness to break the boy's arm" ("Machismo in Washington," reprinted in Pleck and Sawyer, *op. cit.,* 131). Although women are also among the victims of war, I include war in the category of violence against men because I am here referring to the casuality of war.

[39]This is true both of masculinity as an institution and masculinity for the individual. Gay men keep certain parts of the self-oppressive masculine norm intact simply because they have grown up and live in a predominantly heterosexual, male-dominated society.

[40]Horowitz, *op. cit.*, 99.

[41]This formulation was first suggested to me by Charlie Kreiner at a men's counselling workshop in 1982.

[42]D.H. Lawrence, *Women in Love* (Harmondsworth: Penguin, 1960), 304-5; first published 1921.

[43]Fenichel, *op. cit.*, 212.

[44]See Robin Wood's analysis of the film *Raging Bull* in this volume.

[45]Emmanuel Reynaud, *Holy Virility,* translated by Ros Schwartz (London: Pluto Press, 1983), 41-2.

[46]Gabriel Garcia Marquez, *Autumn of the Patriarch,* trans. Gregory Rabassa (Harmondsworth: Penguin, 1972), 111: first published 1967.

[47]Barrett, *op. cit.,* pp. 254-5. Willis follows a similar line of thought in his discussion of the development of the male working class. He says that patriarchy "helps to provide the real human and cultural conditions which . . . actually allow subordinate roles to be taken on 'freely' within liberal democracy" (Willis, *op. cit.,* 151). But then in turn, this reinforces the impediments to change by the maintenance of a division within the working class. As an article in the early 1970s in *Shrew* pointed out, "the tendency of male workers to think of themselves as men (i.e., powerful) rather than as workers (i.e., members of an oppressed group), promotes a false sense of privilege and power, and an identification with the world of men, including the boss," Kathy McAfee and Myrna Wood, "Bread and Roses," quoted by Sheila Rowbotham, *Woman's Consciousness, Men's World* (Harmondsworth: Penguin, 1973).

[48]For a discussion of non–surplus-repressive societies, particularly in the sense of being complementary with Marx's notion of communism, see Horowitz, *op. cit.,* particularly chapter 7, and also Marcuse, *op. cit.,* especially chaps. 7, 10, and 11.

[49]Rowbotham, *op. cit.,* 36.

[50]As is apparent, although I have adopted a Freudian analysis of the unconscious and the mechanisms of repression, these observations on the therapeutic process—especially the importance of a supportive counselling environment, peer-counselling relations, emotional discharge, and the concept of contradiction—are those developed by forms of co-counselling, in particular, Re-evaluation Counselling. But unlike the latter, I do not suppose that any of us can discharge all of our hurt, grief, and anger and uncover an essential self simply because our "self" is created through that process of frustration, hurt, and repression. Rather I feel that some reforming of the ego can take place that allows us to integrate more fully a range of needs and desires, which in turn reduces forms of behavior that are oppressive to others and destructive to ourselves. Furthermore, by giving us greater consciousness of our feelings and the means of discharge, and by freeing dammed-up sources of energy, these changes allow us to act more successfully to change the world.

# Man's Domination and Woman's Oppression: The Question of Origins

## RICHARD LEE
## AND RICHARD DALY

Male domination is one part of a complex of power relations funda-mental to the maintenance of a class society; the other two parts are social inequality and militarism. These three closely interrelated phenomena exist on a large scale in all state societies, including our own. The question is how we account for the pervasiveness of these institutions. There are two explanations among anthropologists, each with a large number of adherents.

The first argument maintains that these forms of power have always existed, that it is, *de facto,* the way of the world, a question of human nature. This position transforms what we would call a histor-ical and cultural question into a question of biology, innateness, and universality. An example of this approach is Steven Goldberg's *The Inevitability of Patriarchy.* Goldberg looks to a physiological explana-tion for what he terms the universality of male dominance:

> The anthropological evidence would force us to postulate a physiologically-engendered emotional and behavioral differentiation. . . . Male physiology is . . . such that the environmental presence of a hierarchy or member of the other sex motivates the male more strongly—makes him feel the need more strongly and more readily—to manifest whatever behavior is, in any given situation the behavior that is required for attainment of dominance in a hierarchy of male-female relationship.[1]

This approach argues that women have always been subordinate to men. It proposes the concept of universal female subordination, of "man the hunter," and "woman the nurturer." Although not all proponents of this view would necessarily subscribe to a so-ciobiological interpretation, they do deal with the question in an essentialist and ahistorical manner.[2]

In criticizing the biological determinist view of men's and women's status, Eleanor Leacock argues that this position not only ignores history but also "transmutes the totality of tribal decision-making structures into the power terms of our own society." She goes on to say,

> Lewis Henry Morgan had a marvellous phrase for such practice. He used it when talking of the term "instinct" but it is generally apt. Such a term, he wrote, is "a system of philosophy in a definition, an installation of the supernatural which silences at once all inquiry into facts." In this instance women are conveniently allocated to their place and the whole inquiry into the structure of the primitive collective is stunted. The primitive collective emerges with no structure, no contradictions of its own; it is merely our society minus, so to speak.[3]

The second explanatory approach to this question—and the approach adopted here—argues that in order to explain this complex of power relation we have to look at it as an aspect of history and not of biology. This view states the matter as follows: male dominance—and for this we could well substitute militarism or social inequality—varies from society to society. It points out that male dominance is strong in some, while it is weak or nonexistent in others. If the degree of male domination varies to such a degree, then it cannot properly be considered to be a product of physiology, hormones, or unchanging human nature. We must look elsewhere for an adequate explanation, to history itself.

To begin this inquiry we might ask whether there was any period of human history when the present hierarchical structure of male-female relations was weaker or even nonexistent. The answer is a qualified yes. If we look at the rise and fall of male dominance and female subordination against the backdrop of evolving world history, the movement from bands and tribes, to chiefdoms and states, we find much less sexual inequality in the simplest societies, bands and tribes than in the later agrarian societies.

Modern states vary considerably: in some, women may be better off than in traditional states; in others they may be worse off. For example, the position of women has improved in some contemporary industrial societies but has actually declined in the Third World owing in no small part to the consequences of the expansion of the world capitalist system. Etienne and Leacock make the very important point in *Women and Colonization* that the status of women in the Third World suffers acutely under imperialism. Case studies from Peru to the Ivory Coast to the Tonga Islands of the South Pacific show that women who enjoyed considerable status under precolonial conditions lost ground when their societies came under the domination of colonialism.[4] At the same time it would not be correct to romanticize the position of women in traditional societies before the advent of capitalism, for some of the most brutal, exploitative examples of male dominance are found in the traditional agrarian states—whether feudal or slave, European or Asiatic—such as Greece, India, China, and the Middle Eastern countries. In attempting to explain the origin of male domination we shall have to beware of simplistic or romantic assumptions of an unspoiled past, or alternatively, of primitive brutality.

Most definitions of the term equality emphasize equality of access to socially valued resources. In hierarchical societies there is differential access to resources, whereas in simpler societies access to resources is more or less equal, though at the individual level it may vary somewhat.

The question of sexual equality is considerably more complicated because, when a husband and wife form a household, both live from the same estate based on lands or herds, and therefore both have similar access to resources. In these situations the question of equal access must be carefully studied and analyzed.

Obviously, women and men are different biologically, and in all societies there is a socially formulated gender division of labor. In no society are men and women equivalent, but in some they enjoy social equality. In primitive communal societies men and women differ not only biologically, but also in rigorous definitions of their respective daily pursuits. However, in spite of being separate they are equal. Without their own social identities and autonomy and their equal access to socially valued resources, they would have no sound basis for the reciprocal relations that bind the sexes and generations together. For example, among the tribally organized Iroquois of pre-colonial times (in what is now upper New York State and southern Ontario) there were, in effect, sex-specific estates: not only were the economic pursuits of the men (hunting and trading) and women (gardening and foraging) separate sectors of the subsistence of the house groupings, but men and women also reciprocated in giving their labor power to the seasonal pursuits of the other sex. The men would lop trees, burn the women's fields, and fence them, as well as construct the houses (which were owned by the women), and the women would assist the men in the hunt by driving game, dressing carcasses, and preparing hides. This was seen by the people as part of the reciprocal relations of the society, the relations that tended to balance over the long term. It can be argued that the reciprocity between men and women was necessitated by their social differences, and that the balancing was made possible by their general equal access to resources by sex.

Thus many scholars argue that in the simplest societies there is a kind of complementarity of roles. This undermines the attempt by others who want to demonstrate the universality of female subordination by setting up, and then shooting down, the straw man of an impossibly pure, abstract equality, which living, breathing societies are unable to achieve.

## MALE AND FEMALE IN A FORAGING SOCIETY

A necessary methodological problem is the question of measurement; that is, how can we say convincingly that women and men are equal, or that women and men are more equal in society A than they are in society B? This is indeed a thorny problem and no matter how unfashionable empiricism is today, we approach this question in a social scientific, almost positivistic way.

If we are to make sense of the real substance of male-female relations we have to leave the abstract level and get down to cases. We will examine the relations between men and women in one society, the !Kung San of Botswana. (One of us did extensive fieldwork among them between 1963 and 1986.) The !Kung, who are, or were until recently, hunter gatherers, display a remarkable sense of gender equality in their daily behavior, a sense that is found in few other societies.[5]

If you ask the !Kung "who really has the power and the strength in their society," many men will say, "Oh, the women have the strength. The women are the strong ones, we're the weak ones." And the women will say, "Oh, no, the men have the strength. Not us!" That is their story and they stick to it. Rather than give a global assessment of male-female relations in !Kung society, we prefer to discuss in turn the various spheres in which men and women interact to show that dominance of one sex in one sphere does not necessarily lead to dominance in another.

In the important area of subsistence, one immediately encounters a marked disparity. !Kung men hunt and !Kung women gather, and gathering provides about two-thirds of the diet. But the men also gather some of the food, and when this contribution is added, the men produce 45 percent, and the women 55 percent, of the total foods.[6] Thus the women have a clear dominance in food production.

Turning to the subjective criteria, it is curious in light of the importance of plant foods that men and women alike agree that meat is a more desirable food than vegetables. They simply say, we want meat. This is a central theme in !Kung consciousness.[7] When meat is scarce in the camp everyone craves it, even when vegetable foods arc abundant. And the killing of large animals is usually marked by feasting, dancing, and the giving of gifts of meat. Since game animals are scarce and unpredictable compared to plant foods, it is perhaps not so surprising that hunting is invested with more symbolic significance than gathering.

Adrienne Zihlmann and Nancy Tanner have proposed that in human evolution vegetable foods gathered by women were primary and that hunting was basically a cultural invention to give the men something to do. On the other hand, we should not lose sight of the fact that meat provides high-quality protein. Even if meat only constitutes 30 percent of the diet, it is nutritionally essential for the !Kung.[8]

Aside from nutritional value, meat has a ceremonial importance for hunters and gatherers, for it is shared more widely and more publicly than vegetable food. Coming in a block of a hundred to four hundred pounds, a kill is a windfall and makes quite a feast. Everybody can take the day off to eat. If a woman were to throw a feast like that, she would have to go out five days in a row and build up a stockpile of plant food.

The second area to assess is marriage and reproductive rights. Who chooses whom at the time of marriage? Is it by mutual agreement, or does the man choose and is the woman chosen? Or do the parents do the choosing? The !Kung have an interesting combination of both ascription and choice in this matter. Most !Kung marriages are arranged by the parents at the instigation of the future husband (who is usually much older than his wife-to-be). Although the girl has very little say in the original choice, many of these marriages fail because the girl is less than enthusiastic about the husband chosen for her. Yet the institution of arranged marriages continues, as a feature of the corporative inter-family nature of marriage in a foraging, kinship-organized society. At marriage, the girl's people insist that the young couple live with them. The reasons given are of three kinds: they say, first, that it must be seen that the man treats the daughter well; second, that he must prove his hunting ability by providing meat; and, third, that the girl is too young to leave her mother. In the majority of cases, the husband leaves his own group and takes up residence with the wife's group, a stay that may last three, five, or ten years, or even a lifetime. This is an area where women exercise power. Furthermore, when we come to the question of divorce, the data we have show that women initiate divorce in !Kung society far more frequently than men.[9]

The question of child care and how it should be divided among mother, father, and others is a controversial issue today in the West. In arguing for a more equitable distribution of household labor, feminists have turned to data on non-Western societies. In some ways the !Kung data offer little support for this view, since over 90 percent of the work involved in directly caring for young children is borne by the mother aided by the other women.[10] This is not to say that !Kung fathers ignore their children; on the contrary, they are attentive and loving and spend part of their leisure hours playing with the young infants and holding them. But the !Kung father rarely takes sole responsibility for the child while the mother is absent, whereas the opposite occurs every day.[11]

For their part the mothers do not consider themselves to be oppressed by this state of affairs. They keenly desire children, are excellent mothers, and often complain that they do not have as many children as they would like.

In interpreting these attitudes one should avoid projecting the disadvantages we associate with child care on an entirely different culture. !Kung women consider childbirth and child care as their sphere of responsibility, and they take steps to guard that prerogative. For example, many !Kung women give birth alone. They go into the bush and insist on excluding men from the childbirth site. The underlying explanation seems to be that it simplifies matters if the woman decides in favor of infanticide. Since the woman will commit a considerable amount of her energy to raising each child, she examines the newborn carefully for evidence of defects; if she finds any, the child is not allowed to live. By excluding men from the childbed, women can report to the camp that the child was born dead without fear of contradiction. But if the child is healthy and wanted by the woman she accepts the major responsibility for raising it. In this way the women exercise control over their own reproduction.

Another important reason why the !Kung woman's share of the child care is not oppressive is that she is not isolated from the community in the same way that modern urban mothers are. She helps and is helped by all the other women in the camp, and there is no necessity to separate her productive work from her child care work. When she gathers and prepares food, her child is on her hip, not at home with babysitters. Moreover, men do participate in the non-child-care aspects of housework: about 20–40 percent of the housework of a four-person household is done by men.[12] For those reasons it does not seem accurate to say that !Kung women are oppressed by the burden of caring for children.

Does the women's predominant role in production, their leverage in marriage and child rearing lead to power in the political arena as well? The answer in a broad sense is yes: !Kung women's participation in group discussions and decision making is probably greater than that of women in most tribal, peasant, and industrial societies. But their participation is not equal to that of the men, who appear to do about two-thirds of the talking in discussions involving both sexes, and to act as group spokespersons far more frequently than women.

This disparity between men and women comes into sharper relief when discussions and arguments turn to violence. In 34 fights occurring in the period 1963–9, a man attacked a woman 14 times, whereas a woman attacked a man only once.[13] Since 11 of these 15 cases involved husbands and wives, it is clear that in domestic scraps the wife is the victim in the great majority of cases. Similarly in cases of homicide there were 25 male killers but no female killers (though it is worth noting that 19 of the 22 victims were males as well).

It is remarkable that one major form of violence against women, rape, is rare among the !Kung. This kind of sexual violence so common in many state societies[14] has been reported to be extremely rare or nonexistent among the !Kung.[15]

In summarizing the evidence for male-female relations, we see that women predominate in some spheres of behavior and men in others, while the overall sense of the relations between the sexes is one of give and take. Both sexes contribute to subsistence. Since women's subsistence work is more efficient and productive than men's, they provide more of the food. In marriage arrangements women exercise some control and they initiate divorce far more frequently than men.

In the political sphere men do more of the talking than women, and it is our impression that their overall influence in "public" matters is greater, though we cannot present any data to confirm this point. Men behave more violently than women, though women are rarely the victims in serious conflicts; and rape, a primary form of violence against women in many societies, is rare among the !Kung.

On balance, the evidence shows a fairly equal role in society for the two sexes, and there is certainly no support in the !Kung data for the view that women in a "state of nature" are oppressed, dominated or sexually exploited by men. However, the comparative evidence suggests that the status of !Kung women may be higher than that enjoyed by women in some other foraging societies such as the Inuit, at least in modern times, and the Australian Aborigines.[16]

In hunter-gatherer societies of the historic period and in the primitive communal societies that predated them, men and women were members of autonomous, self-directed social groups and economies. It should be borne in mind that gender relations were not simply between individuals but between whole corporate kin groupings. Both men and women gained their identity and security from their kin groups. Individual gender roles involved individual decision making by their incumbents, in their areas of competence, for the good of their kinsmen and in-laws. Group decisions were arrived at by seeking unanimity. This feature of corporate kin relations reflected on the individual actors and the relations between specific men and women. Any "measuring" of male dominance or gender inequality must reckon with this inter-corporate *social* reality.

THE ORIGINS OF MALE DOMINATION

It would be foolhardy to argue that the ancestors of all of us were like the !Kung and that early men and women enjoyed a life of gender equality and bliss. However, because of the nature of their productive systems and the widespread evidence of similarities among all or most hunter-gatherer societies, we *can* argue that the gender relations of our ancestors probably resembled those of contemporary hunter-gatherers more than they did the gender relations of our class-stratified patriarchal industrial societies.

The question can now be asked: How did we get from there to here? How, in the course of social evolution, did men come to dominate women? What happened in history, and why?

In responding to these questions it will be useful to distinguish three broad stages of human history before capitalism: first, primitive communism, found in hunting and gathering bands; second, tribal society and chiefdoms; and third, early agrarian states. Speaking generally, two important transformations propelled history from the first stage to the third: (1) the Neolithic revolution and the rise of agriculture, and (2) the rise of the state. This is the basic historical framework in which male domination develops.

*Phase One: Primitive Communism*[17]

In the first stage of human history people lived by hunting and gathering, without domesticated plants or animals; they directly appropriated their subsistence from nature. There was no rich or poor, political leadership was minimal, and the population density was low.[18] Along with Engels, we would argue that in this period men and women were relatively equal.[19] The general conditions of low production coupled with the absence of private property and a minimal production of commodities make possible the relative equality of the sexes. We do not concur, however, with the many nineteenth-century theorists who argued that in the beginning, women dominated men in a matriarchy.[20] There simply is no anthropological evidence for such a view.

It is also important to make the qualification that there is no evidence for primitive promiscuity in the anthropological literature, although this was an important aspect of Morgan's and Engels' view of primitive society. However, primitive communism itself *is* a valid construct: land *was* "owned" collectively or communally, political leadership was minimal, the population density was relatively low, and inequality of status or wealth was minimal. Both men and women contributed to the food supply, and warfare was nonexistent or very modest in scale.

This view of primitive communism and the relative equality between the sexes contrasts sharply with a number of bourgeois ideological constructs in anthropology such as the view of Claude Lévi-Strauss in *Les structures élémentaires de la parenté.* In the beginning, he argues, human society was formed by men agreeing to give away a sister in order to receive someone else's sister, the origin of society being exchange of women by men. He called women the original scarce good, the original medium of exchange.[21] In our view this is an ethnocentric and ideological projection on the material that cannot be convincingly demonstrated from the ethnographic evidence.

It should be added that there *is* variation among hunter-gatherers. The !Kung, and a dozen or so societies like them, seem to represent one pole of sexual egalitarianism. There is another group of hunter-gatherer societies which, while far more egalitarian than we are, nevertheless do display some signs of female subordination, to a greater degree than is found among the !Kung.[22]

## Phase Two: Tribal Society

Tribal society is a product of the first great transformation of human history, the establishment of agriculture, which V. Gordon Childe called the Neolithic Revolution. Here we see three important changes, all of which have implications for the status of men in relation to women.[23]

First of all, we find a change in the mode of production, from a very diffuse direct appropriation from nature to improvement of the land and/or domestication of animals: group livelihood then becomes dependent on the control of a resource, a resource that has been improved by humans—land or livestock. And here we see the germs of the origin of property.

Second, in the tribal society, the population gets larger, a change that has important effects. There is a need for a centralized system of leadership or management. We see, for example the advent of the "Big Man" system in which the Big Man acts as a political catalyst, as spokesperson for the group, and as redistributor of surplus food.

Third, agriculture, in changing the mode of production, increases both the production ceiling of the society, and its need for labor power and economic organization. Land formerly a non-limited component of a hunting and gathering economy now becomes, in arable regions, a subject of dispute. The new mode becomes increasingly successful at the expense of the old. The population grows and the new mode flourishes. Owing to the finite amount of arable land (given the level of Neolithic technology), agricultural peoples come into conflict, not only with one another, concerning the ownership and control of land and resources, but also with peoples who do not embrace the new mode of production. Their object is to obtain both land and labor—by intermarriage, as in earlier times, as well as by trade and warfare. We observe that there is far more warfare in simple horticultural societies around the world than among hunter-gatherers.

As a consequence of these important changes, women's status seems to decline, and the men's to rise, although again there is considerable variation. At this point it is useful to review several arguments.

Eleanor Leacock, following leads given by Engels and other Marxist theorists, argues that the origin of women's oppression is to be found in commodity production: production for exchange instead of production for use. When commodities are being produced for trade outside the local community, women's labor is of critical importance. This means that the *control* of women's labor becomes an area of contestation. Women's freedom of action in divorce and marriage becomes circumscribed. Bride price replaces bride service: that is to say, upon marriage a man no longer provides his labor and skills to his wife and in-laws. The relationship ceased to be one of reciprocal exchange of goods, services, and personnel. Now he and his kin provided a payment to obtain rights over the woman's labor, sexuality and reproduction.

A second argument, and one that has considerable empirical basis, is the study by Patricia Draper of the !Kung San in the process of settling down and adopting agriculture and stock raising. Draper

found that when !Kung settled down and took up agricultural practices, certain subtle changes took place in women's and men's lives
that led to the subordination of the former. While men continued to
travel widely, women became home-bound. Instead of going out and
meeting the "public" in the course of gathering, they were confined to
their homestead. Their work became more socially isolated and more
private, whereas the men, in going out to herd cattle, continued to
meet the public and had a wider view of the world. Draper notes also
the development of segregation of children by sex in tasks. Girls
helped their mothers with their work, and boys helped their fathers
and older brothers with the livestock.[24]

A third view is the position of Marvin Harris that neolithic warfare
is the root cause of women's subordination.[25] He delineates the
complex of warfare and male supremacy of early horticultural societies: males became expendable but also dominant. Female infanticide was practiced and women were given to men survivors as a
reward for bravery in battle. This argument has received a good deal
of justified criticism in feminist circles, since female infanticide is not
nearly as widespread in horticultural societies as warfare is, and there
are warlike tribal societies, such as the Iroquois, in which women had
a high status.[26] On the other hand, among the Yanamamo, for example, a very warlike society (at least in colonial times) in South America, women had low status.[27] We cannot discount warfare as one of
the causes of women's subordination and male domination. But it
seems that the existence of warfare alone does not in itself account for
the subordination of women.

In tribal society we find the phenomenon of social ranking, and we
can no longer make simple statements—which we have been making
so far—about the status of women, because there are high-ranking
men and women, low-ranking men and women, and slaves; we have
to look at the situation of men and women of each status.

One cannot leave this discussion without considering the whole
question of matriarchy, the rule or domination of women over men,
which has been widely discussed by feminists. We accept the prevalent informed view: that matriarchy as far as we know has never
existed. But the question then becomes why the legend of matriarchy
was so persistent and why it appeared in so many mythologies around
the world. The most useful approach to this problem may be the work
of Paula Webster and Esther Newton on matriarchy as a vision of
power for women—a vision of what could be.[28] It has also been
suggested that matriarchy was a scurrilous invention of men to justify

their own domination, because the matriarchy story is always coupled with a world-historical defeat of women by men.

## Phase Three: Early Agrarian States

If patriarchy is defined as the systematic domination of women by men in most or all societies, then pre-state societies, we believe, do not have patriarchy.[29] In order to have real patriarchy we have to go on to the next transformation, which is the origin of the state. Here we observe the development of classes, bureaucracy, and civil administration, together with the decline or destruction of the kin-based social order, which had been universal up to this point. With the origin of the state there is a serious loss of status for women across the board, although again there is a wide variation. Patriarchy, we will argue, needs a state society for its very existence.

Patriarchy can best be understood as the reproduction of state hierarchy within the family. A well-known example of this is the *patria potestas* of the Roman Empire: the emperor rules the empire, the father rules the home and the family. The father was clearly considered the emperor's representative in the home; the emperor was the father's representative in the state. Similar kinds of ideology are found in India, the Middle East, Ancient Greece, and traditional China as well as in Europe—medieval, early modern, and Victorian.

There is an interesting point with which we would like to conclude: recent research on the formation of states makes a distinction between the early state (such as the Incas, the Aztecs, Mesopotamia, and early despotic Egypt) and the mature state (such as fifth-century Athens, the Roman Empire, and the late feudal Kingdoms of Europe). (The capitalist state and socialist state are yet other types.) Building upon a basic point of Morgan and Engels, the proponents of this point of view argue that the mature state is one in which bureaucracy dominates kinship; the early state is one in which kinship still dominates bureaucracy. We have the interesting phenomenon that in early states women may have had higher status than they have in mature states precisely because the kinship system was the source of women's residual power. Destroy it, and you destroy the basis for women's independence. For example, Irene Silverblatt, who has examined the position of women in the pre-columbian Inca state, argues that even though the Incas formed a state and indeed an empire, women enjoyed relatively high status in this state system because the basis of the Inca state was the Andean kin group or "ayllu." This high status was lost when the Spanish conquest destroyed the kin group and, in so doing, destroyed the bases of women's power.[30] The mechanism at work here seems to be that with the destruction of the kinship base women lost their communal autonomy and became isolated and, in a sense, "privatized." In this condition women became more vulnerable to domination or brutalization by husband or fathers. In other words, the extended kin group was a protective device for women.

In conclusion, we might say that women's labor is essential to the reproduction of state power and state organization in a variety of ways, and thus the subordination of women in these early states, which has continued to the present, is essential to the reproduction of state power. Hence, in challenging patriarchy we challenge one of the cornerstones of the state in contemporary capitalist and post-capitalist societies.

It is our contention that male domination arose, not from human biology, but with the evolution of human society, together with institutional inequalities and hierarchies. It gains its full force with the development of state power and the socially sanctioned alienation of women from access to resources and direct production. The question of male dominance is a sociological and cultural question, a product not of animal instincts, but rather, of human history.

## NOTES

[1]Stephen Goldberg, "Response to Leacock and Livingston: Discussion and Debate," *American Anthropologist* 77, no. 1 (1975): 70–1.

[2]Those who argue from a sociobiological perspective tend to ignore these complexities of the biological, and particularly, the primate data, which do not support their arguments. For instance, a considerable body of material has come to light, largely as a result of feminist research, on the ability of females to provide for the family's subsistence and of males to play a significant nurturing role with regard to the young. Cf. L. Leibowitz, *Females, Males, Families: A Biosocial Approach* (North Scituate, Mass.: Duxbury Press, 1978); R. Rohrlich-Leavitt, "Peaceful Primates and Gentle People," in Barbara B. Watson, ed., *Women's Studies: The Social Realities* (New York: Harper's College Press, 1976); and Jane Lancaster, *Primate Behavior and the Emergence of Human Culture* (New York: Holt, Rinehart and Winston, 1975).

[3]Eleanor B. Leacock, *Myths of Male Dominance, Collected Articles on Women Cross-Culturally* (New York: Monthly Review Press, 1981), 18.

[4]Mona Etienne and Eleanor B. Leacock, eds., *Women and Colonization* (New York: Praeger, 1980).

[5]This ethnographic case of a twentieth-century foraging society illustrates not only the contrasts with our own unequal, class-divided society, but also indicates a process of social evolution. While the !Kung are in general an example of a certain evolutionary stage, it must be remembered that they are by no means primitives, in the sense of being a primal, pristine human society. Within the evolutionary stage that they have occupied well into the present century, they have experienced many generations of social variation, development, and change. In a word, they too have a history and heritage as long as our own. Part of this unwritten history, which is virtually impossible to

verify, may well have been a certain degree of moral and ideological influence exerted, by diffusion, on foraging peoples by politically more dominant societies. (The exclamation mark in the word "!Kung" is used to indicate the click sound in their language.) See Richard Lee, *The !Kung San: Men, Women and Work in a Foraging Society* (Cambridge: Cambridge University Press, 1979).

[6]Lee, *op. cit.,* ch. 9.

[7]See Megan Biesele's forthcoming book on !Kung mythology, *Women Like Meat* (Durban: University of Natal Press, in press).

[8]Nancy Tanner and A. Zihlmann, "Women's Evolution. Part I: Innovation and Selection in Human Origins," *Signs* 1, no. 3: 585-608.

[9]Lorna Marshall, *The !Kung of Nyae Nyae* (Cambridge, Mass.: Harvard University Press, 1976), 285-86.

[10]P. Draper, "!Kung women: Contrasts in Sexual Egalitarianism in the Foraging and Sedentary Contexts," in R. Reiter, ed., *Toward an Anthropology of Women* (New York: Monthly Review Press, 1975), 77-109.

[11]Draper, *op. cit.,* and M. West and M. Konner, "The Role of the Father: An Anthropological Perspective," in M. Lamb, ed., *The Role of the Father in Child Development* (New York: Wiley, 1978).

[12]Lee, *op. cit.,* 277-80.

[13]Lee, *op. cit.,* ch. 13.

[14]Susan Brownmiller, *Against Our Will: Men, Women and Rape* (New York: Simon and Schuster, 1975); and Paula Webster, "The Politics of Rape in Primitive Society," paper presented to the 75th Annual Meeting, American Anthropological Association, Washington D.C., 1976.

[15]Marshall, *op. cit.,* 279.

[16]E. Friedl, *Women and Men: An Anthropologist's View* (New York: Holt, Rinehart and Winston, 1975); and F. Gale, ed., *Women's Role in Aboriginal Society,* Australian Aboriginal Studies no. 36 (Canberra: Australian National University Press, 1974).

[17]Long out of favor, the concept of primitive communism appears to be undergoing a revival. See, for example, A. Testart, *Le Communisme primitif. Économie et Idéologie* (Paris: Éditions MSH, 1985).

[18]"Introduction," in E. Leacock and R. Lee, eds., *Politics and History in Band Societies* (Cambridge: Cambridge University Press, 1982) and R. B. Lee, "Reflections on Primitive Communism," in C. Gailey *et al., Festschrift in Honor of Stanley Diamond* (New York: Basic Books, in press). And see E. Leacock, *Myths of Male Dominance* (New York: Monthly Review Press, 1981).

[19]Frederick Engels, *The Origin of the Family, Private Property and the State,* ed. E.B. Leacock, (New York: International Publisher, 1972).

[20]See Paula Webster, "Matriarchy: A Vision of Power," in R. Reiter, ed., *Toward an Anthropology of Women* (New York: Monthly Review Press, 1975). Webster argues that matriarchy should be viewed as an ideological construct rather than an historical fact.

[21]Claude Lévi-Strauss,*Les structures élémentaires de la parenté* (Paris: Presses Universitaires de France, 1949).

[22]See, for example, I. Bern, "Inequality and Australian Aboriginal Society," paper delivered at Symposium on Egalitarian and Hierarchical Tendencies in Aboriginal Social Life, Institute of Aboriginal Studies Conference, Canberra, May 1986.

[23]To some degree a form of tribal society has also developed on a base of fishing where, again, a regular, secure subsistence resource allowed for settled village life. This is discussed by David Aberle, for example, in relation to the distribution and frequency of matriliny. See D. Aberle, "Matrilineal Descent in Cross-cultural perspective," in D.M. Schneider and K. Gough, eds., *Matrilineal Kinship* (Berkeley: University of California Press, 1961), 655-727.

[24]Leacock *op. cit.,* and Draper, *op. cit.*

[25]Marvin Harris, "Why Men Dominate Women," *The New York Times Magazine,* 13 Nov., 1977, 69-73.

[26]George S. Snyderman, "Behind the Tree of Peace: A Sociological Analysis of Iroquois Warfare," *Pennsylvania Archeologist* 18, no. 3-4 (1948): 3-93; and George T. Hunt, *The Wars of the Iroquois:*

*A Study in Intertribal Trade Relations* (Madison: University of Wisconsin Press, 1940).

[27]Napoleon Chagnon, *Yanomamo: The Fierce People* (New York: Holt Rinehart and Winston), 3rd ed., 1983.

[28]Webster, in R. Reiter, *op. cit.*

[29]For the classic statements of the theory of patriarchy, see Sir Henry Maine, *Ancient Law* (1961), reprinted in Everyman's Library (London: Dent, 1917) and in D. McLennan, *The Patriarchal Family,* (London: Macmillan, 1885). For contemporary feminist analyses of patriarchy see, for example, Michele Barrett, *Women's Oppression Today* (London: Verso, 1982) and Rosalind Coward, *Patriarchal Precedents: Sexuality and Social Relations* (London: Routledge and Kegan Paul, 1983).

[30]Irene Silverblatt, "The Universe has turned inside out . . . . There is no justice for us here: Andean Women Under Spanish Rule," in M. Etienne and E. Leacock, eds., *op. cit.,* 149-85.

# Beyond Tarzan and Jane Genes: Toward a Critique of Biological Determinism

## CARMEN SCHIFELLITE

—In a large North American city a pair of Siamese twins are about to be separated. Since they share one set of male genitals, the separation will leave one as a male while the other will have cosmetic and reconstructive surgery done so that "she" can become a "female." The staff that will perform the operation has decided that the twin who will remain a boy will do so because "his" personality is more masculine: "he" is more aggressive, active, and rambunctious than his "sister." "She" will become the "female" because "she" is more feminine, passive, and docile.

—The prime minister of Singapore suggests that "the genetic stock of his nation is about to plummet" and that the educated women of Singapore must have more babies in order to pass on their superior genes.

—A nobel laureate testifies before the United States Congress that head start programs for poor minority children will do no good because 80 percent of intelligence is genetically fixed.

—A mathematics teacher spends more time with the boys in his class than with the girls because everyone knows that girls have more dominant right (emotional) brains and boys more dominant left (analytic) brains; the girls will never be able to do the more abstract and complicated mathematics to come; so he saves his efforts for those who will.

—A doctor listens to a single mother's complaints about her health problems and her worries about money and prescribes a tranquilizer for yet another overly emotional woman.

These incidents—all real—are examples of theories and practices that are considered to be supported by scientific evidence. They are examples of the countless times when people are categorized and decisions made according to biologically deterministic views of what controls and produces human behavior.

Biodeterminist arguments seek to reduce the causes of most human behavior to biological processes or structures. Some make genes the causal factor in their analysis; some arguments see other physical structures and entities as the causes of behavior.[1] Although the details of biologically deterministic arguments may vary, they all assume that there is some complex of genes, proteins, hormones, arrangement of brain cells, structure of the genitals, or any other biological structure that indicates the existence of some heritable trait and that predisposes a person to behave or perform in a preordained, quantifiable, and predictable fashion. (In the nineteenth century, bumps on the head and the shape of the nose were thought to be related to character and behavior.)

These arguments are misleading and simplistic, not to mention dangerous, because they divide human beings into subgroups that are organized on the basis of a supposed relationship between the shared biological makeup of a subgroup and the supposed behavior or traits of that group. Often, this process results in laws and government policies that have damaging consequences for those who have been slotted into one of these subgroups.

Biologically deterministic arguments tend to be used to stigmatize women, various "racial" groups, gays and lesbians, working-class people, and the most economically and socially marginalized, both in the advanced capitalist countries and in the Third World. For people who find themselves on the bottom of the socioeconomic heap, it is not comforting to hear that their position and behavior are normal, and even inevitable, because they have been biologically encoded. Biologically deterministic arguments arise from, and take root in, the structured inequality of the societies that produce them. Whether they pertain to class, sex, race, or sexual orientation, the results are similar. In any social formation in which inequality is structurally and systematically created, it is likely that both the science and the ideology of that society will generate theories that accentuate the apparent differences between different social strata. It is also likely that the causes of these differences in behavior, traits, habits, and customs of the various groups will be attributed to some type of immutable "human nature."

In this article I will examine some of the ways in which biologically deterministic arguments are constructed and legitimized in our society. This is an important aspect of the challenge to patriarchy because these determinist arguments have been used to reinforce male privilege and the oppression of women. There are several possible starting points for such a critique. One is to debunk many of the spurious claims of biodeterminism—that men are naturally this and women are naturally that. This approach is interesting but it leaves many of the underlying assumptions of biodeterminism untouched. As a result, such an approach tends to argue within the same framework as biodeterminism but simply produces different facts or theories. A better approach, even if more abstract, is to challenge these underlying assumptions and biases of biodeterminism. Such is the approach of this article.

## FROM NINETEENTH-CENTURY BIODETERMINISM TO SOCIOBIOLOGY

It was in the second half of the nineteenth century that a very crude theory of evolutionary change emerged and was followed by an equally unrefined theory of genetic transmission. The evolutionary theory borrowed heavily from the leading ideologues of capitalism in its explanations of the process of change, in particular, the stress on competition and the survival of the fittest. This genetic theory ignored the complexities of gene interaction and focused on those genes and traits whose patterns of transmission from one generation to the next occur independently of one another and which are clearly visible, such as eye or hair color. A combination of these two theories was used as the basis of an equally crude set of determinist arguments.

There are a number of reasons why such a determinism could take hold. In the nineteenth century, England ruled a vast colonial empire, and so the idea of genetic or biological inferiority was very useful for legitimizing the subjugation of colonial populations. At home, demands were being made for universal male suffrage, and later for female suffrage, both of which would separate those democratic rights from the ownership of property. Thus a new form of class definition and exclusion was needed to reestablish the lines of class demarcation and social control.[2] In some measure, IQ testing was used to locate and quantify a trait that could be used to redefine who is entitled to succeed. Likewise, such an ideology could be used to legitimize inequality and explain why it persisted in the new supposedly egalitarian society. In addition, public education had been institutionalized and IQ testing became very useful in streaming working-class children into dead-end jobs.[3] In the United States, the emancipation of the slaves meant that they would now be entitled to equal opportunity and representation in the Union. Any theory that would support practices of exclusion on grounds of biological inferiority could be used to help render blacks non-citizens both socially and legally. And finally, the rapid popularization of evolutionary theory by Huxley and Spencer also sped up the popularization of its determinist offshoots.[4]

One of the first forms of these arguments can be traced to the Italian criminologist, Lombroso, who developed a theory that correlated physical types with aggressive behavior. For Lombroso, the criminal tended to be apish and had a primitive brain, long arms, cold eyes, and so on.[5] These were not simply descriptions, but tools of analysis that the police could use to assess the possible criminality of a suspect. Galton, in his book *Hereditary Genius,* took the argument further by observing that parents did pass on their social status to their children and therefore concluding "comfortingly that genius was inherited."[6] His views on the heritability of intelligence put him in a position to lead the eugenics movements that developed in Britain and the United States in the late nineteenth century. In the first decades of the twentieth century, this movement in the United States persuasively lobbied for sterilization laws and, during the 1920s, for restrictions on immigration, believing "that such ills as crime, alcoholism, and prostitution were related to subnormal intelligence" and advocating sterilization "to prevent the unfit from breeding."[7] Many of the approximately fifty thousand who had been sterilized by 1958 were guilty only of suffering from epilepsy, "insanity," and syphilis, or of being prostitutes or alcoholics. This movement also did much to appropriate Binet's intelligence tests and use them for purposes he had never intended:

> the translators and importers of Binet's test, both in the U.S. and in England, tended to share a common ideology, one drastically at variance with Binet's. They asserted that intelligence tests measured an innate and unchangeable quantity, fixed by genetic inheritance.[8]

Other forms of determinist arguments emerged specifically in regard to women. Ehrenreich and English argue that in the transition to capitalism women's roles in society were up for grabs, as were all forms of social relations. A key force in keeping women in unequal and ghettoized positions in society was the various determinist arguments that women's constitutions, thought processes, emotions, and instincts conspired to keep women inferior and therefore unequal.[9] Likewise, it was also during this time that the medical profession took to removing a woman's uterus as a cure for a kind of spontaneous paralysis that affected many women in this epoch. The fact that this surgery sometimes worked seems to attest to the fact that many women unconsciously (and correctly) perceived that scientists and society were making a link between their genital structures and their rights and possibilities in an emerging bourgeois society.

In the middle years of the twentieth century, determinist theories and practices decreased in number and effectiveness. But with the Watson and Crick model of genetic structure came a new synthesis of genetic and evolutionary theory. This new framework was taken up by anthropologists, etymologists, ethnologists, biochemists, neuropsychologists, and neurologists. In the last ten years these different disciplines have been organized under the paradigm of sociobiology.[10] This emergent "science" attributes much human behavior to genetic predisposition. Sociobiology's ability to order so much diverse observation and knowledge into one coherent conceptual framework has allowed it to gain credibility and to be popularized very quickly. It is not crudely formulated as were the nineteenth century theories, and it speaks more of predispositions and tendencies toward certain behavior than of a rigidly biodetermined human nature. Nevertheless, its effects are not altogether different from its nineteenth-century forerunners.

A recent example of this kind of sociobiological thought is a newspaper article entitled "Mystery of love may be genetic." Researchers in England and Canada have advanced a theory that love (that is, attraction) may be genetically determined. Their hypothesis is that "our genes are determined to direct us towards mates who are genetically similar to ourselves." They claim that "there is a lot of animal work showing that in many species, animals prefer relatives that they have never met before to unrelated strangers" and that this "correlates" with "a great deal of evolutionary theory at the moment which argues that altruism is more likely to occur between individuals who are closely related to each other." A Canadian researcher argues that "if like is attracted to like, then there is going to be a greater tendency for altruism to occur between the husband and wife." This will be a selection advantage and together with the children's stronger attraction for their genetically similar children, "will create the bonds that keep family together." While these researchers agree that human behavior is more complicated than it seems, in the end they argue that "similarity did seem to be the general rule governing relationships and marriage, in particular." While they admit that "the strongest similarities are in things like attitudes and socioeconomic status," they still claim that "there is an underlying genetic similarity which draws us together."[11] Here we see the extent to which these theorists will force the social to be subsumed by the biological, even when the evidence is no more than a set of correlations. What this tactic accomplishes, along the way, is to take a number of socially organized institutions—such as monogamy and the nuclear family—and attribute them to evolutionary genetic adaptations.

## BIODETERMINISM: THE CLAIMS FOR MEN AND WOMEN

The literature that makes claims for the biological basis of some of men's and women's behavior tends to concentrate on a few ways in which men and women relate differently to the world and to each other. These differences tend to be posed as mutually exclusive. One such dichotomy is that men are more aggressive and destructive than women, who are more passive and nurturing. A second set of dichotomies centers on male and female thought patterns. Men are seen to be more capable and rational thinkers who can control their emotions, whereas women are seen to act more on intuition, irrationality, and emotion.

Of course, it is not that women cannot think rationally or that men are not capable of irrationality and emotion. It is that men are seen to be more in control. Men are seen to have more control over their bodies, or conversely, men's hormones and genitals are seen to be less prone to getting in their way. Man is aggressive, clever, sometimes destructive, and in control of his emotions. Woman is more of the earth. She is seen to be more passive and nurturing, less likely to attempt to dominate nature or others, and more ruled by her body and emotions. Man therefore is more likely to achieve "greatness" by his own actions and talents; a woman can do so only through the strength of her looks, charm, performing talents, children's achievements, or husband's success. In a nutshell, we can say that men are seen to possess all those abilities and disciplines that allow us to dominate, succeed, and control: that is, to rule the world that we have built. Women are seen to have the talents, intuition, abilities, and emotionality to produce and nurture succeeding generations in this world. What biologically deterministic arguments attempt to do is to locate biological roots for those kinds of behavior, abilities, and weaknesses.

The fundamental question is how these "scientific" conceptions are formed and how they restrict the roles and behavior of men and women by defining the limits of "normality" and "naturalness" in our society. I am not advocating a "sociologism" that sees all behavior as socially produced. Although there is no doubt that our biology establishes the physiological limits to our range of behavior, the relationship between our biology, our behavior, and our social environment is a complex and interdependent one that is not reducible to a simplistic determinism.[12] Whether or not we should even attempt to formulate scientific theories about the relation between biology and society is not at issue. The question is what such theorizing says, how it is organized, how it accounts for its facts and theories, and in whose interests it speaks.

It is not enough to challenge the particular determinist arguments, although this is essential; one must also analyze the concepts and practices that provide the legitimacy for the whole enterprise. A debate like this draws its theoretical integrity and legitimacy from outside the apparent boundaries of its own debates. Likewise, the arguments in favor of biological determinism are so varied and borrow so much from less contentious sciences, like evolutionary and genetic theory, that this study must include an analysis of the ways in which concepts and facts are borrowed and used.

### How Is It Put Together?

The newer versions of biodeterminism are being presented in more sophisticated and more abstract ways than the old ones, and so it is important for its critics also to develop more refined tools for analyzing these positions. Numerous critiques have been made of the various forms of biologically deterministic arguments that have appeared over the years. Although the critics have fought and won many battles by using these methods, they do not challenge the legitimacy of the entire endeavor. That is, they tend not to ask what allows biodeterminism to consider genes and instincts in relation to intelligence, or aggression, or emotionality, or rationality, or sexuality as if they were dealing with the shape of peas or the color of eyes.

The first question in the analysis of the validity of biodeterminist arguments is, "Are the facts accurate?" There are also a number of ways to examine the data that are presented as "the facts." There are all too many cases where scientists have falsified data in order to produce successful, interesting, or predicted results.[13] The area of heritability and genetics has generated a fairly large amount of controversy as well as accusations of and confirmation of falsification of data.

However, let us leave blatant falsification aside, for it is more important that even "true facts"—those for which it is possible to produce repeatable results in research—be treated with suspicion. We must ask: "Is there socially produced bias at play in the production of these results?". Much good research by feminist scholars has revealed the depth to which the inherent sexist biases of researchers and of society in general influence all phases of the production of facts and theories.[14] I am not referring here to an intentional obscuring of reality, but to the general social process of producing information. This category of unintentional bias is probably the category into which the largest number of "facts" would fall. It is also the most difficult to examine critically, precisely because the science used in constructing this information appears to be both objective and accurate. This is an important conceptual point and requires a little more development.

It is commonly believed that the facts and properties of the world exist, self-contained, and preconstituted, waiting for someone to discover them. What is not often brought out is the way in which the accepted facts and interpretations of any phenomenon are socially constructed and influenced by all those forces that influence any human activity. In neuropsychology, it is understood that of all the uncountable sensations impinging on our senses all the time, only a small portion will ever register as stimuli and be incorporated into our conscious and unconscious processes. The ones that we do register have been selected by some filtering process through which they have been rendered recognizable. For example, people who live in the Arctic have developed more categories and distinctions for snow than those who live in temperate zones. It isn't simply a matter of more words; it is a matter of a different process of recognition. This filtering process emerges out of the interplay of biology and social position and generally lets in some sensations as it filters out others. This process occurs not only at the level of individual perceptions, but also with the creation of socially organized perceptions.

Knowledge is a product. It is produced through the same social and discursive practices and social relations that go into producing and reproducing human society. The social biases that are part of these practices and relations are the filters through which we see and make sense of the events that we experience or that are reported to us. The production of biodeterminism, and in fact the production of any knowledge, whether we call it science, ideology, popular culture, discourse, documentary reality, or superstition, is completely rooted in the social field in which it is produced and shaped.[15]

In the case of scientific knowledge, what are constructed are the labs, facts, and theories used in "normal science."[16] Social relations, levels of technique, existing theoretical frameworks, and a whole host of other influences all affect the process. Scientists publish the results of their work in the trade journals, whereupon those results are transformed into entities that can be discussed and considered as if they were "found objects," and not invented ones. The criteria of reproducibility and falsifiability in the scientific method serve to render a phenomenon as interesting, to categorize it, and ultimately to elevate it to the status of a "fact" in what seems to be a disinterested and universally accepted way. It is then an observable phenomenon, which has been given a particular interpretation agreed upon by the scientific community.[17] Through this process, fact and theory become part of an interpretive framework that constructs what Kuhn has called a scientific paradigm.[18]

Once a paradigm or set of interpretations is established, there is a tendency for further research to select facts that fit the theory. For example, Lowe has investigated studies that seek to find a biological basis for male and female differences in mental capacities. She concludes that

> scientists attempt to find tools to measure the differences that are assumed to be there, rather than to examine whether or not the differences actually exist. Results that do not come out as expected are blamed on faulty methodology or bad data and rejected.[19]

Likewise, Sayers found in reviewing some of the literature on the assumed sex-based control of the expression of aggression that many of the connections made rely more on ideology than on "any relevant factual evidence."[20]

There is definitely a difference between those who believe they are doing objective science and those who know they are falsifying data, but no theory and no theoreticians or researchers can rise above their social environment. This environment unconsciously impels the scientist to bring one set of facts "into view," but in doing so other things are rendered invisible. Statistical analysis is just such a process of "fact fixing." That which falls outside the interpretive frame is rendered insignificant and ultimately invisible. (A classic example of this is the labeling of certain effects of drugs as "side effects.")

This process is important because what is made invisible influences and shapes our understanding of the object being studied. When we are the objects being studied, our conceptions can affect our own further developments. How we see the world *influences* how we see the world; it also influences what the world becomes, and therefore, how we see it. These ideas and views of ourselves have power by virtue of their place in the activities and social relations through which we produce and reproduce human society. Who we are, depends on the social world we have created, and that world has the power in turn, to reshape us. As Marian Lowe and Ruth Hubbard have pointed out in some pioneering work on this topic, the evidence suggests "that a great many aspects of biological functioning—including body size and strength, hormone levels, and possibly, brain development—can be changed considerably by changes in the environment."[21] Lowe cites numerous examples of the significant changes in women's physical performance that occur with training, to the extent that "In general, the physical performance of American women athletes differs from that of the average populations of non-athletic women far more than that of men athletes does from non-athletic men."[22] Likewise, it is clear that "sex differences in social roles result in major differences in the ways in which we use our bodies."[23] Thus, even though it is evident that although differences in the performances of men and women in a variety of areas do exist, as Lowe points out,

> The stereotypes we accept about sex roles have far-reaching effects. Ideas about appropriate behaviour for women and men act as powerful constraints on behaviour and often become self-fulfilling prophesies. The effects of sex-role stereotyping can go even further, however; not only behaviour but also biology can be modified by the contraints imposed by rigidly defined sex roles.[24]

And so, even when one finds sex-based differences in physical attributes and performance, the causes of these differences remain unclear.

Thus, when considering the accuracy of "the facts," we are dealing with a threefold problem. The first is that the facts may have been falsified. Second, they are distorted by the biases of researchers and by the biases of society. And finally, our discursive practices—our views of ourselves along with the social practices and social relations that are part of those views—actually control our potential, behavior and performance to a great extent. Both the second and third problems also apply to the causal theories used to explain the existence of these "facts."

## Legitimizing Concepts

The causal theories are very significant because they are the means by which we make sense of the correlative statistics that have been produced.[25] All causal arguments must, to some degree, rely on preexisting categories and concepts. These legitimizing categories are crucial, not only to the process of creating facts, but also to the process of developing the theories that describe these facts.

For example, let us assume that we are attempting to discover the patterns in the inheritance of intelligence. Our interest is differences in intelligence between men and women. This means that first we must have a conception of "trait," a conception of "heritability," and a conception of the mechanisms whereby this transmission occurs, even to conceive of doing such research. Next, we must also have a category called intelligence and a means of measuring it.

The way in which most of the standard research in this area is conducted is by studying, not intelligence, but IQ, simply because the Intelligence Quotient is something that can be measured with a test and something about which we have amassed large numbers of correlative statistics. However, when we substitute IQ for intelligence, we are no longer measuring something we assume to be a genetic trait—something that is a part of one's biological makeup; we are now measuring a socially constructed representation of that object. The IQ test was not discovered, but invented. With the development of the test it became possible to elevate IQ to the level of something that supposedly represents intelligence.

Out of all this comes a very narrow definition of intelligence. The test reveals a person's competence only in the areas that it tests. It reveals nothing about the other kinds of intelligence that are not being tested, or that cannot be revealed by any testing procedures. An IQ test may be accurate in what it assesses, but what it does not assess may be more significant than what it does assess. And the way in which the information gained from the tests is used may have significant effects on the future performance of those who have been tested.

The second part of our imaginary study examines the differences in intelligence (IQ) between male and female. Now, not only do we have to have an interpretive frame that provides for the existence of all of the categories used in the argument but we must also have categories for male and female. At this point most people will say that the differences are pretty self-evident, but are they?

When someone does research on sex-related differences, they would generally refer to male and female as the two populations under investigation. The researcher does not need to qualify this, but will expect the reader to know what is meant by male and female; because it is assumed that we all belong to either one or the other sex. However, there are more than two "sexes."[26] A small proportion of the population is located somewhere between the two. I am not referring to gender socialization here, but to genital morphology and chromosome number and structure. Yet, this group is seldom discussed in the presentation of sex differences. This preexisting schema or interpretive frame has rendered invisible that small percentage of the population born with more than or less than the biological apparati that make it possible for us to slot an individual into either of the two categories we use to cover all the forms. If these "abnormals" were to be presented, it would upset the interpretive framework through which the facts of sex status are created and assigned. This could have repercussions throughout the society for the following reasons.

A rigidly structured sex and gender inequality exists in our society. It is based on the tight linkage of male to masculine and of female to feminine, a linkage in which man equals male-masculine and woman equals female-feminine. The distinctions between masculine and feminine are seen to reflect significant biological differences between males and females. The more the apparent differences between male and female can be developed, the easier it is to administer differential status to men and women, based on sexual distinctions. Any information that could lessen the distinctions between male and female also has the potential to help to delink sex and gender. This example gives some sense of why rendering the invisible visible, or the inaccurate accurate, can make such a large difference for both "the objects of study" (that is, the men and women affected) and the frameworks used to interpret them.

In our hypothetical experiment one can see the ways in which any research experiment must borrow from established facts, techniques, and theories simply to proceed. These provide the legitimacy and foundation for the study. In our experiment, it was necessary to invoke the categories of trait, gene, heritability, intelligence, sex, man, woman, and IQ. The impact of these categories comes from their being more than mere ideas. They are categories that have been woven into the entire social fabric. For example, "females" are not automatically "women." The transformation of "female" into the category "woman" requires an "ensemble of social practices, of institutions, and discourses."[27]

With our experiment, the categories of gene and of heritability had to be invoked simply to conceive the study. When one invokes these categories, one invariably invokes a theory of causation through which intelligence is inherited. Sometimes the theory is not really relevant to the object of study, but a link is made anyway. Thus a discourse is created in which legitimating categories are articulated with the new facts and theories in such a way that inferences can be drawn that go beyond the "evidence" at hand.[28]

This is the key maneuver accomplished in most biodeterminist models. Some complex behavior is transformed into a "trait,"[29] and once this has happened, categories such as "heritability" and "gene" can be invoked. Because these categories draw their legitimacy from the more "neutral" terrain of "pure" natural science, they imbue the deterministic arguments with the same aura of objective truth. At this point in the determinist argument, there is no difference between altruism and eye color, or between aggression and the production of insulin.

E.O. Wilson uses this technique in his writings on sociobiology.[30] In the provocative last chapter of his textbook *Sociobiology,* he uses many legitimating categories in order to cover the spurious correlations he makes. This technique is evident when he discusses the origins of cultural variations in human societies. At first, he cites the view of "conventional wisdom," which holds that there seems to be some evidence that cultural variation is phenotypic (controlled more by environmental factors) rather than simply genotypic (caused mainly by genetic propensities). As examples, he cites two cases of extremely rapid and profound changes in cultural patterns of behavior: "the drastic alteration in Irish society in the first two years of the potato blight (1846-1848)" and "the shift in the Japanese authority structure during the American occupation following World War II." He then presents what he considers a more extreme environmentalist view, which holds that genes contribute only the basic ability of human beings to create and modify culture. "In other words, the capacity for culture is transmitted by a single human genotype." Wilson then presents his own perspective:

> Although the genes have given away most of their sovereignty, they maintain a certain amount of influence in at least the behavioral qualities that underlie variations between cultures.[31]

He has at this point presented three viewpoints: an unscientific common-sense view, an extreme and of course obviously inadequate or politicized view, and a third view, which is Wilson's more "moderate" or compromise position. Thus he appears to hold the rational and scientific view, and he then goes on to support his claims with evidence from two studies. In one, he says, "moderately high heritability has been documented in introversion-extroversion measures, personal tempo, psychomotor and sports activities, neuroticism, dominance, depression, age of first sexual activity, timing of major cognitive development, and the tendency toward certain forms of mental illness such as schizophrenia." In the second example, he states that Freedman and his associates have demonstrated "marked racial differences in locomotion, posture, muscular tone, and emotional responses of newborn infants that cannot reasonably be explained as a result of training or even conditioning within the womb."[32] The important thing to notice about this presentation is the way in which a number of qualitatively different kinds of behavior are considered as possible heritable traits. Those relating to the newborns are not easily assailable, and at the same time they appear to be less contentious. Physical reactions such as muscle tone and posture are not tied so directly with the success and social position of adults. However, the first types of behaviors rely on very subjective measurements and do directly affect the social status of adults and of groups. Yet, in this argument, they are all accorded equal weight to support the argument that cultural differences may be the outcome of genetic dispositions. Even his use of the terms phenotype and genotype in his argument enforce a particular kind of separation between the environmental and the biological.

A large part of the reason why biodeterminist arguments persist and gain prominence is that they justify the structured inequality present to some degree in most of the societies on our planet. Because of this, biologically deterministic arguments have tended to be popularized quickly and have often had very direct and immediate effects upon legal codes, family relations, school curricula, work, and government policy, especially in Great Britain and the United States.

## The XYY Story

We have seen the ways in which falsification is used in biodeterminist arguments, and we have seen how the large scientific paradigms and social biases influence the formation of the facts and theories that provide the basis for biodeterminist arguments. We have also seen how discursive practices, social relations, popular culture, and institutions influence the way in which men and women behave and even the limits to which we can develop. Likewise, we have seen how legitimating categories within science are used to gain credibility for spurious causal positions. We have also seen how categories and institutions outside the strict realm of science can influence the speed with which biodeterminist arguments are taken up. One final example demonstrates all of these factors at work, and the outcome. It is the story of the XYY male.

In the 1960s, violence in cities, on college campuses, and in Vietnam resulted in an increased interest in the United States in the causes of aggressive behavior. Books by Audrey and Lorenz attempted to show the animal and evolutionary-genetic roots of human violence. At the same time, it was "discovered" that a number of males in prison had an extra Y chromosome and that these XYY males were turning up in prisons in higher proportions than would have been predicted. Since males are assumed to be more aggressive than females and since females have no Y chromosome, "it seemed natural to conclude that the Y chromosome carries genes for aggressive behavior."[33] The first case was noted in 1961, and by 1965 XYY had been linked to behavior problems. In the next few years studies in many countries confirmed that the extra Y chromosome produces deviant, aggressive, antisocial behavior. The correlation had become a causal relationship, and these studies all served to validate one another. The suggestive titles and conclusions of these studies brought them public attention. The incorrect identification, in 1968, of mass murderer Richard Speck as an XYY male also served "to fortify the XYY myth" and, despite laboratory results "that showed that Speck was an XY male, the retraction that appeared shortly after the article was published received little attention and the original claim is still generally believed." Some courts and prisons in the U.S. began to screen for XYY males and some inmates were even treated with female hormones "to restore normal behavior."[34]

A former president of the American Association for the Advancement of Science suggested therapeutic abortions to get rid of the XYY deviants, and Ashley Montague recommended typing XYY males at birth so that "it might be possible to institute the proper preventative and other measures at an early age." But by 1974, and more than two hundred research articles later, all that could be affirmed was that "the frequency of antisocial behavior of the XYY male is probably not very different from non-XYY persons of similar background and social class."[35] Yet, articles on the XYY criminal still appear in major newspapers.

The whole story would be fascinating if there had not been serious attempts to use this information to categorize a whole group of people as dangerous. What is clear is that a number of events, interests, and theoretical positions came together around this issue. There was considerable bias on the part of the researchers who chose this area because they entered the research with an eye to using it to solve social problems. Moreover, the studies lacked sufficient controls, conclusions were based on scanty data, very subjective categories were used to classify XYY men, and the causal genetic models were involved in circular arguments. In addition, three interconnected social trends influenced the course of XYY research: "concerns with the problems of crime and violence, expanded medical efforts to alter behavior, and efforts to determine the genetic basis of human behavior."[36]

One can see all of the elements necessary for ideological construction in the making of the XYY myth: the preconceptions of the researchers, the ideology of the funding agencies, the interpreting framework of the public and the legal and penal institutions, and the social construction of the "correlative facts" and causal models of the XYY myth. All this serves to demonstrate that what biological determinist debates say, how they say it, and the ways in which this information is used in the larger sociopolitical context are all aspects of the same process: it is a process of producing and maintaining structured inequality for women and all other groups that find themselves at the lower end of the socioeconomic ladder.

THE NEXT STEP

What can be said at this point about the claims of sociobiology and of biodeterminism in general? This is not an easy question to answer. In the first place, it is unclear that the separation between biology and environment is in any way useful. It may be popular, and it may be politically expedient, but it seems to be only marginally enlightening. Even if measurable differences are found to exist and can be shown to be sex-related and biodetermined, these findings will not automatically justify the inequality between the sexes. They will merely indicate differences. The problem is that difference tends to be transformed into inequality when the "proper functioning" of society is based on the exploitation of structural and relational inequality. Real and apparent physical differences become easy hooks on which to hang the hat of inequality. Even if it can be shown that measurable sex-related differences are determined biologically, the use that this information is put to will depend on who is using it. This is an argument, not for the cessation of research, but for a more complex and sophisticated look at what is a very complex set of issues.

My aim has not been to say that biology does not matter. Rather, I have attempted to show that much of the research conducted to date and the theories constructed and then popularized have little to do with accurate representations of the process of heritability but much to do with our society, political beliefs, and interpretive practices. Men and women must continue to make the process of social construction visible and a part of the object of study in the hope of

rendering the "observable" more visible. We must constantly analyze the interpretive framework in which we operate as producers of
knowledge.

There is a growing literature by feminist and other progressive
scientists that does address the accuracy and legitimacy of the claims
and interests of biologically deterministic theories and practices. Yet
this literature does not find its way into popular treatments of the
issues as readily as the determinist forms. Nonetheless, it is a literature that is seeking new ways to conceptualize this whole question of
the interactions of biological and environmental influences.

In the long run, that is the crucial new terrain onto which we must
shift the debate. For it is no longer enough to continually refute the
claims of biodeterminists; we must find a new way to describe the
relations between biology and environment. A framework that postu-
lates a more complex interaction of genetic and environmental factors will be less useful as a legitimator and producer of structured
inequality. It is crucial for a more progressive synthesis to be constructed because it is very likely that sociobiology and other forms of
biological determinism will be drawn along on the coattails of the
many technological advances that are forthcoming from the new bio-
engineering businesses. The successful manipulation, recombina-
tion, and synthesis of genetic materials and their byproducts will only
legitimate further the theories about the relationships between biology and social organization that emphasize genetic determination.

However, this must not deter us from the goal of constructing a
theoretical framework that will allow for a more sophisticated relationship between our biology and our surroundings. Nor must we
forget that ultimately the proof of the accuracy of this framework will
not lie in abstract discussions and experiments, but in the accomplishments of all those who have been kept down and told that "it was
in their genes." It is our job to help provide the evidence and perspective from which to argue for changes in social policy and legal codes so
that so that this mountain is a little easier to climb.

## NOTES

[1]In one such argument human thought capacities are considered to be located in specific parts of
the cerebral cortex: men are found to be left-hemisphere-dominant and women are right-hemi-
sphere-dominant. The left hemisphere is thought to control speech, as well as analytical and linear
thinking, while the right hemisphere is thought to control visual, holistic, and intuitive thinking.
[2]Cf. P. Corrigan and D. Sayer, The Great Arch (Oxford: Basil Blackwell, 1985).
[3]Ironically, IQ tests became popular for precisely the opposite reasons that its developer, Binet, had

intended. Binet had hoped that such a test could be used to measure the achievement of underprivileged children. He thought that early diagnosis of students who were falling behind their classmates would allow schools to give special attention to these children. He assumed that socioeconomic conditions affected academic achievement and that these measures possibly could mediate against the negative effects that poverty seemed to have. However, with the emergence of complex capitalist industrial economies came the need for compulsory education and with it stratification schemes in schools that mirrored those being created in the general labor market. Thus, the IQ test was transformed, expecially in England and the United States, into a measure, not only of achievement, but also of general aptitude and intelligence. By this time, biologically based theories of all human behavior also had become very popular, and so intelligence became that which was measured by IQ tests and encoded in our genes. *Cf.* R.C. Lewontin, S. Rose, and L. Kamin, *Not in Our Genes* (New York: Pantheon, 1984).

[4]*Cf.* R. Hofstadter, *Social Darwinism in American Thought* (Boston: Beacon Press, 1944).

[5]R. Lewontin *et al., op. cit.,* 53-4.

[6]R. Lewontin *et al., op. cit.,* 71 n.

[7]R. Morris, *Evolution and Human Nature* (New York: Avon Books, 1983), 22.

[8]R. Lewontin *et al.,* 85.

[9]B. Ehrenreich and D. English, *For Her Own Good* (New York: Anchor Press), 1979.

[10]E.O. Wilson, *Sociobiology* (Cambridge: Harvard University Press, 1975).

[11]*Toronto Star,* "Mystery of Love May Be Genetics", 18 Feb. 1985, p. D5.

[12]An excellent treatment of some of the standard biodeterminist positions regarding physical differences is M. Lowe, "Social Bodies: The Interaction of Culture and Women's Bodies," in R. Hubbard, M.S. Henifin, and B. Field, eds., *Biological Women—The Convenient Myth* (Cambridge: Schankman, 1982).

[13]One very important case in the determinist controversy is that of Cyril Burt, whose studies of the patterns of inheritance of intelligence in identical twins were used for years to "prove" that intelligence (IQ) could be inherited. Recently, it was discovered that Burt had faked most of his results. There is no doubt that the stakes in these debates are so high and the consequences so far-reaching that there is enormous pressure on scientists to produce conclusive and enlightening results. For a detailed account of the Burt incident, see S.J. Gould, *The Mismeasure of Man* (New York: W.W. Norton, 1981); R.C. Lewontin *et al., op. cit.*

[14]See for example J. Sayers, "Psychological Sex Differences" in L. Burke, W. Faulkner, S. Bert, D. Janson-Smith, and K. Overfield, eds., *Alice Through the Microscope* (London: Virago, 1980).

[15]The production of scientific theory is often seen as an isolated process. The use of the term "social and discursive practise" is intended to ground this process in our everyday life. Our language, ideas, symbols, and knowledge are not a world apart from our material reality, but are integral to how a society is put together and functions, and how we experience it. *Cf.* D. Smith, "The Ideological Practice of Sociology," *Catalyst,* No. 8 (Winter 1974); D. Smith, "The Social Construction of Documentary Reality," *Sociological Inquiry* 44, no. 4: 257-68; E. Laclau and C. Mouffe, *Hegemony and Socialist Strategy* (London:Verso, 1985).

[16]I use here Kuhn's definition. See further T.S. Kuhn, *The Structure of Scientific Revolutions* (Chicago: University of Chicago Press, 1962).

[17]The strength of the scientific method is seen to be the fact that an experiment must be reproducible and that the experiment and hypothesis must be constructed in such a way that it may be possible to disprove the hypothesis. Thus reproducibility and falsifiability are the twin pillars on which rest the claims of accuracy in scientific investigation.

[18]Kuhn, *op. cit.*

[19]Lowe, *op. cit.,* 100.

[20]Sayers, *op. cit.,* 52.

[21]Lowe, *op. cit.,* 91. These examples illustrate the process that Smith calls an "ideological circle." The social relations through which we produce and reproduce our existence are tied to our activities of interpreting the world. These acts of interpretation tend to view social reality in a way that sees this status quo as natural and timeless. Thus the process of interpretation reinforces what is being interpreted which in turn reinforces the interpretation. (D. Smith, public lectures, 1984.)

As can be seen from Lowe's examples, the effects of these frames and practices do not simply affect how we see, but also the objects themselves.

[22]Lowe, *op. cit.,* 97.

[23]*Ibid.,* 91.

[24]*Ibid.*

[25]For example, it will make a large difference to the way women are treated and a significant difference in the types of social policies that are implemented, if we assume that behavioral and environmental influences are as significant as, or more significant than, biological differences in affecting the "traits" that men and women possess. And as we have seen, these social influences are crucial to the creation of those same "traits."

[26]C.S. Stoll, *Sexism: Scientific Debates* (Reading: Addison Wesley, 1973), 7.

[27]E. Laclau and C. Mouffe, *op. cit.,* 118.

[28]I use Laclau's and Mouffe's conception of "articulation" here. They define it as "any practice establishing a relation among elements such that their identity is modified as a result of the articulatory practice. The structured totality resulting from the articulatory practice, we will call discourse" (*ibid.,* 105).

[29]The category of trait is a very important one in genetic theory, as well as in sociobiology and other biologically deterministic frameworks. This has been so since the rediscovery of Mendel's work on the basic statistical models for the independent assortment of genetic traits in peas. Since that time, much work has been done on things like eye color, pea size, shape and color, size of plant, production of proteins, and so on. These traits are relatively easily quantifiable and do not tend to involve the manifestation of complex social, moral, or political behavior that lends itself to more subjective assessments.

[30]Wilson, *op. cit.*

[31]*Ibid.,* 274.

[32]*Ibid.*

[33]R. Pyeritz, et al., The XYY Male: The Making of a Myth," in, *Biology as a Social Weapon,* eds., The Ann Arbor Science for the People Collective (Minneapolis: Burgess Publishing Company, 1977), p. 85.

[34]*Ibid.,* 88.

[35]R. Pyeritz, *op. cit.,* 89.

[36]*Ibid.,* 92-7.

# Patriarchs and Participants: A Historical Perspective on Fatherhood in the United States

## E. ANTHONY ROTUNDO

An understanding of the nature of contemporary fatherhood in many countries of the world today is stymied by all sorts of conflicting tendencies. Right-wing social critics call for the return to strong patriarchal authority, while feminists and anti-sexist men advocate more participation by fathers in the upbringing of their children. At the same time that a growing percentage of divorced men fail to meet their child-support payments, more and more divorced fathers enjoy joint custody of their children. And even those of us striving for new relationships with our children are often caught between contradictory and conflicting desires and needs.

How can we make sense of these conflicting trends? One way is to seek some historical perspective by examining a particular society and a dominant class within that society. My focus is on the United States, where fatherhood is in a time of dramatic changes. What has set these changes in motion? What is the process by which fatherhood in the United States has changed in the past? How often has it changed, and what form has that change taken? The purpose of this article is to provide some initial answers to these questions. The answers will be drawn from the history of fatherhood among the socially dominant class in the United States—the middle class.

This history can be divided into two major periods, each typified by a particular mode of fathering:[1] patriarchal fatherhood (1620 to 1800) and modern fatherhood (1800 to the present). In considering each of these forms of fathering, we will examine three crucial elements: a father's primary duties; the dominant patterns of emotion in men's relationships with their children; and the social, economic, and intellectual factors that underlie the modes of fatherhood—or that caused them to change. We will then consider the recent development of a third paternal mode, participant fatherhood. Finally, a few thoughts will be offered about the future of fatherhood in the United States.

It should be stressed at the outset that the emphasis of this essay on the middle-class segment of the American population is not to deny the existence, the worth, or the importance of other fathering modes and traditions as part of American history.[2] The focus on middle-class fathering is simply a candid recognition that the dominant modes of fatherhood in the United States have been those practiced by the nation's dominant class. As long as substantial social and ideological (even if not always economic) influence has rested with the middle-class, its form of family life has been held up to other groups as a cultural ideal. Thus middle-class fatherhood has had an importance well out of proportion to the numbers who have actually practiced it. This analysis presents a generalization, then, and one possible starting point for an analysis of fatherhood in the United States. By definition, the emphasis on middle-class fatherhood almost totally leaves out pre–twentieth-century black families. But it appears that the development of the black middle class during the twentieth century has included the widespread adoption of the fathering modes of the white middle-class, even if this has been modified by a range of economic and cultural factors. The same observation appears to hold true for other ethnic or national groups in the United States: class has been the most influential variable on the mode of fathering even though there are differences from group to group. For those reasons the middle-class is a useful starting point in an initial foray into the history of fatherhood in the United States.[3]

PATRIARCHAL FATHERHOOD 1620 to 1800

At the beginning of U.S. history, the father was a towering figure in the family. His authority grew out of the nature of the agricultural world in which he lived. Nearly all colonial men were subsistence farmers who produced for their families and for a limited amount of trade with their neighbors. The family was the basic economic unit in this system, the father was chief of production, and every member beyond early childhood made an active contribution to the common effort for family survival. These farming households formed small villages, in which families were closely linked by intermarriage. Within this narrow world, then, the family was the building block of society and the father served as the family's unquestioned ruler.[4]

One important source of the father's power was his ownership and control of all family property. Through his control of land, a father could direct the rate at which his sons gained their independence. Another major source of paternal authority was his veto power over his children's choice of husband or wife.

But if a father had great power over his children, he also bore a number of weighty responsibilities for their growth and development. It was a man's duty to provide the physical necessities of life for his sons and daughters. He was also responsible for providing them with training for their life's work. In practice, though, the mother taught her daughters the skills of housewifery and child care and the father gave his boys a basic education in farming and—where relevant—business skills.[5]

A father was charged with the moral and spiritual growth of his children. Because colonial fathers were the heads of households and the teachers of morality, they also took on the role of the family disciplinarian. These men relied chiefly on persuasion and sympathy to govern their children; corporal punishment was acceptable only as a last resort and even then in moderation.

But a colonial father's relationship with his children was more than the sum total of his responsibilities to them. These relationships also had patterns of emotional style, tone, and preference, and an examination of these patterns suggests that a father's dealings with his sons were very different from those with his daughters. Both parents treated children in the earliest years of life—regardless of sex—as the mother's children. Colonial fathers often showed a keen interest in the infants and toddlers of the household, but it was the mothers who fed the little ones, cared for them, and established intimate bonds with them. When children reached an age where they could understand what their parents told them (sometime after the age of three), the parent-child connection changed. Fathers began to tutor all their children in moral values at this point. More important, the parents now considered a boy as his father's child and a girl as her mother's.[6]

The father-son relationship was neither explosive nor intimate. In fact, one student of the period has described father-son relations as "distant, didactic, and condescending."[7] A major factor that underlies the absence of strong visible emotions was the colonial belief that too much affection would lead to parental indulgence, which would in turn ruin a child's character. Because men believed that they could control their emotions better than women could, fathers held themselves especially responsible for self-restraint. As a result, fathers tended to express approval and disapproval in place of affection and anger.[8]

There are hints in the historical record that men may have expressed their emotions more freely to their daughters than to their sons. From the few materials that are available, one historian has concluded that fathers openly expressed affection to their daughters in response to good behavior, and threatened to withhold it in response to bad behavior. This pattern was not evident in father-son relationships.[9] A looser rein over affection toward daughters was consistent with a man's feeling about his children of each sex. It was his sons who reflected directly on him; their accomplishments and failures affected his own public reputation. A man was not bound up so closely, emotionally or in the eyes of the community, with his daughters. So a greater display of affection—even if it led to some indulging and spoiling of his daughters—would have affected a man less profoundly than if the same thing happened to his sons.

This patriarchal mode of fathering continued until the beginning of the nineteenth century. But its foundations were being eroded slowly throughout the second half of the eighteenth century, as ideas and conditions of life in society at large began to change. By the middle decades of the century, the growth of the population in the old farming towns near the coast led to a decline in the amount of land available to each man. Thus, fathers could no longer control their sons by promising the gift of a farm later in life. In other words, the father lost power and authority.[10] This gradual change in the middle years of the 1700s paved the way for a new concept of parenting that reached British North America from the mother country in the 1760s and 1770s. In this emerging view, parents were no longer to act as stringent authorities, but rather they were expected to strengthen their roles as moral teachers.[11]

At the same time that traditional ideas of patriarchy were falling into decline, a new notion of womanhood emerged: a belief that women were inherently moral, more spiritual, and more tender than men. Women, in other words, were better suited to carry out the new ideal of the parent as moral tutor, as sympathetic molder of young character. So in the late eighteenth century, a new and more powerful mode of motherhood emerged.[12]

THE EMERGENCE OF MODERN FATHERHOOD, 1800–1880

At the end of the eighteenth century and the beginning of the nineteenth, many farmers in the northeastern United States began for the first time to produce cash crops for a market beyond their own villages. Suddenly, sleepy coastal cities turned into major commercial centers and inland crossroads became market towns.[13] A new urban middle-class rose in these cities and towns to manage the buying and selling of goods from the hinterlands. As it grew, the middle-class developed its own distinctive forms of family life that have remained dominant in American society ever since.

The new commercial life of the cities affected middle-class families by removing paid employment from the home. Farming fathers had worked the family land and passed in and out of the house many times during the day; now the clerks, lawyers, and businessmen of the nineteenth century left home every day to pursue their work in offices and other places of business. Put simply, the middle-class father was less present in the home.[14]

Another factor that undermined paternal importance was the changing role played by the family. The agricultural family was an economic unit; as long as the entire household worked together to produce and survive, the father's place at the heart of the family was secure. In the new commercial society of the 1800s, however, corporations and partnerships emerged as the primary economic units. Within the family, the father became the economic specialist, the member of the work world, the producer.

Women and children in the early nineteenth century spent the day together at home and, as economic functions dropped away, the family came to specialize in nurture and socialization. With the father so often absent from the house, the mother naturally took charge of these special family functions. But a woman did not take up these roles simply because she was left at home with the children. She also assumed these responsibilities because people now believed that women were better suited to tasks of moral education, spiritual uplift, and sympathetic nurture than men were.[15]

Thus, the mother became the core of the middle-class family in the nineteenth century. A man's successes and failures came to reflect more on his mother than his father. This last development happened in great measure because it was now the mother and *not* the father who molded a boy's character.[16]

There were other disruptive new elements that undermined patriarchal authority in the early nineteenth century. A central article of faith in the new commercial capitalism was a belief in individualism, the belief that a man's talent and energy, pitted against those of other men, should determine his wealth and social standing. In this wide-open race for success, young men strove mightily to outdo their fathers. Once sons had waited on the power and authority of their fathers; now they were competitors.[17]

Despite the decline of patriarchy and the expanded importance of mothers in the nineteenth-century family, middle-class fathers still had a significant role to play. More than ever before, the man was *the* provider in the family. That, in turn, reinforced his position as "head of the household." In keeping with this role, the middle-class father retained his place as the ultimate disciplinarian in the family. Corporal punishment, it should be added, was even less in evidence during the nineteenth century than it had been during the colonial era. The father also aided his wife in her role as chief moral tutor in the family. He was expected to conduct family prayers and Bible readings, and he tried to mix moral lessons with the punishments he issued.[18]

Middle-class fathers did specialize as teachers in certain kinds of morality, ones that affected the lives of sons more than daughters. Specifically, it was the father who taught most of the lessons about the ethics of work, property, and money, warning against laziness, theft, extravagance, and so on.[19] These lessons were relevant to children of both sexes but more to sons than daughters; it was assumed that middle-class sons, like their fathers, would be the "economic specialists" in their own families.

In the early nineteenth century, a father had more to do with his sons than with his daughters in a number of other ways. As the person who spent most of the waking day in the world beyond the home, it was inevitably the father who taught practical lessons about survival in the world. A man also served as the chief counselor to his sons regarding their education; and he taught his boys what there was to know about the distinctively male worlds of politics and finance. Finally, and most important, the father was the primary male role model for his sons. In sum, a middle-class father of the nineteenth century still played a part in the lives of his sons that was different from the one he played in the lives of his daughters, even though his power and influence were dwarfed by comparison with those of colonial fathers.

But so far this account covers the *roles* and *functions* of the father. What of his place in the emotional life of this new urban, middle-class family? Apparently, the nineteenth-century father often lived outside the main emotional currents that flowed within his own home. Middle-class fathers were away from the house far too often to take much part in the everyday give-and-take that bred a deep intimacy between parent and child. Family letters of the time provide us with examples of the father's emotional distance. When fathers wrote to absent sons, for instance, they offered advice and stuck to whatever other business prompted the letter. They left the family news, the details of home life, and the expressions of affection to their wives.[20]

Of course, this same tone of formality and distance had characterized the outer surface of men's relations with their sons in the colonial period, too. But that coolness had often masked intense emotional involvement between fathers and sons. In middle-class families of the nineteenth century, the emotional lives of fathers and sons simply did not become so entwined. Men seemed more comfortable expressing emotions to their daughters than to their sons.[21]

In sum, a new mode of fatherhood had emerged within the urban middle-class of the early nineteenth century. Fathers specialized as economic providers, leaving home to work in the world of commerce and the professions and yielding to mothers the burden of responsibility for raising the children. To be sure, men continued to hold the ultimate power within the family, and so it was quite natural that they still functioned as chief disciplinarians for their households. And they acted also as their son's guides to the world beyond the home. But a profound change had nonetheless engulfed middle-class fathers in the nineteenth century—they now stood outside the strongest currents of feeling that flowed between generations in a family. The modern mode of fatherhood was born.

## CHANGING PATTERNS WITHIN MODERN FATHERHOOD: 1880 TO THE PRESENT

The basic form of modern fatherhood has continued from its emergence in the early nineteenth century into the 1980s. During the intervening years, this mode of fatherhood has grown and spread. And, in that same span of time, the inner dynamics of modern fatherhood created two contradictory trends around a central issue: the degree of involvement that a father should have in a family.

In the nineteenth and twentieth centuries, the rise of industrialism, the emergence of bureaucracy, and the arrival of urban ideas in the rural United States all helped to spread the middle-class phenomenon of modern fatherhood.[22] So did the migration of farming folk, from home and abroad, to work in factories and cities. For these people, the separation of the workplace from the home undermined the traditional authority of the father. In addition, immigrant fathers often knew less about the ways of their new world than their children did, and that too was a blow to paternal authority.[23] Thus, modern fatherhood came to large new groups outside the middle class. Of course, the economic pressures of working-class life and the variety of ethnic values produced many variations on the basic form among the different immigrant groups.[24] But modern fatherhood became the norm, the cultural ideal toward which all styles of fathering tended.

At the same time that modern fatherhood was spreading, some of its own internal contradictions became evident as it spawned two opposing trends, the absence of fathers and involvement of fathers. On the one hand, the lack of a commanding paternal role in modern fatherhood made it possible for men to withdraw from the family (in all but economic functions) without immediate disaster. On the other hand, modern fatherhood, unlike the patriarchal style, did not demand lofty restraint and formality; thus, it became easier for men to enjoy warmth, play, and even intimacy with their children. Each of these contradictory trends in modern fatherhood became visible in the late nineteenth century.

Fathers began to be absent from middle-class families in two ways. One was physical. The growth of suburbs moved the home ever farther away from men's workplaces, while the demands of the national corporations that were rising in the late nineteenth century took fathers away on more and more business trips. The other form of absence that came to light in the late 1800s was psychological absence. Critics complained of men who did not involve themselves with their children in any meaningful way. Without a commanding, patriarchal role to play in the family, these men let their wives take full responsiblity for the children, rather than fall into a secondary role and suffer a blow to their masculine pride.[25]

But a contradictory trend did begin to emerge, quietly and with much less notice, at the end of the century. Taking advantage of dwindling demands for patriarchal formality, some men developed new kinds of relationships with their children. Such fathers expressed affection with growing ease, sought close emotional ties with their children, and enjoyed playful hours with sons and daughters.[26]

Most fathers in the late nineteenth and early twentieth centuries, however, steered between these two poles of behavior. What linked these men to the more "removed" fathers and the more involved fathers was a diminished paternal role, a shrunken set of requirements compared with those of patriarchal fatherhood. Breadwinner, certainly; head of household, yes; worldly guide for sons, true—but the mother was the emotional core of the family, the unquestioned molder of the young minds.[27]

Modern fatherhood continued in this form until the 1930s and 1940s, when it was temporarily disrupted by the Great Depression and the Second World War. When men were thrown out of work in the 1930s, they lost their most important function as fathers—that of economic provider.[28] And the war took many fathers out of the household and drew some middle-class mothers into the work force, thus interfering with the basic patterns of family life in which modern fatherhood had its roots.

But the great economic boom of the years after the war restored the father to his positions as provider and head of the household, and modern fatherhood revived. With this revival, the opposing trends of absence and involvement gained renewed momentum. On the one hand, some middle-class men, particularly professionals and corporate managers, put in long weeks of fifty or sixty hours' work. These fathers could not be full members of their families and had a very small part in raising their children.[29]

On the other hand, the slow trend toward more emotional involvement of fathers and more active male participation in child rearing continued in other postwar families. In such households, men tried to befriend their children and take a place in the main currents of home life. Meanwhile, a gradually rising number—but still a distinct minority—of fathers were taking some part in the day-to-day work of tending and feeding their children. And men carved out new functions as fathers. They taught their children, especially their sons, the skills of home repair and yard work. Another new duty that emphasized a father's ties with his sons was the role of coach. Men not only passed on their knowledge of athletics to their boys but also acted as official coaches when Little League sports began to spread.[30]

Some of these roles, obviously, were at the margins of family life. Men had long since abandoned the central position in the family to their wives. They were not trained for household work, much less the emotional tasks of committed parenthood. As a result, the newly involved father of the 1940s, 1950s, and 1960s fitted awkwardly into home life.

The father's basic tasks had changed very little since the emergence of modern fatherhood in the early nineteenth century. Men still functioned as providers and disciplinarians for their children. They served their sons as guides to the man's world of work and achievement, enjoying somewhat more expressive relationships with their daughters. The contradictory trends of absence and involvement that had first emerged in modern fatherhood in the late nineteenth century continued on into the 1960s. And the majority of fathers still took a middle course between these two opposite poles.

But by the 1970s fathers were finding it harder to hold to that middle course. The forces of absence and the forces of involvement have gained strength over the past twenty years. To start with, the steadily rising divorce rate of the late twentieth century has added a whole new dimension to the absence of fathers. A few numbers will suggest the magnitude of this change in the American household. In 1981, 20 percent of all children in the United States were living in one-parent households. The number of such children had increased by more than 50 percent in just over a decade. And of the children living in one-parent households in 1981, fewer than ten percent were living with their fathers. In 1982, the United States Census Bureau found that the percentage of the population living in households headed by married couples had dropped sharply since 1970, from 82 to 73 percent.[31] Nor was household structure the only way in which the rising divorce rate caused fathers to be absent: the growing failure of divorced fathers to make the required child-support payments constituted a form of absence in the extreme. As of 1981, slightly more than half of all men who had been ordered to make child-support payments were not meeting those payments in full. And 28 percent were not making their payments at all.[32]

Recent legislation aimed at these divorced fathers may well force down the rate of non-payment, but the fact remains that their failure to pay represents a dramatic defiance of the ideals of modern fatherhood. It should be noted that this defiance is consistent with a radical form of male individualism that considers family responsibility to be a quiet form of tyranny. Although this feeling ran for many years as a quiet undercurrent in U.S. culture, it has begun to surface during the second half of the twentieth century. One of its organized manifestations is a movement for so-called divorced men's liberation, which seeks to reduce the size and frequency of court-ordered payments in divorce cases.[33]

In many ways, then, the rising divorce rate has pushed the trend toward absent fathers to the point where it is eroding the very duties and values on which modern fatherhood rests. But if divorce has been the most dramatic threat to this established mode of fathering, it is the slackening growth of the U.S. economy that has done the most widespread damage to modern fatherhood. Since the 1970s, rising inflation and unemployment have pushed a growing percentage of women into the labor force.[34] With this new crop of working mothers out in the market place, it became harder for a father to claim a monopoly on knowledge of wordly skills; and his role as sole provider for his children has been disappearing. Meanwhile, as more women entered the work force, the need for fathers to help with basic child care was becoming more acute. Thus economic change has quietly undermined much of the foundation on which modern fatherhood has rested.

At the very same time that economic flux and the absence of fathers were working changes in the family, the long-running trend toward fathers' involvement seemed to accelerate in the 1970s and early 1980s. And as the child-rearing participation of a small but visible minority of fathers became more intensive and devoted, a new mode of fatherhood emerged to challenge the dominance of modern fatherhood. A particular impetus for this change was the growth of the women's liberation movement.

PARTICIPANT FATHERHOOD: POSSIBILITIES AND PROBLEMS

For at least the last two centuries, the men of the professional classes and business elites have set the tone for fatherhood in the United States. They have provided cultural ideals that always touch—even if they do not change—the forms of fatherhood practiced by other social groups. So it is that in the last quarter of the twentieth century a change in fathering among younger men of the upper-middle class has attracted immense attention in the United States. The chief quality of this emergent mode of fathering is the active and engaged participation of a man in all facets of his children's lives—and thus we will call it here participant fatherhood. A participant father is immersed in the tasks of day-to-day child care. His wide-ranging involvement flows from the assumption that after childbirth there are few tasks that cannot be shared interchangeably by mother and father. But participant fatherhood means more than just fulfilling physical responsibilities to children—it means intensive emotional involvement with them, too. This new mode of fathering encourages a man to share in a more expressive and intimate relationship with his children than fathers of previous generations had the time or inclination to do.[35] Thus a man in his role as parent begins in some ways to resemble his mother more than his father. And, indeed, the effect of participant fatherhood is to blur the traditional distinctions between mothering and fathering.

The blurring of gender distinctions plays a part in another key facet of participant fatherhood, for a man who practices this mode of fathering is expected to avoid sex-role stereotypes in dealing with his children. He can encourage girls to be assertive achievers, and he can coach daughters as well as sons in competitive sports. By the same token, the new model of fatherhood involves men in more expressive relationships with their sons; these fathers can encourage their boys to be nurturing as well as assertive.[36]

Clearly, participant fatherhood involves a substantial recasting of American manhood, womanhood, and family life. It demands new patterns of feeling; it entails different notions of male and female; and it requires men to surrender substantial authority to their wives in return for a greater measure of involvement with their children. Will men be willing to make these changes? Will the circumstances of life in the United States in the coming decades support such a radically altered form of fatherhood? There is no clear answer to these questions. We can, however, get some sense of the direction in which events may be headed by exploring the circumstances that have created the participant mode of fatherhood.

First of all, this new mode is really an extension of a quiet historical tendency toward the involvement of middle-class fathers with their children, a tendency that has existed within modern fatherhood for more than a century and a half. For, as we noted earlier, modern fatherhood first emerged as a pared-down version of the older patriarchal mode; this modern version presented a man with fewer specific demands and prescriptions—and so left him with a new freedom to build close personal relationships with his children. Generation after generation, there have been men who eased cautiously into these expressive possibilities that lay hidden in modern fatherhood. By the 1950s and 1960s, it appeared that the number of such middle-class men was growing.

Then, in the 1970s, came the stimulus of the women's movement, which offered social support and intellectual justification for participant fathering. As feminists analyzed traditional sex roles, they envisaged new ideals of womanhood and manhood that would minimize the difference between the sexes. In this new view, women and men are seen as fundamentally alike and qualities such as rationality, nurturance, and assertiveness are considered to be distributed broadly (even randomly) across the boundaries of gender. The implication here is that women should not be confined to child rearing and housework and that a man should not take his identity solely from a career and other worldly pursuits. The new mode of fatherhood is most directly a result of this imaginative redesign of sex roles.[37]

But participant fatherhood is a response to much more practical conditions as well. As noted before, women have entered the labor force in constantly swelling numbers throughout the seventies and eighties. Middle-class women in particular seem to have done so from a mixture of motives. A great number of them, whether avowedly feminist or not, wanted a career and insisted that they had a right to one. And many of them (often the same women) pursued careers for a second reason: given the economic pressures of the time, a career was the only way for these women to maintain the middle-class standard of living they had enjoyed as children. Thus, the two-career marriage—so common now in younger middle-class families—was born out of a combination of economic and personal imperatives. One result of these two-career marriages has been that women are left with much less time to manage the child-rearing duties that for nearly two centuries fell almost exclusively to mothers. This changing situation has put great pressure on "two-career husbands" to play a more active role in child rearing. And this rising urgency has coincided, of course, with the growing interest of middle-class men in raising their children *and* with the development of egalitarian ideals that lend social support to this kind of participation.

But basic questions about the future remain. Will the trends that helped to create participant fatherhood continue? Will they last long enough, in other words, to sustain the mode of fatherhood that they helped to produce? In answering these questions, we should start by noting that the middle-class phenomenon of the two-career couple shows no signs of abating, for the economic conditions that stimulated it will be with us for the foreseeable future. And, in spite of some highly publicized failures of the feminist movement, its cherished beliefs seem to be reaching deeper and deeper cultural levels. For instance, a steadily growing proportion of the young women who go to college assume that they will have full careers. This suggests, in turn, that two-career marriages may be around for a long time. So two of the trends that produced participant fatherhood—a changing economy and the influence of feminist values—seem likely to continue.[38]

Yet in spite of these promising auguries for participant fatherhood, there are several factors that cast doubt on its future. For one thing, the active pursuit of this new mode of fathering is still limited to a very small segment of the population. To be sure, economic change has forced certain men in nearly all social classes to participate extensively in child care. But many of those men view this participation as a temporary—and perhaps unfortunate—deviation from the norm of parental duties. As a concept and as a cultural ideal, participant fatherhood has been accepted mainly by the upper-middle class.[39]

And even within that social group, there are far more men who still practice the traditional mode of fathering than the newer mode that blurs the differences between the two parents. In fact, one can safely guess that there are more *women* who *advocate* participant fatherhood than there are *men* who *practice* it. Many men lack the emotional skills necessary to be deeply and expressively involved with their children, and others have been too thoroughly ingrained with the "male" values of ambition and achievement to devote much time to substantial daily child care. Here, as with many other current trends in fatherhood, the future depends on men's ideas of masculinity. Will there be major changes in definitions of manhood? If so, will they enable men to include the traditional values and skills of the mother in their personal repertoires? The answers to these questions are, at this time, uncertain. But as concepts of manhood change (or resume old forms), they will have an important influence on the future shape of fatherhood in the United States.

Even if the basic concept of manhood does change, and even if the idea of participant fatherhood starts to spread widely across class lines, there are still some serious practical problems that stand in the way of this new mode of fathering. For, although there are men who are able to participate fully and constantly as fathers, they tend to be clustered in the occupations that naturally permit flexible work hours or involve a good deal of work at home. In the meantime, many other men who wish to follow the same participant mode of fatherhood must pursue it as a sort of hobby—one that gets pushed to the margins of their lives by rigid work schedules. In other words, before men who want to participate fully and intensively in fatherhood can do so, the structure and timing of work outside the home will have to change. This would mean changes in employers' definitions of working hours and jobs—changes such as job-sharing and flexible hours. Paternity leave and on-site day care would also enable a participant father to engage himself intensively with his child as early as possible and then maintain regular daytime contact through the child's preschool years. Equal pay for work of equal value and the challenge to the ghettoization of women's wage work is another requirement. Otherwise, when one parent must stay home for protracted periods with a child, it is often economically rational for the father to keep doing the work outside the home. These changes, if they happen, could come by means of employers' initiatives, by collective bargaining, or through the stimulus of a national families policy.

There are other preconditions for the spread of participant fatherhood. To increase the power of women in the household in order to help them demand greater—and indeed, equal—participation from their partners, it is also necessary to challenge the many forms of violence against women in the home and in the streets. Without a challenge to these forms of violence, the balance of emotional and physical power perpetuates the domination of men over women in household decision making and reduces women's potential to discover their own hidden resources. One other precondition for the spread of participant fathering is social support for gay fathers, who face particularly daunting obstacles. Obstacles also exist, although not as daunting, for single heterosexual fathers.

For the moment, it is clear that the underpinnings of modern fatherhood are being eroded by a variety of social and economic forces. It would be an exercise in crystal ball gazing to attempt to predict the future of fatherhood, for we do not know all the forces that will set this course. But among these forces will be those of us—men and women—who are parents or citizens in the late twentieth century. We need to create and maintain the conditions in which participatory fatherhood will flourish, and we must find ways to support men and women who seek to raise children in ways that are more just and non-sexist. Because this is a moment with possibilities for profound change in the mode of fatherhood, it is an auspicious time to make these efforts.

## NOTES

An earlier version of this article appeared under the title "American Fatherhood: A Historical Perspective" in *American Behavioral Scientist* 29, no. 1 (September-October, 1985): 7-25. I wish to thank my wife, Kathleen Dalton, for her help with both versions of this article.

[1] The term "mode" as it is applied here to fatherhood will be used to include two distinct aspects of fathering. The first is the formal social role of "father," which is a role that fits into the larger social structure and is bound by a set of social norms. The second dimension of a "mode of fathering" is a pattern of typical emotional responses and types of behavior that exists without regard to formal social norms but which predominates among fathers at a particular time and place. Although the two different aspects of fathering included in the term "mode" do not necessarily coincide in historical time, it so happens that, in the case of the U.S. middle class examined here, they *do* coincide.

[2] The definition of "middle class" used here is an occupational one. It refers broadly to anyone in a family whose primary breadwinner works in one of the professions, in executive business positions, or in commerce beyond the level of shopkeeper or small storeowner. Two historical qualifications need to be added to that definition. First, the middle class as defined here was very small in the southern states during the nineteenth century. Thus, the generalizations offered here about middle-class fatherhood in the 1800s are drawn largely from the study of the northern states. Secondly, the term "middle class," when applied to the 1600s and 1700s, is anachronistic. However, since family forms in the American colonies were more homogeneous than they are today, generalizations about fatherhood apply equally well to different ranks of colonial society. Again, this is true especially in the northern colonies, where patriarchal forms predominated among the more numerous yeoman-small farmer class and among the more thoroughly documented elite of merchants and large landowners.

[3] The first comprehensive statement of the history of American fatherhood was in J. Demos, "The Changing Face of American Fatherhood: A New Exploration in Family History," in S. Cath, A. Gurwitt, and J. Ross, eds., *Father and Child: Development and Clinical Perspectives* (Boston: Little, Brown, 1982). The author has benefited greatly from many exchanges of ideas with Professor Demos.

[4]The foregoing description of patriarchal fatherhood is based primarily on the practice of this style in the northern colonies. A less studied southern variant of patriarchal fatherhood is described in D.B. Smith, *Inside the Great House: Planter Family Life in Eighteenth-Century Chesapeake Society* (Ithaca: Cornell University Press, 1980).

[5]J. Demos, *A Little Commonwealth: Family Life in Plymouth Colony* (New York: Oxford University Press, 1970), 104-6; E. Morgan, *The Puritan Family: Religion and Domestic Relations in Seventeenth-Century New England,* rev. ed. (New York: Harper and Row, 1966), 65-76.

[6]M.B. Norton, *Liberty's Daughters: The Revolutionary Experience of American Women, 1750-1800* (Boston: Little, Brown, 1980), 92-4; E.A. Rotundo, *Manhood in America: The Northern Middle-Class, 1770-1920* (Doctoral dissertation, Brandeis University, 1982), 76-8.

[7]Norton, *op. cit.,* 102.

[8]P. Greven, *The Protestant Temperament: Patterns of Child-Rearing, Religious Experience, and the Self in Early America* (New York: Alfred A. Knopf, 1977), 164-6; Morgan, *op. cit.,* 77-8; J. Demos, "The Changing Face of American Fatherhood," 3-4.

[9]Norton, *op. cit.,* 99-100.

[10]P. Greven, *Four Generations: Population, Land, and Family in Colonial Andover, Massachusetts* (Ithaca: Cornell University Press, 1970).

[11]J. Fliegelman, *Prodigals and Pilgrims: The American Revolution Against Patriarchal Authority, 1750-1800* (New York: Cambridge University Press, 1982).

[12]L. Kerber, *Women of the Republic: Intellect and Ideology in Revolutionary America* (Chapel Hill: University of North Carolina Press, 1980); N. Cott, *The Bonds of Womanhood: "Woman's Sphere" in New England, 1780-1835,* (New Haven, Yale University Press, 1977).

[13]R. Brown, *Modernization: The Transformation of American Life* (New York: Hill and Wang, 1976).

[14]M. Ryan, *Cradle of the Middle Class: The Family in Oneida County, New York, 1780-1865* (New York: Cambridge University Press, 1981).

[15]B. Welter, "The Cult of True Womanhood: 1820-1860," *American Quarterly* 18, no. 2 (1966): 151-74, also Cott, *op. cit.,* 63–100.

[16]Demos, "The Changing Face of American Fatherhood," 431–2, 439; also Rotundo, *op. cit.,* 180-97.

[17]Demos, "The Changing Face of American Fatherhood," 442-3; also R. Lebeaux, *Young Man Thoreau* (Amherst: University of Massachusetts Press, 1977), 16-17.

[18]Rotundo, *op. cit.,* 207-9; also R. Cramer, *Images of the American Father, 1790-1860* (Senior thesis, Brandeis University, 1980), 51-62.

[19]Rotundo, *op. cit.,* 210-13.

[20]Rotundo, *op. cit.,* 200-3.

[21]E.A. Rotundo, *Manhood in Early Nineteenth-Century America* (unpublished paper, 1981), 23-5.

[22]Men's style of involvement in rural midwestern family life at the middle of the 1800s is described in J.M. Farragher, *Women and Men on the Overland Trail* (New Haven: Yale University Press, 1979).

[23]O. Handlin, *The Uprooted: The Epic Story of the Great Migrations That Made the American People* (New York: Grosset and Dunlap, 1951).

[24]The black family has been a notable exception to this trend. The best history of the black family is H. Gutman, *The Black Family in Slavery and Freedom, 1750-1925.* (New York: Pantheon, 1976). Gutman's book is in part a refutation of the viewpoint expressed in the famous Moynihan Report on the black family in America (D.P. Moynihan, *The Negro Family: The Case for National Action*). That report is published in its entirety along with commentary and critical essays in L. Rainwater and W. Yancey, eds., *The Moynihan Report and the Politics of Controversy,* (Cambridge: MIT Press, 1967). The literature on the history of the family among ethnic groups is extensive. For useful examples of this literature, see Laurence A. Glasco, "The Life Cycles and Household Structure of American Ethnic Groups: Irish, Germans, and Native-Born Whites in Buffalo, New York, 1855," *Journal of Urban History* 3 (May 1975): 339-64; N.D. Humphrey, "The Changing Structure of the Detroit Mexican Family," *American Sociological Review* 9 (December 1944): 622-6; Virginia Yans-McLaughlin, "A Flexible Tradition: South Italian Immigrants Confront a New York Experience," *Journal of Social History* 7 (Summer 1974): 429-45.

[25]J. Dubbert, *A Man's Place: Masculinity in Transition* (Englewood Cliffs, N.J.: Prentice-Hall, 1979), 140-4; Rotundo, *Manhood in America,* 343-4.

[26]Rotundo, *Manhood in America,* 335-47, 344-6.

[27]Rotundo, *Manhood in America,* 335-4; Dubbert, *op. cit.,* 140-4.

[28]M. Komarovsky, *The Unemployed Man and His Family* (New York: Dryden Press, 1940).

[29]P. Filene, *Him/Her/Self: Sex Roles in Modern America* (New York: New American Library, 1975), 176-7.

[30]*Ibid.,* 179–80; "The Changing Face of American Fatherhood," 443.

[31]These are U.S. Census Bureau figures, as reported in R.E. Schmid, "Percentage of Married in U.S. Homes at Low Point," *Boston Globe,* 16 Nov. 1981, and in "Twenty Per Cent of Children Live With One Parent, Study Says," *Boston Globe,* 9 Aug. 1982.

[32]U.S. Bureau of the Census, Current Population Reports, Series P-23, No. 124. *Child Support and Alimony: 1981* (Advance Report). (Washington, D.C.: U.S. Government Printing Office, 1983).

[33]This "men's movement" should not be confused with the activities of many anti-sexist men who seek to support the women's movement and put feminist insights to work in reshaping the male sex role. The surfacing of male rebellion against traditional family roles and forms is discussed perceptively in B. Ehrenreich, *The Hearts of Men: American Dreams and the Flight from Commitment* (New York: Anchor Press/ Doubleday, 1983).

[34]G. Masnick, and M.J. Bane, *The Nation's Families, 1960-1990* (Boston: Auburn House, 1980), 62-64, 100-102.

[35]This new, more involving style of fatherhood was not simply a product of the women's movement and the rethinking of sex roles. There was already historical precedent for a strong male commitment to parenting—the tendency toward fathers' involvement that emerged quietly as a part of modern fatherhood in the late nineteenth century and grew slowly throughout the twentieth century. However, this earlier impulse toward emotional engagement with children never became a full-blown style of fatherhood that rested on a rearranged family as participant fatherhood did. Rather, it was simply an impulse that some men carried out, a tendency within the dominant style of modern fatherhood.

[36]See L. Pogrebin, *Growing Up Free* (New York: McGraw-Hill, 1981).

[37]The best historical summary of the rise of the *current* women's movement is S. Rothman, *Woman's Proper Place: A History of Changing Ideals and Practices, 1870 to the Present,* (New York: Basic Books, 1978), 221-53.

[38]See C. Banas, "More Women Eye 'Male' Careers," *Boston Globe,* 7 Feb. 1981, 4. This article reports on a study that shows the profound impact of the women's movement on the ideas and career plans of college students.

[39]For a compelling account of the values—and the difficulties—surrounding child-rearing in a different social class, see L.B. Rubin, *Worlds of Pain: Life in the Working Class Family* (New York: Basic Books, 1976).

# Male Sexuality: Toward A Theory of Liberation

## GAD HOROWITZ AND MICHAEL KAUFMAN

Until the early 1980s the main trend in feminist presentations of sex and sexuality had to do with sexual oppression and the degradation of women by men. Whether the issue was violence, incest, rape, pornography, or "normal" heterosexual relationships, male sexuality was cast in terms of aggression, objectification, domination, and oppression. The inescapable conclusion of such an analysis was that somehow male sexuality had to be dampened, controlled, and contained.

The converse of all this was a presentation of women's sexuality that either tended to speak of women as sexual victims and objects or that developed concepts of women's sexuality as naturally soft, nurturing, and without conflict. But in recent years a new debate has emerged on women's sexuality. A spate of new books seeks to understand the tensions inherent in female sexuality and sexual expression in patriarchal, industrial societies.[1] Carol Vance, the editor of one such book, clearly summarizes this tension:

> The tension between sexual danger and sexual pleasure is a powerful one in women's lives. Sexuality is simultaneously a domain of restriction, repression, and danger as well as a domain of exploration, pleasure, and agency. To focus only on pleasure and gratification ignores the patriarchal structure in which women act, yet to speak only of sexual violence and oppression ignores women's experience with sexual agency and choice and unwittingly increases the sexual terror and despair in which women live.[2]

Although the feminist discussion of sexuality is making important advances, the understanding by men and women of male sexuality lags woefully behind. Even among gay men, where there has been a continuing affirmation of male sexuality, much more has been written on gay history, identity and culture than on sexuality per se.

Regardless of sexual orientation, most men harbor some confusing feelings about their sexuality. Heterosexual and bisexual men who have become aware of sexism and the oppression of women often feel caught between sexual desire on one side and a pressing confusion about forms of sexual behavior or fantasy that appear to, or actually do, oppress women. For many homosexual and bisexual men there is confusion about the conflict (as determined by our society) between their sexual desire for men and their own gender identity.

As with many questions about men we can profit from recent explorations by feminists. Our starting point can usefully parallel the approach of current writings about female sexuality: the notion of sexuality as a socially constructed system of conflict and inner tension.

Male sexuality is not simply a thing, good, bad, or otherwise. It is a terrain of tension, conflict and struggle. There are a number of internal conflicts as well as a new form of sociopolitical conflict arising from the feminist challenge to patriarchy. The interaction of these conflicts tends to produce anxiety, with guilt and confusion at one extreme and an aggravation of aggression at the other. These two extremes are expressed, at the one extreme, by the guilty feelings of many men sympathetic to feminism and, at the other, by the increase in portrayals of violence against women and perhaps of actual violence itself.[3] But the points of conflict and tension will not be reduced simply by a dampening or suppression of male sexuality or simply by the removal of pornography from newsstands. Rather the solution will be sexual liberation within societies organized to meet as full a range of human needs as possible.

In the most abstract terms, the tension within male sexuality is between pleasure and power. The pleasure is the pleasure of touch, sensation, fantasy, and intimacy. The realm of pleasure is ultimately derived from the body. Power is of two sorts. First is the sheer power of pleasure. Depending on one's feeling of guilt, there may or may not be conflict with the experience of pleasure. But the power of male sexuality also stems from social relations of power: the social power of men over women; the power of social constraint and socially imposed forms of sexual repression; the social power of heterosexuality over homosexuality; the internalization of social and sexual domination in the form of the structures of masculinity and a sense of guilt.

But of course there is no simple dualism of bodily based pleasures and socially constructed power. The pleasure of sensuality cannot be divorced from pleasures derived from relations of power, or, in reverse, inhibitions of sensuality often relate to the existing relations of power. Furthermore the very way our body experiences pleasure is the result of an interaction between the body and the social world.

It is more precise, then, to speak of a series of conflicts. Our sexuality and our sexual lives display conflicts between sexual pleasure per se, the constraints of masculinity, the oppression of women, the repression of an innate polysexuality (that is, repression of a fluid and wide-ranging sexuality), and a generalized fetishism of the objects of desire.

This chapter explores a number of areas in which these conflicts are expressed. The first section examines the split between activity and passivity and the repression of men's innate polysexuality. The purpose is to examine how male sexuality is constructed at the psychological level and to give us some basic concepts with which to examine the conflicts of male sexuality. This first section concludes by sketching the outlines of a theory of male sexual liberation. The second section turns to two interlocking issues—sexual objectification and pornography—to see whether the framework of the first section helps us analyze some of the dilemmas and conflicts faced by men and women as we attempt to understand and change our sexual and social worlds.

Our overall approach is psychoanalytical. One of the great contributions of psychoanalysis is the notion that there is no such thing as a natural form of sexuality. Sexuality is simply the capacity of humans to derive pleasure from the body. The form this takes for the child and adult is a product of biological maturation and historical evolution within the social and natural environments. Our reading of psychoanalysis does not start with the individual as abstracted from society. We start with society and the body—but a body that is part of society. The act of creating a human being is in itself a profoundly social activity, as are the body's experiences from that moment on. Nor do we start with society as abstracted from the body. Society does not exist only in structures external to the human but is embedded within the body. Society is embodied. One need look no farther than the stance of a soldier or the pose of a model to understand this latter point.

There are three problems with using the psychoanalytic model. One is a long history of superficial, sexist, conservative, and otherwise objectionable interpretations. The history of offensive ideological baggage goes back to Freud himself. We do our best to dissociate ourselves from these traditions. Second is the fact that psychoanalysis employs a complex and specialized vocabulary that must be learned to make sense of the whole approach. To make matters worse, this vocabulary itself has been subject to numerous superficial, sexist, and conservative misreadings. We will do our best to limit the use of specialized terminology and, when necessary, to introduce terms as we go along without getting bogged down in terminological debates. A final difficulty is that psychoanalysis is, more than anything, a theory of the unconscious. Many of the matters we will discuss are things that each of us has either forgotten or has never consciously known. These things are only uncovered in the course of psychological analysis, and even when uncovered they are subject to interpretation. We think the best test of the material in the first section will be its application to issues of objectification and pornography in the second. Once unconscious desire is manifested in pictures or in our conscious activities, we can begin to evaluate the usefulness of the concepts we have employed to understand the unconscious.

ACTIVITY/PASSIVITY AND POLYSEXUALITY

## Body and Culture

It is now quite popular to acknowledge that human sexuality is not simply innate and natural, but rather is socially constructed.[4] Sexual desire and sexual behavior vary greatly from society to society, from epoch to epoch, and from person to person. On the other hand, sexuality has to do with the body, bodily pleasure, and physiological responses. Male sexuality may be experienced in the realm of fantasy, and the stuff of our sexuality may be unconscious and deeply repressed, but it isn't constructed out of nothing. Ultimately there is the body, a tingling in the mouth, an erection of the penis, the blush of skin, the sight of an object of desire, the pleasure of taste and sound, or a pressure on the prostate that can take your breath away. Culture does not write on a blank paper.

In order for us to meet our needs in the world our desires must be controlled, organized, and related to external reality. Innate ego capacities—our ability to perceive, to remember, to move purposefully—are the means through which the child's energies are directed out at the world. And it is this world that molds that which is biologically given in the child. This process of molding is the development of the child's ego, the child's personality.

This developmental process is one of organizing, restraining, and repressing the highly malleable energy of human desire. Whereas animal instincts are closely adapted to reality, in humans there is an "organ" of adaption to reality, the ego.[5] Human desires cannot be satisifed without the intervention of the ego. "We are," says Grene, "biologically formed to be cultural animals."[6] Our desires do not take their final form until they have been molded by culture, where biological drives become desire, wish, and pleasure.

This process of transformation is the process that Freud described as repression. The extent and quality of repression is not a biological given or a social constant but changes as societies change and evolve. More specifically, the development of civilization, says Freud, has required an ever greater renunciation of pleasure.[7] Marcuse added to Freud's formulation by drawing a distinction between basic and surplus repression. Basic repression is the renunciation or sublimation of pleasure that is necessary to survive and develop as a human being. On top of this is surplus repression, the forms of repression that increase as civilization develops.[8] This ever increasing renunciation of desire is reexperienced in the development of every human being. As we mature we bring into our developing egos the structures and demands of our society.

Two immediate things concern us here. One is the split between activity and passivity and the superimposition of "masculinity" and "femininity" onto this polarity. The other is the narrowing of the vast expression of sexual desire onto genital pleasure, what Freud saw as the repression of polymorphous bisexuality.

## Activity, Passivity, and Bisexuality

Freud spoke of activity and passivity coexisting in the infant. At the mother's breast, he said, the newborn is the passive recipient of the mother's activities, of her care. But the infant quickly develops the desire and ability to be an active initiator, even though its ability to carry out these activities still depends on nurturing adults. The continuing development of the ego, that is, the increased capacity to master the world, is the developing of one's activity.

As the ego develops, active and passive modes of gratification are extended into general orientations of the ego, what one might call personality types. Generally, activity is associated with an aggressive, outgoing, achieving, or doing orientation; passivity with a more pacific, receptive, being orientation. Psychoanalytic theory stresses that in the first few years of life girls and boys are both active and passive.[9]

Freud also thought that, in the "language" of the unconscious, activity and passivity are related to specific zones of the body. The mouth, anus, and vagina, although capable of being vehicles of activity, have a primarily passive character because they are receptive orifices that can be pleasurably stimulated by another organ—a nipple, thumb, finger, tongue, column of feces, penis.

Although Freud referred to certain organs as essentially active or essentially passive, he did not ignore the distinction between their physiological characteristics and the psychological characteristics that are later associated with them. For example, at the breast a child may appear to be in a state of passive bliss, but active sucking is what brings it to that state. For the newborn, and likely for some time, it is not possible to describe aims as either active or passive. The mouth and vagina may be receptive organs, but this does not necessarily suggest exclusive passivity.

Young children may not consciously understand the world, but as anyone who cares for children knows, they are, without knowing it, incredibly good judges of social and psychological relations. Thus from an early age we bring to our bodies a set of social experiences. We project onto our bodies a whole set of social meanings. In other words, while the vagina is physically a receptive organ and the penis physically an insertive one, it is only through the work of culture that these become passive and active organs. What is the combination of biological and social developments that create these equations?

Boys and girls of one to three years do not seem to experience significantly different sexual desires or gratifications. They can experience both activity and passivity, and they can be erotically interested in humans of either sex; they are essentially bisexual. Very young children are curious about human bodies but do not seem to attach any importance to sex differences.[10]

With maturation this outlook changes, particularly with a growing erotic interest in the genitals. By four or five this new genital interest is impregnated with social meaning. The boy (in a male-dominant society) unconsciously experiences the penis as representing activity. The penis becomes a phallic symbol. The corollary is that an unconscious fear of "castration" develops, a fear that is so strong only because our patriarchal and heterosexist society creates a norm in which one cannot be powerful, active, or a lover of women, without possessing a penis.[11] An antithesis is set up of phallic versus "castrated." The fear of castration is not experienced literally or consciously; rather it is a bodily image associated with a loss of activity and power. Furthermore, in societies of male domination *and* where homosexuality is repressed, most boys cannot escape this castration anxiety without giving up passivity and homosexuality. Homosexuality is equated with passivity—and therefore with castration—because in a patriarchal society men are by definition dominant; thus love for males comes to be equated with passivity. Passivity leads to anxiety about one's masculinity, and thus it is emotionally necessary in such a society for the boy to unconsciously renounce his bisexuality.

Of course the "norms" defined here do not exist in reality. This process of repression is never complete and never without its internal conflicts and tensions. What is repressed lives on, sometimes in the form of active homosexuality or bisexuality as an adult, sometimes in the form of fantasy and dreams, and sometimes in the form of intense fear—homophobia. But what does appear to be a norm for men is the impossibility of simultaneously sustaining active and passive aims without generating conflict and fear.

What occurs, therefore, is a split between activity and passivity and then an imposition on top of it of the phallic/castrated polarity. It is this superimposition that produces "masculinity" and "femininity," which until then, says Freud, "have no psychological meaning."[12] This is the unconscious logic of patriarchy as discovered by Freud.

Even where one's parental figures depart from the patriarchal norms, the boy must experience these superimpositions because of the weight of institutions, the patriarchal family form, and a whole culture that teaches that men = activity.

Children often express their fears through games. One extremely popular game among boys (and many young men) is to tuck their genitals between their legs and out of sight, and then to parade in front of each other or in front of a mirror as a female. In a group of boys the reaction is one of glee; alone, there is amusement, fascination, and terror.

## Freud's Bisexuality versus Polysexuality

In *Repression*, Horowitz uncritically accepted Freud's presupposition that sexual life *must* first be experienced by all human beings in terms of the polarity or antithesis of activity and passivity. It therefore seemed obvious that the lifting of the surplus repression of bisexuality would result in something like androgyny—men and women equally capable of both activity and passivity and of homosexual and heterosexual object choice, like the very young child. We would now take a somewhat different view and would emphasize that the salience of the issue of activity-passivity in the very young child is itself a product of surplus repression.

Earlier in this century, anthropological research on the Trobriand Islands to the east of New Guinea showed a people with no concepts of linear cause and effect—active subject and passive object—in relationships or chronology. Trobrianders did not describe things that happened as a linear series of causes and effects. Paths were not described as leading somewhere or running to and from, but were simply *at*. While we automatically connect events or shapes with lines to indicate relation and continuity, the Trobrianders did not. For example, to us one of their villages would look like a circle of huts; they described it as an aggregate of bumps. Natural and human actions were thought to be set by tradition. But these traditions were not perceived as determining behavior; they were the pattern that indicated what the action was. For example, Trobrianders did not think of work as having a reward outside of, and subsequent to, the act. "We plan future experiences climactically, leading up to future satisfaction or meaning," writes Dorothy Lee. "None of the Trobriand activities is fitted into a climactic line. There is no job, no labor, no drudgery which finds its reward outside the act. All work contains its own satisfaction." There is no radically separate individual acting in linear time as a performer of actions upon objects and invidiously compared with other individuals in terms of the adequacy of the performance. An activity can fail, but not a person. The "outcome" of any action was already determined within an overall pattern of existence and tradition.[13]

Like that of many other tribal peoples, the language of the Trobrianders represents a different description and a different experience of reality than ours. Modern languages and modern societies are deeply imbued with notions of cause and effect and with dualisms such as subject/object and activity/passivity. This can be seen in the basic sentence structure of Indo-European languages, where there is a subject, verb, and object. Whenever anything happens, someone or something is doing something usually to someone or something.

The split between activity and passivity, so fundamental to our appreciation of masculinity and femininity, is a creation of culture and society out of the originally undifferentiated unity of human *being*. Our languages and our historically evolved realities highlight and accentuate a split between subject and object and between active and passive.

Freud posited an original "polymorphous perversity" of the infant, that is, a diverse, diffused capacity for sexual stimulation and satisfaction from all of the body and its senses. Similarly, the Trobrianders conceptualized sexuality as "an aggregate of pleasurable experiences,"[14] not as a series of events leading from forepleasure to genital stimulation to climax; and not as one active person *doing* something *to* a passive person. Not even as two persons doing things to one another alternately or simultaneously.

As we mature our sexuality undergoes a biological maturation and eventually is focused on the genitals. But it is culture and cultural factors that require us to undergo a surplus repression of other sexual aims and desires.

Although Freud spoke of an original polymorphous perversity, he made little use of this notion and tended to assume a natural bisexuality structured around an active/passive split. We feel it is more useful to conceive of human sexual potential as a *polysexuality*—a fluid capacity for sexual excitation and discharge through any part of our body including the brain, with its ability to fantasize, and through the various senses, touch, taste, hearing, sight, and smell. As a capacity rather than a fixed entity, sexuality is originally formless and chaotic. The process of biological maturation narrows this original polysexuality somewhat to a greater focus on genital pleasure. It organizes sexuality around genital sexuality. This appears to be in part a biologically natural process that has much to do with the reproduction of the species. It is a part of what Marcuse called the process of basic repression.

But maturation is also a process of internalizing cultural norms. What isn't natural is the surplus repression of nongenital forms of sexual excitation and expression and of the vast range of physical pleasures that we do not even consider sexual. Within the realm of surplus repression, the notion of social construction of sexuality becomes relevant. The repression and suppression of a wide range of sexual pleasure is not necessary either for biological maturation or for the existence of human culture per se.

What is repressed in the process of maturation and the creation of gender in surplus-repressive societies is not simply bisexuality but our constitutional polysexuality. The developing child internalizes the divisions of society: masculine versus feminine, active versus passive, subject versus object, normal versus abnormal, class versus class, race versus race, human versus nature, and so on. A number of things happen simultaneously to our sexuality:

1. Polysexuality is narrowed down to bisexuality, which in turn is narrowed down to heterosexuality or homosexuality (with a heterosexual norm).

2. Polysexuality is narrowed down to genital sexuality with a surplus repression of other potential forms of sexual desire and expression.

3. Through the process described above, superimposed onto the

natural division between the sexes are masculinity and feminity—surplus aggression and surplus passivity.

These are all norms. When all goes "well," the construction of our sexuality is a selection of certain traits and desires through which our desires and needs can be satisfied. Our ego has to function in synchrony with our social and natural environment in order that our needs will be met. The process of ego development takes place within the norms, the categories, the requirements of a given society. But none of us is the norm because each of us has a unique developmental experience and a unique constitution. Some of us differ widely from the norm, some little. An endless number of different combinations and permutations exist for the three processes mentioned above. In the end there may be an ideological norm, but there is no "real" normal or abnormal; rather there is a range of sexual beings trying to function and find fulfillment in a surplus repressive society.

We can turn this whole process around and begin to conceive of a liberated sexuality, that is, sexuality in a non–surplus-repressive society. The sexually free human being will not experience sexuality as either active or passive or even as *both,* but as "an aggregate of pleasurable experiences." Probably genetic and experiential differences among humans will result in the development of idiosyncracies, habits, and preferences, perhaps even exclusions of one kind or another, perhaps even options for celibacy. But these will be individualized expressions of a multivalent eros rather than compulsive responses to fear and anxiety. There will be many different kinds of sexual expression, many different communities and subcultures with different sexual practices, and freedom for individuals to change and move from one way of life to another in the course of a lifetime.

Freud believed that "progress in civilization" required surplus repression. The Frankfurt school (Adorno, Horkheimer, Marcuse), synthesizing the work of Hegel, Marx, Freud, and Weber, translates "progress in civilization" as the domination of nature. In order to conquer nature, human beings had to dominate their own nature, that is, to repress themselves, to transform themselves into instruments of warfare and labor, to split activity and passivity. Passivity was equated with nature and assigned to women. The *domination* of external nature, of internal nature (sexuality), of women, and of passivity in males are all aspects of an integral process of surplus repression.

Nature is now more than conquered; it is laid waste. It is time for what Marcuse calls a "reconciliation with nature." This means the end of surplus repression and the reclamation of the polysexuality of men and women. It means radically new relations of economic, political, and social organization. Neither women nor men can do it alone. New forms of human association involving both sexes and all sexual orientations can be developed only by men and women struggling together. In its present patriarchal form, male sexuality tends to be the *result* of containment and moral (anti-sexual) reformation. New forms of human sexual association must involve not the containment or the moral reformation of the sexuality of males, but its liberation.

### ZONES OF SEXUAL CONFLICT

The development of masculinity is the development of a surplus-active character type. This implies a repression of passivity. But in our lives a tension between the two continues to exist, even if this tension is disguised and its forms differ widely. One simple example shows how deeply instilled this tension is. One man we know is concerned about his automatic need to operate in a directive, active fashion in relation to women. Nothing he does seems to reduce the tension of this need. For example, if he walks ahead of a woman through a door or along a narrow path he feels he is leading the woman. If he follows, he is aware of "being a gentleman"; he feels he is "letting" the woman go ahead. The active/passive split forms the structure of our psychic reality and determines the categories through which we perceive the world and our activities within it. If such is the tension in so simple an act as walking through a doorway, think of the tremendous forces at work in sexual attraction and relationships.

The analysis in the first section of this article of the repression of polysexuality and the active/passive split can be extended to help us grapple with a number of zones of sexual contradiction and conflict for men in our society. The following are a few comments on two zones of conflict: the sexual objectification of women and heterosexual pornography.

## Sexual Objectification

Sexual desire always has an object. The object may be oneself, it may be another, it may be of a part of another, or it may be a thing. But as we develop and as our ego builds a capacity to meet our needs in the world around us, desire becomes attached to specific objects. The object may be pleasing for its sight, its touch, its taste, its sound, or its smell.

Insofar as the objects of desire are other people, a few things happen. To some extent, particular attributes are abstracted from the total person. For the newborn baby the breast and the voice of the mother represent the whole. Later in life, whether the object of our choice is heterosexual or homosexual, the presence or absence of certain physical characteristics determines whether we will be sexually attracted to a person. The presence of a vagina or a penis is the bottom line across which all but the bisexual dare not step. In other words the part comes to represent the whole. This tendency of the part to represent the whole is also seen in patriarchal societies in the fantastic psychological and cultural investment of energy onto a relatively small and tender bit of tissue that dangles between a man's legs.

Not only the genitals or breasts but any part of the body can come to represent the whole. Further boundaries of sexual attraction are established by a number of secondary sexual characteristics. The touch of relatively hairless skin will excite one man while the feel of a rough beard will do the same for another. And because we do not go around without clothes, even when it would be comfortable to do so, it is usually these secondary sexual characteristics that become the daily currency that represents the whole. The function of fashion, makeup, body language, and what we do with our voices is to accentuate selectively or subdue a number of these secondary characteristics.

Object love is the basic way that our sexuality is expressed. This is intrinsic to the functioning of the human ego. Our ability to experience a part of the body as representative of the whole results from the inherent nature of the unconscious. But beyond these intrinsic features, the shape that object love takes is a product of particular cultures and personal experiences.

One reason why parts of the body come to represent the whole is the repression of polysexuality. With physical maturation, successive zones of the body become the site of particularly intense physical and psychological excitation. The pleasure of a part (part of one's own body or part of another) captures the pleasure of the whole. This is the result of basic repression. In itself this is not a bad thing, so long as the whole person doesn't disappear in the process. The incomparable thrill and excitement attached to particular parts of our bodies or of another's body need not be denigrated. Male or female, if one can touch one's tongue against a lover's nipple or penis or clitoris and for a brief moment through contact with that protuberance capture the vastness of our desire and of our lover's desire, this is clearly a great conquest for human sexuality. This is part of the grandeur of human sexuality as opposed to the simple reproductive instincts of our animal cousins.

But superimposed on this is the surplus repression of nongenital forms of sexual desire. Surplus repression takes place increasingly as civilization "progresses" and this repression is recapitulated in the development of the individual. The primacy of genital sexuality lowers the value of other forms of sexual desire to the extent that they can only exist as elements of "forepleasure" or become taboo or are not seen as sexual at all. The outcome is the fracturing of the whole person into component parts and processes, some of which come to capture all of the sexual energies and desires of a person.

The effect of all this is pernicious as can be seen in the form taken by heterosexual male attraction to women. Even aside from this fracturing, in a society dominated by men, women become socially defined in terms of their reproductive and sexual capacities. Not defined as the brains or brawn of society, they are its reproductive core, its nurturers, its singing flesh. Combined with the tendency of the unconscious to represent the whole by a part, certain physical properties not only are objects of individual sexual desire but are invested with the society's whole definition of women.

The nature of this process and its effects on male sexuality can best be understood by using the psychoanalytic notion of "fixation" and the psychoanalytic and Marxist notions of fetishism. The fixation—an intense preoccupation and focus on certain activities or parts of the body—is a result of a developmental process in which interest and attention have moved from one thing to another and in which earlier delights are incompletely repressed. Some fixations have to do with particularly pleasurable or frightening experiences of childhood. Most often, though, one fixates on experiences or objects that simultaneously provide some form of sexual satisfaction and that give reassurance in the face of some anxiety or fear.[15]

Fetishism is an example of fixation. In psychoanalytic theory, fetishism is the endowment with sexual significance of an inanimate object or a part of the body not normally considered an erotogenic zone. When this reaches neurotic proportions, a person does not experience sexual excitement except as focused on, or in the presence of, that object. This sort of fetishism is almost entirely a phenomenon seen among men. Psychoanalytic investigation suggests that the fetish usually has the unconscious significance of the penis. The symbol, usually developed from childhod experiences, is a response to castration anxieties, in particular the perception that women do not have penises. A part of the woman's body or apparel—classically feet, hair, shoes, or an article of clothing—takes on the significance of the "missing" penis. The *unconscious* "discovery" of this missing penis (that is, of the object so highly valued in patriarchal society) reduces "castration" anxiety—that is, the fear of losing activity and power.

Although Freud discussed fetishism and fixation as neurotic symptoms, the concepts can be used (particularly in conjunction with the discussion in the first section above) to understand "normal" masculine sexuality. Although this discussion could apply with only a few modifications to homosexual masculine sexual desire, we will limit ourselves here to heterosexual attraction.

The heterosexual male fascination with women's bodies represents a number of things. There is a continuing desire to reexperience our first object of love and physical contact. In fact, our original model of object love was with a mother from whom we were inseparable. The fascination is insatiable. It is as if we cannot get enough of the object of desire. In the language of the unconsious this desire to take in, to "get enough of," is ultimately based on experience at the breast. (The process is partially different for a women because she *is* that object of primal desire both in her developed ego and in her physical being.)

The fascination with women's bodies also relates to castration anxiety. The sight of a woman confirms that one is a man. If the root fear of male psychological development is castration, then it follows that as adults we will be fixated on the object of fear, those beings who are without penises. In a society of male domination, the common object (women's bodies) of a common fear (castration) of the dominant group (men) becomes a generalized fetish. As pointed out above, to be a sexual object is not necessarily objectionable. But here the sexual object becomes sexual fetish.

There are two final aspects of this fixation. One is a fascination with what the male has repressed in achieving masculinity. The surplus repression of passivity takes with it the repression of softness and receptivity. Part of the fetishistic fascination with the female body is with what we have lost.

In a society with a heterosexual norm, the fascination with the object of sexual desire takes the form, for the majority of men, of an intense, eroticized, ever-present attraction to women. The development of masculine sexuality, with its prerogative of an active sexual orientation, makes this attraction socially acceptable, indeed, socially celebrated except in the most sexually repressive cultures and subcultures. It is the social norm for men to be sexual actors. In itself there is nothing wrong with that; the problem has to do with the repression of a corresponding sexual activity for women, the loss of men's passivity, and the distortion that sexual attraction and sexual activity undergo in a surplus repressive, patriarchal society. But in spite of these things, one component of what is commonly called the objectification of women is the celebration of sexuality and sexual attraction.

The fixation on and fetishism of women's bodies is a socially constructed psychological form. As a social norm, the objectification of women's bodies represents a progressive distancing from the total personality of the woman. The tendency of patriarchy to reduce women to reproductive and sexual functions is mirrored on the psychological level in the construction of masculinity. The tendency of the unconscious to represent the whole by a part is frozen and the parts *become* the whole. The appreciation of women takes the frozen form of the appreciation of women's form. First women are reduced to their reproductive and sexual functions, and then they are reduced to either one *or* the other. This is the familiar dualism of mother and whore. And in between, the category of virgin is so highly charged in part because it is the only point where the dualism is overcome, or better, it is the point which symbolizes both potentials.

Finally, as a socially mediated fixation that is abstracted from real women, the fascination is with a mythologized being, a collection of parts, a fiction, a mythical part that represents a mythical whole.

In short, what is loosely called men's objectification of women is actually the combination of a series of factors in apparent contradiction. The components so far identified are:

- men's object love for women and the human capacity to represent the whole by a part;
- fascination with what we have repressed (passivity, softness, receptiveness);
- the constant (and not always wanted) intrusion of erotic stimulation into our daily lives;
- confirmation of our own manhood;
- a degradation of women through the fixation on and fetishism of women's bodies and the *reduction* of the whole to some component parts.

## Voyeurism and Pornography

In a capitalist society, a society of commodity production and acquisition, objects of desire become commodities. Wherever it can, capitalism produces objects for sexual consumption and objectifies the subjects of sexuality in order to sell other products.

Marx spoke of the fetishism of commodities. Capitalism breathes illusory life into things. Commodities—the products of social production—are "endowed with a life of their own, [they] enter into relations both with each other and with the human race." The social relations among humans that produce commodities appear, not as a "social relation between persons in their work, but rather as material relations between persons and social relations between things."[16] The fetishism of commodities is in part a process of mystification. But as Norman Geras points out, it is also a process of domination.[17] In a society organized not just around but *for* commodity production, the products of human labor control the lives of the producer. "The definite social relations between men themselves . . . assume here, for them, the fantastic form of a relation between things."[18] Commodity fetishism is mystification, but it also reflects the real life domination of humans by commodities.

This combination of mystification and domination is seen in pornography. Pornography is a prevalent commodity within which sexual objectification is expressed. Like any commodity, pornography presents strong elements of mystification and domination. A form of sexual representation, pornography—by the nature of the commodity form but also as a result of the fixation and fetishism described above—represents distorted and mystified forms of the objects it depicts. But it also accurately portrays the real-life domination of women by men.

As an artifact of a capitalist, patriarchal society, pornography captures a number of the conflicts and contradictions of that society. In an exaggerated and stylized manner, the function and form of pornography depict and portray the conflicts surrounding sexual objectification described above.[19] Of the many questions that relate to the issue of pornography, one interests us here. Why is heterosexual pornography so attractive to so many men? Our emphasis will be on forms of visual representation.

Pornography is a brash statement of male power, of the sexual availability of any woman to any man, of women's vulnerability, of women reduced to sexual parts, of women defiled and even dismembered. As a statement of fetishism, of mystification and domination, pornography reflects and reinforces negative images of women.

The great majority of pornographic images contain this content, and when they do not, the immediate context (the magazine, the porn theatre) and the social context induce these meanings. These contexts are ones of male collusion (in public or in private) in the oppression of women.

These meanings and contexts seem to be one reason for men's attraction to pornography. But in a sense the answer so far begs the question. Why, after all, should these meanings be attractive to men?

As we saw above, the construction of masculinity is inseparable from the repression of bisexuality and passivity. Masculinity is inseparable from a projected, adored, despised, and feared femininity that exists as its opposite. As discussed by Kaufman elsewhere in this volume,[20] masculinity is a fiction in the sense that it is not what it pretends to be: biological reality. It is the ideology of patriarchal, surplus-repressive society captured in the personality of the individual. Because of its real-life distance from biological reality (that is, maleness), masculinity is an elusive and unobtainable goal. From early childhood, every male has great doubts about his masculine credentials. Because one facet of masculinity is the surplus repression of passivity, the confirmation of masculinity can best be found in the trials of manhood (war, fighting, or more refined forms of competition) and in relation to its mirror opposite, femininity. The portrayal of femininity, that is, women in a passive, dominated position in relation to men, is a relatively easy confirmation of one's own masculinity. One reason why the images of pornography are so appealing is that they confirm that one is masculine, which confirms, in gender-based social orders, that one is male.

All this is another way of saying that the fascination with pornography results from the fixation, not only on the object of sexual desire, but also on the object of fear, and this fixation has to do with "castration" anxiety. Needless to say, the viewer of pornography is not conscious of this anxiety.

But while all pornography (immediately or in its context) includes this form and function, it also contains elements that stand in contradiction to sexual repression. The contradiction is to sexual repression both in the sense of social standards and in the sense of the repression of passivity and polysexuality.

In terms of sexual repression in the immediate, social sense, pornography contains elements of sexual celebration. Ann Snitow and others have pointed out that pornography sometimes includes (along with its oppressive features) elements of play, of "thrilling (as opposed to threatening) danger," of defiance, of childlike freedom. For many, particularly the young, pornography is one of the few sources of sexual information.[21] It has become a rather stale joke to say that *Penthouse* is beginning to resemble a gynecology text, but where else can most boys or young men see what a vulva looks like? Of course the sexual information is distorted (particularly the information on sexuality as distinguished from anatomy, although even this is partially distorted), but we are talking here about the contradictory aspects of pornography.

Another part of the attraction of pornography is the attraction to what is socially taboo. Of course the taboo material is expressed in the language of what is not taboo: male dominance and female subservience. But again we are dealing with contradictory images.

Understood in terms of the surplus repression of passivity and bisexuality, pornography has a number of attractive features to men. We noted above that one feature of the male objectification of women is a fascination with what we have lost in the process of masculine development: passivity and receptiveness and all their associated features—softness, the feeling of being loved and adored, and so forth. Pornography represents a yearning for and fascination with those lost qualities. This is true both in what is depicted and in the action of viewing pornography.

The sexual pleasure of looking is one of the most basic of passive-receptive sexual activities. Freud, primarily an observer of adults rather than infants, read back onto infant sexuality from the repressed memories of adults and children. But observe a baby. She or he spends long moments staring, taking in the world, wrapped up in the pleasure of visual sensation. Along with activities of the mouth, seeing is a primary way that the baby takes in the world.

Viewing pornography, like the act of voyeurism, is a regression, a regression to an earlier moment, to an aspect of our polysexual disposition that has undergone surplus repression. "The human child," writes Fenichel, "goes through a prolonged phase of dependence [which] is gradually supplanted by activity; the memory of it, however, always admits of the recurrence of a regressive longing for substituting the earlier receptivity for activity."[22]

And it is the male, in male-dominated societies, who has undergone a surplus repression of passive aims. This repression does not destroy the passive aims (for they are intrinsic to the organism), but it forces them into disguised, distorted, derivative channels. Pornography not only presents a passive, receptive object to marvel at; it offers a form of sexual pleasure in which men can be passive and receptive (to the image, to the object of desire). In a real-life situation, with real contact with a woman in her full subjective, directive, active presence, passivity would arouse all sorts of anxieties. And of course part of what allows the passive pleasure of viewing pornography is that the object is often portrayed as passive and unthreatening. In terms of the repression of bisexuality, because the focus of our passive attention has no penis, it is not threatening. In terms of social power, the viewer also retains his dominance.

Of course the pornographic image varies widely. Much pornography shows an active, sexually aggressive, vampish woman. Some shows the subjection of men: the classic photo of a man under her stiletto heel. Both images provide a safe portrayal of female activity in the context of male passivity, either as viewer or as an object in a picture. But as noted by Mariana Valverde, in this case the presentation of female activity and male passivity is just the surface appearance. "In fact what is going on is that the male camera eye is creating a version of female active desire (as an evil form of desire, vampire-like), and then proceeding to appropriate that representation of female desire. This is best seen in so-called lesbian porn, which is unintelligible unless we understand that masculine desire is intent on appropriating not just women's bodies but women's own active desires."[23]

For some men passivity in face of the pornographic picture can still be threatening, so insecure is their purchase on maleness, so great is the unconscious tug of repressed passivity or repressed homosexuality or both, so great is their surplus aggressiveness. In this case pornography is pleasurable only if it portrays the active and explicit domination of women through images of bondage, torture, even murder. In the language of the unconscious, the dismemberment of the woman (the dismembered, that is, "castrated" object) is the only thing that can quiet one's anxiety and increase one's self-esteem.

There are many economic and social reasons for the current proliferation of pornography. But what is the psychological basis of this trend? The desires expressed by looking at pornography are insatiable, not only because sexual desire itself is insatiable, but because pornography in itself cannot provide an integrated expression of passive and active sexual aims. Pornography proliferates as profit-makers see they have an insatiable market. The more you look the more the passive, receptive urges are restimulated, looking becomes ever more intense, and the aims become ever more insatiable. Viewing pornography is ultimately an unfulfilling activity. It leads to greater frustration and to greater tensions between activity and passivity. And all this leads to the increasing tendency for pornography to portray sadistic actions.

It becomes sadistic because looking provides insufficient mastery of the object of desire. Part of the pleasure of looking is a regression to the omnipotence of childhood. The visual taking in of the object is not only passive: it is a mastery of the object because by looking, knowledge is acquired. For the unconscious, knowledge is power. As noted above, the viewer of pornography is looking for more than a pleasurable object of desire: he is looking for confirmation of his masculinity and confirmation that what he fears cannot be true, that castration is not a possibility. These are very contradictory desires, which in themselves fuel the insatiable desire. As long as the object of view remains partially unknown, the male childhood castration fears are not confirmed. The more clothes are removed and the more is seen, the more there is that has to be seen to find out that what he fears (castration) is not really true. At a certain point nothing more can be shown: already women's legs are pulled apart at ridiculous angles to show "everything." And thus the only thing left is to increase one's surplus aggressiveness (as a defense against the much feared equation of passivity with castration) and to pull the woman apart—figuratively in depictions of explicit domination or literally in snuff movies.

The proliferation of pornography is also what Marcuse called a "repressive desublimation." Over the past fifteen years there has been a certain freeing of instinctual energies occasioned by the spread of effective means of birth control, by the rise of feminism and women's activity, by the development of gay and lesbian pride, by the rejection of lifelong monogamy and premarital viginity, and by the rejection of the most blatant forms of social sexual repression, particularly in the advanced capitalist countries. But in our societies that nevertheless remain authoritarian and surplus-repressive, these released energies are channeled into distorted and unsatisfying forms in order to perpetuate the overall regime of surplus repression.

Since pornography functions to meet a number of contradictory needs and demands created by a society of surplus sexual repression and commercialization, the mere censorship of pornography will do next to nothing to reduce the degradation of women in all its myriad forms. Viewing pornography does not create the problem, it represents and in some sense helps perpetuate the problem. And the problem described here is not only the degradation of women but also the surplus repression of the full range of sexual desires, activities, and aims. The root of the problem is a patriarchal, profit-oriented, commodity-producing, surplus-repressive culture that represses polysexuality and superimposes masculinity and femininity onto the dualism of activity and passivity; such are the ultimate sources of the sexual degradation of women and the surplus repression of all humanity.

The struggle against such an imposing problem has many fronts.

One is the struggle against sexist representation and spectacle. As representations of a problem they codify, symbolize, make tangible, and help propagate the problem. Strategies that demonstrate opposition and rage are far different from state censorship. This opposition must be combined with sexual education that is antisexist and prosex (without, of course, socially imposing sexual activity as a mark of normality.) Active opposition and education must be combined with support for alternatives on the visual and personal fronts.[24]

Pornography represents the problem. But in a very distorted way it also represents the solution. In a distorted and oppressive manner it demonstrates that men's passive aims do not disappear, that polysexual urges do not disappear, that there remains in men a deep longing for the free and full expression and celebration of sexual desire. To say the least, pornography is not this full expression and celebration. But what do we expect from a patriarchal society of generalized commodity production?

And this leads us back to the essential problem. The solution to the problems presented in the discussion of objectification and pornography are to be found in the broad struggle against a patriarchal, surplus-repressive, class society. The prehistorical foundations of these structures are scarcity and the struggle to tame nature. For the first time in human history humans have the capacity to step beyond societies of scarcity. This certainly does not mean a future where machines continue to run amok and environmental pillage continues along its perilous course. Of necessity, the struggle will be an integrated one against all forms of sexual, class, gender, and human oppression informed by a keen ecological sensitivity. The goal is liberation and integration: social, political, economic—and sexual.

## NOTES

[1]See for example, Ann Snitow, Christine Stansell, and Sharon Thompson, eds., *Powers of Desire* (New York: Monthly Review Press, 1983); Carol S. Vance, ed., *Pleasure and Danger: Exploring Female Sexuality* (Boston: Routledge and Kegan Paul, 1984); Sue Cartledge and Joanna Ryan, eds., *Sex and Love: New Thoughts and Old Contradictions* (London: The Women's Press, 1983); and Mariana Valverde, *Sex, Power, and Pleasure* (Toronto: Women's Press, 1985).

[2]Carol S. Vance, "Pleasure and Danger: Toward a Politics of Sexuality," in Vance, *op. cit.,* 1.

[3]It is very difficult to analyze the statistical increase in rape and wife battering over the last decade in a number of countries, because the statistics do not necessarily indicate an increase in these forms of assault but might be accounted for by the increased willingness of women to report these crimes.

[4]This is one of the themes of many articles in the collections mentioned above, as well as in Michel Foucault, *The History of Sexuality* (New York: Pantheon, 1978), vol. 1, *An Introduction.*

[5]Heinz Hartmann, "Comments on the Psychoanalytic Theory of the Ego" in *Essays on Ego Psychology* (New York: International Universities Press, 1964), 120.

[6]Marjorie Grene, *Approaches to a Philosophical Biology* (New York: Basic Books, 1968), 44. For Freud's analysis of the drives, see his "Instincts and their Vicissitudes, " in *Standard Edition of the Complete Psychological Works of Sigmund Freud* (London: Hogarth Press), 14: 121-2.

[7]See Sigmund Freud, *Civilization and Its Discontents* (1930), trans. James Strachey (New York: W.W. Norton, 1961).

[8]See Herbert Marcuse, *Eros and Civilization* (New York: Vintage Books, 1962).

[9]For a detailed discussion of the problems in the psychoanalytic use of the terms active and passive, see David Rapaport, "Some Metapsychological Considerations Concerning Activity and Passivity" (1953), in *The Collected Papers of David Rapaport* (New York: Basic Books, 1967), 530-68.

[10]Many references in this subsection (such as to "castration" anxiety) are to unconscious processes, associations, and knowledge. One is not aware of these mental processes. The dominance of the unconscious over one's life is much greater for children than for adults. The language of this article does not refer to the conscious experience of children. Rather they have involuntary, powerful, emotional, dreamlike images of things happening bodily to themselves.

[11]For a detailed look at the issues presented in this section see Gad Horowitz, *Repression: Basic and Surplus Repression in Psychoanalytic Theory* (Toronto: University of Toronto Press, 1977), 81-125. For Freud's views on childhood sexuality see, for example, "Three Essays on the Theory of Sexuality" (1905), in *Standard Edition of the Complete Psychological Works of Sigmund Freud* (London: Hogarth Press), vol. 7.

[12]Sigmund Freud, "Instincts and their Vicissitudes" (1915) in Freud, *op. cit.,* 14: 134.

[13]Dorothy Lee, *Freedom and Culture* (New York: Prentice-Hall, 1959), esp. 89-120. These studies by Lee are based on the transcripts of Bronislaw Malinowski. Although current research by feminist anthropologists calls a number of Malinowski's conclusions and techniques into question, it does not appear that these criticisms would affect his actual records of the spoken language, particularly in the matters discussed here.

[14]*Ibid,* 119.

[15]See Otto Fenichel, *The Psychoanalytic Theory of Neurosis* (New York: W.W. Norton, 1945), 65-6, 327.

[16]Karl Marx, *Capital,* trans. Ben Fowkes (New York: Vintage, 1977), 1: 165-6.

[17]Norman Geras, "Marx and the Critique of Political Economy," in Robin Blackburn, ed., *Ideology in Social Science* (London: Fontana/Collins, 1972), 287.

[18]Marx, *op. cit.,* 165.

[19]We are indebted to various contributions in the collection *Women Against Censorship,* edited by Varda Burstyn (Toronto: Douglas and McIntyre, 1985), for a number of the observations in these paragraphs. Particularly relevant to the issues addressed here were the essays by Sara Diamond, "Pornography: Image and Reality" (40-57); Myrna Kostash, "Second Thoughts" (32-9); Ann Snitow, "Retrenchment Versus Transformation: The Politics of the Antipornography Movement" (107-20); and Varda Burstyn, "Political Precedents and Moral Crusades: Women, Sex and the State," (4-31).

[20]Michael Kaufman, "The Construction of Masculinity and the Triad of Men's Violence," in this volume.

[21]Snitow, *op. cit.,* 114-16.

[22]Fenichel, *op. cit.,* 468.

[23]Mariana Valverde, personal communication. We would also like to thank her for her comments on an earlier draft of this paper.

[24]See Varda Burstyn, "Beyond Despair: Positive Strategies," in Burstyn *op. cit.,* 152-80, for a discussion of some aspects of the struggle against forms of sexist representation and the sexual exploitation of women.

# Men Loving Men:
# The Challenge of
# Gay Liberation

## GARY KINSMAN

The limits of "acceptable" masculinity are in part defined by comments like "What are you, a fag?"[1] As boys and men we have heard such expressions and the words "queer," "faggot," and "sissy" all our lives. These words encourage certain types of male behavior and serve to define, regulate, and limit our lives, whether we consider ourselves straight or gay. Depending on who is speaking and who is listening, they incite fear or hatred.

Even among many heterosexual men who have been influenced by feminism, the taboo against loving the same sex remains unchallenged. Lines like "I may be anti-sexist, but I am certainly not gay" can still be heard. These men may be questioning some aspects of male privilege, but in attempting to remake masculinity they have not questioned the institution of heterosexuality.[2] As a result their challenge to male privilege is partial and inadequate.

Gay men have often found much support in the "men's movement" or in groups of men against sexism. At the same time we have also seen our concerns as gay men marginalized and pushed aside and have often felt like outsiders. Joe Interrante expresses some of the reservations of gay men about the "men's movement" and its literature:

> As a gay man . . . I had suspicions about the heterocentrist bias of this work. It told me that my gayness existed "in addition to" my masculinity, whereas I found that it colored my entire experience of manhood. I distrusted a literature which claimed that gay men were just like heterosexual men except for what they did in bed.[3]

The literature of the men's movement has tended to produce an image of men that is white, middle-class, and heterosexual. As Ned Lyttleton has pointed out, "an analysis of masculinity that does not deal with the contradictions of power imbalances that exist between men themselves will be limited and biased, and its limits and biases will be concealed under the blanket of shared male privilege."[4] A series of masculinities becomes subsumed under one form of masculinity that becomes "masculinity." As a result, socially organized power relations among and between men based on sexuality, race, class, or age have been neglected. These power relations are major dividing lines between men that have to be addressed if progressive organizing among men is to encompass the needs and experiences of all men. The men's movement has reached a turning point.[5] It has to choose whether it is simply a movement for men's rights—defending men's rights to be human too—or whether it will deepen the challenge to an interlocked web of oppression: sexism, heterosexism, racism, and class exploitation. We have to choose between a vision of a world in which men are more sensitive and human but are still "real" men at the top of the social order, and a radically new vision that entails the transformation of masculinity and sexuality and the challenging of other forms of domination.

In developing this radical vision—radical in the sense of getting to the roots of the problem—the politics of gay liberation and the politics of lesbian feminism are important. So too are the experiences of those of us who have been made into outsiders, people labelled "faggot," "queer," or "dyke" who have reclaimed these stigmatized labels as ways of naming experiences of the world and as weapons of resistance to heterosexual hegemony. The struggle against the institutionalized social norm of heterosexuality opens up the door to other kinds of social and personal change.

## GAY LIBERATION VERSUS HETEROSEXUAL PRIVILEGE

In our society heterosexuality as an institutionalized norm has become an important means of social regulation, enforced by laws, police practices, family and social policies, schools, and the mass media. In its historical development heterosexuality is tied up with the institution of masculinity, which gives social and cultural meaning to biological male anatomy, associating it with masculinity, aggressiveness, and an "active" sexuality. "Real" men are intrinsically heterosexual; gay men, therefore, are not real men.

While gay men share with straight men the privilege of being in a dominant position in relation to women, we are at the same time in a subordinate position in the institution of heterosexuality. As a result, gay men's lives and experiences are not the same as those of heterosexual men. For instance, while we share with straight men the economic benefits of being men in a patriarchal society, we do not participate as regularly in the everyday interpersonal subordination of women in the realms of sexuality and violence. Although, like other men, we have more social opportunities, we are not accepted as open gays in corporate boardrooms or in many jobs, sports, and professions. We can still be labeled "national security risks" and sick, deviant, or abnormal. Consequently, gay men experience a rupture between the presumably universal categories of heterosexual experience and their own particular experience of the world, a rupture that denies many of our experiences; for gay men exist in social situations that allow us to see aspects of life, desire, sexuality, and love that cannot be seen by heterosexual men.[6]

Gay men have had to question the institution of masculinity—which associates masculinity with heterosexuality—in our daily lives. We have experimented with and developed new ways of organizing our sexual lives and our love and support relations, of receiving and giving pleasure. Heterosexual men interested in seriously transforming the fabric of their lives have to stop seeing gay liberation as simply a separate issue for some men that has nothing to say to them. They should begin to ask what the experience of gay men can bring into view for them. As we break the silence and move beyond liberal tolerance toward gays and lesbians, we can begin to see how "queer baiting" and the social taboo against pleasure, sex, and love between men serves to keep all men in line, defining what proper masculinity is for us. Gay liberation suggests that heterosexuality is not the only natural form of sexuality but has instead been socially and culturally made the "normal" sexual practice and identity. As the Kinsey Institute studies suggested, the actual flux of human desire cannot be easily captured in rigid sexual categories. Many men who define themselves as straight have had sexual experiences with other men.[7] This has demonstrated the contradictions that can exist between our actual experiences and desires and the rigid social categories that are used to divide normal from deviant and that imply that any participation in homosexual activity automatically defines one as a homosexual.

Breaking the silence surrounding homosexuality requires challenging heterosexism and heterosexual privilege. Lesbian-feminist Charlotte Bunch once explained to heterosexual women that the best way to find out what heterosexual privilege is all about is to go about for a few days as an open lesbian:

> What makes heterosexuality work is heterosexual privilege—and if you don't have a sense of what privilege is, I suggest that you go home and announce to everybody that you know—a roommate, your family, the people you work with—everywhere that you go—that you're a queer. Try being a queer for a week.[8]

This statement could also be applied to the situation of straight men, and any heterosexual man can easily imagine the discomfort, ridicule, and fear he might experience, how his "coming out" would disrupt "normal" relations at work and with his family. Such experiences are the substance of gay oppression that make our lives different from those of straight men. Gay men in this heterosexist society are labeled with many terms of abuse. Young boys hurl the labels "queer," "fag," or "cocksucker" at each other before they know what the words mean. As we grow up we are denied images of men loving men and any models for our lives outside heterosexuality. In the United States, the age of consent varies from state to state, usually from sixteen to eighteen, although in some states all homosexual acts remain technically illegal. Under Canadian and British law males under twenty-one are denied the right to have sexual relations with other boys and men. Many members of the medical and psychiatric professions still practice psychological and social terrorism against us by trying to adjust us to fit the norm. We are excluded as open lesbians and gay men from most activities and institutions. When the mass media does cover us they use stereotypes or other means to show us to be sick, immoral, indecent, as some sort of social problem or social menace, or they trivialize us as silly and frivolous.[9] The police continue to raid our bookstores and seize our magazines. In 1983-6, the media fostered fear and hatred against gay men by associating all gay men with AIDS. Such media stories shift and mold public opinion against us. On city streets we are often violently attacked by gangs of "queerbashers." Most countries deny lesbians and gay men the basic civil and human rights, leaving us open to arbitrary firings and evictions.

A variety of sexual laws are used to regulate and control gay men's sexual and community lives. Police in many cities have a policy of systematically entrapping and harassing gays. In recent years hundreds of men across North America have been arrested and often entrapped by the police in washrooms and parks. These campaigns—especially in small towns and cities—and the associated media attention have torn apart the lives of these men, many of whom define themselves as heterosexual and are married with families.

In fact, the society in which we have all grown up is so profoundly heterosexist that even many gays have internalized the social hatred against us in forms of "self-oppression."[10] This fear keeps many of us isolated and silent, hiding our sexuality. One of the first steps in combating this self-oppression is to reject this denial of our love and sexuality by affirming our existence and pride publically. Assertions that "gay is good" and affirmations of gay pride are the beginnings of our resistance to heterosexual hegemony on the individual and social levels.

## THE HISTORY OF SEXUALITY

In addressing the matter of gay and lesbian oppression, we have to ask where this oppression has come from. How did heterosexuality come to be the dominant social relation? How did homosexuality come to be seen as a perverse outcast form of sexuality? If we can answer those questions, we can begin to see how we could break down the institution of heterosexuality and its control over our lives.

As a result of numerous cross-cultural and historical studies that have demonstrated that there is no natural or normal sexuality, we can no longer see sex as simply natural or biologically given. Our biological, erotic, and sexual capabilities are only the precondition for the organization of the social and cultural forms of meaning and activity that compose human sexuality. Our biological capabilities are transformed and mediated culturally, producing sexuality as a social need and relation. As Gayle Rubin explained, each social system has its own "sex/gender system," which

> is the set of arrangements by which a society transforms biological sexuality into products of human activity, and in which these transformed sexual needs are satisfied.[11]

Recent historical studies have challenged the assumed natural categories of heterosexuality and homosexuality themselves.[12] Gay, lesbian, and feminist historians have expanded our understanding of sexual meaning and identity, contesting the dominant ways in which sexuality has been discussed and viewed in our society.[13] The dominant perspective for looking at sexuality is what has been called the "repression hypothesis," which assumes that there is a natural sexuality that is repressed to maintain social and moral order. Many leftists argue that sexuality is repressed by the ruling class—to maintain class society because of capitalism's need for the family and a docile work force. This interpretation was popularized in the writings and activities of Wilhelm Reich,[14] who called for the end of sexual repression through the liberation of natural sexuality, which was for him completely heterosexual. Variations of this repression theory, and its corresponding call for the liberation of natural sexuality, have inspired sexual liberationist politics, including much of the gay liberation movement, which sees homosexuality as a natural sexuality that simply needs to be released from social repression.

The experience by women of the male sexual (i.e., heterosexual) revolution of the sixties and seventies has led much of the feminist movement to a more complex understanding of sexuality than simple theories of sexual repression. Feminism has exposed the contradictions in a sexual revolution that increased women's ability to seek sexual satisfaction but only within male-dominated heterosexual relations. Feminism has also begun to explore how sexuality and social power are bound together and how sexuality has been socially organized in male-dominated forms in this society.[15] This view of sex opens up new possibilities for sexual politics—our sexual lives are no longer seen as divorced from human and social activity but as the results of human praxis (the unity of thought and activity). Sexual relations are therefore changeable and are themselves the site of personal and social struggles. We can then begin to question the natural appearance of such sexual categories as heterosexual and homosexual and to make visible the human activity that is involved in the making of sexuality. This opens up a struggle, not for the liberation of some inherent sexuality that just has to be freed from the bonds of capitalism or repressive laws, but for a much broader challenge to the ways our sexual lives are defined, regulated, and controlled. It opens up questions about the very making and remaking of sex, desire, and pleasure.

## Enter the Homosexual

The historical emergence of the "homosexual" required a number of social preconditions, which can be summarized as three interrelated social processes: first, the rise of capitalist social relations, which created the necessary social spaces for the emergence of homosexual cultures;[16] second, the regime of sexuality that categorized and labeled homosexuality and sexual "deviations"; and third, the activities, cultural production, and resistance to the oppression of men in these same-sex desire-based cultures.

The rise of capitalism in Europe between the fifteenth and nineteenth centuries separated the rural household economy from the new industrial economy and undermined the interdependent different-sex household economy. The working class was made, and made itself, in the context of this industrialization, urbanization, and commercialization. This separation of "work" from the household and the development of wage labor meant that it became possible for more men in the cities to live outside the family, earning a wage and living as boarders. Later they would be able to eat at restaurants or taverns and rent their own accommodation. This created the opportunities for some men to start organizing what would become, through a process of development and struggle, the beginnings of a homosexual culture, from the eighteenth century on.[17]

A regime of sexuality has emerged as part of a series of social struggles over the last two centuries. The transition from feudalism to capitalism in the western countries meant a transition in the way kinship and sexual and class relations were organized. The new ruling class was no longer able to understand itself or organize its social life simply through the old feudal ties of blood or lineage.[18] New forms of family and state formation led to new forms of self-understanding, class consciousness, and notions of moral and social order. Sexuality emerged as an autonomous sphere separate from household production. A proper, respectable sexual and gender identity became an essential feature of the class unity of the bourgeoisie. This process is linked to the emergence of the ideology of individual identity. The regime of sexual definitions was first applied to the bodies of the bourgeoisie itself through its educational and medical systems and through the sexological knowledge that was generated by the new professional groups of doctors and psychiatrists and that served to draw a boundary between bourgeois respectability and the "bestial" sexual practices of the outcast poor and "lower orders." These norms of sex and gender definition helped organize the relations of the bourgeois family and its sexual morality.

Later these same norms of sexual identity and morality were used against the urban working class and poor, who were considered a threat to social order by middle-class and state agencies. The working class both resisted this enforcement of social norms and at the same time adopted them as its own. The male-dominated "respectable" sections of the working class developed their own norms of family and sexual life that incorporated the socially dominant norms of masculinity, femininity, and reproductive heterosexuality. The uneven and at times contradictory development of sexual identity in different classes, genders, races, and nationalities is a subject that remains to be more fully explored.

In the big cities sexuality becomes an object to be studied and a terrain for the expanding male-dominated fields of medicine, psychiatry, and sexology. Various forms of sexual behavior were categorized, classified, and ranked, with heterosexuality on the top and homosexuality and lesbianism near the bottom. The norm and the perversions were defined, separating normal and abnormal behavior. In this context sex in the ruling discourses became the truth of our being.[19]

The heterosexual man was no longer simply carrying out the types of activities he had to carry out in the sexual division of labor, or the activities that would lead to the reproduction of the species; rather he had become someone with a particular erotic, sexual, and gender identity that linked his masculinity to an exclusively heterosexual way of life. The heterosexual and the homosexual emerged in relation to each other as part of the same historical and social process of struggle and negotiation.

Men who engaged in sexual relations with other men in this emerging regime of sexuality (and who were affected by the ideology of individualism) began to organize their lives around their sexuality and to see themselves as separate and different from other men. They fought against campaigns by religious fundamentalists and the police who wished to curtail their activities.[20] In the last century, the emergence of sexology, increased police regulation of sexual behavior, and the passing of laws against sexual offenses combined with the development of these same-sex desire-based cultures to make the new social experience and social category of homosexuality.

The term homosexual itself was not devised until 1869, when Károly Mária Benkert, a Hungarian, coined the term in an appeal to the government to keep its laws out of peoples lives.[21] The category of homosexuality was originally elaborated by some homosexuals themselves, mostly professional men it seems, in order to name their "difference" and in order to protect themselves from police and legal prohibitions. The word was taken up by the various agencies of social regulation from the medical profession to the police and courts. Homosexuality was defined as an abnormality, a sickness, and a symptom of degeneracy. The efforts of medical and legal experts

were chiefly concerned with whether the disgusting breed of perverts could be physically identified for courts and whether they should be held legally responsible for their acts.[22]

An early Canadian reference—in 1898—to same-sex "perversion" among men by a Dr. Ezra Stafford (which refers to the work of Krafft-Ebing, one of the grandfathers of sexology) linked sex between men with prostitution in a theory of degeneracy. Stafford wrote that these things "may lead to the tragedy of our species."[23] This connection between homosexuality and prostitution as stigmatized social and sexual practices continued even to England's Wolfenden report of 1957, which linked these topics, and it continues to this day, in, for example, the use by the Canadian police of bawdy-house legislation, originally intended to deal with houses of female prostitutes, against gay men.

Simultaneously the needs of capitalism for a skilled labor force and a continuing supply of wage-laborers led to an emphasis on the heterosexual nuclear family. The rise of modern militarism and the scramble for colonies by the western powers led to demands for a larger and healthier supply of cannon fodder at the beginning of the twentieth century. An intensification of military discipline resulted in stiff prohibitions against homosexuality, which was seen as subversive of discipline and hierarchy in the armed forces. As a result, reproductive heterosexuality was reinforced for men, and motherhood further institutionalized for women.[24]

The category of the male homosexual emerged in sexology as an "invert" and was associated with some form of effeminacy and "gender inversion." A relation between gender dysfunction and abnormal sexuality was established:

> As defined by the ancient civil or canonical codes, sodomy was a category of forbidden acts. . . . The nineteenth century homosexual became a personage, a past, a case history, and a childhood, in addition to being a type of life, a life form, and a morphology, with an indiscreet anatomy and possibly a mysterious physiology. Nothing that went into his total composition was unaffected by his sexuality. . . . Homosexuality appeared as one of the forms of sexuality when it was transposed from the practice of sodomy onto a kind of interior androgyny, a hermaphrodism of the soul. The sodomite had been a temporary aberration; the homosexual was now a species.[25]

The categorization of "perverse" sexual types also provided a basis for resistance. Sexual categorization, as Foucault puts it,

> also made possible the formation of a "reverse" discourse: homosexuality began to speak on its own behalf, to demand that its legitimacy or "naturality" be acknowledged, often in the same vocabulary, using the same categories by which it was radically disqualified.[26]

Homosexuals themselves used this category to name their experiences, to articulate their differences and cultures, moving this category in a more progressive direction. There has been a century-long struggle over the meaning of homosexuality that has involved sexologists, the police, lawyers, psychiatrists, and homosexuals, a struggle that continues today. The regime of sexuality and the specification of different sexual categories in an attempt to buttress the emerging norm of heterosexuality has unwittingly also provided the basis for homosexual experiences, identities, and cultures. Through these experiences a series of new social and sexual needs, human capacities, and pleasures have been created among a group of men. This homosexual experience, along with the slightly later emergence of a distinct lesbian experience,[27] and the feminist movement have created the basis for contemporary challenges to the hegemony of heterosexuality.

## Enter Gay Liberation and the Gay Community

Recent social changes in the western capitalist countries have put in question the patriarchal, gender, and sexual relations established during the last century. A prolonged crisis in sexual and gender relations and in the meaning of sexuality has occurred. The feminist and gay liberation movements, for example, have challenged the relegation of sexual relations and particularly "deviant" forms of sexuality to the socially defined private realm, subverting the public/ private categories that have been used to regulate our sexual lives. The development of contraceptive and reproductive technologies has made it more and more possible to separate heterosexual pleasure and procreation, although the struggle continues about who will have access to, and control over, this technology. The expansion of consumer markets and advertising in the post-war period has led to an increasing drawing of sexuality and sexual images into the marketplace and the public realm.[28] This increasing public visibility of sexual images and sexual cultures has led to objections from those who would wish to reprivatize sexuality, in particular its "deviant" strains. And feminists have challenged the patriarchal values that are visible in much advertising and heterosexual male pornography.

The social ferment of the sixties—particularly the civil rights, black power, and feminist movements—combined with earlier forms of homosexual activism and the expansion of the gay commercial scene and culture to produce the gay liberation movement, which erupted in 1969 in the Stonewall Riot in New York City.[29] The movement developed a new, positive identity that has served as a basis for our resistance to heterosexual hegemony. The movement's most significant achievements were its contesting of the psychiatric definition of homosexuality as a mental illness and its creation of a culture and community that have transformed the lives of hundreds of thousands of men and women. As usual in a patriarchal society, many more opportunities have opened up for men than for women.

In a challenge to the "universality" of heterosexuality, gays have affirmed that gay is just as good as straight, calling on lesbians and gay men to affirm themselves and their sexualities. This has challenged the gender and social policies of the state, suggesting that sexual activity does not have to be solely for reproduction, but can also be for play, pleasure, love, and support, and questioning the very right of the state to regulate people's sexual lives. We have affirmed our right to sexual self-determination and control over our own bodies and sexuality and have affirmed this right for others as well.

The growth of a visible gay community and the emergence of gay streets and commercial areas in many big cities have led to a reaction from the police, conservative political parties, and the new right. These groups fear the breakdown of "traditional" sexual and family relations, which they associate with social and moral order, and see the challenge that gay liberation presents to heterosexual hegemony as a threat to the ways in which their lives and institutions are organized. They want lesbians and gay men out of public view and back in the closets, threatening our very existence as a public community.

In a sense the gay ghetto is both a playground and a potential concentration camp. While it provides people a place to meet and to explore and develop aspects of their lives and sexuality, it can also separate people from the rest of the population in a much larger closet that can be isolated and contained. The ghetto can tend to obscure the experiences gay men share with other men in their society. Locking people into the new categorization of gays as minority group or community may weaken the critique of sex and gender relations in society as a whole. As Altman explains, the "ethnic homosexual" has emerged, "the widespread recognition of a distinct cultural category which appears to be pressing for the same sort of 'equality,' in Western society as do ethnic minorities."[30] However, lesbians and gay men are not born into a minority group, but like heterosexuals assume a sexual identity through social and psychological processes.[31] Gays and lesbians are not only a minority group but also an oppressed and denied sexuality. The position that gays are simply a new minority group can deflect our challenges to the dominant way of life.

In challenging heterosexuality as the social norm gays have brought into question aspects of the institutions of masculinity and male privilege. Over the last decade images of gay men have shifted from the effeminacy of the "gender invert" to the new macho and clone looks that have dominated the gay men's community. This imagery challenges the previous stereotypes of homosexuals that associated our sexuality with gender nonconformity and has asserted that we can be both homosexual and "masculine" at the same time.[32] In defining ourselves as masculine we have had to make use of and transform the existing images of straight masculinity we find around us. These new images challenge heterosexual norms that associate "deviant" gender stereotypes with sexual "deviancy," for instance effeminacy with male homosexuality, but at the same time also tend to create new standards and stereotypes of what gay men are supposed to be like. These images and styles themselves continue to be imprisoned within the polarities of gender dichotomy. While gay men often believe we have freed ourselves from the social organization of gender, what we have actually done is exchange "gender inversion" for a situation where homosexuality can be organized through "normal" gender identifications. This assertion of masculinized imagery can to some extent lead us away from the critique of the institution of masculinity and its effects in our lives and persuade us that gender is no longer a problem for gay men.

It is ironic that some forms of resistance to past ways in which we were stigmatized can serve to accommodate us to aspects of the existing order of things. It is in this context that some of the challenges to masculinity and gender norms by straight men fighting against sexism will also be valuable to gay men. To be successful, gay liberation must challenge not only the institutionalization of heterosexuality as a social norm but also the institution of masculinity.

## GAY LIBERATION AND THE RULING REGIME OF SEX

Gay liberation has emerged from the contradictions within the ruling system of sexual regulation and definition. It is fundamentally a struggle to transform the norms and definitions of sexual regulation. Gay liberation strives for the recognition of homosexuality as socially equal to the dominant social institution of heterosexuality. Yet as Weeks suggests,

> the strategic aim of the gay liberation movement must be not simply the validation of the rights of a minority within a heterosexual majority but the challenge to all the rigid categorizations of sexuality. . . . The struggle for sexual self-determination is a struggle in the end for control over our bodies. To establish this control we must escape from those ideologies and categorizations which imprison us within the existing order.[33]

The struggle to transform our sexual norms and to end the control of the institution of heterosexuality over our lives holds out the possibility of beginning to disengage us from the ruling regime of sex and gender. As Foucault suggested, movements that have been called sexual liberation movements, including gay liberation, are movements that start with sexuality, with the apparatus of sexuality in the midst of which they are caught and which make it function to the limit; but, at the same time, they are in motion relative to it, disengaging themselves and surmounting them.[34]

The struggle for gay liberation can be seen as a process of transformation. The assertion that gay is just as good as straight—which lies at the heart of gay liberation—is formally within the present regime of sexual categorization, for it still separates gay from straight as rigid categories and assigns value to sexuality, thus mirroring the limitations of the current sexual regime. However, the gay liberation movement operates both within *and* against this regime of sexual regulation. In asserting equal value for homosexuality and lesbianism, it begins to turn the ruling practices of sexual hierarchy on their head. Resistance begins within the present regime of sexual definitions, but it begins to shift the sexual boundaries that they have defined, opening up the possibility of transcending their limitations. By naming our specific experiences of the world, gay liberation provides the basis for a social and political struggle that can transform, defy, cut across, and break down the ruling regime of sex and gender.

The gay and lesbian communities, like other oppressed social groups, oscillate between resistance and accommodation to oppression. This is a struggle on two closely interrelated fronts. First, the gay community itself needs to strengthen cultures of resistance by building on sexual and cultural traditions that question gender norms and the relegation of erotic life to the state-defined private sphere. This will involve challenging the internalization and reproduction of sexism, racism, ageism, and class divisions within the gay community, as well as building alliances with other social groups fighting these forms of domination. Secondly, it requires a struggle outside the gay and lesbian communities for the defense of a community under attack by the police, government, and media. A key part of this strategy would be campaigning for new social policies that uproot heterosexuality as *the* social norm.

OPENING UP EROTIC CHOICES FOR EVERYONE

In developing a radical perspective we need to draw on the insights of lesbian feminism about the social power of heterosexuality and also on the historical perspectives provided by the new critical gay history, which reveals the social and historical process of the organization of heterosexual hegemony and the present system of sexual regulation more generally. These understandings create the basis for alliances between feminists, lesbians, gay liberationists, anti-sexist men, and other groups against the institution of heterosexuality, which lies at the root of the social oppression of women, lesbians, and gays. This alliance would contest the hegemony of heterosexuality in the legal system, state policies, in forms of family organization, and in the churches, unions, and other social bodies. The struggle would be for women, gays, and others to gain control over our bodies and sexuality and to begin to define our own eroticism and sexuality. A fundamental aspect of such an approach would be the elaboration and exploration of the experiences and visions of those of us living outside institutionalized heterosexuality.

Proposals for new and different ways of living (including collective and nonsexist ways of rearing children) are particularly vital since the new right and moral conservatives in their various incarnations are taking advantage of people's fears about changes in family organization and sexual mores to campaign in support of patriarchal and heterosexist social norms. The defense of a male-dominated heterosexuality is not only central to the policies of the new right and moral conservatives regarding feminism and gay liberation, but is a central theme of their racial and class politics as well.[35] The progressive movement's failure to deal with people's real fears, concerns, and hopes regarding sexual and gender politics is an important reason why right-wing groups are able to gain support. Feminism, gay liberation, and all progressive movements will have to articulate a vision that will allow us to move forward beyond the confines of institutionalized heterosexuality.

Gay liberation enables heterosexual men who question heterosexism to contribute to this new social vision. The issues raised by gay liberation must be addressed by all men interested in fundamental change because heterosexism limits and restricts the lives of all men. This challenge will only be effective, however, if heterosexual privilege is challenged in daily life and in social institutions. This could help begin the long struggle to disentangle heterosexual desire from the confines of institutionalized masculinity and heterosexuality. Together we could begin to redefine and remake masculinity and sexuality. If sexuality is socially produced, then heterosexuality itself can be transformed and redefined and its pleasures and desires separated from the social relations of power and domination. Gay liberation can allow all men to challenge gender and sexual norms and redefine gender and sex for ourselves in alliance with feminism; it can allow all men to explore and create different forms of sexual pleasures in our lives. This redefining of masculinity and sexuality will also help destroy the anxieties and insecurities of many straight men who try so hard to be "real men." But the success of this undertaking depends on the ability to develop alternative visions and experiences that will help all people understand how their lives could be organized without heterosexuality as the institutionalized social norm. Such a goal is a radically transformed society in which everyone will be able to gain control of his or her own body, desires, and life.

## NOTES

Special thanks to Ned Lyttelton, Brian Conway, and Bob Gardner for comments on this paper. For more general comments on matters that pertain to topics addressed in this paper I am indebted to Varda Burstyn, Philip Corrigan, Bert Hansen, Michael Kaufman, Ian Lumsden, Dorothy E. Smith, George Smith, Mariana Valverde, and Lorna Weir.

[1] See G.K. Lehne, "Homophobia Among Men," in Deborah David and Robert Brannon, *The Forty Nine Per Cent Majority* (Reading, Mass.:Addison-Wesley, 1976), 78.

[2] On the notion of institutionalized heterosexuality see Charlotte Bunch, "Not For Lesbians Only," *Quest* 11, no. 2 (Fall 1975). Also see Adrienne Rich, "Compulsory Heterosexuality And Lesbian Existence," in Snitow, Stansell and Thompson, eds., *Powers of Desire: The Politics of Sexuality* (New York: Monthly Review Press, 1983): 177-205.

[3] Joe Interrante, "Dancing Along the Precipice: The Men's Movement in the '80s," *Radical America* 15, no. 5 (September-October 1981): 54.

[4] Ned Lyttelton, "Men's Liberation, Men Against Sexism and Major Dividing Lines," *Resources for Feminist Research* 12, no. 4 (December/January 1983/1984): 33. Several discussions with Ned Lyttelton were very useful in clarifying my ideas in this section and throughout this paper.

[5] Interrante, *op. cit.,* 54.

[6] For further elaboration see my forthcoming book entitled *The Regulation of Desire* (Montreal: Black Rose, 1986).

[7] See Kinsey, Pomeroy, and Martin, *Sexual Behavior in the Human Male* (Philadelphia: W.B. Saunders, 1948) and Mary McIntosh, "The Homosexual Role," in Plummer, ed., *The Making Of The Modern Homosexual* (London: Hutchinson, 1981), 38-43.

[8] Bunch, "Not For Lesbians Only."

[9] See Frank Pearce, "How to be Immoral and Ill, Pathetic and Dangerous all at the same time: Mass Media and the Homosexual," in Cohen and Young, eds., *The Manufacture of News: Deviance, Social Problems and the Mass Media* (London: Constable, 1973), 284-301.

[10] See Andrew Hodges and David Hutter. *With Downcast Gays, Aspects of Homosexual Self-Oppression* (Toronto: Pink Triangle Press, 1977).

[11] Gayle Rubin, "The Traffic In Women: Notes on the Political Economy of Sex," in Reiter, ed., *Towards An Anthropology Of Women* (New York: Monthly Review Press, 1975), 159. I prefer the use of sex and gender relations to sex/gender system since the notion of system tends to conflate questions of sexuality and gender and suggests that sex/gender relations are a separate system from other social relations rather than an integral aspect of them.

[12] See Joe Interrante, "From Homosexual to Gay to ?: Recent Work in Gay History," in *Radical America* 15, no. 6 (November-December 1981); Martha Vicinus, "Sexuality and Power: A Review of Current Work in the History of Sexuality," *Feminist Studies* 8, no. 1 (Spring 1982): 133-56; and Robert A. Padgug, "Sexual Matters: On Conceptualizing Sexuality In History," *Radical History Review,* "Sexuality in History" Issue, no. 20 (Spring/Summer 1979): 3-23.

[13] See for instance Michel Foucault, *The History Of Sexuality* (New York: Vintage, 1980), vol. 1, *An Introduction;* Jeffrey Weeks, *Sex, Politics and Society: The Regulation of Sexuality since 1800* (London: Hutchinson, 1981); and Jonathan Ned Katz, *Gay/Lesbian Almanac* (New York: Harper

and Row, 1983). For recent feminist explorations of sexuality see Snitow, Stansell and Thompson, *Powers of Desire* (New York: Monthly Review, 1983); Carol Vance, ed., *Pleasure and Danger, Exploring Female Sexuality* (Boston: Routledge and Kegan Paul, 1984); Rosalind Coward, *Female Desire, Women's Sexuality Today* (London: Routledge and Kegan Paul, 1984); and Mariana Valverde, *Sex, Power and Pleasure* (Toronto: Women's Press, 1985).

[14]See Wilhelm Reich, *The Sexual Revolution* (New York: Straus and Giroux, 1974) and Baxandall, ed., *Sex-Pol. Essays, 1929-1934, Wilhelm Reich* (New York: Vintage, 1972).

[15]Unfortunately, over the last few years some anti-pornography feminists have suggested that sexuality is only a realm of danger for women, obscuring how it can also be a realm of pleasure. Some anti-porn feminists have been used by state agencies in attempts to clamp down on sexually explicit material including sexual material for gay men and lesbians. See Vance, *Pleasure and Danger;* Varda Burstyn. ed., *Women Against Censorship* (Vancouver and Toronto: Douglas and McIntyre, 1985); and Varda Burstyn, "Anatomy of a Moral Panic" and Gary Kinsman, "The Porn Debate," *Fuse* 3, no. 1 (Summer 1984).

[16]On this see the work of John D'Emilio, for instance his "Capitalism and Gay Identity," in Snitow, Stansell and Thompson, eds., *Powers of Desire,* 100-13, and his *Sexual Politics, Sexual Communities* (Chicago: University of Chicago Press, 1983).

[17]See Randolph Trumbach, "London's Sodomites: Homosexual Behaviour and Western Culture in the 18th Century," *Journal of Social History,* Fall 1977, 1-33; Mary McIntosh, "The Homosexual Role," in Plummer, ed., *The Making of The Modern Homosexual;* Alan Bray, *Homosexuality in Renaissance England* (London: Gay Men's Press, 1982); and Jeffrey Weeks, *Sex, Politics and Society.*

[18]See Foucault, *The History of Sexuality.* vol. 1 and Kinsman, *The Regulation of Desire.*

[19]This idea comes from the work of Foucault.

[20]See Bray, *Homosexuality in Renaissance England* for the activities of the Society for the Reformation of Morals, which campaigned against same-sex desire-based networks in the early eighteenth century.

[21]John Lauritsen and David Thorstad, *The Early Homosexual Rights Movement* (New York: Times Change Press, 1974), 6.

[22]Arno Karlen, *Sexuality and Homosexuality* (New York: W.W. Norton, 1971), 185.

[23]Ezra Hurlburt Stafford, "Perversion," the *Canadian Journal of Medicine and Surgery* 3, no. 4 (April 1898).

[24]On this see Anna Davin. "Imperialism and Motherhood," *History Workshop,* no. 5 (Spring 1978).

[25]Foucault, *op. cit.,* 43.

[26]*Ibid.,* 101.

[27]See Lillian Faderman, *Surpassing The Love Of Men* (New York: William Morrow, 1981); Christina Simmons, "Companionate Marriage and the Lesbian Threat," in *Frontiers* 4, no. 3 (Fall 1979); Martha Vicinus, "Sexuality and Power"; and Ann Ferguson, "Patriarchy, Sexual Identity, and the Sexual Revolution," *Signs* 7, no. 1 (Fall 1981): 158-72.

[28]See Gary Kinsman, "Porn/Censor Wars And The Battlefields Of Sex," in *Issues of Censorship* (Toronto: A Space, 1985), 31-9.

[29]See John D'Emilio, *Sexual Politics, Sexual Communities.*

[30]Dennis Altman, "What Changed in the Seventies?," in Gay Left Collective, eds., *Homosexuality, Power and Politics* (London: Allison and Busby, 1980), 61.

[31]One prejudice that is embodied in sexual legislation and social policies is the myth that lesbians and gay men are a special threat to young people and that gay men are "child molesters." Most studies show, on the contrary, that more than 90 percent of sexual assaults on young people are committed by heterosexual men and often within the family or home. Breines and Gordon state that, "approximately 92 per cent of the victims are female and 97 percent of the assailants are males." See Wini Breines and Linda Gordon, "The New Scholarship on Family Violence," *Signs* 8, no. 3 (Spring 1983): 522. Also see Elizabeth Wilson, *What Is To Be Done About Violence Against Women* (London: Penguin, 1983), particularly 117-34. We have to eliminate special age restrictions on the right to participate in consensual lesbian and gay sex so that lesbian and gay young people can express their desires and instead challenge the principal source of violence against

children and young people—the patriarchal family and straight-identified men. We have to propose changes in family relations and schooling and alternative social policies that would allow young people to take more control over their own lives, to get support in fighting unwanted sexual attention *and* to be able to participate in consensual sexual activity.

[32]See John Marshall, "Pansies, Perverts and Macho Men: Changing Conceptions of Male Homosexuality" and Greg Blachford, "Male Dominance In The Gay World," in Plummer, ed., *The Making of The Modern Homosexual;* and also Seymour Kleinberg's article elsewhere in this volume for a different approach.

[33]Jeffrey Weeks, "Captialism and the Organization of Sex," Gay Left Collective, eds., *Homosexuality, Power and Politics* 19-20.

[34]Michel Foucault, "Power and Sex," *Telos,* no. 32 (Summer 1977): 152-61.

[35]See Allen Hunter, "In the Wings, New Right Ideology and Organization," *Radical America* 15, no. 1-2 (Spring 1981): 127-38.

# The New Masculinity
# of Gay Men, and Beyond

## SEYMOUR KLEINBERG

*teaching astray morally*

One week after Labor Day 1977, I made a trip to the Anvil Bar, a gay club in New York City. For a long time I had wanted to know whether the legends of debauchery one heard with some skepticism were accurate. No one I knew was a member, and I had been told by those who claimed to be informed that I was not a likely type to crash successfully. I presumed they meant that my only leather jacket, tailored like a blazer, would not pass muster. Then a close friend became enamored of a go-go boy who danced there, joined the Anvil, and took me along to meet Daniel.

The bar nearly lived up to its fame. The boys do dance continually on top of the four-sided bar, they do strip naked, not counting construction shoes or cock rings. There is a back room where no-nonsense, hard-core porno films silently and continually flicker, shown by a mesmerized projectionist wearily perched on the ledge of the back wall. A small pitch-dark cubicle called the fuck room opens off the rear wall. In the middle of the front-room bar is a stage raised five feet where fist-fucking demonstrations used to be held at 3 a.m. if the crowd was enthusiastic, but those spontaneous shows were stopped when they began to draw tourists from the uptown discos. Now it is used by the dancers, who take turns exhibiting their specialities in the limelight. The boys range from extraordinary to middling, from high-schoolers to forty-year-olds, from professionals (everything) to amateurs who move awkwardly but who are graceful and stunning when they don't move at all. There are types for every taste and some for none. Hispanic and black, WASP and Italian, the boys dance three hours of a six-hour stint for $25 a night, three or four times a week. There are always new faces, and the management is liberal about letting anyone with a good body try out. Usually, there is one dancer who has had some ballet training and is naive enough to make that clear; he is invariably the least favored by the clientele.

My friend's Daniel is unusual. He is one of the few boys who can use the trapeze bars bolted to the ceiling with real expertise. Without breaking the rhythm of his dance, he leaps for a trapeze and spends four or five minutes hanging on or swinging from one bar to another in the most daring manner. When he alights, it is with a sure flip back onto the bar, where he continues to dance with an unbroken stride. Daniel has never fallen, as some of the boys have (a broken nose or a fractured arm is not unheard of), nor has he crashed into a customer since he holds his drugs well.

His other specialty is his ability to grab with his buttocks the folded one-dollar or five-dollar tips the men at the bar hold between their teeth, a variation on the skill of the Cotton Club girls of Harlem in the twenties and thirties. His perfect behind descends in time to the music over the customer's uplifted face, and there is a round of applause when the money disappears into those constricted rosy cheeks.

Like most of the clientele, Daniel looks like a college athlete or construction worker, two favored images these recent seasons. Clothed, he wears the uniform of the moment: cheap plaid flannel shirts and jeans, or if it is really warm just overalls, and boots or construction worker's shoes no matter what the weather is. With the first signs of frost, boots and heavy leather bomber jackets are *de rigueur*.

Daniel is also typical of one type of club client in that he is a masochist, a "slave" who sleeps with other men only with the permission of his master (who instructs him to charge a hefty fee). While Daniel's masochism has taken a pecuniary turn, he is not really a whore, for he is indifferent to money, keeping only what he needs for his uppers and poppers, his grass and coke. He dances frenetically four nights a week and does what he is told because he finds that exciting. There is little that he has not experienced sexually, and at twenty-two, his tastes are now as perverse as any possibilities Western civilization has devised.

To look at him, one would hardly suspect that this Irish kid from Queens with his thatch of reddish hair, cowlick and all, this sweet-faced boy built like a swimmer in his blue-collar uniform, lives a life more sexually extreme than anything described by the Marquis de Sade. When he discusses his life, it appears to be an endless dirty movie, but the anecdotes tend to leave his listeners in a moral vacuum. While it is possible to become erotically excited hearing his adventures, it is difficult to judge them without feeling prudish. Conventional moral standards are tangential, psychological ones almost as irrelevant. One is not really shocked; rather, one feels adrift, puzzled, perhaps bemused. Most of all, this nice boy seems very remote.

The values of his generation, acted out as theater of the absurd, are even more histrionic in Daniel's life. Just as one does not expect experimental theater or avant-garde art to live up to the standards of naturalism, one does not try to understand Daniel's life from the lessons of one's own experience: the collective sanity of the past is momentarily dumb.

What one struggled to learn and call "adult" as the final approbation now looks somewhat priggish. If one wanted to use such standards, why go to the Anvil at all? But once one *is* there or at the Mine Shaft or any of half a dozen bars just like them, what does one use to understand this spectacle of men? Some, like me, are clearly audience at a drama where only the actors understand the play. Intuition is not trustworthy, and easy judgments make one feel like a tourist. But whether or not one wishes to refrain from judgment, one thing is clear, if not glaring. The universal stance is a studied masculinity. There are no limp wrists, no giggles, no indiscreet hips swiveling. Walk, talk, voice, costume, grooming are just right: this is macho country. It is a rigorous place where one destroys oneself in drugs and sexual humiliation.

The same impulses are evident in other scenes. Fire Island Pines is as besotted and extreme as the leather and Levis world, and often they overlap, but the Pines is playful. Like its shabbier neighbor, Cherry Grove, the Pines enjoys the long legacy of camp. It loves to dictate next year's chic to café society, for novelty, flair, and sophistication are as paramount in this scene as they are in the world of women's fashion. For a time, the place seemed to veer toward egalitarianism; only youthful beauty was required if one were not rich. But with inflation, the freeloading beauty has to be spectacular indeed. The dance halls of the Pines and the Grove, like the waterfront bars, are filled with handsome men posing in careful costumes, and no matter how elegant or expensive, they are all butch.

As a matter of fact, young gay men seem to have abjured effeminacy with universal success. Muscular bodies laboriously cultivated all year round are standard; youthful athletic agility is everyone's style. The volleyball game on the beach is no longer a camp classic; now it takes itself as seriously as the San Francisco gay softball team. Hardness is in.

But talk to these men, sleep with them, befriend them, and the problems are the old familiar ones: misery when they are in love, loneliness when they are not, frustration and ambitiousness at work, and a monumental self-centeredness that exacerbates the rest. These have been the archetypes of unhappiness in homosexual America for as long as I can remember.

What is different from anything else I remember, however, is the relentless pursuit of masculinity. There are no limits; the most oppressive images of sexual violence and dominance are adopted unhesitatingly. Though the neo-Nazi adorations—fascinating fascism as Susan Sontag termed them—are more sinister than the innocuous ideals of the weight-lifting room, they are equally mindless. The offense is not aesthetic; it is entirely political. The homosexuals who adopt images of masculinity, conveying their desire for power and their belief in its beauty, are in fact eroticizing the very values of straight society that have tyrannized their own lives. It is the tension between this style and the content of their lives that demands the oblivion of drugs and sexual libertinism. In the past, the duplicity of closeted lives found relief in effeminate camping; now the suppression or denial of the moral issue in their choice is far more damaging. The perversity of imitating their oppressors guarantees that such blindness will work itself out as self-contempt.

## Sex and Sexual Politics

This is the central message of the macho bar world: manliness is the only real virtue; other values are contemptible. And manliness is not some philosophical notion or psychological state; it is not even morally related to behavior. It lies exclusively in the glamorization of physical strength.

This idea of masculinity is so conservative it is almost primitive. That homosexuals are attracted to it and find it gratifying is not a total surprise. Gay male sexual preference has always favored a butch boyish beauty, and only in artistic or intellectual circles has beauty been allowed a certain feyness. Butchness is always relative; the least swishy man in the room is the most butch. It usually meant one looked straight, one could pass. In the past, an over-enthusiasm for butchness translated itself into a taste for rough trade. Those who were too frightened or sane to pursue that particular quarry could always find a gay partner who would accommodatingly act the part.

There is a special eroticism in the experience of pretending to be degraded that is by no means rare in adult sexual behavior of whatever persuasion. The homosexual whose erotic feelings are enhanced by the illusion that his partner holds him in contempt, who is thrilled when told his ass or mouth is just like a cunt, is involved in a complicated self-deception. What appears to be happening is a homosexual variation of masochism: the contempt of the "straight" partner emblazes gay self-contempt, which in turn is exploited as an aphrodisiac. Why this process works is less clear than how it does.

The complex tie between the need for degradation and sexual excitement has never been satisfactorily explored, though Freud began the effort over eighty years ago and writers and artists have always intuitively understood it. It seems to be prominent in societies that are advanced, where sexual mores are liberal or ambivalent, and where intellectual life is very sophisticated. In times like ours, when women are redefining their roles and images, men must also redefine theirs. As women forgo in dress and appearance the *style* of their oppression (it is the easiest to abandon and thus one of the first aspects to go), and as glamor falls under a suspicious light, men, increasingly accused of being the symbol of sexism, are forced to confront their own ideas of masculinity.

While straight men define their ideas from a variety of sources (strength, achievement, success, money), two of those sources are always their attitudes toward women and toward paternity. It is no coincidence that the same decade that popularized liberation for women and announced that the nuclear family was a failure also saw men return to a long-haired, androgynous style. If straight men are confused about their maleness, what is the dilemma for gay men, who rarely did more than imitate these ideas?

It is no accident that the macho gesture is always prominent in those gay bars and resorts where women are entirely absent. Certain gay locales have always catered exclusively to one sex: porno movie houses and bookstores, baths, public toilets. The new bars are often private clubs as much for the sake of legally barring women as for screening male customers. Their atmosphere is eerily reminiscent of the locker room. And, of course, while they are there, the men live as if there were no women in the world. This is a useful illusion. It allows some of them to get gang-banged in the back rooms and still evade the self-reproach that derives from the world's contempt for homosexual men who behave sexually like women. If there are no women in the world, some men simply must replace them. With women absent, whether one is sexually active or passive is no longer the great dividing issue.

In fact, some of the men who look most butch are the most liberated in bed, the least role-oriented. While there is still much role preference for passivity, it no longer has the clear quality it had in the past. Then, gay men made unmistakable announcements: those who liked to be fucked adopted effeminate mannerisms; those who were active tried to look respectable.

Quentin Crisp in his autobiography, *The Naked Civil Servant,* epitomized these attitudes. He documents the anger of an acquaintance railing at the misfortune of having picked up a young soldier who wanted to be fucked: "All of a sudden, he turned over. After all I'd done—flitting about the room in my wrap . . . camping myself silly. My dear, I was disgusted."[1] Today, to replace the usually reliable information that straight or campy behavior conveyed in the past, gay men at the leather bars have taken to elaborate clothing signals: key chains or handkerchiefs drooping from left or right pocket in blue or yellow or red all have coded meanings. Occasionally, some of the *cognoscenti* lie and misalliances occur. Of course, one could ask a prospective partner what his preferences are, but that is the least likely behavior between strangers.

If I am critical of the present style, it is not because I advocate a return to the denigrations of the past. Quentin Crisp's rebelliousness testifies to the hourly misery of gay life when all the sexual roles are petrified. He considered all his friends "pseudo men in search of pseudo women." That is not an improvement on pseudo men in search of nothing. Nor is his sense of inferiority: "I regard all heterosexuals, however low, as superior to any homosexual, however noble." Such estimates were commonplace for men subjected to lifelong ridicule because they could not or would not disguise their effeminacy.

But camping for Crisp and for the entire homosexual world until the end of the 1950s was not just the expression of self-contempt by men pretending to be women and feeling pseudo as both. Camping also gave homosexual men an *exclusive* form of behavior that neither women nor straight men could adopt. Some women and straight men are camp, but that is another story.

Camping in the gay world did not mean simply behaving in a blatantly effeminate manner; that was camp only when performed in the presence of those it irritated or threatened or delighted. Swishing is effective only if someone else notices, preferably registering a sense of shock, or ideally, outrage. In discreet bars like the Blue Parrot in 1950, men impeccably Brooks Brothers and as apparently WASP as one's banker could, in a flicker, slide into limpness. They had available a persona that mixed ironic distance, close observation, and wit, all allies of sanity.

Camping did express self-denigration, but it was a complex criticism. For example, the women whom these men imitated were themselves extraordinary; androgynous idols like Garbo or Dietrich symbolized an ambiguous and amoral sexuality. But more important, in their campy behavior, gay men revealed an empathic observation of women and feminine interests.

When camping also released for gay men some of their anger at their closeted lives, it became a weapon as well as a comment. The behavior chosen for imitation or ridicule was usually evidence of sexist attitudes, of positions women had taken or were forced to take that had effeminized them out of their humanity. It is for this reason that feminists object to drag queens who still try to resemble the slavish emblems of the past, and their criticism would be valid if the imitations were sincere. But men in drag are not swept up in the delusion that they are women; only insane men in drag believe that. The rest are committed to ambiguity; they are neither men nor women and are only rarely androgynous—the aura of drag is neuter.

When a gay man said, "Oh, Mary, come off it," he was sneering at pretension, self-deceit, or prudery. That it took the form of reminding one's fellow faggot that he was in reality no better than a woman, and often not as good with his "pseudo" sexual equipment, is not politically commendable, but why should gay men have had a special consciousness about sexism? At least they had a sure recognition of it: they imitated women because they understood that they were victims in sisterhood of the same masculine ideas about sexuality. Generations of women defined themselves entirely in men's terms, and homosexual men often seemed to accept the same values.

But there was also a chagrined recognition that they just could not live up to expectations. They could not be men as heterosexuals defined manhood; most of all they could not be men because they did not sleep with women or beget children. No amount of manliness could counterbalance that. Between the values of virility that they did not question and their rage at having no apparent alternatives, gay men would camp out their frustration. It was not a particularly effective means of ending oppression, but it was a covert defiance of a society that humiliated them.

With the political and social changes of the sixties, a new androgyny seemed to be on the verge of life. Heterosexual and homosexual suddenly became less interesting than just sexual. Getting out of the closet was more than announcing one was gay; it was a pronouncement that one was free of sexual shame. The new mood fostered this: even straight boys looked prettier than girls. The relief at seeing male vanity in the open, surrendered to and accepted, made it possible for homosexuals to reconsider some of their attitudes toward themselves. It was no longer extraordinary to look effeminate in a world where most sexual men looked feminine and where sexually liberated women were the antithesis of the glamorous and fragile.

Sexual style had become a clear political issue. Conventional manliness was properly identified with reaction and repression. The enemy had a crewcut, was still posturing in outmoded chivalric stances, while his wife and daughter and son embraced the revolutionary notion of rolelessness. To some extent, this is where American society still is: searching for a sense of what roles, if any, are appropriate for adult men and women. Only the betrayed patriarch still refuses to acknowledge the permanence of these changes, since for him they are pure deprivations, erosions of his long, long privilege.

## Homosexuality and Masculinity

"Feminist" is a term that increasing numbers of gay men apply to themselves as they come to recognize the common oppression of homosexuals and women. The empathy of gay men in the past is the foundation for this newer understanding, and it is heartening to discover that a mutual sense of victimization need not always lead to self-denigration. If in the past women were less likely to self-contempt at being women than gay men felt at being homosexual, it was partly because women were rewarded for their acquiescence and partly because they did not have to experience the sense of having betrayed their birthright. Homosexual men usually gave up paternity as well as other prerogatives for their gayness and too often felt gypped for what they got. They exchanged the simplicity of being phallic oppressors for advantages much more dubious, and the sense that they had betrayed their best interests was haunting. As more gays come to realize the bankruptcy of conventional ideas of masculinity, it is easier for them to forgo the sexism they shared with heterosexual men.

Unfortunately, heterosexuals cling to their sexual definitions with even greater tenacity. For example, the Save Our Children slogan is not as banal as it sounds; the phobic hostility behind it expresses a genuine fear that some children will be lost, lost to patriarchy, to the values of the past, to the perpetuation of conventional ideas of men and women. There is a fear of homosexuality that is far beyond what the surface can explain.

Many gays, especially apolitical ones, are dismissive of Anita

Bryant and what she represents. Remarks like "Straights will just have to hope that heterosexuality can hold its own on the open market" express a contempt for the fears, but not much understanding of them. It *is* puzzling: where does this idea of the frailty of heterosexuality come from, the assumption that a mere knowledge that teachers or ordinary people are gay will automatically seduce children? It comes from the panic about new sexual ideas, but most of all, about the identity of women.

It often sounds absurd when conservatives accuse feminist women of attempting to destroy the family, though it does not stop them from making the accusation. It is easier to appear sensible talking about the seduction of children by homosexuals. I suggest that much of the recent vehemence about the children is deflected from a much more central rage against women who are redefining their ideas about child rearing. The political issue is always hottest when women's connection with motherhood is raised. Thus, the issues of child rearing and anti-abortion gather a conservative support that puzzles liberal America. What these issues have in common is the attempt of women to free themselves from conventional roles, crucially their roles as mothers. That liberation is the first wave; the secondary one, far more perilous, lies beneath the surface: it demands that men liberate themselves from their notions as well, since the central ideas about masculinity have always been related to the unquestioned responsibilities of men as husbands and fathers.

It is curious that lesbians are never mentioned when child molestation is raised as an issue, and when lesbians are attacked, as they were at Houston, it is in relation to their militant feminism, not in relation to their being school teachers. Lesbians have usually been exempt from heterosexual fears about seduction, partly because they are women and, like all women, traditionally powerless. When they are attacked, when the press notices lesbian issues, it is often in connection with custody cases. There the issue of saving the children for heterosexuality and precisely for patriarchy is clear. These lesbians who once lived as straight women, who married and had children, are objects of the most extreme wrath, and one that has used the judicial system as its instrument to punish them.

But most lesbians are not mothers, and most lesbian mothers do not end up, fortunately, as victims in custody hearings. Lesbians are usually dismissed as unimportant, as nuisances. It is the lowest rung on the ladder of social contempt. But gay men who have abdicated their privileges, who have made sexual desire a higher priority than power over women, are indeed not men at all.

Bryant's keynote is that homosexuals should return to the closet. That would solve the problem for straights, since it is *visibility* that is terrifying. To be openly gay without contrition or guilt or shame is to testify that there are viable alternative sexual styles. But the real alternative for the children is not necessarily homosexuality; it is to reject the old verities of masculine and feminine.

Ironically, the men at the Anvil have not rejected those verities at all. Their new pseudo-masculinity is a precise response to the confusions of a society venturing toward sexual redefinition. But it is in its way as reactionary as the hysteria that Anita Bryant's campaign consolidated.

The men of the macho bars will not buy Quentin Crisp's book, or if they do, they will not read it sympathetically, whereas they *are* part of the audience that made the story of football player David Kopay a best seller.[2] I do not want to belittle Kopay's modest effort, but its success depends more on his image than on his courage. Effeminate men like Crisp who have the courage to defy society are eccentric; butch men are heroic. Of course, what is left unsaid is that Kopay could have passed: no one would have known if he hadn't told them, and having once announced it, he can still pass. What could sissies like Crisp do even if they didn't flaunt it? Crisp's *life* is an act of courage.

Ex-soldier Leonard Matlovich is also a respectable image.[3] When media reporters treat him and Kopay just like the mainstream Americans they have always been, they make a point many gays approve of: homosexual men are really like everyone else. If beneath Matlovich's conservative, bemedalled chest beat aberrant yearnings, the public, if not the army, can accommodate them. What makes Kopay and Matlovich seem acceptable to gays and straights alike, while the Quentin Crisps remain pitiful?

Crisp was defiant and miserable, an acknowledged victim, and unrepentant: it was all agony, but it couldn't have been any other way. Even more, Crisp made his sexuality the obsession of his life. His whole existence was devoted to proclaiming his homosexuality; it is the meaning of his life. Today, his heir is Daniel, who is as absorbed in the same singular definition of himself. Daniel's life seems consecrated to pleasure while Crisp's was miserable, and that is an enormous difference. But the source of his pleasure in sexuality is as extreme, as dangerous and defiant as the quest for pleasure in Crisp's life. I may feel that Crisp is morally superior because he has suffered and Daniel refuses to, but that is only a sentimental notion. What is stunning in both their lives is the exclusivity of sexuality, and while

Daniel is not heroic, his life demands that one refrain from easy judgment. The drama of such displays is filled with meaning for them and us. These lives are not like others'.

Kopay and Matlovich are fighting to be like everyone else. They claim that they are just like other football players or professional soldiers, and I do not dispute them. Compared to their conventionality, their homosexuality is almost incidental. Neither of them has gotten off quite free, nor have they seemed to expect to. For reasons they articulate with unquestionable credibility, they could not tolerate the duplicity of being conservative, rather ordinary men and secret homosexuals. Ironically, to some extent they have now become extraordinary men if somewhat commonplace homosexuals.

The men in leather watching naked go-go boys and having sex in back-room bars are not like Crisp or Daniel whom they regard as a kind of erotic theater; they are much closer to Kopay and Matlovich with whom they can identify. The rock-bottom premise of such sympathy is that all forms of traditional masculinity are respectable; all symptoms of effeminacy are contemptible. Real sexual extremism, like Daniel's, belongs to a netherworld; it is not regarded as liberated but as libertine. Daniel is the complete sexual object, and his presence makes the bar world the psychological equivalent of the brothel for the men who watch him. He turns them on, and then they can play whore or client or both.

Most men who are ardent for leather defend it as play. Dressing butch is another version of the gay uniform. What is the harm of walking through the world dressed like a construction worker? What does it matter what costume you wear to the ball? Go as Cinderella's fairy godmother, and you may break the law. But go as Hell's Angels, and you risk breaking your own spirit.

It is no coincidence that in the macho bar world and the libertine baths the incidence of impotence is so high that it is barely worth remarking, or that gay men increasingly rely on the toys and trappings of sadomasochism. It is not irrelevant that the new gay image of virility is most often illustrated in pornography.

Manly means hot, and hot is everything. Why then isn't it working better? Men tell me that I do not appreciate this new celebration of masculinity, that I am overlooking the important "fact": "We fell for masculinity when we were twelve; there must be something to it because it made us gay. Most of us didn't become gay because we fell in love with sissies; we became sissies because we fell in love with men, usually jocks."

It sounds familiar. And so what if one chooses to make one's life pornographic? Isn't that only the most recent version of sexual devotion, of incarnating Eros in one's life? Besides, it's too late to be a do-gooder. Obviously, as soon as one sets up notions of propriety, no matter how well intended, they will be preempted by the worst, most coercive forces in our society. One is then forced to accept all choices of style; the alternative is to find oneself allied with oppression. In the arena of sexual politics, there is the left and the right. Those who think they are in the middle will ultimately discover that the center is the right.

But my feelings tell me that there is another version; that macho is somehow another closet, and not a new one—many have suspected that it's the oldest closet in the house. Macho cultures have always had more covert homosexuality. Without belaboring the analogy, there is one consistency. In those cultures, homosexuality is not a sexual identity; it is defined as role. Only the passive partner, which means anally passive or orally active, is homosexual; the other role is reserved for men, because one either is a man or one is not; that is, one is a woman, and a woman who cannot bear a child and attest to a man's virility is beneath contempt, at best a whore.

The men in the macho bars are not like this. They have adopted a style and abandoned its psychic origin in sexual role playing. Apparently they have rescued the best and discarded the worst. But it is an appearance that resonates with unexamined yearnings. It says I am strong and I am free, that gay no longer means the contemptibleness of being nelly, which is the old powerless *reactiveness* to oppression. Insofar as it does that—strong is better than weak, free is always good––it is an improvement on the past. But it claims more: it says that this is a choice, a proper fulfillment of those initial desires that led us to love men, and even at its oddest, it is only playful.

But it is not free, not strong, and it is dangerous play. It is dangerous to dress up like one's enemy, and worse, it can tie one to him as helplessly as ever. It still says that he, the powerful brute, is the definer, to which we then react. It is the other side of nelly, and more helpless because it denies that one is helpless at all. Effeminacy acknowledged the rage of being oppressed in defiance; macho denies that there *is* rage and oppression. The strength of those new bodies is a costume designed for sexual allure and for the discotheque. Passing for the enemy does not exempt one from the wrath. Men in leather are already the easiest marks for violent teenagers on a drunken rampage in Greenwich Village or on Mission Street on a Saturday night. Macho is another illusion. The lessons of Negroes who disliked blackness, or Jews who insisted they were assimilated, really *German,* are ignored. To some whites, everything not white is black; to Nazis, Jews are Jews, sidelocks or no. Telling the enemy one is as good as he is because one is like him does not appease him; often it makes him more vicious, furious because somehow his victim seems to approve his scorn. And the freedom—that too is illusory except as sexual taste. In that area alone, there has been real change. Compared to their counterparts in the past gay men today have found a freedom to act out their erotic tastes. But taste is not a choice; usually, it is a tyrant.

Homosexuals at their most oppressed have not been in love with men; they have been in love with masculinity. The politics of the New Left and the sexual aesthetics of androgyny have not lasted, but they seemed to be offering alternatives that were authentic, better choices than the ones we had. The new style seems both inauthentic and barely better than the old options. Sometimes it seems worse.

That is what is disturbing and enraging: to find it the growing choice in the 1980s. Does it seriously matter that some men choose to imitate their worst enemies? What is remarkable about such an old story? For one, it is so unnecessary. For the first time in modern history, there are real options for gays. The sissies in the Blue Parrot had little choice other than to stay home. They could only pretend their lives were ordinary. That pretense was survival, but one that led fatally to rage and self-contempt. The theatricality of camping helped to keep some sanity and humanity because it was an awareness of one's helplessness. Macho values are the architects of closeted lives, and adopting that style is the opposite of awareness. Whatever its ironies, they are not critical ones.

Fortunately, gay men are less helpless than they have ever been before, and because of that they are more threatened. What is worth affirming is not bravura, but political alliance with women and with a whole liberal America that is dedicated to freedom of personal choice. *That* is worth celebrating.

LIFE AFTER DEATH: A VIEW FROM THE LATE 1980s

These days the mood of the gay community ranges from cloudy optimism to crystal-clear despair, depending on whom you talk to. I've been talking to gay activists, journalists, academics, therapists and medical doctors, businessmen, poets and painters, working-class men, and men who don't work, either because they don't need to or because they can't find a job. Some are Marxists, some lesbian feminists, and some have no politics but sexual politics. The term "gay community" refers partly to a discernible group of homosexual men and lesbians in large cities, and partly to a political idea. The media made it a term to reckon with long before anyone could say what it was. In 1969 "gay community" was largely a political idea and a myth. Even then there was a community in the simplest sense of the word, but what it looked like, as in the case of the blind men describing the elephant, depended on what you touched.

Seventeen years later, there are listings in the Yellow Pages. Coherent and representative groups have emerged, particularly in San Francisco, Los Angeles, and New York. They differ enough to be unable to provide a national leadership, and persistent closetry makes estimates of their numbers and their members rough at best, but a gay man or woman would likely feel at home in any of those three cities. The real differences are geographical, not political or social, and there is no single lifestyle or even a dominant one. The promiscuous one that became the hallmark of urban gay life in the early seventies—newsworthy because it was commercial and outrageous and because it gradually became the self-defining image of so many gay men—no longer prevails as it once did.

Today the general mood is grim. Everyone is either melancholy or anxious, afraid not only of AIDS but of the growing signs of hostility toward gay men and women. It is chilling when the *New York Times,* purportedly in the interests of balanced journalism, publishes William F. Buckley in support of tatooing homosexual men and intravenous-drug users, while the word "quarantine" quivers between the lines of the article. (I naively waited for letters of protest from both the Jewish and gay communities. Wouldn't Jews be disgusted by the parodic horror of the suggestion?) Though Buckley is absurd, the fears he touches on are not.

Helplessness about AIDS and uncertainty about the social future are exacerbated for gay men and women by their memories of the past. This is one reason so many are eager to be involved with gay organizations, to be tangibly connected to a real, not an ideological community. To be passive again is to stress one's helplessness, to be waiting for the next blow and wondering if the humiliation will be bearable.

Most of society is less concerned about who is responsible for the AIDS epidemic than with how gay men are going to behave in order to inhibit its spread. That issue, it should be said at once, arose in the gay community almost as soon as it was clear that AIDS was regarded as a gay disease. The closing of the bathhouses in San Francisco and New York was the occasion for raising the question in public. Publicly and privately it was admitted that the issue of accountability and social responsibility would have to be addressed. Obviously, this meant altering sexual behavior and style of life. Efforts were made in every large North American city with a gay community to inform and educate gay men about "safe sex," hoping that would be enough to halt the spread of AIDS. It is not yet clear how much deprivation this entails or how successful the educational campaign has been. History does not offer much ground for optimism: venereal epidemics of the past ended not with altered sexual behavior but with the discovery of penicillin.

But another issue, internal and not yet explored in any public way, has now arisen and needs attention, an issue that the symptoms of the crisis sometimes hint at: what does it mean to be homosexual in the modern world? This question is not about grievances and injustices, and it cannot be answered on the barricades, especially the barricade of rhetoric. As long as the subject of gay identity is argued in terms of whether it is good or bad, legitimate or illegitimate, there is no energy left to address the question of what it is. The new activism cannot address the more important internal questions the crisis has raised. The sources of change are elsewhere, in behavior and in thought about the homosexual condition that most men and women are reluctant to embrace.

## Promiscuity and Liberation

Some have refused to change; they search for safe places to practice old pleasures. Latin America and the Caribbean have long accommodated homosexual men with their informal bordellos, their "muchachos" who are partners to passive men but who do not think of themselves as homosexual. It is only a question of time before these gay men spread AIDS to other islands near Haiti, from which they probably first brought it to the mainland. It is hard to gauge the state of mind of such men. They may be filled with rage and seeking revenge. They may fatalistically believe that their behavior doesn't matter. They don't feel they are doing anything wrong, or they don't care. They have no moral sense, or they are immoral. It's bad enough to live in dread of dying an awful premature death. Yet to be filled with desire for revenge, or to be without desire at all, even for ordinary dignity, is a terrible way to live or die. I assume that such men act less from conscious indecency than from pure evasion. To emphasize sexual desire and desirability is a very effective way to mask anxiety. The habit of promiscuity doesn't allow much room for introspection.

Promiscuity is a broad term. For some men, it means serial affairs or brief erotic relationships. For others, there are no relationships at all; sexual encounters begin and end with momentary arousal. And for some men, promiscuity is all of these—having a lover, and having someone else, and having anyone else. Promiscuity is time consuming and repetitious. Still, it also has another history and meaning for gay men; and it is that history, and that meaning, with which gay men in the shadow of AIDS must grapple.

In the last fifteen years or so, until AIDS appeared, promiscuity had been a rich if not invaluable experience for gay men, uniting a sense of liberation with a politics of resentment, a feeling of living at the modern edge with an outlet for aggressions created by long-held grievances. Such a combination is explosive, of course, and anti-intellectual. But gay men did not invent sexual liberation. They merely stamped it with their hallmark of aggressive display. Casual sex, freed from commercialism, seemed a glamorous portent of a society free from sexism. After "Stonewall," the riot at a New York bar in which gay men successfully resisted arrest and inadvertently inaugurated gay liberation, gay activists felt they were going to re-define the old terms, junk the guilt and the remorse. They were already discarding with contempt the shrinks and the moralists, paying some of them back for the years of misery they had helped to create, the self-dislike they had urged gays to internalize for the sake of what now seemed merely propriety. Out the window went "sick" and "bad." Many could hardly believe they were jettisoning that dismal baggage.

Those years of sexual opportunism were a time of indifference to psychological inquiry. Description was a higher priority. After so much silence, the need to explain and the desire to shock were first on the agenda of gay writers and intellectuals, while the majority of gay men were exploring an exhilarating sense of relief in discos, bars with back rooms, and the baths. The politics of that eroticism had as much to do with ego as with eros: gay men said that sexuality did not diminish social status, to say nothing of intellectual or professional stature—no matter how vividly it was practiced.

In the early seventies, when movement politics was at the zenith of its popularity, the values it promoted were very seductive. It said the old romantic pieties were a slavish imitation of straight society, where they were already undergoing vigorous scrutiny from feminists. If women and blacks could use politics to demand that society acknowledge they had been unjustly treated, why not gay men? If the acknowledgment of that injustice took the form of striking down old laws and replacing them with better ones, then that, obviously, was the agenda. But for the most part, neither the victories nor the defeats changed the daily lives of gay men and women very much. With or without sodomy laws, most lived without concern for legality. It was understood that the principal struggle was psychological, a demand first for recognition, then for acceptance; the bold terms in which that demand was couched guaranteed the right to pursue a sexual lifestyle of their own choosing. After Stonewall, gays chose to be very visible.

Before Stonewall, promiscuous sex was illegal, but it was no particular threat to health. If the heart and heat of gay politics has been to ensure the right to fuck who, when, and where one pleases, then the consequences now for the movement have a rough poetic justice. The more that sex dominated the style of life, from discos to parades, with rights secured or not, the less need most men felt they had for politics––and the less others, such as lesbians, feminists, and minorities, felt the gay movement offered them. For gay men sexual politics became something oddly literal. Both before and after the movement, promiscuity was honored as the sign of an individual's aggressiveness (no matter how passive he was in bed). To fuck was to defy, as bad girls of the past did, dismantling some of society's dearest notions about virtue. But most homosexuals want to be conventional. They are no more imaginative, courageous, or innovative than their neighbors. They want a good life on the easiest terms they can get. Many regard as uninteresting the activism that a handful of men and women are devoted to.

By the late seventies, movement politics displaced flamboyant effeminacy. The piece of trade (a man who is fellated by another but pretends to be heterosexual) whose very pose of masculinity ensured his contempt for his homosexual partner, had been replaced by that formerly groveling queen himself, now looking more virile than his proletarian idol. The dominant image of rebellion was no longer the defiant queens with their merciless ironies but powerful, strong bodies modeled on working-class youth. This new image exposed the erotic ideal of gay male life more clearly and responsively than anything since classical Greece. It was a vast improvement. Liberation freed gays from a lot of burdens, and one of the biggest was to end the search for masculinity among the enemy.

But paralleling the rise of the macho body has been the decline of the health of the male community—a nasty coincidence, if you believe in coincidence. The deeper truth, however, is that the very values that motivated us to look strong rather than be strong are the same values that elevated promiscuity as the foundation of a social identity. AIDS is mobilizing many to work in agencies caring for the ill, allowing them opportunities for sympathy and generosity—but that, too, is not the basis of an identity. What is killing you is not likely to give you a sense of self.

Even if AIDS were cured tomorrow, the style and identity of gay life in the seventies and mid-eighties would be as dated as the sexual mores of closeted homosexual life are now. Many men may rush back to the baths, but it can no longer be the liberating experience it once was. AIDS has nullified promiscuity as politically or even psychologically useful and has replaced one set of meanings with another. It has now become mythic as the dark side of sexuality, Thanatos to Eros. The life force that is the sexual drive has always had its counterpart, and AIDS is the most dramatic juxtaposition of the need for another and the fear of the other, of pain and pleasure, of life and death, in modern medical history. From the ancient Greeks on down, without a moment's interruption, the interpretation has been the same: unfettered sexuality means death, whether through dishonor, the wrath of the gods, or nature itself. We are the heirs of those legends. AIDS, like a blotter, has absorbed those old meanings.

## Life After Death

There is much, then, that gay men must give up. The loss of sexual life, nearly as much as the grief and fear, is a deprivation for which no amount of civic work or marching to banners of Gay Pride can compensate. The most dramatic changes have occurred among those large numbers of men who have become abstinent, assuming a sense of responsibility to themselves if not to others. Not only must gay men refrain from what alone gave them a powerful enough identity to make a mark on the consciousness of society, a behavior that replaced society's contempt with the much more respectable fear and anger, but they must cease to think of themselves as unloved children. They must do both before they can have social acceptance or before their own behavior can have meaning for each other more nurturing than it has been. It is very hard to give up a sense of deprivation when little that created it has disappeared, and worse, when one is beset with fear.

One thing, however, is clear: gay men are not acting in concert. If gay men sensed they belonged to a recognized community, instead of struggling still to assert their legitimacy, the task would be simpler. If they felt the larger society was no longer so adamantly adversarial, they could give up the sense of injustice that makes talk of social responsibility seem hypocritical. And if their own experiences with each other had provided them with bonds deeper than momentary pleasure, they could trust themselves to act as a group in which members assumed responsibility for each other.

As long as the larger society continues to prefer the old homosexual invisibility, the nice couple next door to whom anyone can condescend, as long as that society fails to express its responsibilities to gay men, the harder it will be for gay men to give up their seductive sense of grievance. Those men who act irresponsibly in the midst of this crisis betray their isolation, their failure to feel they belong either to a gay community or to a larger one. They perceive the demand for accountability as a demand from strangers. Society has not acted as the surrogate family in which we all develop our loyalties and moral sense. In fact, too often it acts just like the family of gay men: filled with contempt or indifference.

Many gays are now relieved that sex is no longer a banner issue. It is not even so important that we all stand up to be counted; enough of us have stood up to satisfy the curious. Instead, much as other groups in U.S. society have done, the gay community has had to reassess more profoundly its relationship to the larger society. Customarily, that relationship has been adversarial. Now, for the first time in my memory, the gay community expects help. It hopes for sympathy from heterosexual society. It expects that those who are ordinarily silent will be uncomfortable with such neutrality when orthodox religious leaders proclaim AIDS the scourge of God upon homosexuals, or when politicians exploit and promote fear.

AIDS has made it necessary for gay men to begin questioning themselves. For too long we have lived as if we were driven, too impelled to know what we were doing and what, consequently, was happening to us. It takes perhaps half a lifetime before one is capable of the introspection (not self-absorption) necessary to make sense of the past and thus act as a morally free adult. The same is true of groups. There are moments in history when groups, too, must tell the truth about themselves.

## NOTES

"The New Masculinity of Gay Men," written in 1978, was originally published as a chapter of Kleinberg's book *Alienated Affections* (New York: St. Martin's Press, 1980). "Life After Death: A View From the Late 1980s" is excerpted from an article in the New Republic, 11 and 18 Aug., 1986.

[1]Quentin Crisp. *The Naked Civil Servant* (New York: New American Library, 1983).
[2]David Kopay and Perry D. Young, *The David Kopay Story* (New York: Arbor House, 1980).
[3]Leonard Matlovich was formerly a sergeant in the U.S. Army.

# Hard and Heavy: Toward a New Sociology of Masculinity

TIM CARRIGAN, BOB CONNELL, AND JOHN LEE

The upheaval in sexual politics of the last twenty years has mainly been discussed as a change in the social position of women. Yet change in one term of a relationship signals change in the other. From very early in the history of women's liberation it was clear that its politics had radical implications for men. A small "men's liberation" movement developed in the 1970s among heterosexual men. Gay men became politicized as the new feminism was developing, and gay liberation politics have continued to call in question the conventional understanding of what it is to be a man. Academic sex role research, though mainly about women in the family, was easily extended to the "male role." From several different directions in the 1970s, critiques and analyses of masculinity appeared. Quite strong claims about the emergence of a new area of study, and a new departure in sexual politics, were made. The purpose of this article is to bring together these attempts, evaluate them, and propose an alternative.

We think it important to start with the "prehistory" of this debate—early attempts at a sociology of gender, the emergence of the "sex role" framework, and research on masculinity *before* the advent of women's liberation. In this dusty literature are the main sources of the framework that has governed most recent writing on masculinity. It includes an agenda about modernization, a characteristic blindness about power, and a theoretical incoherence built into the "sex-role" paradigm. There are also, in some nearly forgotten writing, pointers to a much more powerful and interesting analysis.

Approaching the recent literature, we were concerned with three things: its empirical discoveries, its political assumptions and implications, and its theoretical framework. Its empirical content turns out to be slight. Though most social science is indeed about men, good-quality research that brings *masculinity* into focus is rare. Ironically, most recent studies are not up to the standard set by several researchers in the 1950s. There is however a notable exception, a new body of work on the history of homosexual masculinity, which has general implications for our understanding of the historical construction of gender categories.

The political meaning of writing about masculinity turns mainly on its treatment of power. Our touchstone is the essential feminist insight that the overall relationship between men and women is one involving domination or oppression. This is a fact about the social world that must have profound consequences for the character of men. It is a fact that is steadily evaded, and sometimes flatly denied, in much of the literature about masculinity written by men—an evasion wittily documented by Barbara Ehrenreich in *The Hearts of Men*.[1]

There are, however, some accounts of masculinity that have faced the issue of social power, and it is here that we find the bases of an adequate theory of masculinity. But they too face a characteristic danger in trying to hold to feminist insights about men. For a powerful current in feminism, focusing on sexual exploitation and violence, sees masculinity as more or less unrelieved villainy and all men as agents of the patriarchy in more or less the same degree. Accepting such a view leads to a highly schematic view of gender relations and leads men in particular into a paralyzing politics of guilt. This has gripped the "left wing" of men's sexual politics since the mid-1970s.

It is necessary to face the facts of sexual power without evasion but also without simplification. A central argument of this article is that the theoretical bases for doing so are now available and that a strong radical analysis of masculinity has become possible. Three steps open this possibility up. First, the question of sexual power has to be taken more seriously and pursued *inside* the sex categories. In particular the relations between heterosexual and homosexual men have to be studied to understand the constitution of masculinity as a political order, and the question of what forms of masculinity are socially dominant or hegemonic has to be explored. The writings of gay liberation theorists already provide important insights about this problem. Second, the analysis of masculinity needs to be related as well to other currents in feminism. Particularly important are those that have focused on the sexual division of labor, the sexual politics of workplaces, and the interplay of gender relations with class dynamics. Third, the analysis needs to use those developments in social theory in the last decade or so that offer ways past the dichotomies of structure versus individual, society versus the person, that have plagued the analysis of gender as much as the analysis of class. These developments imply a focus on the historical production of social categories, on power as the ability to control the production of people (in both the biological and psychological senses), and on large-scale structures as both the objects and effects of collective practice. In the final section we sketch a sociology of masculinity that draws on these sources.

We hope for a realistic sociology of masculinity, built on actual social practices rather than discussion of rhetoric and attitudes. And we hope for a realistic politics of masculinity, neither fatuously optimistic nor defeatist. We see such an enterprise as part of a radical approach to the theory of gender relations in general, made possible by convergences among feminism, gay liberation, contemporary socialism, psychoanalysis, and the history and sociology of practice. The theme of masculinity makes sense only in the context of that larger project. At the same time it is, we think, an important part of it.

ORIGINS

### The Early Sociology of Gender and the "Sex Role" Framework

"The problem of women" was a question taken up by science generally in the second half of the nineteenth century, at first in a mainly biological framework. This was not simply part of the widening scope of scientific inquiry. It was clearly also a response to the enormous changes that had overtaken women's lives with the growth of industrial capitalism. And, toward the end of the century, it was a response to the direct challenge of the women's emancipation movement.

The relationship of the emerging social sciences to this nineteenth- and early twentieth-century discourse on women was profound. In a useful sociology of knowledge investigation of the growth of the discourse, Viola Klein observed that

> There is a peculiar affinity between the fate of women and the origins of social science, and it is no mere co-incidence that the emancipation of women should be started at the same time as the birth of sociology.[2]

The political stakes were particularly evident in psychological research. The area usually referred to today as "sex difference research" has been a major component in the development of social science work on gender. In the view of one prominent observer of the field, this work was originally

> motivated by the desire to demonstrate that females are inherently inferior to males . . . But from 1900 on, the findings of the psychologists gave strong support to the arguments of the feminists.[3]

Rosalind Rosenberg has documented the pioneering, and subsequently forgotten, research by American women into sex differences in the first two decades of this century. She established the importance of the work of Helen Thompson, Leta Hollingworth, Jessie Taft, Elsie Clews Parsons, and others across a range of disciplines into questions of intelligence, the socialization of women, and American sexual mores. There were serious obstacles in the way of the academic careers of these women, but Rosenberg revealed the influence they had on such social theorists as W.I. Thomas, Robert Lowie, John Dewey, and Margaret Mead.[4]

Establishing the social basis of sex differences was one thing (though biological claims and assumptions recur in this work right up to the present). Developing a sociological account of femininity was quite another. The "marginal man" perspective, for example, was used by Park and other sociologists at the University of Chicago from the late 1920s to refer to the ways in which groups such as Jewish and black people experienced the conflict of living in two cultures. As Rosenberg observed, this was quite comparable to how Taft had conceived the position of women a decade before. Yet it was not until the 1950s that the "marginal man" or "minority" perspective was applied to women, by Helen Hacker.[5] By then, however, the development of an adequate sociology of femininity was inhibited by the ascendancy of functionalism; for this meant that the radical implications of the early research into femininity were pretty well lost.

By the mid-century, functionalist sex role theory dominated the western sociological discourse on women. The key figure in this development was Talcott Parsons, who in the early 1950s wrote the classic formulation of American sex role theory, giving it an intellectual breadth and rigor it had never had before. The notion of "role" as a basic structural concept of the social sciences had crystallized in the 1930s, and it was immediately applied to questions of gender. Two of Parsons's own papers of the early 1940s talked freely of "sex roles." In the course of his argument he offered an interesting account of several options that had recently emerged within the female role. There was, however, little sense of a power relation between men and women; and the argument embedded the issue of sex and gender firmly in the context of the family.[6]

For the rest of the 1940s Parsons was mainly occupied with the system building for which he is now famous. When he returned to the theme of sex it was with questions of structure behind him, and questions of how people were fitted into structures—what he called "socialization"—uppermost in his mind. The main tool he used on this problem was psychoanalysis, and his work thus is the first important encounter of Freudian thought on sexuality with the American sociology of gender—even if it was the rather bland version of psychoanalysis being naturalized in the United States at the time.

In the two chapters of the collaborative volume *Family, Socialization and Interaction Process* (1953) that represent the culmination of this development, Parsons achieved a notable synthesis. He brought together a structural account of kinship, the socialization problem in sociology, psychoanalytic accounts of personality formation, the internal interaction patterns of the household, and the sexual division of labor into a coherent argument. The theme of the differentiation and learning of sex roles provided the solvent that blended all these ingredients. It follows that in most of Parsons's argument "sex roles" themselves were a taken-for-granted fact. What was at issue was the processes and structures that called them into play.

At a key point, however, Parsons did make sex role differentiation the problem, asking how it was to be explained. He rejected the biological-difference argument as utterly incapable of explaining the social pattern of sex roles. Rather, he derived it from a general sociological principle, the imperative of structural differentiation. Its particular form here was explained by the famous distinction between "instrumental" and "expressive" leadership. Parsons treated sex roles as the instrumental/expressive differentiation that operated within the conjugal family. And he treated the conjugal family both as a small group and as the specific agency of the larger society entrusted with the function of socializing the young. Thus he deduced the gender patterning of roles and their reproduction across generations from the structural requirements of any social order whatever.

To this tour de force of reasoning Parsons added a sophisticated account of role acquisition, in the sense of how the role is *internalized.* This is where psychoanalysis, with its account of the production of masculinity and femininity through different patternings of the oedipal crisis, came into play. In effect, sex role becomes part of the very constitution of the person, through the emotional dynamics of development in the nuclear family.

Thus Parsons analyzed the acquisition of sex roles as a matter of the production, from one generation to the next, of what we might call *gender personalities.* For example:

> relative to the total culture as a whole, the masculine personality tends more to the predominance of instrumental interests, needs and functions, presumably in whatever social system both sexes are involved, while the feminine personality tends more to the primacy of expressive interests,

needs and functions. We would expect, by and large, that other things being equal, men would assume more technical, executive and "judicial" roles, women more supportive, integrative and "tension-managing" roles.[7]

This notion provided Parsons then, as it provides role theorists still, with a powerful solution to the problem of how to link person and society. But its ability to do so was based on a drastic simplification. As phrases like "the masculine personality" show, the whole argument is based on a normative standard case. Parsons was not in the least concerned about how many men (or women) are actually like that. Even the options within a sex role that he had cheerfully recognized in the earlier papers had vanished. All that was left in the theory was the normative case on the one hand and, on the other, deviance. Homosexuality, he wrote only a couple of pages after the passage just quoted, is universally prohibited so as to reinforce the differentiation of sex roles.

Apart from being historically false (homosexuality was and is institutionalized in some societies), such a theory fails to register tension and power processes *within* gender relations. Parsons recognizes many forms of "role strain," but basically as a result of problems in the articulation of the different subsystems of society. For instance, in his account the relation between the family and the economy is the source of much of the change in sex roles. The underlying structural notion in his analysis of gender is always differentiation, not relation. Hence his automatic assumption is that the connection between the two sex roles is one of complementarity, not power.

This version of the role framework fitted comfortably with the intense social conservatism of the American intelligentsia in the 1950s and with the lack of any direct political challenge from women. For functionalist sociology "the problem of women" was no longer how to explain their social subordination. It was how to understand the dysfunctions and strains involved in women's roles, primarily in relation to the middle-class family. Given the normative emphasis on the family, the sociological focus was strongly on "social problems": the conflicts faced by working wives, "maternal deprivation," divorce rates and juvenile delinquency, and intergenerational family conflict. The sense of conflict is strong in the work of Mirra Komarovsky, who, after Parsons, made the most impressive application of the functionalist framework to sex roles in the 1940s. She developed a general argument about modernization producing a clash between a feminine "homemaker" ideal and a "career girl" ideal. The implications remained vague, but there was much more sense of complexity within sex roles than in Parsons's grand theorizing.[8]

Through the 1950s and 1960s the focus of sex role research remained on women in the family. And the field of sex role research remained a distinctly minor one within the overall concerns of sociology. This changed dramatically with the impact of second-wave feminism. There was a spectacular growth in the volume of work produced under the general rubric of "sex role research," and this field also claimed a much greater proportion of sociological research interest.

It was not only a matter of establishment social science registering the issues raised by the new feminism. Academic feminists themselves began a process of rejuvenating the discourse. On the one hand there was a huge increase in the volume of research on women, feeding into the growth of women's studies courses. On the other, attention was directed to the way an analysis of the subordination of women had been "contained" by the social-scientific discourse itself. For although sex role theory was nominally about both sexes, the conventional pattern had been an almost exclusive concentration on women's roles, ignoring their relation to men's roles and to larger social structures. Thus one immediate reform called for was a greater attention to men's roles. Research and writing on men's roles did in fact rise markedly from the late 1960s, producing about half the volume of the work on women's.

The institutional power that role theory enjoyed in sociology, especially in the United States—where as recently as the mid-seventies Komarovsky could describe it simply as "the generally accepted arsenal of sociological conceptual tools"[9]—ensured that feminist questions would be posed in that framework, at least at the start. Could this framework encompass feminist propositions? Especially could it incorporate the notion of *oppression,* or as it was more often called in this literature, the power differential between men and women?

Some feminist sociologists argued that this was perfectly possible; that role theory had been misapplied or misunderstood, or had not been extended to its full potential.[10] Yet by the late 1970s, other feminist sociologists were arguing that the sex role framework should be abandoned. Not only had the notion of "role" been shown to be incoherent. The framework continued to mask questions of power and material inequality; or worse, it implied that women and men were "separate but equal."[11]

These criticisms underlined a more general problem: the discourse lacked a stable theoretical object. "Sex role" research could, and did, wobble from psychological argument with biological assumptions, through accounts of interpersonal transactions, to explanations of a macro-sociological character, without ever having to resolve its boundaries. The elusive character of a discourse where issues as important as that of oppression could appear, disappear and reappear in different pieces of writing without anything logically compeling authors to stick with and solve them no doubt lies behind much of the frustration expressed in these criticisms. As we shall see, this underlying incoherence was to have a devastating influence on the sociological literature about men.

### The "Male Role" Literature before Women's Liberation

A sociology of masculinity, of a kind, had appeared before the "sex role" paradigm. Specific groups of boys and men had become the object of research when their behavior was perceived as a "social problem." Two notable instances are juvenile delinquency and educational underachievement—topics whose significance in the history of sociology can hardly be exaggerated. Studies such as Thrasher's *The Gang* (1927) and Whyte's *Street Corner Society* (1943) talked extensively about masculinity without directly proclaiming sex roles as their object.[12]

Through the 1950s and 1960s the most popular explanation of such social problems was "father absence," especially from poor or black families. The idea of "father absence" had a broader significance, since the historical tendency of capitalism has been to separate home from workplace. Most fathers earning wages or salaries are therefore absent from their families much of the time. This imbalance was the focus of one of the first sociological discussions of the conflicts involved in the construction of masculinity.

Ruth Hartley, in a paper published in 1959, related the absence of fathers and the overwhelming presence of mothers to a widespread anxiety among American boys, which was centered in the whole area of sex-connected role behavior,

> an anxiety which frequently expresses itself in an overstraining to be masculine, in virtual panic at being caught doing anything traditionally defined as feminine, and in hostility toward anything even hinting at "femininity," including females themselves.[13]

Hartley's interviews produced a picture of boys who had distant relationships with their fathers, who had been taught to eschew everything feminine from a very early age while having to live in an environment dominated by women, and who consequently constructed an oversimplified and overemphasized understanding of masculinity within their peer groups. For Hartley, the basic problem was not "father absence" as such, so much as a pattern of masculine socialization rigidly upheld by adults in a society where feminine roles were changing rapidly and the emancipation of women was well advanced.

Other sociologists, including David Riesman, proposed that in the modern male role, expressive functions had been added to the traditional instrumental ones.[14] The idea was clearly formulated by Helen Hacker in a notable paper called "The New Burdens of Masculinity," published in 1957:

> As a man, men are now expected to demonstrate the manipulative skills in interpersonal relations formerly reserved for women under the headings of intuition, charm, tact, coquetry, womanly wiles, et cetera. They are asked to bring patience, understanding, gentleness to their human dealings. Yet with regard to women they must still be sturdy oaks.[15]

This argument has become virtually a cliché in more recent writing. Hacker's paper is striking in its emphasis on conflict within masculinity. She pointed out that, though the husband was necessarily often absent from his family, he was "increasingly reproached for his delinquencies as father." To compound the problem, men were also under pressure to evoke a full sexual response on the part of women. The result was the growing social visibility of impotence.

Male homosexuality was also becoming increasingly visible, and this was further evidence that "all is not well with men." It is notable that Hacker did not conceive of homosexuality in terms of the current medical model but in relation to the strong differentiation between masculine and feminine social roles.

> The "flight from masculinity" evident in male homosexuality may be in part a reflection of role conflicts. If it is true that heterosexual functioning is an important component of the masculine role in its social as well as sexual aspects, then homosexuality may be viewed as one index of the burdens of masculinity.[16]

Though Hacker probably viewed (more equal) heterosexual relations as the natural order of things, her remark in fact prefigured the perspective reached within the gay liberation movement twelve years later. Almost all subsequent sociological writing, however, has ignored Hacker's brief comments, as well as the gay movement's arguments, and has continued to take the heterosexual definition of masculinity for granted.

The consideration of male homosexuality suggested the need to establish empirically "a typology of men, perhaps according to family constellation or social class position, in terms of their interpretation of the demands of masculinity and their felt capacity to fulfill them."[17] In short, masculinity varies as it is constructed in different situations.

Hacker never lost sight of the fact that masculinity exists as a power relation. Her appreciation of the effects of power led her to describe the possible range of masculine types as more restricted than that of feminine types. It also led to the suggestion (reminiscent of Chodorow's later work) "that masculinity is more important to men than femininity is to women."[18]

There is something motherly in Hacker's approach to men. Her feminism, if advanced at the time, certainly seems tame twenty-five years later. But the striking fact is that most research on masculinity in the meantime has not improved on her analysis. Indeed much of it has been a good deal more primitive. For instance, *The Male in Crisis* (1970), by the Austrian author Karl Bednarik, suggests that alienation at work, bureaucracy in politics and war, and the commercialization of sexuality all undermine masculinity. Bednarik made some acute observations on the way the commercialization of sexuality connects it with aggressiveness. And his stress on the contradiction between the hegemonic male image and the real conditions of men's lives is notable. But he never questioned that the traditional image *is* the primordial, true nature of men.[19] Nor did the American Patricia Sexton in her widely quoted book *The Feminized Male* (1969).

> What does it mean to be masculine? It means, obviously, holding male values and following male behavior norms . . . Male norms stress values such as courage, inner direction, certain forms of aggression, autonomy, mastery, technological skill, group solidarity, adventure, and a considerable amount of toughness in mind and body.[20]

In her account, however, the main force pushing American boys away from true masculinity was women. Schoolteachers and mothers, through their control of child rearing and rewarding of conformity and academic success, were making them into sissies. It is not surprising to find that Sexton romanticized working-class boys and their "boy culture," and was hostile to the "visibly feminized" soft men of the new left and counter-culture ("a new lumpen leisure-class of assorted hippies, homosexuals, artistic poseurs, and 'malevolent blacks' ").[21]

But there was something more here: an appreciation of power that had a distinctly feminist flavor. The reason women were engaged in feminizing boys, Sexton argued, was that women have been excluded from all *other* positions of authority. She documented not only the hazards of being male, citing statistics on the higher death and illness rates among men that were soon to become another cliché of the literature. She also recited at length the facts of men's power. Basically the reform she wanted was a change in the sexual division of labor, and in this regard her argument was in line with the feminism of ten years later. But she had no sense that the "male values" and "male norms" she admired are as much effects of the structure of power as the women's behavior she condemned.

Lionel Tiger's *Men in Groups,* published in the same year in Britain, was also a paradigmatic treatment of masculinity. It extensively documented men's control of war, politics, production, and sport, and argued that all this reflected a genetic pattern built into human beings at the time when the human ancestral stock took up cooperative hunting. Greater political participation by women, of the kind argued for by Sexton, would be going against the biological grain.

The notion that there is a simple continuity between biology and the social has been very powerful as ideology. So has another important feature of Tiger's argument, the way *relations* are interpreted as *differences.* The greater social power of men and the sexual division of labor are interpreted as "sexual dimorphism" in behavior. With this, the whole question of social structure is spirited away. Tiger's scientific-sounding argument turns out to be pseudo-evolutionary speculation, overlaying a more sinister political message. Its drift becomes obvious in the book's closing fantasy about masculinity and Tiger's concern with "hard and heavy phenomena," with warmongering being part of "the masculine aesthetic," and with arguments about what social arrangements are and are not "biologically healthy."[22]

It will be obvious from these cases that there was a reasonably complex and sometimes sophisticated discussion about masculinity going on before the main impact of feminism. It is also clear that this discussion was intellectually disorganized, even erratic. What coherence it had was provided by role concepts; and in one case this framework did give rise to a notable piece of research. Komarovsky's *Blue Collar Marriage* is one of the best pieces of empirical research on any topic produced by American sociology in its heyday.[23] Based on long interviews conducted in the late 1950s, the study yielded a vivid account of the interactions that actually constitute the politics of everyday life. From a bitter sketch of the sexual frustration of one heavily subordinated wife, to reflections on husbands' violence, to an illuminating (if over-moralistic) account of the emotional importance of mothers-in-law, Komarovsky traced the construction of relationships under pressure. She delivered some shrewd knocks to the bland assumptions made by conventional theorists, Parsons among them, about how "the American family" worked.

Out of this came a picture of masculinity that was both more subtle and harsher than anything else written in its period. Though she did not use this terminology, she painted a picture of masculinity as something constructed in a very complex and often tense process of negotiation, mostly with women, that stretched right through adult life. The outcomes are never guaranteed; and there is a lot of variation in the patterns Komarovsky found. Nevertheless there was a general sense of unease. The working men she found in her American steel town were on the whole an unhappy lot, with little real communication with their wives, and constricted views of the world outside. There was a lot of prejudice and aimless anger around. Ten years later these themes were to be made a centerpiece of the "men's movement" account of masculinity in general.

Unlike most role research, Komarovsky did have a lot to say about power. She was sensitive to the significance of family violence and to the economic resources of husband and wife. Like the slightly earlier Australian research by Fallding, much less known though similar in style, and Bott's *Family and Social Network*,[24] she was able to show a difference between more patriarchal and more egalitarian patterns of marriage. Nevertheless this variation was limited. Komarovsky acutely observed that in the case where the husband's power had been so far eroded that the wife was dominant in the marriage, it still was not acceptable for the wife to deny her husband's supremacy in public or among friends, neighbors, or relations. But here the analysis stopped. To push further required the concepts that were still to be provided by second-wave feminism.

THE MALE SEX ROLE AND MEN'S LIBERATION

## The "Male Role" Literature in the 1970s

The first effect of the new feminism on the study of men's roles was a dramatic increase in its volume. Grady, Brannon, and Pleck, in an annotated bibliography on "the male sex role" published in 1979, listed over 250 items; and the Massachusetts Institute of Technology in the same year listed about 1,300 items in a "Men's Studies Bibliography," the catalogue of their collection. The vast majority of items in both bibliographies are from the 1970s and of U.S. origin.[25]

There was also a distinct change in mood. The advent of women's liberation and feminist critiques of patriarchy gave a focus to the literature on masculinity that it had never had before. There was now a degree of coherence to the discussion as a whole, a common set of issues, and for many of the authors a distinct new genre of writing.

. Much of this work could hardly be described as feminist. One of the most prominent themes in the "male role" literature of the 1970s was the restrictions, disadvantages, and general penalties attached to being a man. "Do men need women's liberation?" was a common question or point of reference, and the response was resoundingly "Yes"—for the benefit of men. This was sometimes so that men too could become complete, authentic human beings. The title of one early paper, "The Inexpressive Male: A Tragedy of American Society," captured the tone. But there were also more specific hazards in being male, not least being men's high rates of death and illness relative to women's. Problems for men given attention ranged from the threatening nature of their sex role for men as they age and the role strain experienced by athletes and non-athletes, to the maladaptive effects of men's sexual socialization.[26]

Most of this literature remained within a rather narrow range of ideas. There was general acceptance of the picture of mainstream masculinity that had already been drawn by authors like Patricia Sexton. This was commonly called "the male role," "the masculine value system," "traditional masculinity," or words to that effect. The great difference was that in most of the new literature this was seen as bad rather than good, or at best inappropriate and insupportable. The crux of the change was that such masculinity was no longer thought to express the true nature of men.

The new literature viewed traditional masculinity as bad for two main reasons. First, it leads men to do nasty things, like compete with each other, oppress women, destroy the environment, and ruin the Third World, notably by bombing Vietnam. (That masculinity among the Vietnamese might have had a different significance did not occur to anyone; the ethnocentrism of this literature was almost total.) Second, men are themselves uncomfortable with it. There is "role strain," a "male dilemma," a "crisis of masculinity"; men can't live up to their images. This was evidently a deeply felt point. The autobiographical sketches that peppered the 1970s books about men regularly remarked how the author had been taught the conventional male role, found it hard to inhabit, and eventually discovered the trouble was not in him but in the role.

Where then does masculinity come from? There were two starkly different views. The minority of authors who continued to reject feminism clung to the idea that masculinity is a product of genetic programming, derived from far back in our evolutionary history. Society might attempt to modify this, but did better just expressing it. The much more common view was that masculinity is the artificial product of conditioning, with biological differences of only minimal importance. Vilar put this most memorably:

> There is virtually no difference between an unmade-up, bald, naked woman and an unmade-up bald, naked man—apart from the reproductive organs. Any other differences between them are artificially produced.[27]

Accounts of how this artificial production of masculinity occurs usually relied on a simplified social-learning theory. Parents' injunctions, school curricula, peer example, TV sports programs, and car and cigarette advertising, were all laid out side by side as influences. They were usually assumed to be all pointing the same way. "Conditioning," "modeling," "influence" were the terms used to describe the acquisition of the male role. Psychoanalytic accounts of gender were quite strikingly ignored.

Much of the literature did recognize the point argued by Hacker, that there is variation within masculinity and femininity, not just between them. This was usually understood as people ranging on some kind of scale from hard to soft. Steinmann and Fox offered a classic version in 1974. They asked the reader to think of men as lined up on a football field with the Marlboro Man at one end, Caspar Milquetoast at the other; and to think of women as lined up on-stage in a femininity contest, with the hard-nosed career woman at one end, and the meek housewife at the other.[28] There is a technical basis for this understanding of variation, in the dimensional logic that underlies the construction of masculinity and femininity tests, which as Pleck notes, have a long history in American psychology.[29] A refinement of this notion became very popular in the 1970s, with variation in masculinity and femininity explained by postulating combinations of the two kinds of characteristics within the one individual, "androgyny." The degrees of androgyny were also measured by a scale, devised by Bem.[30]

Another, rather more subtle, distinction was also often made. When authors complained about the restrictiveness of the male role and said, for instance, "Some of us are searching for new ways to work that will more fully express ourselves rather than our learned desire for masculinity,"[31] they were clearly assuming that there is an inner "self" separate from, and sometimes opposed to, the motives of behavior that form the package of "masculinity." Where this "self" might come from and how it came to be in tension with that other part of the personality remained unexplored. The social-learning approach that dominated the discussion of the acquisition of masculinity gave no grip on this issue at all. So conflict within masculinity, though recognized, remained untheorized in social terms.

As all of this suggests, there was a definite tendency in the masculinity literature to psychologize the feminist critique of men's oppression of women, and men's competition with each other. It usually located the source of the trouble in the heads of men, in their character structure, not in a structure of relationships. The feminist critique of the family was generally ignored. There was a very general reinterpretation of feminism to mean women breaking out of their roles, rather than women contesting men's power. The notion of the prevailing relationship between the sexes was therefore often one of "segregation," not oppression. A very clear example of this is Jack Nichols's widely read book *Men's Liberation,* in which he was careful to distance himself from feminism, though approving of it. The personal-political relations described by many feminists as "patriarchy" became "sex role stereotyping," and the cure, freer thinking.[32]

The central theoretical proposition of the 1970s masculinity literature, even if it sometimes remained implicit, was that men are oppressed in a fashion comparable to women. But the oppressor was not taken to be women (except in the view of the right wing of the men's movement and in satirical pieces like Vilar's *The Manipulated Man*). Rather, it was taken to be the *male role.* The real self is squashed, strained, or suppressed by the demands of this role. In one way this theory rejected the first proposition of feminism, the fact of women's subordination. Herb Goldberg's book *The Hazards of Being Male* was subtitled *Surviving the Myth of Male Privilege,* and he meant it, arguing that men are not privileged over women. The Berkeley Men's Center had arrived there as early as 1973: "All liberation movements are equally important; there is no hierarchy of oppression." Not many authors went as far as that, but most went some distance in that direction.[33]

There was, however, a more positive side to the masculinity literature. It not only argued men are oppressed; it argued they need not be. A good deal of it was in fact devoted to the theme of changes in male character and to rationalizing the idea of a modernized masculinity. In this, the notion of "androgyny" came into its own, as a translation to the level of the individual of the earlier idea that the modern male role comprised expressive as well as instrumental elements. The "healthy" modern man possesses, not exclusively gender-consonant traits, but a mixture of masculine and feminine. It all rather sounds, as Mary Daly remarked, like "John Travolta and Farrah Fawcett-Majors scotch-taped together." But its popularity showed that the concept of androgyny met a widely felt need for an image of change in sexual character. As another writer observed. "The initial response clearly indicated that the concept expressed the zeitgeist in sex-role research."[34]

Perhaps the most striking feature of this writing was the appearance, alongside the "woman book industry,"[35] of a small industry of books about men, the male role, and masculinity. By our present count, the years 1971 to 1980 saw no less than thirty-eight English-language nonfiction books published that were wholly or mainly on this subject (excluding medical works, general texts on sexuality and sex roles, books on fathering and the family, and books on specific topics such as men aging, which would doubtless treble the count). While some were aimed at the "general reader" and others at the college textbook market, there was a lot of overlap and mutual quotation. Many of the authors were self-conscious about doing something new, and all were very much aware of the new context created by the advent of women's liberation. Though there had been books about masculinity before the 1970s, there had not been a *genre* debating the nature of masculinity and its social expression. There is such a genre now.

Its scope and general character can be seen from the titles. With some pushing and shoving they can be sorted (at least the twenty-nine we have found and read) into the following categories, according to their style or principal impulse:

Men's liberation:[36]      *Unbecoming Men* (Men's Consciousness Raising Group, 1971), *The Liberated Man* (Farrell, 1974), *Men and Masculinity* (Pleck and Sawyer, 1974), *Men's Liberation* (Nichols, 1975), *Sex: Male Gender: Masculine* (Petras, 1975), *The Forty-nine Percent Majority* (David and Brannon, 1976).

Offended or satirical:[37]      *The Prisoner of Sex* (Mailer, 1971), *The Difference Between a Man and a Woman*

|  | (Lang, 1971), *The Manipulated Man* (Vilar, 1972), *Free the Male Man!* (Mead, 1972), *The Inevitability of Patriarchy* (S. Goldberg, 1973). |
| Liberal commentary:[38] | *Male Chauvinsim* (Korda, 1973), *The Male Machine* (Fasteau, 1974), *A Book About Men* (Goodman and Walby, 1975). |
| Growth movement:[39] | *The Male Dilemma* (Steinmann and Fox, 1974), *The Hazards of Being Male* (H. Goldberg, 1976), *Sex and the Liberated Man* (Ellis, 1976), *Male Sexuality* (Zilbergeld, 1978). |
| Feminist women:[40] | *Below the Belt* (Bishop and McNeill, 1977), *About Men* (Chesler, 1978). |
| Radical men:[41] | *For Men Against Sexism* (Snodgrass, 1977), *The Limits of Masculinity* (Tolson, 1977), *White Hero, Black Beast* (Hoch, 1979). |
| The academy:[42] | *A Book of Men* (Firestone, 1975), *Dilemmas of Masculinity* (Komarovsky, 1976), *A Man's Place* (Dubbert, 1979), *Be a Man!* (Stearns, 1979), *The Male Sex Role* (Grady, Brannon and Pleck, 1979), *The American Man* (Pleck and Pleck, 1980). |

The genre had four principal themes. The first, which we have already encountered, is the evils of traditional masculinity and men's discomfort in it. In a number of key texts this became the theoretical proposition that men are oppressed too, by their roles. This implied the second theme: men too need liberating. The redefinition of "liberation" from meaning a struggle against the powerful to breaking free from conventions was very general (though not quite universal) and was a move with large political implications. It enabled men to approve of feminism as a worthy parallel endeavor, rather than an assault on *them*. It was part of the general drift by which new left became counter-culture, more concerned with personal lifestyle than with questions of social exploitation, personal "liberation" meaning an expansion of the pleasures of already privileged groups. A rationalization of this drift was provided by the growth-movement psychology that was becoming extremely popular with the American middle classes at the time. As one of its proponents suggested: "The humanistic growth movement and the feminist movement have both helped to create a climate that is conducive to altering rigid and harmful patterns of behavior."[43] Men could draw dividends on both.

To do so, of course, they needed techniques of change. The ways in which masculinity has been formed and ways it might be reformed were the third main theme of the genre. As we have seen, there is a debate about biological versus social determination that goes back to the first days of the sex difference literature, and this debate was faithfully reproduced in the books about men. Opinion leaned heavily to the social side, even Norman Mailer's: "humans-with-phalluses, hardly men at birth, must work to become men."[44]

And it is social convention that was addressed by the techniques for change out of the male role that these books generally, though vaguely, recommended. Among them were being more expressive and more vulnerable, forming support groups and consciousness-raising groups, low-key group therapy, change of occupation, role sharing with one's wife, and meditation.

Though some of these notions seem a bit like trying to dig up the Pyramids with a spoon, at least they show the genre addressing the question of change in masculinity; and this was its fourth main theme. There was a very general sense that some sea-change had come over the world of sexuality and gender in the age of women's liberation and, like it or not, we have to grapple with it. Masculinity does move, sex roles have a history, and we are at one of its turning points. On the one hand this sent a number of authors back down the years to try to write the history of masculinity. (The results were abysmal as historiography; Stearns was the only one that had basic competence in historical research technique, and even his argument was thin.) On the other hand it fed a sense of excitement and purpose about the current situation and its prospects. Most of these books were tracts, and most of them were optimistic.

The intellectual content of the books-about-men genre is slender. With a couple of exceptions it never gets beyond a rather simplified version of role theory; and even with that, such elementary points of role theory as the distinction between expectation and behavior are rarely consistently maintained. And the research base of the genre is so slight as to be embarrassing, given the repeated claims about establishing "a new area of study." The only substantial research contribution in the twenty-nine books listed above is Komarovsky's, and even she is not at her best. A few others, like Tolson and Stearns, are decent compilations; Korda's *Male Chauvinism* and Goodman and Walby's *A Book About Men* are crisp and perceptive pieces of journalistic writing. The rest, to put it kindly, do not make a great contribution to the growth of knowledge.

Though most of these books were ephemeral, the 1970s did see some more substantial attempts to develop the sex role perspective. Perhaps the most interesting is the work of Joseph Pleck. Pleck has built an academic career as a social psychologist primarily concerned with the male sex role; he is also one of the most prominent "men's movement" publicists. He is editor or co-editor of several books of readings, bibliographies, and special issues of journals about masculinity; has written a couple of dozen articles and papers about masculinity since he completed a Ph.D. on the subject in 1973; and has recently published a monograph.

Pleck's work has three main components: theoretical writing about how to understand sex roles, a program of empirical research, and practical arguments about gender politics and associated social issues. His theoretical interests were announced in an article published in the first volume of the new journal *Sex Roles* in 1975.[45] He wished to understand masculinity, not as something permanently fixed by childhood experiences, but as a role that changes over the lifespan of the individual and as a role that is itself not stable but undergoes significant cultural changes.

Pleck's most substantial treatment of these themes is in his 1981 monograph *The Myth of Masculinity*. The title is curiously inapt; the main argument is not about masculinity, let alone myths, but is a critique of one version of sex role theory and an attempt to replace it with another. (The basic terms of role theory—roles, norms, sanctions, conformity and deviance, role strain—are taken for granted.)

It is clear enough what he wants to reject: biological determinism, depth psychology, simple masculinity/femininity divisions, and the notion of "identity" as a key to the psychology of gender. Broadly, he wishes to replace this with a more thoroughgoing role perspective, emphasizing the importance of social expectations, the way both conformity to them and violation of them may be "psychologically dysfunctional," and the strains arising from the fact that they change in history. Here, as elsewhere,[46] the essentialist understanding of the self that is common in much of the male role literature is clear.

The inconclusiveness of all this is partly a result of muddled argument. Pleck tries to grasp historical change, for instance, by contrasting "the modern male role" with "the traditional male role"; in the "traditional" basket are included not only the working class and American ethnics but also "primitive societies," making a theoretical category that should have quite a few anthropologists (Margaret Mead not least) turning in their graves. But more generally, the indeterminacy lies in the basic concepts of role theory itself; the more rigorously Pleck applies them, the more their underlying inadequacy appears.

We will pass over Pleck's empirical research: it is neither better nor worse than the generality of paper-and-pencil role studies.[47] It is when he puts on his "men's movement" cap that Pleck is at his most interesting. In an important paper called "Men's power with women, other men, and society: A men's movement analysis," he proposes a connection between the subordination of women and the hierarchy of power among men. This hierarchy is maintained in terms of wealth, physical strength, age, and heterosexuality, and the competition among men to assert themselves in these terms produces a considerable amount of conflict:

> Thus, men's patriarchal competition with each other makes use of women as symbols of success, as mediators, as refuges and as an underclass. In each of these roles, women are dominated by men in ways that derive directly from men's struggle with each other.[48]

Further, Pleck connects men's power to the sexual division of labor. Discussing the apparent contradiction of men exercising power in their families but enduring jobs where they are relatively powerless and that the great majority find meaningless, he argues:

> They experience their jobs and themselves as worthwhile only through priding themselves on the hard work and personal sacrifice they are making to be breadwinners for their families. Accepting these hardships reaffirms their role as family providers and therefore as true men.[49]

Though criticisms could be made of both these formulations, the connections are important and the implications large. Here Pleck was beginning to move beyond "role" notions altogether. But it was not sustained. Two later papers on the sexual division of labor lost all sense of power in gender relations, talking instead of sex-segregation "norms." In the second of these, Pleck had become quietly optimistic that men with working wives were now increasing their share of domestic work. A survey (based on men's self-reporting) found that these men did half an hour more of domestic work a day than other men. Pleck concluded that the "changing role perspective" was more accurate than the "exploitation perspective" as an approach to the question of men's domestic work. Comment seems unnecessary.[50]

Pleck's political stance and, to a significant degree, his theoretical orientation, seem to vary with his readership. The article just noted was published in *The Family Coordinator,* and here Pleck spoke to public-policy makers and social workers as a practical liberal commentator who was confident that "men can and will change if appropriate educational and social policies are implemented."[51] This is quite different from what he had to say as a "men's movement" publicist, and different again from his approach as a hard-nosed professional social psychologist. The fundamental intellectual incoherence of the general approach to masculinity is strikingly illustrated in his work.

One thing Pleck does hold onto firmly, as most of the books-about-men do, is the idea that we are currently going through a major transformation in the male sex role. There is surprisingly little research that directly investigates whether that is true. The question does come into focus in the later research of Komarovsky. In an interview study of sixty-two male students in an elite American university, which might be expected to register such cultural changes early, Komarovsky indeed found the majority reporting no intellectual insecurity or strain with their "dates." She concluded that "the normative expectation of male intellectual superiority appears to be giving way on the campus to the ideal of intellectual companionship between equals."[52] This finding might have been taken as evidence of a movement toward androgyny, or at least acceptance of feminism. But more detailed probing modified this picture considerably. Only 7 percent were willing to modify their own roles significantly to facilitate their future wives' careers. Among the remainder Komarovsky found a variety of contradictory values and sentiments, but concluded that there remained a

> deeply rooted norm that the husband should be the superior achiever in the occupational world and the wife, the primary child rearer.... Even equality of achievement of husband and wife is interpreted as a defeat for the man. The prospect of occupational rivalry with one's wife seems intolerable to contemplate.[53]

Though many supported a woman's right to a career, the issue was not a source of any particular tension or strain; the "career or marriage" problem was assumed to be solved by the wife's withdrawing from and returning to work. The idea of a major transformation of the male sex role, in this milieu at least, seems premature.

Russell's more recent research on Australian couples who actually have reversed the sexual division of labor likewise suggests the reversal is at best unstable and often reflects no change in basic assumptions at all.[54] A recent American survey of a range of empirical findings concluded that most "large-scale, objective measures of men's roles show little change over the past decade, but men do feel now and then that their position is in question."[55] This is not all the available evidence, of course. But findings of this kind (combined with feminist perceptions of reactions *against* feminism by men) are numerous enough to raise serious doubts that the changes that are undoubtedly occurring can be understood as the changing definition of a male role.

### "Men's Liberation" and Its Opponents

Most of the books-about-men are less contributions to a new science than responses to a practical exigency, and this both gave a distinctive character to the sex role literature of the 1970s and provoked the beginnings of a move beyond it. The exigency was the impact of second-wave feminism on the heterosexual men in the white, affluent, college-educated intelligentsia of the United States and other advanced capitalist countries. In the Books about Men, author after author spoke of having been forced to confront the question of masculinity by his wife or girlfriend, who had become a feminist and joined a consciousness-raising group. The Author's Wife is a strong collective presence in this genre; and although it was mainly written by men, the political practice of women's groups was its major practical basis. The genre was emotionally structured around heterosexual men's reactions to feminism.

One of these reactions was the development that came to be called the "men's liberation movement" or just the "men's movement." Women's liberation, as a visible political movement, took off in the United States in 1968, rapidly followed by the other advanced capitalist countries.[56] One of its first creations was a network of consciousness-raising (CR) groups; in the very early days, some of these were mixed. By 1970 there were some all-men CR groups in the United States. We do not know how many, but they certainly existed in both New York and Berkeley. If the one that published the booklet *Unbecoming Men* the following year is any guide, they were drawn from university-educated new-left activists. The connection with the radical wing of the anti-war movement is confirmed from other sources—positively in the case of Jack Sawyer, the author of what was regarded as the first article on "male liberation," published in 1970 in the new-left magazine *Liberation,* and negatively by Warren Farrell, soon to emerge as the most active organizer of men's groups, who records in *The Liberated Man* his discomfort with the political radicalism of his early customers. He saw radicalism as irrelevant to men's liberation and wanted to get beyond it.

And that indeed happened. In the next four or five years the connection with the left faded as a network of men's CR groups expanded across the United States. The flavor was increasingly counter-cultural rather than radical, and sometimes not even that—rather, therapeutic or concerned with self-improvement. Several "men's centers" were established to parallel women's ones, and there was a spate of publishing, both in the ordinary press and in newly created newsletters. Men's liberation had arrived; men's oppression was a recognized problem.

The impression of a spontaneous upsurge that is cultivated in the books-about-men is misleading. Much of this was consciously organized, using the mass media and the main organization of American liberal feminism, the National Organization of Women. Farrell was involved in setting up a NOW "task force" on "the masculine mystique" and travelled around the country organizing men's groups using NOW local branches as the basis. By 1974 things were big enough to hold a national conference, where in Farrell's somewhat hyperbolic words,

> hundreds of facilitators were trained to return to their local communities to form a nationwide network of men's and joint consciousness-raising groups and to carry out national demonstrations and "actions."[57]

A national organization, called the "Men's Awareness Network" was set up. And this activity began to be reproduced overseas. Men's CR groups appeared in Britain, followed by national conferences and newsletters; in the late 1970s there was a "men's centre" in London and a good-quality magazine called *Achilles' Heel.*

In the mid 1970s, however, differences were emerging in the United States that deepened in the second half of the decade. The connection with the left had not been entirely lost, as it continued to be a major source of recruits for men's groups. Radical men, organizing under the name of "Men Against Sexism," were sharply critical of the complacency and egocentricity of much of the "men's movement," its failure to confront patriarchy, its blindness to race and class. In 1977 Jon Snodgrass brought out *For Men Against Sexism,* a comprehensive attack on the politics of "men's liberation" from the left. In Britain many of the same themes were picked up by Andrew Tolson, whose book *The Limits of Masculinity* was published in the same year.

But it was a hardening in the opposite direction that attracted much more public attention. The notion of women's and men's parallel struggles in some cases concealed a latent anti-feminism. The notion of "men's liberation," in the context of American liberal individualism, rapidly led to the notion of "men's rights"; and "men's rights," logically, can only be defined against women. David and

Brannon's *Forty-Nine Percent Majority,* a vintage men's liberation piece published in 1976 and presumably compiled a year or two earlier, already included a long article on legal aspects of "discrimination against men," for instance in divorce and legal procedures. By 1976-7 there was some organized support in the United States for men fighting custody cases, with "father's rights" groups forming. By the end of the decade another national organization, calling itself "Free Men," was in existence campaigning on such issues, and opposing feminist positions on abortion as well.[58]

The growth of the "men's movement" sounds impressive, as its main chroniclers, Farrell and the Plecks, tell it. But what was its real scale? It is difficult to be certain at this distance, but we have the impression that the notion of a *movement* is much too strong for what happened in North America and Britain, if this activity is compared with movements like gay liberation and women's liberation.[59] An intermittent, thinly spread collection of support groups, therapeutic activities, and ephemeral pressure-group campaigns might be nearer the real picture; and it is hard to think of any significant political effect it has had in any country over ten years.[60]. What it has done, very successfully, is produce publicists.

The critique of "men's liberation" made in the Snodgrass anthology *For Men Against Sexism* is the most systematic American attempt to move outside the genre's political conventions and, implicitly, the sex role analysis of masculinity. It is explicitly an attempt to respond to feminism without falling into the men-are-equally-oppressed trap. It insists on the importance of the concept of patriarchy and tries to relate men's oppression of women to the oppression of workers, blacks, and—almost uniquely among books-about-men—gay men. It tries to reckon with the ambivalences of counter-sexist attitudes among men, and face, rather than evade, the political difficulties. It is in many ways an impressive book, especially as critique. But its own positive positions are much less convincing.

The most striking thing about *For Men Against Sexism* is the massive guilt that runs through its major pieces. Authors bewail their own past sexism; the editors flirt with "effeminism" (a New York confection of 1973 in which men declare themselves cooks and bottlewashers for feminism and humbly follow the nearest woman's lead in everything). The book insists that men must accept radical feminism as the basis for their CR groups and have them started and supervised by women; and even this is immediately followed by a paper on "dangers with men's CR groups." The guilt is compounded by the influence of the "growth movement," strong even in this book;

its simple-minded voluntarism makes the writers and readers of the book the direct and deliberate authors of women's oppression. The theme is neatly summarized in the title of a chapter by Schein, "All men are misogynists." One gets the impression that being subject to constant criticism by feminists is the emotional center of this book, and that the response is to bend over backwards, and backwards again. A relationship with feminism is indeed crucial to any counter-sexist politics among heterosexual men; but a series of back somersaults is not a strong position from which to confront the patriarchal power structure.

In most ways Tolson's *Limits of Masculinity* is the best thing yet written on the whole subject. It is, for one thing, a real attempt at a *sociology* of masculinity, concerned with the organization of power on a large scale. Tolson goes through the research literature on family, community, and workplace, mining it for evidence about the situation and activities of men; and in consequence is able to make the first serious attempt to explore class differences in the construction and expression of masculinity. The book's central theme, unlike most writing on masculinity, is the social relations of the workplace, and Tolson presents very interesting material on what he calls the "culture of work" and the ways masculinity is both constructed and undermined by the dynamics of the capitalist labor process. More, he offers an account of the psychodynamics of masculinity, focusing on both father-son and peer relations as sources of the emotional reactions that sustain masculinity.

Not all of this is successful. Though the description of workplaces, and especially working-class daily life, is vivid, the underlying sociology is rather structuralist. Tolson's account of the oedipal crisis is confused. His notion of masculinity is still mainly based on a trait notion of personality, and the consequence of that is a good deal of stereotyping. But he goes a long way to showing what can be done when the interaction of capitalism and patriarchy, rather than a search for the real self, is taken as the starting point for and understanding of masculinity.

The context of Tolson's thought is the British left of the early 1970s and the experience of a men's CR group of which he was a founding member. He brings them together at the end of the book in what remains the most sophisticated assessment of "men's liberation" and counter-sexist politics among heterosexual men. And the overall conclusion is quite pessimistic. Small-group techniques certainly open up areas of personal life; but since ultimately masculinity is the product of large-scale social structures, they do not generate any leverage on the real problems. Further, Tolson argues, masculinity simply is not a position from which one can engage in a politics of sexual liberation. The *dominant* group in a power structure cannot do that. The best that heterosexual men can do in the long run is try to make the socialist movement more receptive to the kind of initiatives women's and gay groups are working for.

Tolson at least lends support to gay liberation; but it is notable that in formulating this conclusion, he treats "gay" and "masculine," "gays" and "men," as quite separate concepts. In this, he is very much in the tradition of the books-about-men. Works in the genre range between generally ignoring homosexuals and homosexuality, and totally ignoring them. Snodgrass in *For Men Against Sexism* names "gay oppression" and gives it a short section, but separates it from the general dicussion of patriarchy, anti-sexist practice, and men's liberation. Though Snodgrass's treatment is markedly better than the rest, he too has marginalized the issue.

In this evasion is a final confirmation of the political meaning of the "men's movement" and the books-about-men genre. It is not, fundamentally, about uprooting sexism or transforming patriarchy, or even understanding masculinity in its various forms. When it comes to the crunch, what it is about is *modernizing* hegemonic masculinity. It is concerned with finding ways in which the dominant group—the white, educated, heterosexual, affluent males we know and love so well—can adapt to new circumstances without breaking down the social-structural arrangements that actually give them their power.

Yet the weakness and incoherence of the literature of this modernizing process, which we have documented in the last two sections, strongly implies that it is not working very well. There are possibilities for better practices, as well as worse. An internal dialectic has produced the critique set out by Snodgrass and Tolson. The logic of this critique is to abandon "men's movement" politics; but that leaves a void, both conceptually and practically. For however spurious the answers that have been given, the questions posed in the sex role literature of the early 1970s were real enough. Sexual politics continues to implicate men, all of them; and if people don't have good new ideas, they will make do with bad old ones. What positive alternative can be offered? We will suggest later that the most important new resources for constructing an adequate account of masculinity are to be found in the arguments of the movement so studiously ignored by the books-about-men, gay liberation.

TOWARD REDEFINITION

## Sex Roles Revisited

We have shown the massive influence of "sex-role" notions in both formal social science and the informal literature associated with the "men's movement" of the 1970s. We have offered reasons to be dissatisfied with particular formulations, and we now turn to the general critique of the "sex role" framework.

Broadly, the "role" framework has been used to analyze what the difference is between the social positions of women and men, to explain how they are shaped for those positions, and to describe the changes and conflicts that have occurred in and about those positions. At the simplest level, it is clear that the sex role framework accepts that sexual differentiation is a social phenomenon: sex roles are learnt, acquired, or "internalized." But the precise meaning of the social relations proposed by the framework is not nearly as simple as its proponents assume.

The very idea of a "role" implies a recognizable and accepted standard, and sex role theorists posit just such a norm to explain sexual differentiation. Society is organized around a pervasive differentiation between men's and women's roles, and these roles are internalized by all individuals. There is an obvious common-sense appeal to this approach. But the first objection to be made is that it does not actually describe the concrete reality of people's lives. Not all men are "responsible" fathers nor "successful" in their occupations, and so on. Most men's lives reveal some departure from what the "male sex role" is supposed to prescribe.

The problem here is that the sex role literature does not consistently distinguish between what is expected of people and what they in fact do. The framework often sees variations from the presumed norms of male behavior as "deviance," as a "failure" in socialization. This is particularly evident in the functionalist version of sex role theory, where "deviance" becomes an unexplained, residual, and essentially non-social category.

When variation and conflict in the male role are recognized to be more typical, there are two possible explanations for sex role theorists. Some see this conflict as a result of the blurring of men's and women's roles, so that men find they are expected to add expressive elements to their traditional instrumental roles. It is not obvious why men, perhaps allowing for some initial confusion, could not internalize this new male role just as they did the original one. The answer for authors such as Bednarik and Sexton was that these changes in men's lives go against the grain.[61] Hegemonic masculinity *is* the true nature of men, and social harmony arises from promoting this idea, not impeding it. "Masculinity" in these terms is a non-social essence —usually presumed to arise from the biological makeup or genetic programming of men.

In the alternative explanation of role conflict, the focus is more narrowly on the individual. There is a variation in masculinity, arising from individual experiences, that produces a range of personalities—ranging in one conception along a dimension from "hard" to "soft," in another from higher to lower levels of androgyny. Conflict arises when society demands that men try to live up to an impossible standard at the hard or gynephobic ends of the scales; this is "dysfunctional." The "male role" is unduly restrictive because hegemonic masculinity does *not* reflect the true nature of men. The assumption is of an essential self whose needs would be better met by a more relaxed existence nearer the soft or androgynous poles. In this argument, masculinity is fundamentally the social pressure that, internalized, prevents personal growth.

The role framework, then, depending on which way one pushes it, can lead to entirely opposite conclusions about the nature of masculinity. One is reminded of the wax nose mentioned by Marc Bloch, which can be bent either to the right or to the left.[62] Role theory in general and sex role theory in particular lacks a stable theoretical object; there is no way that these different lines of argument about masculinity can be forced to meet. As argued in detail elsewhere, this is a consequence of the logical structure of the role framework itself; it is internally incoherent.[63]

As social theory, the sex role framework is fundamentally static. This is not to say that it cannot recognize social change. Quite the contrary: change has been a leading theme in the discussion of men's sex roles by authors such as Pleck and Brannon.[64] The problem is that they cannot grasp it as history, as the interplay of praxis and structure. Change is always something that *happens to* sex roles, that impinges on them—whether from the direction of the society at large (as in discussions of how technological and economic change demands a shift to a "modern" male sex role) or from the direction of the asocial "real self" inside the person, demanding more room to breathe. Sex role theory cannot grasp change as a dialectic arising within gender relations themselves.

This is quite simply inherent in the procedure by which any account of "sex roles" is constructed: generalizing about sexual norms and then applying this frozen description to men's and women's lives. This is true even of the best role research. Komarovsky in *Blue Collar Marriage* gives a wonderful account of the tangled process of constructing a marriage, the sexual dilemmas, the struggles with in-laws over money and independence, and so on; and then describes this as "learning conjugal roles," as if the scripts were just sitting there waiting to be read. Because the framework ultimately takes sex roles for granted, it remains trapped within the ideological context of what it is attempting to analyze.

The result of using the role framework is an abstract view of the differences between the sexes and their situations, not a concrete one of the relations between them. As Franzway and Lowe observe in their critique of the use of sex role theory in feminism, the role literature focuses on attitudes and misses the realities that the attitudes are about.[65] The political effect is to highlight the attitudes and pressures that create an artificially rigid distinction between men and women and to play down the power that men exercise over women. (As some critics have observed, we do not speak of "race roles" or "class roles" because the exercise of power in these areas of social relations is more immediately evident to sociologists.) Where sex role analysis does recognize power it is usually in a very restricted context. Once again Komarovsky, because her field research is very good, provides a clear example. She recognizes power as a balance within marriage; her analysis of this is subtle and sophisticated. And she reports that in the cases where the wife had achieved dominance within the marriage, it was still not acceptable for this to be shown in public. But she cannot theorize this, though it is a very important point. The notion of the overall social subordination of women, institutionalized in the marital division of labor, but consistent with a fluctuating and occasionally reversed power situation in particular relationships, is not a conception that can be formulated in the language of role theory.

The consequence of the evasion and blurring of issues of power is, we feel, a persistent and serious misjudgment of the position of heterosexual men in the sexual politics of the advanced capitalist countries. The interpretation of oppression as over-rigid role requirements has been important in bolstering the idea, widely argued in the "men's movement" literature of the 1970s, that men in general stand to gain from women's liberation. This notion is naive at best, and at worst dishonest. The liberation of women must mean a loss of power for most men; and given the structuring of personality by power, also a great deal of personal pain. The sex role literature fairly systematically evades the facts of men's resistance to change in the distribution of power, in the sexual division of labor, and in masculinity itself, a point about which we shall have more to say in a moment.

The role framework, then, is neither a conceptually stable nor a practically and empirically adequate basis for the analysis of masculinity. Let us be blunt about it. The "male sex role" does not exist. It is impossible to isolate a "role" that constructs masculinity (or another that constructs femininity). Because there is no area of social life that is not the arena of sexual differentiation and gender relations, the notion of a sex role necessarily simplifies and abstracts to an impossible degree.

What should be put in its place? Partly that question is unanswerable; the only thing that can occupy the conceptual and political place of sex role theory is sex role theory itself. It has a particular intellectual pedigree. It is connected with a definite politics (liberal feminism and its "men's movement" offshoot), to which it supplies answers that seem to satisfy. And it is, of course, now institutionalized in academia and plays a very material part in many academic careers. Nothing else will do just that.

But we may still ask for alternatives in another sense. We have argued that the questions that were posed in the language of role theory and in the rhetoric of the "men's movement" are real and important questions. If so, they should arise in other approaches to gender relations and sexual politics, though they may take a different shape there.

## Resistance and Psychoanalysis

How are we to understand the deep-seated resistance to change in masculinity that has become steadily more evident since the mid-1970s? As we have noted, the sex role literature mainly analyzes the acquisition of masculinity by means of a simple social-learning, conformity-to-norms, model. This gives no grip on the general question of resistance, let alone such specifics as the violence experienced by gay men and many women at the hands of heterosexual men. (Both of these are notable absences in one of the rare discussions of men's resistance, by Goode, which remains staunchly optimistic that men will finally accept the equality of women despite being unable to find very much evidence of such a tendency at present.)[66] But since Parsons's work thirty years ago, role literature has had available a more complex and powerful tool for work on this issue, psychoanalysis.

It is instructive to see what has become of this. Parsons himself made a very selective reading of Freud, taking the theory of the oedipus complex as the psychological side of role differentiation in the family and leaving out much of the emotional complexity Freud had documented within masculinity.[67] Later sex role theorists have taken even less. On the whole they have simply ignored psychoanalytic work on gender. The influences of the "growth movement" on the masculinity literature of the 1970s is part of this story: there is no room for the unconscious, let alone intractable unconscious conflict, within its woolly-minded voluntarism. Another part is the blinkering effect of the research conventions in role research: if you can't measure it, then it can't exist. Some sex role theorists, such as Pleck, are however quite explicit about the expulsion of depth psychology from the domain of their argument.[68]

There has been rather more receptiveness to psychoanalysis in accounts of masculinity given by writers on the political left, though not very much clarity. Tolson has a rather confused reference to the oedipal relationship between father and son. Hoch presents a sub-Reichian argument about the links between capitalism, sexual repression, and the production of masculinity that is so scrambled it is difficult to take seriously. Psychoanalytic ideas appear and disappear more or less randomly in the French men's movement treatise *Holy Virility* by Reynaud.[69]

Zaretsky provides a more substantial account in a paper called "Male Supremacy and the Unconscious." To our knowledge, he is the only author to consider what Mitchell's interpretation of Freud might mean for the psychology of masculinity. While his treatment of "male supremacy" is fairly cursory, Zaretsky usefully marshals Freud's explicit arguments about the unconscious workings of masculinity. The three main ones concern men's disparagement of women as castrates, the structured tension in masculinity between love and desire, and the high level of resistance among men to expressing passive attitudes toward other men. Quite how this picture fits into a broader conception of masculinity as a continuous process with variable expressions Zaretsky does not ask; but he does provide a clear case for the relevance of psychoanalysis for making psychological sense of masculinity.[70]

The more imaginative use of Freudian concepts has been by feminist women, among whom psychoanalysis came into widespread use in the 1970s as a tool for the analysis of femininity. Chesler suggests one line of thought on masculinity, though only in very general terms: a connection between fear of the father, male-to-male violence, and the subordination of women as a way of absorbing that violence.[71] Stockard and Johnson argue for a different emphasis. In a brief survey of psychoanalytic work they distinguish a "gynecentric" approach, which takes the construction of masculinity to be problematic, from a "phallocentric" approach (illustrated by Mitchell and Rubin), which stresses instead the problematic nature of femininity. Stockard and Johnson emphasize a connection between the exclusive care of children by women and men's subsequent difficulty in establishing a masculine identity after their initial "feminine" identification—an argument in some ways reminiscent of Sexton's. But they argue that there is a general reaction from this. Men's urge to domination is thus a result of their assertion of a tenuous identity in the face of a continuing fear of the power of the mother and their envy of women's reproductive capacity.[72]

The most detailed feminist argument moves away from the high but cloudy territory of men's lust for power to the concrete reality of diaper changing. Chodorow's *The Reproduction of Mothering* is an ambitious synthesis of psychoanalysis and sociology that attempts to explain why men do not mother, as well as why women do. The argument involves her in developing a general theory of the production of masculinity, drawing mainly on the "object relations" school of psychoanalysis. Given primary parenting by women, the rupture of the little boy's primary identification with his mother (in contrast to the continuity of the girl's) is central to the emotional dynamics of adult masculinity. It produces a personality with reduced capacity for relationships, stronger ego boundaries, and less motive to find completeness in constructing new relationships with the young. The family sexual division of labor in child care thus reproduces itself from one generation to another by the formation of gender personalities.[73]

On this point, as on others, the similarity to Parsons's argument is quite striking. The difference is mainly in the evaluations. Chodorow infers from the analysis that a changed sexual division of labor in child care is crucial to any strategy for major change in masculinity or femininity. Much the same criticisms can be made of her argument as of Parsons's, the concentration on a normative standard case in particular. It is therefore appropriate to turn to what is emphatically not a normative standard case and look at the analysis of masculinity offered by homosexual men.

### Gay Liberation and the Understanding of Masculinity

The masculinity literature before women's liberation was frankly hostile to homosexuality, or at best very wary of the issue. What is post-women's-liberation is also post-gay-liberation. Gay activists were the first contemporary group of men to address the problem of hegemonic masculinity outside of a clinical context. They were the first group of men to apply the political techniques of women's liberation and to align themselves with feminists on issues of sexual politics—in fact to argue for the importance of sexual politics.

As we noted earlier, none of the 1970s books-about-men made a serious attempt to get to grips with gay liberation arguments, or to reckon with the fact that mainstream masculinity is heterosexual masculinity. Nor did the "men's movement" publicists ever write about the fact that beside them was another group of men active in sexual politics, or discuss their methods, concerns, or problems. The reason is obvious enough. Homosexuality is a theoretical embarrassment to sociobiologists and social-learning theorists alike, and a practical embarrassment to the "men's movement." How they got away with it is another matter. It required them to avert their gaze not only from gay liberation but also from contemporary developments in women's liberation (Jill Johnston's *Lesbian Nation* came out in 1973, for instance) and from basic concepts in the analysis of sexuality (notably the theory of bisexuality).[74]

The gay movement has been centrally concerned with masculinity as part of its critique of the political structure of sexuality. In this, it should be noted, the contemporary movement represents a distinct break with previous forms of homosexual activism. It has gone well beyond earlier campaigns for the social rights of homosexual people and the accompanying efforts to foster tolerance in the heterosexual population toward a "sexual minority." Instead, gay liberationists attacked the social practices and psychological assumptions surrounding gender relations, for a prominent theme in their arguments is an attempt to explain the sources of homosexual oppression in these terms. The British gay liberation newspaper *Come Together* declared in 1970:

> We recognize that the oppression that gay people suffer is an integral part of the social structure of our society. Women and gay people are both victims of the cultural and ideological phenomenon known as sexism. This is manifested in our culture as male supremacy and heterosexual chauvinism.[75]

Activists argued that homosexual people were severely penalized by a social system that enforced the subservience of women to men and that propagated an ideology of the "natural" differences between the sexes. The denial and fear of homosexuality were an integral part of this ideology because homosexuals were seen to contradict the accepted characteristics of men and women and the complementarity of the sexes that is institutionalized within the family and many other areas of social life.[76]

Not surprisingly then, the gay movement has been particularly critical of psychiatric definitions of homosexuality as a pathology and of the concern with "curing" homosexuals, a phenomenon of twentieth-century medicine marked by both theoretical incoherence and practical failure. Activists readily observed the ways in which notions such as "gender inversion" were a transparent rationalization of the prevailing relationship between men and women. For the whole medical model of homosexuality rested upon a belief in the biological (or occasionally socially functional) determination of heterosexual masculinity and femininity. The gay-liberation tactic in this and many other areas was one of a defiant reversal of the dominant sexual ideology. In affirming a homosexual identity, many gay liberationists embraced the charge of effeminacy and declared that the real problem lay in the rigid social definitions of masculinity. It was society, not themselves, that needed to be cured.[77]

For some, this led to experiments with what was known as "radical drag." An American activist declared, "There is more to be learned from wearing a dress for a day than there is from wearing a suit for life."[78] The point was not to imitate a glamorous image of stereotypical femininity (à la Danny La Rue or Les Girls), but to combine feminine images with masculine ones, such as a dress with a beard. The aim was described as gender confusion, and it was advocated as a means both for personal liberation from the prescriptions of hegemonic masculinity and for subverting the accepted gender categories by demonstrating their social basis, as indicated by its technical name, a "gender fuck." Radical drag was hardly an effective strategy for social change, but it contained far more political insight than did the notion of androgyny that was beginning to be popularized by sex role theorists at about the same time.

To understand gay liberation's political responses, we should observe how the gender dichotomy acts to define homosexual men not only as "outside" patriarchal sexual relations but "within" them as well. In the first case, as we have just noted, homosexual men are penalized for failing to meet the criteria of masculinity and are told that they are weak, effeminate, maladjusted, and so on. But they have often been defined "within" patriarchal sexual relations by being divided into "active" and "passive" types. Gay activists argued very strenuously that when homosexual men consequently organized a relationship in terms of husband and wife "roles," they were expressing self-hatred in a futile attempt to win heterosexual tolerance. More centrally, activists attacked sexual "role playing" or concepts of oneself as "butch" or "femme." The objection was not simply that this was sexist and bizarrely conformist; there was an agonizing personal trap for homosexual men in such a conception.

If a man identified himself as "femme," could he ever be satisfied to love a "butch" partner who returned his love? Would not a "real" man love only women (the homosexual "tragedy" explored by Proust and to an extent also by Genet)? The gay-liberation response was to urge homosexual men to love each other and to direct considerable criticism and satire at the masculine posturing of straight men. In these terms, the assertion of a strong gay identity that incorporates a confidence that homosexual men are perfectly capable of giving each other sexual pleasure is an attack on the power of heterosexual men.

The gay movement, then, did not speak only to homosexual people. A common sentiment, especially in the early days of the movement, was that "every straight man is a target for gay liberation." Activists often drew on Freud's conviction of universal bisexuality and claimed that heterosexual men suffered from their repressed homosexual desire; to reject it they had constantly to prove their manliness, which resulted in their oppression of women.

There are serious theoretical problems in these early gay-liberation arguments, but their significance remains. Consider this contrast. Quentin Crisp has described his conviction during the inter-war years that to have sexual relations with a man he desired would destroy the relationship; that man would have revealed a fatal flaw in his masculinity.[79] Forty years later, gay liberationists had sexual relations, on occasion, with heterosexual men who in this way hoped to liberate their repressed homosexuality and to prove they were politically on side. This is a minor, though striking, aspect of a larger process in which gay liberationists have contested the power in gender relations; a process in which resistance among homosexual men has been generated and in which identities have changed.

The most general significance of the gay-liberation arguments (and no doubt a central reason that the "men's movement" ignored them) was that they challenged the assumptions by which heterosexuality is taken for granted as the natural order of things. It is, for example, a fundamental element of modern hegemonic masculinity that one sex (women) exists as potential sexual object, while the other sex (men) is negated as a sexual object. It is women, therefore, who provide heterosexual men with sexual validation, whereas men exist as rivals in both sexual and other spheres of life. The gay-liberation perspective emphasized that the institutionalization of heterosexuality, as in the family, was achieved only by considerable effort, and at considerable cost not only to homosexual people but also to women and children. It is, then, precisely within heterosexuality as it is at present organized that a central dimension of the power that men exercise over women is to be found.

The gay movement's theoretical work, by comparison with the "sex role" literature and "men's movement" writings, had a much clearer understanding of the reality of men's power over women, and it had direct implications for any consideration of the hierarchy of power among men. Pleck was one of the few writers outside gay liberation to observe that the homosexual/heterosexual dichotomy acts as a central symbol in *all* rankings of masculinity. Any kind of powerlessness or refusal to compete among men readily becomes involved with the imagery of homosexuality.[80]

What emerges from this line of argument is the very important concept of hegemonic masculinity, not as "the male role," but as a particular variety of masculinity to which others—among them young and effeminate as well as homosexual men—are subordinated. It is particular groups of men, not men in general, who are oppressed within patriarchal sexual relations and whose situations are related in different ways to the overall logic of the subordination of women to men. A consideration of homosexuality thus provides the beginnings of a dynamic conception of masculinity as a structure of social relations.

Gay liberation arguments further strengthen a dynamic approach to masculinity by providing some important insights into the historical character of gender relations. Homosexuality is a historically specific phenomenon, and the fact that it is socially organized becomes clear once we distinguish between homosexual behavior and a homosexual identity. While some kind of homosexual behavior may be universal, this does not automatically entail the existence of self-identified or publicly labeled "homosexuals." In fact, the latter are unusual enough to require a historical explanation. Jeffrey Weeks and others have argued that in Western Europe, male homosexuality did not gain its characteristically modern meaning and social organization until the late nineteenth century.[81] That period witnessed the advent of new medical categorizations, homosexuality being defined as a pathology by the German psychiatrist Westphal in 1870. There were also new legal proscriptions, so that all male homosexual behavior was subject to legal sanctions in Britain by the end of the century (one of the first victims of these laws being Oscar Wilde). Such medical and legal discourses underlined a new conception of the homosexual as a specific type of person in contrast to the older one of homosexuality as merely a potential in the lustful nature of all men— or indeed a potential for disorder in the cosmos.[82] Correspondingly, men with same-sex preferences had more reason than previously to think of themselves as separate and distinct; and the homosexual subculture of the time in cities such as London gained its recognizably modern form.

These developments have yet to be fully explained. But they do highlight an important change in gender relations. It is clear that the early medical categorizations of homosexuality usually relied upon the idea of gender inversion, and what is known of the early homosexual subcultures (say in the "Molly houses" of London from the late seventeenth century[83]) suggests that they were characterized by a high degree of effeminacy and what is now known as "transvestism." Thus the emergence of both the medical discourses on homosexuality and the corresponding self-conception of homosexuals in the nineteenth century need to be related to particular social conceptions of masculinity and the process of its social reorganization. Just as "the housewife," "the prostitute," and "the child" are historically specific "types" that should be understood in the context of gender relations of the time, so too "the homosexual" is the modern definition of a new "type" of adult male. It was a man who was classified as an invert and who, frequently at least, understood himself to possess a "woman's soul in a man's body."

The subsequent career of the category of homosexuality and of the identities of homosexual men similarly point to broader changes in masculinity. For the idea of inversion has now been theoretically discredited, and male homosexuals generally identify themselves as men (however problematic they may find the general social elaboration of masculinity). The changes that have taken place in the definition of the gender of homosexual men, in their own identities, and in the level of their oppression need to be understood in the light of changes in the general power relationship between men and women. The "social space" that homosexuals at present occupy and that the gay movement has struggled to expand reflects a contestation of the subordination of women to men. For it is now possible to depart publicly from the prescriptions of hegemonic masculinity without being defined, and accepting oneself, as "really" a woman. Homosexual relationships are now much less marked, to borrow Rubin's terms, by the rules of the gender division and obligatory heterosexuality.[84] The distinctions between the "invert"/"pervert," the "active"/"passive," and the "masculine"/"feminine" homosexual man, all of which acted to give heterosexual meaning to an anomalous relationship, have lost their former salience. So long as a very rigid distinction is maintained between the social categories of "man" and "woman," there is relatively little space in which homosexual men can exist; the very idea of a homosexual man may be inconceivable if "man" is a strictly heterosexual category. Thus it can scarcely be an accident that the first wave of feminism in nineteenth-century Europe was accompanied by some substantial efforts to achieve the emancipation of homosexuals, just as over the past fifteen years there has been an indispensable link between the gay and women's movements.

The emerging history of male homosexuality, then, offers the most valuable starting point we have for constructing a historical perspective on masculinity at large. The technical superiority of the work of gay historians over the histories of masculinity and the "male role" to be found in works like Hoch, Dubbert, Stearns, and Pleck and Pleck, is so marked as to be embarrassing. Conceptually, gay history moves decisively away from the conception underlying those works, that the history of masculinity is the story of the modulation, through time, of the expressions of a more or less fixed entity.[85]

The history of homosexuality obliges us to think of masculinity, not as a single object with its own history, but as being constantly constructed within the history of an evolving social structure, a structure of sexual power relations. It obliges us to see this construction as a social struggle going on in a complex ideological and political field, in which there is a continuing process of mobilization, contestation, resistance, and subordination. It forces us to recognize the importance of violence, not as an expression of subjective values or of a type of masculinity, but as a constitutive practice that helps to make all kinds of masculinity—and to recognize that much of this violence comes from the state, so that the historical construction of masculinity and femininity is also a struggle for the control and direction of state power. Finally it is an important corrective to the tendency, in left-wing thought especially, to subordinate the history of gender to the history of capitalism. The making of modern homosexuality is plainly connected to the development of industrial capitalism, but equally clearly it has its own dynamic.

OUTLINE OF A SOCIAL ANALYSIS OF MASCULINITY

## Men in the Framework of Gender Relations

The starting point for any understanding of masculinity that is not simply biologistic or subjective must be men's involvement in the social relations that constitute the gender order. In a classic article Rubin has defined the domain of the argument as "the sex/gender system," a patterning of social relations connected with reproduction and gender division that is found in all societies, though in varying shapes.[86] This system is historical, in the fullest sense; its elements and relationships are constructed in history and are all subject to historical change.[87] It is also internally differentiated, as Mitchell argued more than a decade ago.[88] Two aspects of its organization have been the foci of research in the past decade: the division of labor and the structure of power. (The latter is what Millett originally called "sexual politics,"[89] and is the more precise referent of the concept "patriarchy.") To these we must add the structure of cathexis, the social organization of sexuality and attraction—which as the history of homosexuality demonstrates is fully as social as the structures of work and power.

The central fact about this structure in the contemporary capitalist world (like most other social orders, though not all) is the subordination of women. This fact is massively documented and has enormous ramifications—physical, mental, interpersonal, cultural—whose effects on the lives of women have been the major concerns of feminism. One of the central facts about masculinity, then, is that men in general are advantaged through the subordination of women.

To say "men in general" is already to point to an important complication in power relations. The global subordination of women is consistent with many particular situations in which women hold power over men or are at least equal. Close-up research on families shows a good many households where wives hold authority in practice.[90] The fact of mothers' authority over young sons has been noted in most discussions of the psychodynamics of masculinity. The intersections of gender relations with class and race relations yield many other situations where rich white heterosexual women, for instance, are employers of working-class men, patrons of homosexual men, or politically dominant over black men.

To cite such examples and claim that women are therefore not subordinated in general would be crass. The point is, rather, that contradictions between local situations and the global relationships are endemic. They are likely to be a fruitful source of turmoil and change in the structure as a whole.

The overall relations between men and women, further, are not a confrontation between homogeneous, undifferentiated blocs. Our argument has perhaps established this sufficiently by now; even some role theorists, notably Hacker,[91] recognized a range of masculinities. We would suggest, in fact, that the fissuring of the categories of "men" and "women" is one of the central facts about a patriarchal power and the way it works. In the case of men, the crucial division is between hegemonic masculinity and various subordinated masculinities.

Even this, however, is too simple a phrasing, for it suggests a masculinity differentiated only by power relations. If the general remarks about the gender system made above are correct, it follows that masculinities are constructed not just by power relations but by their interplay with a division of labor and with patterns of emotional attachment. For example, as Bray has clearly shown, the character of men's homosexuality, and of its regulation by the state, is very different in the mercantile city from what it was in the pre-capitalist countryside.[92]

The differentiation of masculinities is psychological—it bears on the kind of people that men are and become—but it is not only psychological. In an equally important sense it is institutional, an aspect of collective practice. In a notable recent study of British printing workers, Cynthia Cockburn has shown how a definition of compositors' work as hypermasculine has been sustained despite enormous changes in technology.[93] The key was a highly organized practice that drove women out of the trade, marginalized related labor processes in which they remained, and sustained a strongly marked masculine "culture" in the workplace. What was going on here, as many details of her study show, was the collective definition of a hegemonic masculinity that not only manned the barricades against women but at the same time marginalized or subordinated other men in the industry (e.g., young men, unskilled workers, and those unable or unwilling to join the rituals). Though the details vary, there is every reason to think such processes are very general. Accordingly we see social definitions of masculinity as being embedded in the dynamics of institutions—the working of the state, of corporations, of unions, of families—quite as much as in the personality of individuals.

## Forms of Masculinity and Their Interrelationships

In some historical circumstances, a subordinated masculinity can be produced collectively as a well-defined social group and a stable social identity, with some well-recognized traits at the personal level. A now familiar case in point is the "making of the modern homosexual" (to use Plummer's phrase[94]) in the late nineteenth and early twentieth centuries. One aspect of the collective process here was a change in forms of policing that criminalized homosexuality as such, creating a criminal sexual "type." And one aspect of the psychological process was the creation of "camp" personal style, both internalizing and sardonically transforming the new medical and clinical definition of the homosexual as a type of person.

In other circumstances, a subordinated masculinity may be a transient identity. The printing apprentices in Cockburn's study provide one example of this. Another is provided by the New Guinea culture studied by Herdt, where younger men gain their masculinity through ritualized homosexuality under the guardianship of older men.[95] In other cases again, the collective and individual processes do not correspond. There may be stable enough personalities and configurations of motive produced, which for various reasons do not receive a clear social definition. A historic case of this is the vague social identity of English homosexuality before the advent of "Molly" at the end of the seventeenth century. Closer to home, another example would seem to be the various forms of effeminate heterosexual masculinity being produced today. There are attempts to give such masculinities an identity: for instance by commercial exploitation of hippie styles of dress and by conservative transvestite organizations such as the Beaumont Society (in the UK) or the Seahorse Club (in Australia). But for the most part there is no very clear social definition of heterosexual effeminacy. It is popularly assimilated to a gay identity when it is noticed at all—an equation its publicists furiously but unavailingly protest.

The ability to impose a particular definition on other kinds of masculinity is part of what we mean by "hegemony." Hegemonic masculinity is far more complex than the accounts of essences in the masculinity books would suggest. It is not a "syndrome" of the kind produced when sexologists like Money reify human behavior into a "condition"[96] or when clinicians reify homosexuality into a pathology. It is, rather, a question of how particular groups of men inhabit positions of power and wealth and how they legitimate and reproduce the social relationships that generate their dominance.

An immediate consequence of this is that the culturally exalted form of masculinity, the hegemonic model so to speak, may only correspond to the actual characters of a small number of men. On this point at least the "men's liberation" literature had a sound insight. There is a distance and a tension between collective ideal and actual lives. Most men do not really act like the screen image of John Wayne or Humphrey Bogart; and when they try to, it is likely to be thought comic (as in the Woody Allen movie *Play It Again, Sam*) or horrific (as in shoot-outs and "sieges"). Yet very large numbers of men are responsible for sustaining the hegemonic model. There are various reasons: gratification through fantasy, compensation through displaced aggression (e.g., gay bashing by police and working-class youths), etc. But the overwhelmingly important reason is that most men benefit from the subordination of women, and hegemonic masculinity is centrally connected with the institutionalization of men's dominance over women. It would hardly be an exaggeration to say that hegemonic masculinity is hegemonic insofar as it embodies a successful strategy in relation to women.

This strategy is necessarily modified in different classes, a point that can be documented in the research already mentioned on relationships inside families. A contemporary ruling-class family is organized around the corporate or professional career of the husband. In a typical case the well-groomed wife is subordinated, not by being under the husband's thumb—he isn't in the house most of the time—but by her task of making sure his home life runs on wheels to support his self-confidence, his career advancement, and their collective income. In working-class homes, to start with, there is no "career"; the self-esteem of men is eroded rather than inflated in the workplace. For a husband to be dominant in the home is likely to require an assertion of authority without a technical basis; hence a reliance on traditional ideology (religion or ethnic culture) or on force. The working man who gets drunk and belts his wife when she doesn't hold her tongue and belts his son to make a man of him, is by no means a figure of fiction.[97]

To think of this as "working-class authoritarianism" and see the ruling-class family as more liberal would be to mistake the nature of power. Both are forms of patriarchy, and the husbands in both cases are enacting a hegemonic masculinity. But the situations in which they do so are very different, their responses are not exactly the same, and their impact on wives and children is likely to vary a good deal.

The most important feature of this masculinity, alongside its connection with dominance, is that it is heterosexual. Though most literature on the family and masculinity takes this entirely for granted, it should not. Psychoanalytic evidence goes far to show that conventional adult heterosexuality is constructed, in the individual life, as one among a number of possible paths through the emotional forest of childhood and adolescence. It is now clear that this is also true at the collective level, that the pattern of exclusive adult hetero-sexuality is a historically constructed one. Its dominance is by no means universal. For this to become the hegemonic form of masculine sexuality required a historic redefinition of sexuality itself, in which undifferentiated "lust" was turned into specific types of "perversion"—the process that is documented, from the under side, by the historians of homosexuality already mentioned. A passion for beautiful boys was compatible with hegemonic masculinity in renaissance Europe, but it was emphatically not at the end of the nineteenth century. In this historical shift, men's sexual desire was to be focused more closely on women—a fact with complex consequences for them—while groups of men who were visibly not following the hegemonic pattern were more specifically labeled and attacked. So powerful was this shift that even men of the ruling classes found wealth and reputation no protection. It is interesting to contrast the experiences of the Chevalier d'Eon, who managed an active career in diplomacy while dressed as a woman (in a later era he would have been labeled a "transvestite"), with that of Oscar Wilde a hundred years later.

"Hegemony," then, always refers to a historical situation, a set of circumstances in which power is won and held. The construction of hegemony is not a matter of pushing and pulling between ready-formed groupings, but is partly a matter of the *formation* of those groupings. To understand the different kinds of masculinity demands, above all, an examination of the practices in which hegemony is constituted and contested—in short, the political techniques of the patriarchal social order.

This is a large enterprise, and we can only note a few points about it here. First, hegemony means persuasion, and one of its important sites is likely to be the commercial mass media. An examination of advertising, for instance, shows a number of ways in which images of masculinity are constructed and put to work: amplifying the sense of virility, creating anxiety and giving reassurance about being a father, playing games with stereotypes (men washing dishes), and so on.[98] Studying versions of masculinity in Australian mass media, Glen Lewis points to an important qualification to the usual conception of media influence.[99] Commercial television in fact gives a lot of airplay to "soft" men, in particular slots such as hosts of daytime quiz shows. What comes across is by no means unrelieved machismo; the inference is that television companies think their audiences would not like that.

Second, hegemony closely involves the division of labor, the social definition of tasks as either "men's work" or "women's work," and the definition of some kinds of work as more masculine than others. Here is an important source of tension between the gender order and the class order, as heavy manual labor is generally felt to be more masculine than white-collar and professional work (though perhaps not management).[100] Third, the negotiation and enforcement of hegemony involves the state. The criminalization of male homosexuality as such was a key move in the construction of the modern form of hegemonic masculinity. Attempts to reassert it after the struggles of the last twenty years, for instance by fundamentalist right-wing groups in the United States, are very much addressed to the state— attempting to get homosexual people dismissed as public school teachers, for instance, or to erode court protection for civil liberties. Much more subtly, the existence of a skein of welfare rules, tax concessions, and so on that advantage people living in conventional conjugal households and disadvantage others,[101] creates economic incentives to conform to the hegemonic pattern.

*Psychodynamics*

To argue that masculinity and femininity are produced historically is entirely at odds with the view that sees them as settled by biology, and thus as being pre-social categories. It is also at odds with the now most common view of gender, which sees it as a social elaboration, amplification, or perhaps exaggeration of the biological fact of sex—where biology says "what" and society says "how." Certainly, the biological facts of maleness and femaleness are central to the matter; human reproduction is a major part of what defines the "sex/gender system." But all kinds of questions can be raised about the nature of the relation between biology and the social. The facts of anatomical and physiological variation should caution us against assuming that biology presents society with clear-cut categories of people. More generally, it should not be assumed that the relation is one of continuity.

We would suggest that the evidence about masculinity, and gender relations at large, makes more sense if we recognize that the social practice of gender arises—to borrow some terminology from Sartre— in *contradiction* to the biological statute.[102] It is precisely the property of human sociality that it transcends biological determination. To transcend is not to ignore: the bodily dimension remains a presence within the social practice, not as a "base," but as an object of practice. Masculinity invests the body. Reproduction is a question of strategies. Social relations continuously take account of the body and biological process and interact with them. "Interact" should be given its full weight. For our knowledge of the biological dimension of sexual difference is itself predicated on the social categories, as the startling research of Kessler and McKenna makes clear.[103]

Sexuality and desire are constituted in the field of this interaction, being both bodily pain and pleasure, and social injunction and prohibition. Where Freud saw the history of this interaction only as a strengthening prohibition by an undifferentiated "society," and Marcuse as the by-product of class exploitation,[104] we must now see the construction of the unconscious as the field of play of a number of historically developing power relations and gender practices. Their interactions constitute masculinities and femininities as particular patterns of cathexis.

Freud's work with his male patients produced the first systematic evidence of one key feature of this patterning. The repressions and attachments are not necessarily homogeneous. The psychoanalytic exploration of masculinity means diving through layers of emotion that may be flagrantly contradictory. For instance in the "Wolf Man" case history,[105] the classic of the genre, Freud found a promiscuous heterosexuality, a homosexual and passive attachment to the father, and an identification with women, all psychologically present though subject to different levels of repression. Without case-study evidence, many recent authors have speculated about the degree of repression that goes into the construction of dominant forms of masculinity: the sublimated homosexuality in the cult of sport, repressed identification with the mother, and so on. Homosexual masculinity as a pattern of cathexis is no less complex, as we see for instance in Genet. If texts like *Our Lady of the Flowers* are, as Sartre claims, masturbatory fantasies,[106] they are an extraordinary guide to a range and pattern of cathexes—from the hard young criminal to Divine herself—that show, among other things, that Genet's homosexuality is far from a mere "inversion" of heterosexual object-choice.

In this perspective the unconscious emerges as a field of politics, and not just in the sense that a conscious political practice can address it or that practices that do address it must have a politics, as argued (against Freud) by the Red Collective in Britain.[107] More generally, the organization of desire is the domain of relations of power. When writers of the books-about-men speak of "the wisdom of the penis" (H. Goldberg thinks the masculine ideal is a rock-hard erection), or when they dilate on its existential significance ("a firm erection on a delicate fellow was the adventurous juncture of ego and courage"— Mailer), they have grasped an important point, though they have not quite got to the root of it. What is at issue here is power over women.

This is seen by some authors, such as Lippert in an excellent paper exploring the connections of the male-supremacist sexuality of American automobile workers with the conditions of factory work. Bednarik's suggestion about the origins of popular sadism in the commercialization of sex and the degradation of working life is a more complex case of how the lines of force might work.[108]

The psychodynamics of masculinity, then, are not to be seen as a separate issue from the social relations that invest and construct masculinity. An effective analysis will work at both levels; and an effective political practice must attempt to do so too.

## Transformations

An "effective political practice" implies something that can be worked on and transformed. The question of transformation and its possibilities, sources, and strategies should be central to the analysis of masculinity.

It has had a very ambiguous status in the literature so far. The "male role" literature has spoken a lot about changes in the role, but has had no very clear account of how they come about. Indeed this literature generally implies, without arguing the point very explicitly, that once a man has been socialized to his role, that is more or less the end of it. On the other side, the gay movement, in its contest with psychiatrists who wished to "cure" homosexuality, has had its own reasons for claiming that homosexual masculinity, once formed, is settled.

The strength of sexual desire as a motive is one reason why a pattern of cathexis may remain stable for most of a lifetime. Such stability can be found even in the most implausible patterns of cathexis, as the literature of sexual fetishism has abundantly shown, ever since Krafft-Ebing introduced his middle-European hair, handkerchief, corset, and shoe enthusiasts back in the 1880s.[109] Yet the strength of desire can also be a mighty engine of change, when caught up in contradiction. And as the last two sections have suggested, contradiction is in fact endemic in the processes that construct masculinity.

The psychodynamics of change in masculinity is a question that so far has attracted little attention. There is one exception: the highly publicized, indeed sensationalized, case of male-to-female "transsexuals." Even this case has not brought the question quite into focus, because the transsexuals are mostly saying they are really women and their bodies should be adjusted to match, while their opponents say their bodies show they are really men and their psyches should be adjusted to match. Both look on masculinity and femininity as pure essences, though of different kinds. Roberta Perkins's fascinating study shows the true situation is much more complex.[110] The conviction of being really a woman may grow, rather than being present from the start. It may not be complete; ambiguity and uncertainty are common. Those who push on must negotiate their way out of the social position of being a man and into that of being a woman, a process liable to corrode family relationships, lose jobs, and attract police attention. (The social supports of conventional masculine identities are very much in evidence.) Sexual ambiguity is exciting to many people, and one way of surviving—if one's physique allows it— is to become a transsexual prostitute or show girl. But this tends to create a new gender category—one becomes known as "a transsexual"—rather than making a smooth transition into femininity. There is, in short, a complex interplay between motive and social circumstance; masculinity cannot be abandoned all at once, nor without pain.

Although very few are involved in a process as dramatic and traumatic as that, a good many men feel themselves to be involved in some kind of change having to do with gender, with sexual identity, with what it is to be a man. The "androgyny" literature of the late 1970s spoke to this in one way, the literature about the importance of fathering in another.[111] We have already seen some reasons to doubt that the changes discussed were as decisive as the "men's movement" proclaimed. But it seems clear enough that there have been recent changes in the constitution of masculinity in advanced capitalist countries, of at least two kinds: a deepening of tensions around relationships with women, and the crisis of a form of heterosexual masculinity that is increasingly felt to be obsolete.

The psychodynamics of these processes remain obscure; we still lack the close-up research that would illuminate them. What is happening on the larger scale is somewhat clearer. Masculinities are constituted, we argued above, within a structure of gender relations that has a historical dynamic as a whole This is not to say it is a neatly defined and closely integrated system—the false assumption made by Parsons, Chodorow, and a good many others.[112] This would take for granted what is currently being fought for. The dominion of men over women and the supremacy of particular groups of men over others are sought by constantly reconstituting gender relations as a system within which that dominance is generated. Hegemonic masculinity might be seen as what would function automatically if the strategy were entirely successful. But it never does function automatically.

The project is contradictory, the conditions for its realization are constantly changing, and, most importantly, there is resistance from the groups being subordinated. The violence in gender relations is not part of the essence of masculinity (as Fasteau, Nichols, and Reynaud, as well as many radical feminists, present it)[113] so much as a measure of the bitterness of this struggle.

The emergence of women's liberation at the end of the 1960s was, as feminists are now inclined to see it, the heightening of a resistance that is much older and has taken many other forms in the past. It did nevertheless represent two new and important things: first, the transformation of resistance into a liberation project addressed to the whole gender order; and second, a breakdown of masculine authority, if not in the society as a whole, at least in a substantial group, the younger professional intelligentsia of western cities. Though it has not widened its base as fast as activists expected, the new feminism has also not succumbed to the reaction that gained momentum in the late 1970s. Like gay liberation, it is here to stay; and at least in limited milieux the two movements have achieved some changes in power relations that are unlikely to be reversed.

This dynamic of sexual politics has met up with a change in class relations that also has implications for masculinity. In a very interesting paper, Winter and Robert suggest that some of the familiar economic and cultural changes in contemporary capitalism—the growth of large bureaucratized corporations, the integration of business and government, the shift to technocratic modes of decision making and control—have implications for the character of "male dominance."[114] We think they over-generalize, but at least they have pointed to an important conflict within and about hegemonic masculinity. Forms of masculinity well adapted to face-to-face conflict and the management of personal capital are not so well suited to the politics of organizations, to professionalism, to the management of strategic compromises and consensus.

One dimension of the recent politics of capitalism, then, is a struggle about the modernization of hegemonic masculinity. This has by no means gone all one way. The recent ascendancy of the hard-liners in the American ruling class has involved the systematic reassertion of old-fashioned models of masculinity (not to mention femininity—*vide* Nancy Reagan).

The politics of "men's liberation" and the search for androgyny have to be understood in this field of forces. They are, explicitly, a response to the new feminism—accepting feminism in a watered-down version, hoping that men could gain something from its advent. This required an evasion of the issue of power, and the limits were clearly marked by the refusal of any engagement with gay liberation. Yet there was an urgency about what the "men's movement" publicists were saying in the early 1970s, which drew its force partly from the drive for the modernization of hegemonic masculinity already going on in other forms.[115] The goal (to simplify a little) was to produce forms of masculinity able to adapt to new conditions, but sufficiently similar to the old ones to maintain the family, heterosexuality, capitalist work relations, and American national power (most of which are taken for granted in the books-about-men). The shift in the later 1970s that produced "Free Men" campaigning for fathers' rights and the ponderings of conservative ideologues like Stearns on how to revive intelligent paternalism is clearly connected with the anti-modernist movement in the American ruling class. This offered strategies for repairing men's authority in the face of the damage done by feminism, much as the Reagan foreign policy proposed to restore American hegemony internationally and monetarism proposed a drastic disciplining of the working class. The political appeal of the whole package—mainly to men, given the "gender gap"—is notable.

The triumph of these ideas is not inevitable. They are strategies, responding to dilemmas of practice, and they have their problems too. Other responses, other strategies, are also possible; among them much more radical ones. The ferment that was started by the new left, and that produced the counter-culture, the new feminism, gay liberation, and many attempts at communal households and collective child care, has also produced a good deal of quiet experimentation with masculinity and attempts to work out in practice unoppressive forms of heterosexuality. This is confined at present to a limited milieu, and has not had anything like the shape or public impact of the politics of liberation among gay men.

The moment of opportunity, as it appeared in the early 1970s, is past. There is no easy path to a major reconstruction of masculinity. Yet the initiative in sexual politics is not entirely in the hands of reaction, and the underlying tensions that produced the initiatives of ten years ago have not vanished. There are potentials for a more liberating politics, here and now. Not in the form of grand schemes of change, but at least in the form of coalitions among feminists, gay men, and progressive heterosexual men that have real chances of making gains on specific issues.

# NOTES

This article was originally published in *Theory and Society* 14 (1985): 551-603.

The authors are grateful for the help of Cynthia Hamilton, Helen Easson, Margaret Clarke and other secretarial staff of the School of Behavioural Sciences at Macquarie University; and for technical assistance from the staff of the Kuring-gai College of Advanced Education Resources Centre. The work was funded by a grant, "Theory of Class and Patriarchy," from the Australian Research Grants Scheme.

[1] B. Ehrenreich, *The Hearts of Men: American Dreams and the Flight from Commitment* (London: Pluto Press, 1983).

[2] V. Klein, *The Feminine Character: History of an Ideology* (London: Routledge and Kegan Paul, 1971), 17; first published 1946.

[3] L. Tyler, *The Psychology of Human Differences* (New York: Appleton Century Crofts, 1965), 240.

[4] R. Rosenberg, *Beyond Separate Spheres: Intellectual Roots of Modern Feminism* (New Haven, Conn.: Yale University Press, 1982).

[5] H. M. Hacker, "Women as a Minority Group," *Social Forces* 30 (October 1951): 60-9.

[6] T. Parsons, "Age and Sex in the Social Structure of the United States" in *Essays in Sociological Theory* (New York: The Free Press, 1964), 89-103; and, in the same volume, "The Kinship System of the Contemporary United States," 177-96.

[7] T. Parsons and R. F. Bales, *Family, Socialization and Interaction Process* (London: Routledge and Kegan Paul, 1953), 101.

[8] M. Komarovsky, "Cultural Contradictions and Sex Roles," *American Journal of Sociology* 52 (November 1946): 184-9; and Komarovsky, "Functional Analysis of Sex Roles," *American Sociology Review* 15 (August 1950): 508-16.

[9] M. Komarovsky, *Dilemmas of Masculinity* (New York: Norton, 1976), 7.

[10] See, for example, M. Komarovsky, "Presidential Address: Some Problems in Role Analysis," *American Sociological Review* 38 (December 1973): 649-62; M. Millman, "Observations on Sex Role Research," *Journal of Marriage and the Family* 33 (November 1971): 772-6; and E. Peal, "Normal Sex Roles: An Historical Analysis," *Family Process* 14 (September 1975): 389-409.

[11] See, for example, A. R. Edwards, "Sex Roles: A Problem for Sociology and for Women," *Australian and New Zealand Journal of Sociology* 19 (1983): 385-412; S. Franzway and J. Lowe, "Sex Role Theory, Political Cul-de-sac?" *Refractory Girl* 16 (1978): 14-16; M. Gould and R. Kern-Daniels, "Toward a Sociological Theory of Gender and Sex," *American Sociologist* 12 (November 1977): 182-9; and H. Z. Lopata and B. Thorne, "On the Term 'Sex Roles,' " *Signs* 3, (Spring 1978): 718-21.

[12] F. M. Thrasher, *The Gang* (Chicago: University of Chicago Press, 1927); W. F. Whyte, *Street Corner Society* (Chicago: University of Chicago Press, 1943).

[13] R. E. Hartley, "Sex Role Pressures in the Socialization of the Male Child," *Psychological Reports* 5 (1959): 458.

[14] D. Riesman, *The Lonely Crowd* (Garden City: Doubleday and Anchor Books, 1953).

[15] H. M. Hacker, "The New Burdens of Masculinity," *Marriage and Family Living* 19 (August 1957): 229.

[16] *Ibid.,* 231.

[17] *Ibid.,* 232.

[18] *Ibid.,* 231.

[19] K. Bednarik, *The Male in Crisis* (New York: Knopf, 1970).

[20] P. Sexton, *The Feminized Male* (New York: Random House, 1969), 15.

[21] *Ibid.,* 204.

[22] L. Tiger, *Men in Groups* (London: Nelson, 1969), 209.

[23] M. Komarovsky, *Blue Collar Marriage* (New York: Vintage, 1964).

[24] H. Fallding, "Inside the Australian Family" in A. P. Elkin, ed., *Marriage and the Family in Australia* (Sydney: Angus and Robertson, 1957); E. Bott, *Family and Social Network* (London: Tavistock, 1957).

[25]K. E. Grady, R. Brannon and J. H. Pleck, *The Male Sex Role: A Selected and Annotated Bibliography* (Rockville, Md: U.S. Dept. of Health, Education and Welfare, 1979); Massachusetts Institute of Technology Humanities Library, *Men's Studies Bibliography;* 4th ed. (Cambridge: *MIT,* 1979).

[26]J. O. Balswick, "The Inexpressive Male: A Tragedy of American Society" (paper at meeting of American Sociological Association, 1970); C.E. Lewis and M.A. Lewis, "The Potential Impact of Sexual Equality on Health," *New England Journal of Medicine* 297 (October 1977): 863-9; J. K. Burgess-Kohn, "A Note on Role Changes that Prepare Men for the Ageing Process," *Winconsin Sociologist* 13 (1976): 85-90; P.J. Stein and S. Hoffman, "Sports and Male Role Strain," *Journal of Social Issues* 34 (Winter 1978): 136-50; A.E. Gross, "The Male Role and Heterosexual Behaviour," *Journal of Social Issues* 34 (Winter 1978): 87-107.

[27]E. Vilar, *The Manipulated Man* (New York: Farrar, Strauss and Giroux, 1972), 110.

[28]A. Steinmann and D.J. Fox, *The Male Dilemma* (New York: Aronson, 1974), 69-70, 95-6.

[29]J.H. Pleck, *The Myth of Masculinity* (Cambridge: *MIT* Press, 1981), 32 ff.

[30]S.L. Bem, "The Measurement of Psychological Androgyny," *Journal of Consulting and Clinical Psychology* 42 (1974): 155-62.

[31]J.H. Pleck and J. Sawyer, eds., *Men and Masculinity* (Englewood Cliffs: Prentice Hall, 1974), 95.

[32]J. Nichols, *Men's Liberation* (New York: Penguin, 1975).

[33]H. Goldberk, *The Hazards of Being Male* (New York: Nash, 1976); Berkeley Men's Center, in Pleck and Sawyer, *Men and Masculinity,* 174.

[34]M. Daly, *Gyn/Ecology* (Boston: Beacon Press, 1978), xi; E. Lenney, "Androgyny: Some Audacious Assertions Toward Its Coming of Age," *Sex Roles* 5 (December 1979): 704.

[35]C. Ehrlich, "The Woman Book Industry," *American Journal of Sociology* 78 (1973): 1031-44.

[36]Men's Consciousness Raising Group, *Unbecoming Men* (New York: Times Change Press, 1971); W. Farrell, *The Liberated Man* (New York: Random House, 1974); J.W. Petras, ed., *Sex: Male, Gender: Masculine* (Pt. Washington N.Y.: Alfred,1975); D.S. David and R. Brannon, *The Forty-Nine Percent Majority* (New York: Random, 1976); Pleck and Sawyer, n. 31; Nichols, n. 32.

[37]The books in this section are the least secure candidates for the new genre: Lang's book, for instance, was researched before the 1970s, and Vilar (n. 27) is more a variation of the old battle-of-the-sexes genre. But it seemed important to register the presence of this strain too. N. Mailer, *The Prisoner of Sex* (London: Weidenfeld and Nicholson, 1971); T. Lang, *The Difference Between a Man and a Woman* (New York: John Day, 1971); S. Mead, *Free the Male Man!* (New York: Simon and Schuster, 1972); S. Goldbert, *The Inevitability of Patriarchy* (New York: William Morrow, 1973).

[38]M. Korda, *Male Chauvinism* (New York: Random House, 1973); M. Fasteau, *The Male Machine* (New York: McGraw-Hill, 1974); A. Goodman and P. Walby, *A Book About Men* (London: Quartet, 1975).

[39]A. Ellis, *Sex and the Liberated Man* (Secaucus: Lyle Stuart, 1976); B. Zilbergeld, *Male Sexuality* (Boston: Little, Brown, 1978); Steinmann and Fox, n. 28; Goldberg, n. 33.

[40]B. Bishop and P. McNeill, *Below the Belt* (London: Coventure, 1977); P. Chesler, *About Men* (London: Women's Press, 1978).

[41]J. Snodgrass, ed., *For Men Against Sexism* (Albion: Times Change Press, 1977); A. Tolson, *The Limits of Masculinity* (London: Tavistock, 1977); P. Hoch, *White Hero, Black Beast* (London: Pluto Press, 1979).

[42]R. Firestone, ed., *A Book of Men* (New York: Stonehill, 1975); J.L. Dubbert, *A Man's Place* (Englewood Cliffs: Prentice Hall, 1979); P.N. Stearns, *Be a Man!* (New York: Holmes and Meier, 1979); E.H. Pleck and J.H. Pleck, eds., *The American Man* (Englewood Cliffs: Prentice Hall, 1980); Komarovsky, n. 9; Grady, Brannon and Pleck, n. 25.

[43]Goldberg, *The Hazards of Being Male,* 11.

[44]Mailer, *The Prisoner of Sex,* 169.

[45]J.H. Pleck, "Masculinity-Femininity: Current and Alternative Paradigms," *Sex Roles* 1, (June 1975): 161-78.

[46]J.H. PLeck, "The Male Sex Role: Definitions, Problems and Sources of Change," *Journal of Social Issues* 32 (1796): 155-64.

[47]For example, J.H. Pleck, "Male Threat From Female Competence," *Journal of Consulting and*

*Clinical Psychology* 44 (1976): 608-13; and "Men's Traditional Perceptions and Attitudes About Women: Correlates of Adjustment and Maladjustment," *Psychological Reports* 42 (February-June 1978): 975-83.

[48]J.H. Pleck, "Men's Power With Women, Other Men, and Society: A Men's Movement Analysis," in Pleck and Pleck, *The American Man,* 427.

[49]*Ibid.,* 428.

[50]J.H. Pleck, "The Work-Family Role System," *Social Problems* 24 (April 1977): 417-27; and "Men's Family Work: Three Perspectives and Some New Data," *The Family Coordinator* 28 (October 1979): 481-8.

[51]*Ibid.,* 485.

[52]M. Komarovsky, "Cultural Contradictions and Sex Roles: The Masculine Case," *American Journal of Sociology* 78 (January 1973): 884.

[53]*Ibid.,* 880-1.

[54]G. Russell, *The Changing Role of Fathers?* (St. Lucia: University of Queensland Press, 1983).

[55]W.J. Goode, "Why Men Resist," in B. Thorne and M. Yalom, eds., *Rethinking The Family: Some Feminist Questions* (New York: Longman, 1982), 145.

[56]For U.S. chronology see R. Morgan, ed., *Sisterhood is Powerful* (New York: Random House, 1970), xxi-xxv; and for the spread of the movement internationally see J. Mitchell, *Woman's Estate* (Harmondsworth: Penguin, 1971).

[57]Farrell, *The Liberated Man,* 141.

[58]J. Interrante, "Dancing Along the Precipice: The Men's Movement in the '80's," *Radical America* 15 (September-October 1981): 53-71.

[59]Farrell claims personally to have organized about a hundred CR groups; American newspaper reports on the existence of a "men's liberation movement" can be found from 1972 on; one such piece in late 1973 mentions a figure of three hundred men's groups (Pleck and Sawyer, *Men and Masculinity,* 152). Tolson reckons there were about forty in Britain in 1973-5 *(The Limits of Masculinity,* 143). Given the ephemerality of CR groups, it is very unlikely that all were active at the same time; and the American figures also have to be considered an exaggeration. The MIT *Men's Studies Bibliography* of 1979 listed only about fifteen local newsletters published at any time between 1973 and 1979, and doubtless some of these were ephemeral too.

[60]The personal effects are another matter, and we would take them much more seriously. For good discussions of the personal politics of men's groups and conferences, see Tolson *The Limits of Masculinity,* Interrante, "Dancing Along the Precipice,' and M. Gilding, "Men's Groups: Their Radical Possibilities," *Gay Information* 9/10 (1982): 35-9.

[61]Bednarik, *The Male in Crisis;* Sexton, *The Feminized Male.*

[62]M. Bloch, *The Historian's Craft* (Manchester: The University Press, 1984).

[63]R.W. Connell, "The Concept of 'Role' and What To Do With It," *Australian and New Zealand Journal of Sociology* 15 (1979): 7-17; reprinted in Connell, *Which Way Is Up?* (Sydney: Allen and Unwin, 1983), ch. 10.

[64]Pleck, "The Male Sex Role"; Pleck, *The Myth of Masculinity;* David and Brannon, *The Forty-Nine Percent Majority.*

[65]Franzway and Lowe, "Sex Role Theory."

[66]Goode. "Why Men Resist."

[67]Parsons and Bales, *Family, Socialization and Interaction Process.*

[68]Pleck, "Masculinity-Femininity"; Pleck, *The Myth of Masculinity,* 112.

[69]Tolson, *The Limits of Masculinity;* Hoch, *White Hero, Black Beast;* E. Reynaud, *Holy Virility* (London: Pluto Press, 1983).

[70]E. Zaretsky, "Male Supremacy and the Unconscious," *Socialist Revolution* 4 (1975): 7-55.

[71]Chesler, *About Men.*

[72]J. Stockard and M. Johnston, *Sex Roles* (Englewood Cliffs: Prentice Hall, 1980), ch. 9; J. Mitchell, *Psychoanalysis and Feminism* (Harmondsworth: Penguin, 1974); G. Rubin, "The Traffic in Women: Notes on the 'Political Economy' of Sex," in R. Reiter, ed., *Toward an Anthropology of Women* (New York: Monthly Review Press, 1975), 157-210.

[73]N. Chodorow, *The Reproduction of Mothering* (Berkeley: University of California Press, 1978).

[74]J. Johnston, *Lesbian Nation* (New York: Simon and Schuster, 1973).

[75]A. Walter, ed., *Come Together* (London: Gay Men's Press, 1980), 49.

[76]M. Mieli, *Homosexuality and Liberation* (London: Gay Men's Press, 1980); D. Fernbach, *The Spiral Path* (London: Gay Men's Press, 1981).

[77]R. Bayer, *Homosexuality and American Psychiatry* (New York: Basic Books, 1981).

[78]Miele, *Homosexuality and Liberation,* 193.

[79]Q. Crisp, *The Naked Civil Servant* (London: Jonathon Cape, 1968).

[80]Pleck, "Men's Power with Women."

[81]J. Weeks, *Coming Out* (London: Quartet, 1977); J. Weeks, *Sex, Politics and Society* (London: Longman, 1981); K. Plummer, ed., *The Making of the Modern Homosexual* (London: Hutchinson, 1981).

[82]A. Bray, *Homosexuality in Renaissance England* (London: Gay Men's Press, 1982).

[83]M. McIntosh, "The Homosexual Role," *Social Problems* 16 (Fall 1968): 182-92; Bray, *Homosexuality in Renaissance England,* ch. 4.

[84]Rubin, "The Traffic in Women."

[85]Hoch, *White Hero, Black Beast;* Dubbert, *A Man's Place;* Stearns, *Be a Man!;* Pleck and Pleck, *The American Man.*

[86]Rubin, "The Traffic in Women."

[87]R.W. Connell, "Theorising Gender," *Sociology* 19 (May 1985): 260-72.

[88]Mitchell, *Woman's Estate.*

[89]K. Millett, *Sexual Politics* (New York: Doubleday, 1970).

[90]Dowsett, "Gender Relations in Secondary Schooling," *Sociology of Education* 58 (January 1985): 34-48.

[91]Hacker, "The New Burdens of Masculinity."

[92]Bray, *Homosexuality in Renaissance England.*

[93]C. Cockburn, *Brothers: Male Dominance and Technological Change* (London: Pluto Press, 1983).

[94]Plummer, *The Making of the Modern Homosexual.*

[95]G.H. Herdt, *Guardians of the Flutes* (New York: McGraw-Hill, 1981).

[96]J. Money, "Social Dimorphism and Homosexual Gender Identity," *Psychological Bulletin* 74 (1970): 425-40.

[97]See, for example, Kessler *et al.,* "Gender Relations in Secondary Schooling"; V. Johnson, *The Last Resort* (Ringwood: Penguin, 1981).

[98]R. Atwan, D. McQuade, and J.W. Wright, *Edsels, Luckies and Frigidaires* (New York: Delta, 1979).

[99]G. Lewis, *Real Men Like Violence* (Sydney: Kangaroo Press, 1983).

[100]Tolson, *The Limits of Masculinity.*

[101]C.V. Baldock and B. Cass, eds., *Women, Social Welfare and the State* (Sydney: Allen and Unwin, 1983).

[102]R. W. Connell "Class, Patriarchy and Sartre's Theory of Practice," *Theory and Society* 11 (1982): 305-20.

[103]S.J. Kessler and W. McKenna, *Gender: An Ethnomethodological Approach* (New York: Wiley, 1978).

[104]S. Freud, "Civilization and its Discontents," *Standard Edition of the Complete Psychological Works* (London: Hogarth, 1930), vol. 21; H. Marcuse, *Eros and Civilization* (London: Sphere Books, 1955).

[105]S. Freud, "From the History of an Infantile Neurosis," *Standard Edition of the Complete Psychological Works* (London: Hogarth, 1918), vol. 17.

[106]J.P. Sartre, *Saint Genet* (London: W.H. Allen, 1964).

[107]Red Collective, *The Politics of Sexuality in Capitalism* (London: Red Collective PDC, 1978).

[108]Goldberg, *The Hazards of Being Male;* Mailer, *The Prisoner of Sex;* J. Lippert, "Sexuality as Consumption," in Snodgrass, *For Men Against Sexism,* 207-13; Bednarik, *The Male in Crisis.*

[109]R. von Krafft-Ebing, *PPsychopathia Sexualis* (New York: Paperback Library, 1965); first published in 1886.

[110]R. Perkins, *The Drag Queen Scene* (Sydney: Allen and Unwin, 1983).

[111]Bem, "The Measurement of Psychological Androgyny"; Russell, *The Changing Role of Fathers?*

[112]Parsons and Bales, *Family, Socialization and Interaction Process;* Chodorow, *The Reproduction of Mothering.*

[113]Fasteau, *The Male Machine;* Nichols, *Men's Liberation;* Reynaud, *Holy Virility;* A. Dworkin, *Pornography: Men Possessing Women* (London: The Women's Press, 1981).

[114]M.F. Winter and E.R. Robert, "Male Dominance, Late Capitalism, and the Growth of Instrumental Reason," *Berkeley Journal of Sociology* 24/25 (1980): 249-80.

[115]Ehrenreich, *The Hearts of Men.*

# PART II

# Men, Work, and Cultural Life

# Patriarchy, Scientists, and Nuclear Warriors

## BRIAN EASLEA

In a lecture at the University of California in 1980, the Oxford historian Michael Howard accused the world's scientific community, and particularly the Western scientific community, of an inventiveness in the creation and design of weapons that has made, he believes, the pursuit of a "stable nuclear balance" between the superpowers virtually impossible. At the very least, he found it curious that a scientific community that had expressed great anguish over its moral responsibility for the development of the first crude fission weapons "should have ceased to trouble itself over its continuous involvement with weapons-systems whose lethality and effectiveness make the weapons that destroyed Hiroshima and Nagasaki look like clumsy toys."[1] On the other hand, in the compelling pamphlet *It'll Make a Man of You: A Feminist View of the Arms Race,* Penny Strange expresses no surprise at the militarization of science that has occurred since the Second World War. While acknowledging that individual scientists have been people of integrity with a genuine desire for peace, she tersely states that "weapons research is consistent with the attitudes underlying the whole scientific worldview" and that she looks forward to "an escape from the patriarchal science in which the conquest of nature is a projection of sexual dominance."[2] My aim in this article is to explore the psychological attributes of patriarchal science, particularly physics, that contribute so greatly to the apparent readiness of scientists to maintain the inventive momentum of the nuclear arms race.

My own experiences as a physicist were symptomatic of the problems of modern science. So I begin with a brief account of these experiences followed by a look at various aspects of the masculinity of science, particularly physics, paying special attention to the ideology surrounding the concept of a scientific method and to the kinds of sexual rhetoric used by physicists to describe both their "pure" research and their contributions to weapons design. I conclude with some thoughts on the potential human integrity of a life in science—

once patriarchy and its various subsystems have become relics of history.

A PERSONAL EXPERIENCE OF PHYSICS

Growing up in the heart of rural England, I wanted in my early teens to become a professional bird-watcher. However, at the local grammar school I was persuaded that boys who are good at mathematics become scientists: people just don't become bird-watchers. I did in fact have a deep, if romantic, interest in physics, believing that somehow those "great men" like Einstein and Bohr truly understood a world whose secrets I longed to share. So I went to University College London in 1954 to study physics and found it excruciatingly boring. But I studied hard and convinced myself that at the postgraduate level it would be different if only I could "do research" —whatever that mysterious activity really was. It didn't seem remarkable to me at the time that our class consisted of some forty men and only three or four women. At that time, I was both politically conservative and politically naive, a situation not helped by the complete absence of any lectures in the physics curriculum on "science and society" issues.

In my final year it was necessary to think of future employment. Not wanting to make nuclear weapons and preferring to leave such "dirty" work to other people, I considered a career in the "clean and beautiful" simplicity of the electronics industry. I came very close to entering industry but in the end, to my great happiness, was accepted back at University College to "do research" in mathematical physics. It was while doing this research that I was to begin my drift away from a career in physics.

One event in my graduate years stands out. As an undergraduate I had only twice ever asked about the nature of reality as presented by modern physics, and both times the presiding lecturer had ridiculed my question. However, one day a notice appeared announcing that a famous physicist, David Bohm, together with a philosopher of science were inviting physics students to spend a weekend in a large country house to discuss fundamental questions of physics. That weekend was an enlightening experience that gave me the confidence to believe that physics was not solely a means for manipulating nature or a path to professional mundane achievement through the publication of numerous, uninteresting papers, but ideally was an essential part of human wisdom.

In the early 1960s, while I was on a two-year NATO Fellowship at the Institute of Theoretical Physics in Copenhagen, the first cracks and dents began to appear in my worldview. I met scientists from around the world, including the Soviet Union, who engaged me in animated political discussions. With a group of physicists I went on a ten-day tour of Leningrad and Moscow and, equipped with a smattering of Russian, I left the group to wander about on my own and kept meeting people who, at this high point of the Cold War, implored me to believe that Russia wanted peace. I couldn't square this image of Russia and the Russian people with what I had become accustomed to in Britain and would soon be exposed to while teaching at the University of Pittsburgh.

It seemed to be a world gone mad: my new university in Pittsburgh awarded honorary degrees to Werner von Braun, the former Nazi missile expert, and to Edward Teller, the father of the H-bomb. The Cuban blockade followed; Kennedy, Khrushchev, and physics were going to bring about the end of the world. I kept asking myself how the seemingly beautiful, breathtaking physics of Rutherford, Einstein, Heisenberg, and Niels Bohr had come to this.

New experiences followed which deepened my frustration with physics and increased my social and philosophic interests. University appointments in Brazil gave me a first-hand experience with the type of military regime that the United States so liked to support to save the world from communism. In the end I returned to the University of Sussex, where I taught "about science" courses to non-science students and "science and society" courses to science majors.

The more I learned, the more I became convinced that the reason physics was so misused and the reason the nuclear arms race existed was the existence of capitalist societies, principally the United States, that are based on profit making, permanent war economies, and the subjugation of the Third World. My pat conclusion was that if capitalism could be replaced by socialism, human behavior would change dramatically. But I felt uneasy with this belief since oppression and violence had not first appeared in the world in the sixteenth century. As the years went by and the feminist movement developed, I came to explore the profound psychological connections between the discipline of physics and the world of the warriors—connections that are ultimately rooted in the social institutions of patriarchy. That is the focus of this paper.

THE MASCULINITY OF PHYSICS

Indisputably, British and American physics is male-dominated. In Britain in the early 1980s women made up only 4 percent of the membership of the Institute of Physics, and in the United States women made up only 2 percent of the faculty of the 171 doctorate-awarding physics departments.[3] This male domination of physics has obviously not come about by chance; not until recently have physicists made serious attempts to encourage women to study the discipline and enter the profession. Indeed, in the first decades of the twentieth century strenuous attempts by physicists to keep women out of their male preserve were not unknown. Symbolic of such attempts in the 1930s was that of no less a man than the Nobel laureate Robert Millikan, who in 1936 wrote to the President of Duke University questioning the wisdom of the University's appointment of a woman to a full physics professorship.[4] As the statistics amply demonstrate, the male domination of physics continues despite publicized attempts by physicists to eliminate whatever prejudice still exists against the entry of women into the profession.

A second aspect of the masculinity of physics is that the men who inhabit this scientific world—particularly those who are successful in it—behave in culturally masculine ways. Indeed, as in other hierarchical male-dominated activities, getting to the top invariably entails aggressive, competitive behavior. Scientists themselves recognize that such masculine behavior, though it is considered unseemly to dwell upon it, is a prominent feature of science. The biologist Richard Lewontin even goes so far as to affirm that "science is a form of competitive and aggressive activity, a contest of man against man that provides knowledge as a side-product."[5] Although I wouldn't agree with Lewontin that knowledge is a mere "side-product" of such competition, I would, for example, agree with the anthropologist Sharon Traweek, who writes that those most prestigious of physicists—the members of the high-energy physics "community"—display the highly masculine behavioral traits of "aggressive individualism, haughty self-confidence, and a sharp competitive edge."[6] Moreover, Traweek's verdict is supported by the remarks of the high-energy physicist Heinz Pagels, who justifies such masculine behavior by explaining that a predominant feature in the conduct of scientific research has to be intellectual aggression, since, as he puts it, "no great science was discovered in the spirit of humility."[7] Scientists, then, physicists included, behave socially in a masculine manner.

A third aspect of the masculinity of physics is the pervasiveness of the ideology and practice of the conquest of nature rather than a human goal of respectful interaction and use. Although, of course, many attitudes (including the most gentle) have informed and continue to inform the practice of science, nevertheless a frequently stated masculine objective of science is the conquest of nature. This was expressed prominently by two of the principal promoters and would-be practitioners of the "new science" in the seventeenth century, Francis Bacon and René Descartes, the former even claiming that successful institutionalization of his method would inaugurate the "truly masculine birth of time." Although modern scientists usually attempt to draw a distinction between "pure" and "applied" science, claiming that pure science is the attempt to discover the fundamental (and beautiful) laws of nature without regard to possible application, it is nevertheless widely recognized that it is causal knowledge of nature that is sought, that is, knowledge that in principle gives its possessors power to intervene successfully in natural processes. In any case, most "pure" scientists know very well that their work, if successful, will generally find application in the "conquest of nature." We may recall how the first investigators of nuclear energy wrote enthusiastically in the early years of the twentieth century that their work, if successful, would provide mankind with an almost limitless source of energy. Both the "pure" and the technological challenges posed by the nucleus proved irresistible: the nucleus was there to be conquered and conquest was always incredibly exciting. Even in today's beleaguered domain of nuclear power for "peaceful" purposes, the ideology and practice of the conquest of nature has not disappeared. Thus, rallying the troops in 1979 at the twenty-fifth anniversary of the formation of the UK Atomic Energy Authority, the physicist chairman of the Authority, Sir John Hill, said that we will be judged "upon our achievements and not upon the plaintive cries of the faint-hearted who have lost the courage and ambitions of our forefathers, which made mankind the master of the earth."[8]

The masculine goal of conquest undoubtedly makes its presence felt in our images of nature and beliefs about the nature of reality; this constitutes a fourth aspect of the masculinity of physics and of science in general. That which is to be conquered does not usually emerge in the conqueror's view as possessing intrinsically admirable properties that need to be respected and preserved. Much, of course, could be written on specific images of nature, particularly with respect to "pure" and "applied" research objectives, and the subject does not lend itself to obvious generalizations. Nevertheless, it is clear that from the seventeenth century onwards, natural philosophers, men of science, and scientists tended to see the "matter" of nature as having no initiating, creative powers of its own (a point of view maintained only with some difficulty after the development of evolutionary theory in the nineteenth century). The historian of science, R.S. Westfall, is certainly not wrong when he writes that "whatever the crudities of the seventeenth century's conception of nature, the rigid exclusion of the psychic from physical nature has remained as its permanent legacy."[9] No matter what the cognitive arguments in favor of science's generally reductionist conception of "matter" and nature, it is clear that a nature that is seen as "the mere scurrying of matter to and fro" is a nature not only amenable to conquest but also one that requires no moral self-examination on the part of its would-be conqueror. "Man's place in the physical universe," declared the Nobel laureate physical chemist (and impeccable Cold-War warrior) Willard Libby, "is to be its master . . . to be its king through the power he alone possesses—the Principle of Intelligence."[10]

A fifth aspect of the masculinity of physics lies in the militarization the discipline has undergone in the twentieth century. Optimistically, Francis Bacon had expressed the hope in the seventeenth century that men would cease making war on each other in order to make collective warfare on nature. That hope has not been realized, nor is it likely to be. We may, after all, recall C.S. Lewis's opinion that "what we call Man's power over nature turns out to be a power exercised by some men over other men [and women] with nature as its instrument."[11] In the overall militarization of science that has occurred largely in this century and that was institutionalized during and after the Second World War, physics and its associated disciplines have indeed been in the forefront. For example, in a courageous paper to the *American Journal of Physics,* the physicist E.L. Woollett reported that at the end of the 1970s some 55 percent of physicists and astronomers carrying out research and development in the United States worked on projects of direct military value and he complained bitterly that physics had become a largely silent partner in the nuclear arms race.[12] It is estimated that throughout the world some half million physical scientists work on weapons design and improvement. As the physicist Freeman Dyson has reported, not only is the world of the scientific warriors overwhelmingly male-dominated but he sees the competition between physicists in weapons creation, allied to the (surely masculine) thrill of creating almost limitless destructive power, as being in large part responsible for the continuing qualitative escalation of the nuclear arms race.[13] Moreover, competition between weapons physicists is still a powerful motivating force in the nuclear arms race. Commenting on the rivalry at the Livermore Weapons Laboratory between two physical scientists, Peter Hagelstein and George Chapline, as to who would be the first to achieve a breakthrough in the design of a nuclear-bomb-powered X-ray laser, the head of the Livermore "Star Wars" Group, Lowell Wood, alleged: "It was raw, unabashed competitiveness. It was amazing—even though I had seen it happen before . . . two relatively young men . . . slugging it out for dominance in this particular technical arena."[14] And he then went on to agree with Richard Lewontin's unflattering description of motivation throughout the world of science:

> I would be very surprised if very many major scientific endeavors, maybe even minor ones, happen because a disinterested scientist coolly and dispassionately grinds away in his lab, devoid of thoughts about what this means in terms of competition, peer esteem, his wife and finally, prizes and recognition. I'm afraid I'm sufficiently cynical to think that in excess of 90 percent of all science is done with these considerations in mind. Pushing back the frontiers of knowledge and advancing truth are distinctly secondary considerations.[15]

One might, no doubt naively, like to believe that male scientists do not compete among themselves for the privilege of being the first to create a devastating new weapon. That belief would certainly be quite wrong.

Given such a sobering description of the masculine world of physics in Britain and North America, it isn't altogether surprising if girls, whose gender socialization is quite different from that of boys, are reluctant to study physics at school. What's more, it is in no way irrational, as British science teacher Hazel Grice points out, for girls to reject a subject that appears to offer "as the apex of its achievement a weapon of mass annihilation."[16]

## SCIENTIFIC METHOD FOR SCIENTISTS AND WARRIORS

One common description of physics is that it is a "hard," intellectually difficult discipline, as opposed to "soft" ones, such as English or history. The hard-soft spectrum spanning the academic disciplines is, of course, well-known, and within the sciences themselves there is also a notorious hard-soft spectrum, with physics situated at the hard end, chemistry somewhere toward the middle, biology toward the soft end, and psychology beyond. Insofar as mind, reason, and intellect are (in a patriarchy) culturally seen as masculine attributes, the hard-soft spectrum serves to define a spectrum of diminishing masculinity from hard to soft.

But what is held to constitute intellectual difficulty? It seems that the more mathematical a scientific discipline, the more intellectually difficult it is believed to be and hence the "harder" it is. Mathematics not only makes a discipline difficult, it seems: it also makes it rigorous; and the discipline is thus seen to be "hard" in the two connecting senses of difficult and rigorous. The fact that physics, and especially theoretical physics, makes prodigious use of sophisticated mathematics no doubt contributes to their enviable position at the masculine end of the hard-soft spectrum. It is perhaps of more relevance, however, that mathematics and logical rigor are usually seen as essential components of the "scientific method" and it is the extent to which a discipline is able to practice the "scientific method" that determines its ultimate "hardness" in the sense of intellectual difficulty, the rigor of its reasoning, and the reliability and profundity of its findings. Physics, it is widely believed, is not only able to but does make excellent use of the "scientific method," which thus accounts for its spectacular successes both in the understanding of physical processes and in their mastery. While, of course, all the scientific disciplines aspire to practice the "scientific method," it is physics and related disciplines that are held to have succeeded best.

But does such a procedure as the "scientific method" really exist? If it does, it is deemed to enjoy masculine rather than feminine status insofar as it rigorously and inexorably arrives at truth about the natural world and not mere opinion or wishful thinking. Such a method must therefore, it seems, be ideally characterized by logically rigorous thinking aided by mathematics and determined by experimental, that is, "hard" evidence with no contamination by feminine emotion, intuition, and subjective desires. "The scientific attitude of mind," explained Bertrand Russell in 1913, "involves a sweeping away of all other desires in the interests of the desire to know—it involves the suppression of hopes and fears, loves and hates, and the whole subjective emotional life, until we become subdued to the material, able to see it frankly, without preconceptions, without biases, without any wish except to see it as it is."[17] Such a view of the scientific method remains incredibly influential. In 1974 the sociologist Robert Bierstedt could confirm that "the scientist, *as such,* has no ethical, religious, political, literary, philosophical, moral, or marital preferences. . . . As a scientist he is interested not in what is right or wrong, or good and evil, but only in what is true or false."[18] Numerous examples could be given. Emotion, wishful thinking, intuition, and other such apparent pollutants of cognition are held to betray and subvert the objectivity of the scientific method, which is the hard, ruthless application of logic and experimental evidence to the quest to understand and master the world. Thus while the philosopher of science Hans Reichenbach could tell the world in 1951 that "the scientific philosopher does not want to belittle the value of emotions, nor would he like to live without them" and that the philosopher's own life could be as passionate and sentimental as that of any literary man, nevertheless the truly scientific philosopher "refuses to muddle emotion and cognition, and likes to breathe the pure air of logical insight and penetration."[19] Perhaps that is why the Nobel laureate physicist, Isidor Rabi, then eighty-four years of age, could confide in the early 1980s to Vivian Gornick that women were temperamentally unsuited to science, that the female nervous system was "simply different." "It makes it impossible for them to stay with the thing," he explained. "I'm afraid there's no use quarrelling with it, that's the way it is."[20]

Now the view of successful "scientific method" as masculine logic, rigor, and experimentation necessarily untainted and uncontaminated with feminine emotion, intuition, and wishful thinking is completely and hopelessly wrong. Such a scientific method is as elusive as "pure" masculinity. If nothing else, the invention of theories demands considerable intuition and creative imagination, as every innovative scientist knows and often has proclaimed. Does this therefore mean that the masculine "objectivity" of scientific method is intrinsically compromised? The philosopher of science, Carl Hempel, explains that it doesn't, since "scientific objectivity is safeguarded by the principle that while hypotheses and theories may be freely invented and *proposed* in science [the so-called context of discovery], they can be *accepted* into the body of scientific knowledge only if they pass critical scrutiny [the context of justification], which includes in particular the checking of suitable test implications by careful observation and experiment."[21] Alas for this typical defense of scientific objectivity, for ever since the work of Thomas Kuhn in his 1962 essay *The Structure of Scientific Revolutions,* it is generally accepted that no hard and fast distinction can be readily drawn between such a feminine context of discovery and a masculine context of justification.[22]

For this is what seems to be at issue. Not only does the notion of scientific objectivity appear to entail a clear-cut distinction between the masculine investigator and the world of "feminine" or "female" matter, within the psyche of the masculine investigator there also appears to be a pressing need to establish an inviolable distinction between a masculine mode of "hard," rigorous reasoning determined by logic and experimental evidence and, should it operate at all, a feminine mode characterized by creative imagination, intuition, and emotion-linked preferences. However, such clear-cut distinctions neither exist nor are possible in scientific practice, no matter how much the masculine mode appears paramount in normal research. What certainly does exist (although not uniformly so) is a very impassioned commitment to deny an evaluative subjective component to scientific practice; we may see such a masculine commitment as stemming from an emotional rejection and repudiation of the feminine within masculine inquiry. In other words, the impassioned claim that there exists an unemotional, value-free scientific method (or context of justification) may be interpreted as an emotional rejection and repudiation of the feminine and, if this is so, it would mean that scientific practice carried out (supposedly) in an "objective," value-free, unemotional way is in fact deeply and emotionally repressive of the feminine. This is a hornets' nest with all kinds of implications, but it may help to explain why much of modern science has, I shall argue, been embraced so uncritically by a society that is misogynistic and, in the case of the war industries, misanthropic as well. It is partly because patriarchal science is fundamentally antifeminine that its practitioners are psychologically vulnerable to the attractions of the "defense" industry.

We learn from Freeman Dyson that the world of the warriors, which comprises military strategists, scientists, and Pentagon officials, is ostentatiously defined by a "deliberately cool," quantitative style that explicitly excludes "overt emotion and rhetoric"—it is a style modelled on "scientific method" and directly opposed to, for example, the "emotional, anecdotal style of the anti-nuclear campaigner Helen Caldicott, whose arguments, according to Dyson, the warriors find unacceptable even when they manage to take them seriously.[23] For her part, Helen Caldicott believes that great rage and hatred lie suppressed behind the seemingly imperturbable, "rational" mask of scientific military analysis.[24] The military historian Sue Mansfield has posed the problem at its starkest: the stress placed in the scientific world on "objectivity" and a quantitative approach as a guarantee of truth, together with the relegation of emotions to a peripheral and unconscious existence, has, she maintains, carried "from its beginnings in the seventeenth century the burden of an essential hostility to the body, the feminine, and the natural environment."[25]

SEXUAL RHETORIC BY SCIENTISTS AND WARRIORS

The stereotype of the sober male scientist dispassionately investigating the properties of matter with, obviously, not a single sexual thought in mind is singularly undermined by the extent to which scientists portray nature as female in their informal prose, lectures, and talks. Indeed, according to the historian of science, Carolyn Merchant, the most powerful image in Western science is "the identification of nature with the female, especially a female harbouring secrets."[26] Physicists often refer to their "pure" research as a kind of sexual exploration of the secrets of nature—a female nature that not only possesses great subtlety and beauty to be revealed only to her most skilful and determined admirers and lovers, but that is truly fearsome in her awesome powers.

"Nature," wrote the high-energy physicist Frank Close in the *Guardian,* "hides her secrets in subtle ways." By "probing" the deep, mysterious, unexpectedly beautiful submicroscopic world, "we have our eyes opened to her greater glory."[27] The impression is given of a non-violent, male exploration of the sexual secrets of a mysterious, profoundly wonderful female nature. From the end of the nineteenth century to the middle 1980s such sentiments have frequently been expressed by famous physicists. Thus, addressing the annual meeting of the British Association in 1898, the physicist Sir William Crookes announced to his audience, "Steadily, unflinchingly, we strive to pierce the inmost heart of nature, from what she is to reconstruct what she has been, and to prophesy what she yet shall be. Veil after veil we have lifted, and her face grows more beautiful, august, and wonderful, with every barrier that is withdrawn."[28]

But no matter how many veils are lifted, ultimately the fearsome and untameable "femaleness" of the universe will remain.[29] Even if female nature is ultimately untameable, scientific research and application can reveal and make usable many of nature's comparatively lesser secrets. It is striking how successful scientific research is frequently described in the language of sexual intercourse, birth, and claims to paternity in which science or the mind of man is ascribed the phallic role of penetrating or probing into the secrets of nature— with the supposed hardness of successful scientific method now acquiring an obvious phallic connotation. Accounts of the origins of quantum mechanics and nuclear physics in the first decades of the twentieth century illustrate this well. In 1966 the physicist, historian, and philosopher of science, Max Jammer, admiringly announced that those early achievements of physicists in quantum mechanics clearly showed "how far man's intellect can penetrate into the secrets of nature on the basis of comparatively inconspicuous evidence"; indeed, Victor Weisskopf, Nobel laureate, remembers how the physicists at Niels Bohr's institute were held together "by a common urge to penetrate into the secrets of nature."[30] While Frederick Soddy was already proudly convinced by 1908 that "in the discovery of radioactivity . . . we had penetrated one of nature's innermost secrets,"[31] it was Soddy's collaborator in those early years, Sir Ernest Rutherford, who has been adjudged by later physicists and historians to have been the truly masculine man behind nuclear physics' spectacular advances in this period. Referring to Rutherford's triumphant hypothesis in 1911 that the atom consisted of an extremely concentrated nucleus of positively charged matter surrounded by a planetary system of orbiting electrons, one of Rutherford's assistants at the time, C.G. Darwin, later wrote that it was one of the "great occurrences" of his life that he was "actually present half-an-hour after the nucleus was born."[32] Successful and deep penetration, birth, and ensuing paternity: these are the hallmarks of great scientific advance.

At first sight it might seem that there is little untoward in such use of sexual, birth, and paternity metaphors, their use merely demonstrating that nuclear research, like scientific research in general, can be unproblematically described by its practitioners as a kind of surrogate sexual activity carried out by male physicists on female nature. However, not only did all the early nuclear pioneers (Rutherford included) realize that enormous quantities of energy lay waiting, as it were, to be exploited by physicists—"it would be rash to predict," wrote Rutherford's collaborator, W.C.D. Whetham, "that our impotence will last for ever"[33]—but, ominously, some of the sexual metaphors were extremely aggressive, reminding one forcibly of the ideology of (masculine) conquest of (female) nature. Indeed, since Rutherford's favorite word appears to have been "attack," it does not seem startling when one of the most distinguished physicists in the United States, George Ellery Hale, who was convinced that "nature has hidden her secrets in an almost impregnable stronghold," wrote admiringly to Rutherford in astonishingly military-sexual language. "The rush of your advance is overpowering," he congratulated him, "and I do not wonder that nature has retreated from trench to trench, and from height to height, until she is now capitulating in her inmost citadel."[34]

The implications of all this were not lost on everyone. Well before the discovery of uranium fission in 1939, the poet and Cambridge historian Thomas Thornely expressed his great apprehension at the consequences of a successful scientific assault on nature's remaining nuclear secrets:

> Well may she start and desperate strain,
> To thrust the bold besiegers back;

> If they that citadel should gain,
> What grisly shapes of death and pain
> May rise and follow in their track![35]

Not surprisingly, just as military scientists and strategists have adopted the formal "scientific style" of unemotional, quantitative argument, so they also frequently make informal use of sexual, birth, and paternity metaphors in their research and testing. Now, however, these metaphors become frighteningly aggressive, indeed obscene: military sexual penetration into nature's nuclear secrets will, the metaphors suggest, not only shake nature to her very foundations but at the same time demonstrate indisputable masculine status and military paternity. We learn that the first fission bomb developed at the Los Alamos laboratory was often referred to as a "baby"—a baby boy if a successful explosion, a baby girl if a failure. Secretary of War Henry Stimson received a message at Potsdam after the successful Trinity test of an implosion fission weapon which (after decoding) read:

> Doctor has just returned most enthusiastic and confident that the little boy [the uranium bomb] is as husky as his big brother [the tested plutonium bomb]. The light in his eyes discernible from here to Highhold and I could have heard his screams from here to my farm.[36]

Examples are abundant: the two bombs (one uranium and one plutonium) exploded over Japanese cities were given the code names "Little Boy" and "Fat Man"; a third bomb being made ready was given the name "Big Boy." Oppenheimer became known as the Father of the A-Bomb and indeed the National Baby Institution of America made Oppenheimer its Father of the Year. Edward Teller, publicly seen as the principal physicist behind the successful design of the first fusion weapon or H-bomb, seemingly takes pains in his memoirs to draw readers' attention to the fact that it was a "phallic" triumph on his part.[37] After the enormous blast of the first H-bomb obliterated a Pacific island and all its life, Teller sent a triumphant telegram to his Los Alamos colleagues, "It's a boy."[38] Unfortunately for Teller, his paternity status of "Father of the H-Bomb" has been challenged by some physicists who claim that the mathematician Stanislaw Ulam produced the original idea and that all Teller did was to gestate the bomb after Ulam had inseminated him with his idea, thus, they say, making him the mere Mother.

Following the creation of this superbomb, a dispute over two competing plans for a nuclear attack against the Soviet Union occurred between strategists in the RAND think tank and the leading generals of the Strategic Air Command (SAC) of the U.S. Air Force. In a circulated memorandum the famous strategist Bernard Brodie likened his own RAND plan of a limited nuclear strike against military targets while keeping the major part of the nuclear arsenal in reserve to the act of sexual penetration but with withdrawal before ejaculation; he likened the alternative SAC plan to leave the Soviet Union a "smoking radiating ruin at the end of two hours" to sexual intercourse that "goes all the way."[39] His colleague Herman Kahn coined the term "wargasm" to describe the all-out "orgastic spasm of destruction" that the SAC generals supposedly favored.[40] Kahn's book *On Escalation* attempts, like an elaborate scientific sex manual, a precise identification of forty-four (!) stages of increasing tension culminating in the final stage of "spasm war."[41] Such sexual metaphors for nuclear explosions and warfare appear to be still in common use. In 1980 General William Odom, then a military adviser to Zbigniew Brzesinski on the National Security Council, told a Harvard seminar of a strategic plan to release 70 to 80 percent of America's nuclear megatonnage "in one orgasmic whump,"[42] while at a London meeting in 1984, General Daniel Graham, a former head of the Defense Intelligence Agency and a prominent person behind President Reagan's Strategic Defense Initiative, brought some appreciative chuckles from his nearly all-male audience in referring to all-out nuclear "exchange" as the "wargasm."[43]

What is one to make of such metaphors and in particular of an analogy that likens ejaculation of semen during sexual intercourse (an act, one hopes, of mutual pleasure and possibly the first stage in the creation of new life) with a nuclear bombardment intended to render a huge country virtually lifeless, perhaps for millenia to come? And what conception of pleasure was foremost in Kahn's mind when he coined the term "wargasm"—surely the most obscene word in the English language—to describe what he sees as the union between Eros and Thanatos that is nuclear holocaust? I find such comparisons and terminology almost beyond rational comment. Simone de Beauvoire's accurate observation that "the erotic vocabulary of males" has always been drawn from military terminology becomes totally inadequate.[44] Brodie's and Kahn's inventiveness has surely eclipsed Suzanne Lowry's observation in the *Guardian* that "fuck" is the prime hate word" in the English language.[45] Indeed, given the sexual metaphors used by some of the nuclear warriors, one can understand Susan Griffin's anguished agreement with Norman Mailer's (surprising) description of Western culture as "drawing a rifle sight on an open vagina"—a culture, Griffin continues, "that even within its worship of the female sex goddess hates female sexuality."[46] We may indeed wonder why a picture of Rita Hayworth, "the ubiquitous pin-up girl of World War II," was stenciled on the first atomic bomb exploded in the Bikini tests of 1946.[47]

UNCONSCIOUS OBJECTIVES OF PATRIARCHY AND PATRIARCHAL PHYSICS

There has been much analysis of the Catholic Church's dichotomization of women into two stereotypes: the unattainable, asexual, morally pure virgin to which the Christian woman could aspire but never reach and the carnal whore-witch representing uncontrollable sexuality, depravity, wickedness, and the threat of universal chaos and disorder. During the sixteenth and seventeenth centuries such a fear and loathing of women's apparent wickedness came to a head in the European witch craze that was responsible for the inquisition and execution of scores of thousands of victims, over 80 percent of them female. A major historian of the witch craze, H.C.E. Midelfort, has noted that "one cannot begin to understand the European witch craze without recognizing that it displayed a burst of misogyny without parallel in Western history."[48]

Whatever the causes of the European witch craze, what may be particularly significant is that it coincided with the first phase of the scientific revolution, the peak of the witch craze occurring during the decades in which Francis Bacon, René Descartes, Johannes Kepler, and Galileo Galilei made their revolutionary contributions. In *one* of its aspects, I believe that the scientific revolution may be seen as a secularized version of the witch craze in which sophisticated men either, like Francis Bacon, projected powerful and dangerous "femaleness" onto nature or, like René Descartes, declared nature to be feminine and thus totally amenable to manipulation and control by (the mind of) man. We recall how Simone de Beauvoir declared that woman is seemingly "represented, at one time, as pure passivity, available, open, a utensil"—which is surely Descartes's view of "feminine" matter—while "at another time she is regarded as if possessed by alien forces: there is a devil raging in her womb, a serpent lurks in her vagina, eager to devour the male's sperm"—which has more affinity to Francis Bacon's view of "female" matter.[49] Indeed, Bacon likened the experimental investigation of the secrets of "female" nature to the inquisition of witches on the rack and looked forward to the time when masculine science would shake "female" nature to her very foundations. It is, I believe, the purified natural magical tradition advocated by Bacon (with considerable use of very aggressive sexual imagery) that contributed in a major way to the rise of modern science. Believing firmly in the existence of the secrets of nature that could be penetrated by the mind of man, Bacon predicted that eventually the new science would be able to perform near miracles. And indeed the momentous significance of the scientific revolution surely lies in the fact that, unlike the rituals of preliterate societies which in general failed to give their practitioners power over nature (if this is what they sought), the male practitioners of modern science have been rewarded with truly breathtaking powers to intervene successfully in natural phenomena (we have become blasé about the spectacular triumphs of modern science, but what a near miracle is, for example, a television picture). Bacon's prediction that the new science he so passionately advocated would inaugurate the "truly masculine birth of time" and eventually shake nature to her very foundations has been triumphantly borne out by the achievements of modern physics and the sad possibility of devastating nature with environmental destruction, nuclear holocaust, and nuclear winter.

Clearly modern science possesses what might be called a rational component. In this article I am taking for granted the fact that modern science produces knowledge of nature that "works" relative to masculine (and other) expectations and objectives and that the intrinsic interest and fascination of scientific inquiry would render a non-patriarchal science a worthy and central feature of a truly human society. What I am here concerned with is the "truly masculine" nature of scientific inquiry involving the discipline's would-be rigid separation between masculine science and "female" nature and the possibility of an underlying, if for the most part unconscious, hostility to "dangerous femaleness" in the minds of some, or many, of its practitioners—a hostility presumably endemic to patriarchal society. A case can be made—and has been both by Carolyn Merchant and myself—that a powerful motivating force, but not the only one, behind the rise of modern science was a kind of displaced misogyny.[50] In addition a case can be made that a powerful motivating force behind some (or much) modern science and particularly weapons science is a continuation of the displaced misogyny that helped generate the scientific revolution.

Certainly a counterclaim is possible that modern science might have had some misogynistic origins, but that this has no relevance today. In disagreement with such a counterclaim, however, it can be plausibly argued that the industrialized countries have remained virulently misogynistic, as seen in the prevalence of violence practiced and depicted by men against women. If there is indeed a link between misogyny, insecure masculinity, and our conceptions of science, particularly weapons science, then we are given a way to understand why nuclear violence can be associated in warriors' minds with sexual intercourse and ejaculation. Moreover, not only does Sue Mansfield suggest that at a deep level the scientific mentality has carried from its inception in the seventeenth century "the burden of an essential hostility to the body, the feminine, and the natural environment," but she also points out that, if human life survives at all after a nuclear holocaust, then it will mean the total restoration of the power of arm-bearing men over women. This leads her to make a significant comment that "though the reenslavement of women and the destruction of nature are not conscious goals of our nuclear stance, the language of our bodies, our postures, and our acts is a critical clue to our unexamined motives and desires."[51]

Of course, at the conscious level the scientific warrior today can, and does, offer a "rational" explanation for his behavior: his creation of fission and fusion weapons, he maintains, has made the deliberate starting of world war unthinkable and certainly has preserved peace in Europe for the last forty years. Whatever financial gain comes his way is not unappreciated but is secondary to the necessity of maintaining his country's security; likewise whatever scientific interest he experiences in the technological challenge of his work is again secondary to the all-important objective of preserving the balance of terror until world statesmen achieve multilateral disarmament. While well-known arguments can be made against the coherence of such a typical rationalization, what I am suggesting is that at a partly conscious, partly unconscious, level the scientific warrior experiences not only an almost irresistible need to separate his (insecure) masculinity from what he conceives as femininity but also a compulsive desire to create the weapons that unmistakably affirm his masculinity and by means of which what is "female" can, if necessary and as a last resort, be annihilated. (And it must be noted that scientific warriors can be supported by women or even joined by female warriors in their largely unconscious quest to affirm masculine triumph over the feminine and female.)

CONCLUSION

Looking over the history of humanity—the "slaughter-bench of history" as Hegel called it—I feel compelled to identify a factor—beyond economic and territorial rationales—that could help explain this sorry escalation of weaponry, oppression, and bloodshed. It seems to me of paramount importance to try to understand why men are generally the direct oppressors, oppressing other men and women, why in general men allow neither themselves nor women the opportunity to realize full humanity.

While the political scientist Jean Bethke Elshtain may well be correct when she writes skeptically that no great movement will ever be fought under the banner of "androgyny," I suggest that it could well be fought under the banner of "a truly human future for everyone."[52] And that would entail the abolition of the *institutionalized* sexual division of labor. Men and women must be allowed the right to become complete human beings and not mutilated into their separate masculine and feminine gender roles. At the same time, I agree with Cynthia Cockburn when she writes in her book *Machinery of Dominance* that "men need more urgently to learn women's skills than women need to learn men's" and that "the revolutionary step will be to bring men down to earth, to domesticate technology and reforge the link between making and nurturing."[53]

In such a world "education" could not remain as it is now in Britain and the United States (and elsewhere). Certainly there would be no "physics" degree as it exists today, although there would be studies that would eventually take "students" to the frontiers of research in "physics." Needless to say, such an educational system would not be male-dominated (or female-dominated), it would not institutionalize and reward socially competitive aggressive behavior, and there would be no objective in "physics" education of the "conquest of nature," although it would certainly recognize the need to find respectful, ecologically sound ways of making use of nature. Moreover, images of nature would, I suspect, undergo some profound changes (with probably major changes to some theories as well), and clearly in a truly human world there would be no militarization of physics. As for the "scientific method," this would be recognized to be a somewhat mysterious activity, perhaps never completely specifiable, certainly an activity making use of the full range of *human* capacities from creative intuition to the most rigorous logical reasoning.

As for sexual imagery, that would surely thrive in the new truly human activity of scientific research, given that sexual relations—deprived of the hatred that now so greatly distorts sexuality—would continue to provide not only much of the motivation but also the metaphors for describing scientific activity (and much else). Consider, for example, the language of a woman who was awarded just about every honor the discipline of astrophysics could bestow (but only after she spent years challenging blatant sexism and discrimination). The images invoked by Cecilia Payne-Gaposchkin are more directly erotic than the "equivalent" sexual imagery used by male scientists and physicists (not to mention their frequent aggressive imagery); her language was of her friendship, her love, her delight, her ecstasy with the world of "male" stars and galaxies. Writing of nature as female, Payne-Gaposchkin advises her fellow researchers: "Nature has always had a trick of surprising us, and she will continue to surprise us. But she has never let us down yet. We can go forward with confidence,

> Knowing that nature never did betray
> The heart that loved her."[54]

But it was an embrace of relatedness that Payne-Gaposchkin had sought and which had given her great satisfaction throughout her life, the satisfaction arising, in the words of Peggy Kidwell, from a sustained impassioned, loving endeavor "to unravel the mysteries of the stars."[55] In a truly human world, the principal purpose and result of science, as Erwin Schrödinger once said, will surely be to enhance "the general joy of living."[56]

## NOTES

I am most grateful to Michael Kaufman for his extremely skilful pruning of a very long manuscript.

[1]Michael Howard, "On Fighting a Nuclear War," in Michael Howard, *The Causes of War and Other Essays* (London: Temple Smith, 1983), 136.

[2]Penny Strange, *It'll Make a Man of You* (Nottingham, England: Mushroom Books with Peace News, 1983), 24-5.

[3]These statistics are taken from *Girls and Physics: A Report by the Joint Physics Education Committee of the Royal Society and the Institute of Physics* (London, 1982), 8, and Lilli S. Hornig, "Women in Science and Engineering: Why So Few?" *Technology Review* 87 (November/December, 1984), 41.

[4]See Margaret W. Rossiter, *Women Scientists in America: Struggles and Strategies to 1940* (Baltimore: Johns Hopkins University Press, 1982), 190-1.

[5]Richard Lewontin, " 'Honest Jim' Watson's Big Thriller, about DNA," Chicago *Sun Times,* 25 Feb. 1968, 1-2, reprinted in James D. Watson, *The Double Helix . . . A New Critical Edition,* edited by Gunther S. Stent (London: Weidenfeld, 1981), 186.

[6]Sharon Traweek, "High-Energy Physics: A Male Preserve," *Technology Review* (November/December, 1984), 42-3; see also her *Particle Physics Culture: Buying Time and Taking Space* (1987), forthcoming.

[7]Heinz Pagels, *The Cosmic Code: Quantum Physics as the Language of Nature* (London: Michael Joseph, 1982), 338.

[8]Sir John Hill, "The Quest for Public Acceptance of Nuclear Power," *Atom,* no. 273 (1979): 166-72.

[9]Richard S. Westfall, *The Construction of Modern Science* (1971; Cambridge: Cambridge University Press, 1977), 41. It should be noted, however, that quantum mechanics is essentially an anti-reductionist theory; see, for example, the (controversial) book by Fritjof Capra, *The Tāo of Physics* (London: Fontana, 1976).

[10] Willard Libby, "Man's Place in the Physical Universe," in John R. Platt, ed., *New Views of the Nature of Man* (Chicago: University of Chicago Press, 1965), 14-15.

[11] C.S. Lewis, *The Abolition of Man* (1943; London: Geoffrey Bles, 1946), 40.

[12] E.L. Woollett, "Physics and Modern Warfare: The Awkward Silence," *American Journal of Physics* 48 (1980): 104-11.

[13] Freeman Dyson, *Weapons and Hope* (New York: Harper and Row, 1984), 41-2.

[14] William J. Broad, *Star Warriors: A Penetrating Look into the Lives of the Young Scientists Behind Our Space Age Weaponry* (New York: Simon and Schuster, 1985), 204.

[15] *Ibid.*

[16] Hazel Grice, letter to the *Guardian,* 9 Oct. 1984, 20.

[17] Bertrand Russell, "Science in a Liberal Education," the *New Statesman* (1913) reprinted in *Mysticism and Logic and Other Essays* (Harmondsworth: Penguin, 1953), 47-8.

[18] Robert Bierstedt, *The Social Order* (1957; New York: McGraw-Hill, 1974), 26.

[19] Hans Reichenbach, *The Rise of Scientific Philosophy* (1951; Berkeley and Los Angeles: California University Press, 1966), 312.

[20] Vivian Gornick, *Women in Science: Portraits from a World in Transition* (New York: Simon and Schuster, 1984), 36.

[21] Carl Hempel, *Philosophy of Natural Science* (Englewood Cliffs, N.J.: Prentice-Hall, 1966), 16.

[22] See, for example, Imre Lakatos and Alan Musgrave, eds., *Criticism and the Growth of Knowledge* (Cambridge: Cambridge University Press, 1970), Sandra Harding, "Is Gender a Variable in Conceptions of Rationality? A Survey of Issues," *Dialectica: International Journal of Philosophy of Knowledge* 36 (1982): 225-42, and Harry M. Collins, ed., special issue of *Social Studies of Science* 11 (1981): 3-158, "Knowledge and Controversy: Studies of Modern Natural Science."

[23] Freeman Dyson, *Weapons and Hope,* 4-6.

[24] Helen Caldicott, "Etiology: Missile Envy and Other Psychopathology," in her *Missile Envy: The Arms Race and Nuclear War* (New York: William Morrow, 1984).

[25] Sue Mansfield, *The Gestalts of War: An Inquiry into Its Origins and Meaning as a Social Institution* (New York: Dial Press, 1982), 224.

[26] Carolyn Merchant, "Isis' Consciousness Raised," *Isis* 73 (1982): 398-409.

[27] Frank Close, "And now at last, the quark to top them all," the *Guardian,* 19 July 1984, 13, and "A shining example of what ought to be impossible," the *Guardian,* 8 Aug. 1985, 13.

[28] Sir William Crookes, quoted in E.E. Fournier d'Albe, *The Life of Sir William Crookes* (London: Fisher Unwin, 1923), 365.

[29] See, for example, the physicist Paul Davies's account of "black holes," "naked singularities," and "cosmic anarchy" in his *The Edge of Infinity: Naked Singularities and the Destruction of Space-time* (London: Dent, 1981), especially 92-3, 114, 145.

[30] Max Jammer, *The Conceptual Development of Quantum Mechanics* (New York: McGraw-Hill, 1966), 61, and Victor Weisskopf, "Niels Bohr and International Scientific Collaboration," in S. Rozenthal, ed., *Niels Bohr: His Life and Work as Seen by His Friends and Colleagues* (Amsterdam: North Holland, 1967), 262.

[31] Frederick Soddy, *The Interpretation of Radium* (London, 1909), 234.

[32] C.G. Darwin quoted in A.S. Eve, *Rutherford* (Cambridge: Cambridge University Press, 1939), 199, 434.

[33] W.C.D. Whetham, *The Recent Development of Physical Science* (London: Murray, 1904), 242.

[34] G.E. Hale quoted in Helen Wright, *Explorer of the Universe: A Biography of George Ellery Hale* (New York: Dutton, 1966), 283, and in A.S. Eve, *Rutherford,* 231.

[35] "The Atom" from *The Collected Verse of Thomas Thornely* (Cambridge: W. Heffer, 1939), 70-1, reprinted in John Heath-Stubbes and Phillips Salmon, eds., *Poems of Science* (Harmondsworth: Penguin, 1984), 245.

[36] Richard G. Hewlett and Oscar E. Anderson, *A History of the United States Atomic Energy Commission* (Pennsylvania State University Press, 1962), vol. 1, *The New World, 1939-1946,* 386.

[37] Edward Teller with Allen Brown, *The Legacy of Hiroshima* (London: Macmillan, 1962), 51-3.

[38] Edward Teller, *Energy from Heaven and Earth* (San Francisco: W.H. Freeman, 1979), 151. See also Norman Moss, *Men Who Play God* (Harmondsworth: Penguin, 1970), 78. For general detail

see my *Fathering the Unthinkable: Masculinity, Scientists and the Nuclear Arms Race* (London: Pluto Press, 1983), ch. 3.

[39]Bernard Brodie's memorandum is referred to by Fred Kaplan in *The Wizards of Armageddon* (New York: Simon and Schuster, 1983), 222. I have not seen the text of Brodie's memorandum. The chilling phrase "smoking, radiating ruin at the end of two hours" comes from a declassified Navy memorandum on a SAC briefing held in March 1954; see David Alan Rosenberg, " 'A Smoking Radiating Ruin at the End of Two hours': Documents on American Plans for Nuclear War with the Soviet Union 1954-55," *International Security* 6 (1981/82), 3-38.

[40]Herman Kahn, *On Escalation: Metaphors and Scenarios* (London: Pall Mall, 1965), 194.

[41]Note that Gregg Herken in *Counsels of War* (New York: Knopf, 1985), 206, writes that Bernard Brodie objected to Herman Kahn's "levity" in coining the term "wargasm."

[42]Quoted in Thomas Powers, "How Nuclear War Could Start," *New York Review of Books,* 17 Jan. 1985, 34.

[43]Roger Hutton, (personal communication) who attended the meeting when researching the Star Wars project.

[44]Simone de Beauvoir, *The Second Sex* (1949; Harmondsworth: Penguin, 1972), 396.

[45]Suzanne Lowry, "O Tempora, O Mores," the *Guardian,* 24 May 1984, 17.

[46]Susan Griffin, *Pornography and Silence: Culture's Revenge Against Nature* (London: Women's Press, 1981), 217.

[47]Paul Boyer, *By the Bomb's Early Light: American Thought and Culture at the Dawn of the Atomic Age* (New York: Pantheon, 1985), 83.

[48]H.C.E. Midelfort, "Heartland of the Witchcraze: Central and Northern Europe," *History Today* 31 (February 1981): 28.

[49]Simone de Beauvoir, *The Second Sex,* 699.

[50]See, for example, Carolyn Merchant, *The Death of Nature: Women, Ecology and the Scientific Revolution* (San Francisco: Harper and Row, 1980), and my *Science and Sexual Oppression: Patriarchy's Confrontation with Woman and Nature* (London: Weidenfeld, 1981), ch. 3 and *Fathering the Unthinkable,* ch. 1.

[51]Sue Mansfield, *The Gestalts of War,* 223.

[52]Jean Bethke, Elshtain, "Against Androgyny," *Telos* 47 (1981), 5-22.

[53]Cynthia Cockburn, *Machinery of Dominance* (London: Pluto Press, 1985), 256-7.

[54]Katherine Haramundanis, ed., *Cecilia Payne-Gaposchkin: An Autobiography and Other Recollections* (Cambridge: Cambridge University Press, 1984), 237.

[55]*Ibid.,* 28.

[56]"Science, Art and Play," reprinted in E.C. Schrödinger, *Science, Theory and Man* (New York: Dover, 1957), 29; see, for example, Evan Squires, *To Acknowledge the Wonder: The Story of Fundamental Physics* (Bristol: Adam Hilger, 1985).

# Sharing the Shop Floor

## STAN GRAY

On an October evening in 1983, a group of women factory workers from Westinghouse came to the United Steelworkers hall in Hamilton, Ontario, to tell their story to a labor federation forum on affirmative action. The women told of decades of maltreatment by Westinghouse—they had been confined to job ghettoes with inferior conditions and pay, and later, when their "Switchgear" plant was shut down, they had fought to be transferred to the other Westinghouse plants in the city. They had to battle management and the resistance of some, though not all, of their brothers in the shops. They won the first round, but when the recession hit, many were laid off regardless of seniority and left with little or no income in their senior years.

By the night of the forum I had worked at Westinghouse for ten years and had gone through the various battles for equality in the workplace. As I listened to the women, I thought of how much their coming into our plant had changed me, my fellow workers, and my brother unionists.

The women were there to tell their own story because the male staff officials of their union, United Electrical Workers, had prevented the women's committee of the local labor council from presenting their brief. The union claimed it was inaccurate, the problems weren't that bad, and it didn't give union officials the credit for leading the fight for women's rights. The Westinghouse women gave their story and then the union delivered a brief of its own, presenting a historical discussion of male-female relations in the context of the global class struggle, without mentioning Westinghouse or Hamilton or any women that it represented.[1]

This kind of thing happens in other cities and in other unions. The unanimous convention resolutions in support of affirmative action tend to mask a male resistance within the unions and on the shop floor. Too many men pay lip service to women's rights but leave the real fighting to the women. They don't openly confront the chauvinism of their brothers on the shop floor and in the labor movement. Yet an open fight by men against sexism is an important part of the fight for sexual equality. It is also important because sexism is harmful for working men, in spite of whatever benefits they gain in the short term: it runs counter to their interests and undermines the quality of their trade unionism.

I was one of those unionists who for years sat on the fence in this area until sharp events at work pushed me off. I then had to try to deal with these issues in practice. The following account of the debates and struggles on the shop floor at Westinghouse concentrates on the men rather than on the women's battle; it focuses on the men's issues and tries to bring out concretely the interests of workingmen in the fight against sexism.

### MY EDUCATION BEGINS

My education in the problems of the Westinghouse women began in November 1978, when I was recalled to work following a bitter and unsuccessful five-month strike. The union represented eighteen hundred workers in three plants that produced turbines, motors, transformers, and switchgear equipment. When I was recalled to work it wasn't to my old Beach Road plant—where I had been a union steward and safety rep—but to an all-female department in the Switchgear plant and to a drastic drop in my labor grade. The plant was mostly segregated; in other words, jobs (and many departments) were either male or female. There were separate seniority lists and job descriptions. The dual-wage, dual-seniority system was enshrined in the collective agreement signed and enforced by both company and union.

At Switchgear I heard the complaints of the women, who worked the worst jobs in terms of monotony, speed, and work discipline but received lower pay, were denied chances for promotion, and were frequently laid off. They complained too of the union, accusing the male leadership of sanctioning and policing their inferior treatment. In cahoots with management, it swept the women's complaints under the carpet. From the first day it was obvious to me that the company enforced harsher standards for the women. They worked harder and faster, got less break time, and were allowed less leeway than the men. When I was later transferred to the all-male machine shop, the change was from night to day.

Meanwhile the men's club that ran the union made its views known to me early and clearly. The staff rep told me that he himself would never work with women. He boasted that he and his friends in the leadership drank in the one remaining all-male bar in the city. The local president was upset when he heard that I was seriously listening to the complaints of the women workers. He told me that he always just listened to their unfounded bitching, said "yes, yes, yes," and then completely ignored what he had been told. I ought to do the same, was his advice. Although I had just been elected to the executive in a rank-and-file rebellion against the old guard, he assumed that a common male bond would override our differences. When I persisted in taking the women's complaints seriously, the leadership started to ridicule me, calling me "the Ambassador" and saying they were now happy that I was saving them the distasteful task of listening to the women's bitching.

Then in 1979 the boom fell at Switchgear: the company announced it would close the plant. For the women, this was a serious threat. In the new contract the seniority and wage lists had been integrated, thanks to a new Ontario Human Rights Code. But would the women be able to exercise their seniority and bump or transfer to jobs in the other Hamilton plants, or would they find themselves out in the street after years at Switchgear?

## DIVIDE AND CONQUER

By this time I had been recalled to my old department at the Beach Road plant, thanks to shop-floor pressure by the guys. There was a lot of worry in the plants about the prospect of large-scale transfers of women from Switchgear. A few women who had already been transferred had met with harassment and open hostility from the men. Some of us tried to raise the matter in the stewards' council, but the leadership was in no mood to discuss and confront sexism openly. The union bully boys went after us, threatening, shouting, breast beating, and blaming the women for the problems.

Since the union structures weren't going to touch the problem, we were left to our own resources in the shop. I worked in the Transformer Division, which the management was determined to keep all male. As a steward I insisted that the Switchgear women had every right to jobs in our department, at least to training and a trial period as stipulated by seniority. Since this was a legal and contractual right, management developed a strategy of Divide and Rule: present the women as a threat to men's jobs; create splits and get the hourly men to do the bosses' dirty work for them. Management had a secondary objective here, which was to break our shop-floor union organization. Since the trauma of the strike and post-strike repression, a number of stewards and safety reps had patiently rebuilt the union in the plant, block by block—fighting every grievance, hazard, and injustice with a variety of tactics and constructing some shop-floor unity. We did so in the teeth of opposition from both company and union, whose officials were overly anxious to get along peacefully with each other. A war of the sexes would be a weapon in management's counter-offensive against us.

For months before the anticipated transfers, foremen and their assorted rumor mongers stirred up the pot with the specter of the Invasion of the Women. Two hundred Switchgear women would come and throw all Beach Road breadwinners out in the street; no one's job would be safe. Day after day, week after week, we were fed the tales: for example, that fourteen women with thirty years' seniority were coming to the department in eight days and no male would be protected. Better start thinking now about unemployment insurance.

In the department next to mine a few transfers of women were met with a vicious response from the men. Each side, including the militant steward, ended up ratting on the other to the boss. The men were furious and went all over the plant to warn others against allowing any "cunts" or "bitches" into their departments.

Meanwhile I had been fighting for the women to be called into new jobs opening up in the iron-stacking area of my department. The union's business agent had insisted that women couldn't physically handle those and other jobs. But I won the point with the company. The major influx of women would start here.

For weeks before their arrival, the department was hyper-alive, everyone keyed to the Invasion of the Women. I was approached by one of the guys, who said that a number of them had discussed the problem and wanted me, as their steward, to tell management the men didn't want the women in here and would fight to keep them out.

The moment was a personal watershed for me. As I listened to him, I knew that half measures would no longer do. I would now have to take the bull by the horns.

Over the years I had been dealing with male chauvinism in a limited fashion. As a health and safety rep, I had to battle constantly with men who would knowingly do dangerous work because it was "manly" to do so and because it affirmed their masculine superiority. The bosses certainly knew how to use guys like that to get jobs done quickly. With a mixture of sarcasm, force, and reason, I would argue, "It's stupidity not manliness to hurt yourself. Use your brains, don't be a hero and cripple yourself; you're harming all of us and helping the company by breaking the safety rules we fought so hard to establish, rules that protect all of us."

From this I was familiar with how irrational, self-destructive, and anti-collective the male ego could be. I also felt I had learned a great deal from the women's movement, including a never-ending struggle with my own sexism. Off and on I would have debates with my male co-workers about women's liberation. But all this only went so far. Now with the approaching invasion and the Great Fear gripping the department, I had to deal with an angry male sexism in high gear. I got off the fence.

I told this guy, "No. These women from Switchgear are our sisters, and we have fought for them to come into our department. They are our fellow workers with seniority rights, and we want them to work here rather than get laid off. If we deny them their seniority rights, it hurts us, for once that goes down the drain, none of us has any protection. It is our enemies, the bosses, who are trying to do them out of jobs here. There's enough work for everyone; even if there weren't, seniority has to rule. For us as well as for them. The guys should train the women when they come and make them feel welcome."

And with that reply, the battle was on. For the next few weeks the debate raged hot and heavy, touching on many basic questions, drawing in workers from all over the plant. Many men made the accusation that the women would be the bosses' fifth column and break our unity. They would side with the foremen, squeal on us, outproduce us, and thereby force speed-ups. The women were our enemy, or at least agents of the enemy, and would be used by *them* against *us*. Many of them pointed to the experience of the next department over, where, since the influx of a few women, the situation had been steadily worsening.

The reply was that if we treated the women as sisters and friends they'd side with us not the boss. Some of us had worked in Switchgear and knew it was the *men* there who got favored treatment. What's more, our own shop-floor unity left a lot to be desired and many of our male co-workers engaged in squealing and kowtowing to the boss. Some of us argued sarcastically that women could never equal some of our men in this area.

We argued that we had common class interests with our sisters against the company, particularly in protecting the seniority principle.

It was easy to tease guys with the contradictions that male double standards led them to. Although they were afraid the women would overproduce, at the same time they insisted that women wouldn't be physically strong enough to do our "man's work." Either they could or they couldn't was the answer to that one, and if they could, they deserved the jobs. It would be up to us to initiate them into the department norms. Many of the guys said that the women would never be able to do certain of the heavy and rotten jobs. As steward and safety rep I always jumped on that one: we shouldn't do those jobs either. Hadn't we been fighting to make them safer and easier for ourselves? Well, they answered, the women would still not be able to do all the jobs. Right, I would say, but how many guys here have we protected from doing certain jobs because of back or heart problems, or age, or simply personal distaste? If the women can't do certain jobs, we treat them the same way as men who can't. We don't victimize people who can't do everything the company wants them to. We protect them: as our brothers, and as our sisters.

By pointing out the irrationalities of the sexist double standards, we were pushing the guys to apply their class principles—universal standards of equal treatment. Treat the women just as we treat men regarding work tasks, seniority, illness, and so on.

COUNTERING SEXISM

Male sexist culture strives to degrade women to nothing but pieces of flesh, physical bodies, mindless animals . . . something less than fully human, which the men can then be superior to. Name-calling becomes a means of putting women in a different category from *us,* to justify different and inferior treatment.

Part of the fight to identify the women as co-workers was therefore the battle against calling them "cunts" or "bitches." It was important to set the public standard whereby the women were labeled as part of us, not *them.* I wouldn't be silent with anyone using these sexist labels and pushed the point very aggressively. Eventually everyone referred to "the women."

After a while most of the men in the department came to agree that having the women in and giving them a chance was the right thing to do by any standard of fairness, unionism, or solidarity, and was required by the basic human decency that separates *us* from *them.* But then the focus shifted to other areas. Many men came back with traditional arguments against women in the work force. They belong at home with the kids, they're robbing male breadwinners of family income and so forth. But others disagreed: most of the guys' wives worked outside the home or had done so in the past; after all a family needed at least two wages these days. Some men answered that in bad times a family should have only one breadwinner so all would have an income. Fine, we told them, let's be really fair and square: you go home and clean the house and leave your wife at work. Alright, they countered, they could tolerate women working who supported a family, but not single women. And so I picked out four single men in our department and proposed they be immediately sacked.

Fairness and equality seemed to triumph here too. The guys understood that everyone who had a job at Westinghouse deserved equal protection. But then, some men found another objection. As one, Peter, put it, "I have no respect for any women who could come in to work here in these rotten conditions." The comeback was sharp: "What the hell are *you* putting up with this shit for? Why didn't you refuse to do that dirty job last month? Don't *you* deserve to be treated with respect?[2]

As the Invasion Date approached I got worried. Reason and appeals to class solidarity had had a certain impact. Most of the guys were agreeing, grudgingly, to give the women a chance. But the campaign had been too short; fear and hostility were surfacing more and more. I was worried that there would be some ugly incident the first day or two that would set a pattern.

Much of the male hostility had been kept in check because I, as the union steward, had fought so aggressively on the issue. I decided to take this one step further and use some intimidation to enforce the basics of public behavior. In a tactic I later realized was a double-edged sword, I puffed myself up, assumed a cocky posture, and went for the jugular. I loudly challenged the masculinity of any worker who was opposed to the women. What kind of man is afraid of women? I asked. Only sissies and wimps are threatened by equality. A *real man* has nothing to be afraid of; he wants strong women. Any man worth his salt doesn't need the crutch of superiority over his sisters; he fears no female. A real man lives like an equal, doesn't step on women, doesn't degrade his sisters, doesn't have to rule the roost at home in order to affirm his manhood. Real men fight the boss, stand up with self-respect and dignity, rather than scapegoat our sisters.

I was sarcastic and cutting with my buddies: "This anti-woman crap of yours is a symbol of weakness. Stand up like a real man and behave and work as equals. The liberation of the women is the best thing that ever came along. . . . It's in *our* interests." To someone who boasted of how he made his wife cook his meals and clean his floors, I'd ask if she wiped his ass too? To the porno addicts I'd say, "You like that pervert shit? What's wrong with the real thing? Can you only get it up with those fantasies and cartoon women? Afraid of a real woman?" I'd outdo some of the worst guys in verbal intimidation and physical feats. Then I'd lecture them on women's equality and on welcoming our sisters the next week. I zeroed in on one or two of the sick types and physically threatened them if they pulled off anything with the women.

All of this worked, as I had hoped. It established an atmosphere of intimidation; no one was going to get smart with the women. Everyone would stand back for a while, some would cooperate, some would be neutral, and those I saw as "psycho-sexists" would keep out.

The tactic was effective because it spoke directly to a basic issue. But it was also effective because it took a leaf from the book of the psycho-sexists themselves.

At Westinghouse as elsewhere, some of the men were less chauvinistic and more sensible than others, but they often kept quiet in a group. They allowed the group pattern to be set by the most sexist bullies, whose style of woman baiting everyone at least gave in to. The psycho-sexists achieved this result because they challenged, directly or by implication, the masculinity of any male who didn't act the same way. All the men, whatever their real inclinations, are intimidated into acting or talking in a manner degrading to women. I had done the same thing, but in reverse. I had challenged the masculinity of any worker who would oppose the women. I had scared them off.

### THE DAY THE WOMEN ARRIVED

The department crackled with tension the morning The Women arrived. There were only two of them to start with. The company was evidently scared by the volatile situation it had worked so hard to create. They backed off a direct confrontation by assigning my helper George and me to work with the women.

The two women were on their guard: Betty and Laura, in their late thirties, were expecting trouble. They were pleasantly shocked when I said matter-of-factly that we would train them on the job. They were overjoyed when I explained that the men had wanted them in our department and had fought the bosses to bring them here.

It was an unforgettable day. Men from all corners of the plant crept near the iron-stacking area to spy on us. I explained the work and we set about our tasks. We outproduced the standard rate by just a hair so that the company couldn't say the women weren't able to meet the normal requirements of the job.

My strategy was to get over the hump of the first few days. I knew that once the guys got used to the women being there, they'd begin to treat them as people, not as "women" and their hysteria would go away. It was essential to avoid incidents. Thus I forced the guys to interact with them. Calling over one of the male opponents, I introduced him as Bruce the Slinger who knew all the jobs and was an expert in lifts and would be happy to help them if asked and could always be called on to give a hand. This put him on the spot. Finally he flashed a big smile, and said, "Sure, just ask and I'd be pleased to show you anything, and to begin with, here's what to watch out for. . . . "

The morning went by. There were no incidents. From then on it was easy. More guys began to talk to the two women. They started to see them as Betty with four kids who lived on the mountain and knew wiring and was always cheerful; or Laura, who was a friend of John's uncle and was cranky early in the morning, who could easily operate the crane but had trouble with the impact gun, and who liked to heat up meat pies for lunch. After all, these men lived and worked with women all of their lives outside the plant—mothers, sisters, wives, in-laws, friends, daughters, and girlfriends. Having women at work was no big deal once they got over the trauma of the invasion of this male preserve. Just like helping your sister-in-law hang some wallpaper.

As the news spread, more and more women applied to transfer to our department. They were integrated with minimum fuss. The same thing happened in several adjoining departments. Quickly, men and women began to see each other as people and co-workers, not as enemies. Rather than man vs. woman it was John, Mary, Sue, Peter, Alice, George, and Laura. That Christmas we had a big party at someone's home—men and women of the department, drinking and dancing. The photos and various raucous tales of that night provided the basis for department storytelling for the next three months.

Was this, then, peace between the sexes? The integration of men and women as co-workers in the plant? Class solidarity triumphing over sex antagonism? Not quite. Although they were now together, it was not peace. The result was more complicated, for now the war between the sexes was being extended from the community into the workplace.

WORKPLACE CULTURE

As our struggle showed, sexism coexists and often is at war with class consciousness and with the trade union solidarity that develops among factory men. Our campaign was successful to the extent that it was able to sharply polarize and push the contradictions between these two tendencies in each individual. With most of the men, their sense of class solidarity triumphed over male chauvinism.

Many of the men had resisted the female invasion of the workplace because for them it was the last sanctum of male culture. It was somewhere they could get away from the world of women, away from responsibility and children and the civilized society's cultural restraints. In the plant they could revel in the rough and tumble of a masculine world of physical harshness, of constant swearing and rough behavior, of half-serious fighting and competition with each other and more serious fighting with the boss. It was eight hours full of filth and dirt and grease and grime and sweat—manual labor and a manly atmosphere. They could be vulgar and obscene, talk about football and car repairs, and let their hair down. Boys could be boys.

The male workplace culture functions as a form of rebellion against the discipline of their society. Outside the workplace, women are the guardians of the community. They raise the kids and enforce some degree of family and collective responsibility. They frequently have to force this upon men, who would rather go drinking or play baseball while the women mind the kids, wash the family's clothes, attend to problems with the neighbors and in-laws, and so on. Like rebellious teenage sons escaping mother's control, male wage earners enter the factory gates, where in their male culture they feel free of the restraints of these repressive standards.

Even if all factory men don't share these attitudes, a large proportion do, to a greater or lesser degree.

The manly factory culture becomes an outlet for accumulated anger and frustration. But this is a vicious circle because the tedious work and the subordination to the bosses is in large part the very cause of the male worker's dissatisfaction. He is bitter against a world that has kept him down, exploited his labor power, bent him to meet the needs of production and profit, cheated him of a better life, and made the daily grind so harsh. Working men are treated like dirt everywhere: at work they are at the bottom of the heap and under the thumb of the boss; outside they are scorned by polite society. But, the men can say, we are better than them all in certain ways; we're doing men's work; it's physically tough; women can't do it; neither can the bankers and politicians. Tough work gives a sense of masculine superiority that compensates for being stepped on and ridiculed. All that was threatened by the Women's Invasion.

However, this male workplace culture is not one-sided, for it contains a fundamentally positive sense of class value. The workingmen contrast themselves to other classes and take pride in having a concrete grasp of the physical world around them. The big shots can talk fancy and manipulate words, flout their elegance and manners. But we control the nuts and bolts of production, have our hands on the machines and gears and valves, the wires and lathes and pumps, the furnaces and spindles and batteries. We're the masters of the real and the concrete; we manipulate the steel and the lead, the wood, oil, and aluminum. What we know is genuine, the real and specific world of daily life. Workers are the wheels that make a society go round, the creators of social value and wealth. There would be no fancy society, no civilized conditions if it were not for our labor.

The male workers are contemptuous of the mild-mannered parasites and soft-spoken vultures who live off our daily sweat: the managers and directors, the judges and entertainers, the lawyers, the coupon clippers, the administrators, the insurance brokers, the legislators . . . all those who profit from the shop floor, who build careers for themselves with the wealth we create. All that social overhead depends upon our mechanical skills, our concrete knowledge, our calloused hands, our technical ingenuity, our strained muscles and backs.

The Dignity of Labor, but society treats us like a pack of dumb animals, mere bodies with no minds or culture. We're physical labor power; the intelligence belongs to the management class. Workers are sneeringly regarded as society's bodies, the middle class as society's mind. One is inferior; the other is superior and fully human. The workers are less than human, close to animals, society's beasts of burden.

The male workplace culture tends to worship this self-identity of vulgar physicalness. It is as if the men enjoy wallowing in a masculine filth. They brag of being the wild men of the factory. Say it loud: I'm a brute and I'm proud.

Sexism thus undermines and subverts the proud tradition of the dignity of labor. It turns a class consciousness upside down by accepting and then glorifying the middle-class view of manual labor and physical activity as inferior, animalistic, and crude. When workers identify with the savages that the bosses see them as, they develop contempt for themselves. It is self-contempt to accept the scornful labels, the negative definitions, the insulting dehumanized treatment, the cartoon stereotypes of class chauvinism: the supermasculine menials, the industrial sweathogs.

Remember Peter; who couldn't respect a woman who would come to work in this hellhole. It was obviously a place where he felt he had lost his own self-respect. My reply to him was that he shouldn't put up with that rotten treatment, *that the men also deserved better.* We should be treated with dignity. Respect yourself—fight back like a man, not a macho fool who glorifies that which degrades him.

Everything gets turned inside out. It is seen as manly to be treated as less than a man, as just a physical, instinctual creature. But this is precisely how sexist society treats women: as mindless bodies, pieces of flesh . . . "biology is destiny." You would think that male factory workers and the women's movement would be natural allies, that they'd speak the same language. They share a common experience of being used as objects, dehumanized by those on top. Men in the factory are treated not as persons, but as bodies, replaceable numbers, commodities, faceless factors of production. The struggles of workingmen and of women revolve around similar things. The right to choice on abortion, for example, revolves around the right for women to control their own bodies. Is this not what the fight for health and safety on the shop floor is all about? To have some control over our bodies, not to let the bastards do what they want with our lives and limbs, to wreck us in their search for higher profits.

But male chauvinism turns many workingmen away from their natural allies, away from a rational and collective solution to their problems, diverting them from class unity with their sisters into oppressors and degraders of their sisters. Robbed of their real manhood—their humanity as men—they get a false sense of manhood by lording over women.

PLAYING THE FOREMAN AT HOME

Many men compensate for their wage-labor status in the workplace by becoming the boss at home. Treated terribly in the factory, he plays foreman after work and rules with authority over his wife and kids. He thus gains at home that independence he loses on the shop floor. He becomes a part-time boss himself with women as his servants. This becomes key to his identity and sense of self-esteem. Working-class patriarchs, rulers of the roost.

This sense of authority has an economic underpinning. The male worker's role as primary breadwinner gives him power over the family and status in society. It also makes him the beneficiary of the woman's unpaid labor in the household.

A wage laborer not only lacks independence, he also lacks property, having nothing but his labor power to sell. Sexism gives him the sense of property, as owner of the family. His wife or girlfriend is his sexual property. As Elvis sang, "You are my only possession, you are my everything." This domination and ownership of a woman are basic to how he sees himself.

These things are powerful pressures toward individualism, a trait of the business class: foreman of the family, man of property, possessiveness. They elevate the wage earner above the category of the downtrodden common laborer, and in doing so divert him from the collective struggle with his brothers and sisters to change their conditions. Capitalism is based on competitiveness and encourages everyone to be better than the next guy, to rise up on the backs of your neighbors. Similarly the male chauvinist seeks superiority over others, of both sexes. Men tend to be competitive, always putting one another down, constantly playing one-upmanship. Men even express appreciation and affection for each other through good-natured mutual insults.

Sexist culture thus undermines the working-class traditions of equality and solidarity and provides a recruiting ground for labor's adversaries. Over the years at Westinghouse I had noticed that a high proportion of workers who became foremen were extreme chauvinists—sexual braggarts, degraders of women, aggressive, individualistic, ambitious, ever willing to push other workers around. Male competition is counterproductive in the shop or union, where we ought to cooperate as equals and seek common solutions. The masculine ego makes for bad comradeship, bad brotherhood. It also makes it difficult for chauvinistic men to look at and deal objectively with many situations because their fragile egos are always on the line. They have to keep up a façade of superiority and are unable to handle criticism, no matter how constructive. Their chauvinistic crutches make them subjective, irrational, unreliable, and often self-destructive, as with men who want to work or drive dangerously.

Workingmen pay a high price for the limited material benefits they get from sexist structures. It is the bosses who make the big bucks and enjoy the real power from the inferior treatment of women.

THE NEXT ROUND AND A PEEK INTO THE WOMEN'S WORLD

Battles continued about the women getting a crack at the more skilled and high-paying assembly jobs up the floor. Next we won the fight against the company, which was trying to promote junior men. This time women were there to fight for themselves, and there were male stewards from other departments who backed them up. The shop floor was less hostile, many of the men being sympathetic or neutral.

But despite the general cooperation, most men still maintained that the women were inferior workers. The foremen did their best to foster sex divisions by spreading stories of all the mistakes the women supposedly made. They would reserve the worst jobs for the men, telling them the women couldn't do them. The men would thus feel superior while resenting the women's so-called privileges and the women would feel grateful for not having to do these jobs. The supervisors forged a common cause with some of the guys against the women. They fed their male egos and persuaded them to break safety rules, outproduce, and rat on other workers. The male bond often proved stronger than the union bond, and our collective strength suffered as a result.

As for myself, I was learning and changing a lot as a result of my experiences. I would often meet with the women at the lunch table to plan strategy. These sessions affected me in many ways. They were good talks, peaceful and constructive, with no fighting and argument, no competition, all of us talking sensibly about a common problem and figuring out how to handle it as a group. It was a relaxed and peaceful half hour, even when we had serious differences.

This was in marked contrast to the men's lunch tables, which were usually boisterous and raucous during those months. There was a lot of yelling and shouting, mutual insults, fist pounding, and throwing things at one another. When you ate at the women's table, you sat down to rest and relax. When you ate at the men's table, you sat down to fight.

I had read and heard a lot from my feminist friends about this so-called woman's world of warmth, cooperation, and friendship, as contrasted to men's norm of aggression, violence, and competition. Although I had always advocated women's liberation and respected the women's movement, I paid only lip service, if that, to this distinction, and was in fact more often scornful of this "women's world." Over the years I had become a more aggressive male, which I saw as distinct from being a chauvinist or sexist male. In the world of constant struggle, I thought, you had to be aggressive or go under. We'd have peace and love in the socialist future, some distant day.

As a unionist it became very clear to me that the women almost automatically acted like a collective. And in those months of going back and forth between the men's and women's tables, I took a long and serious look at this women's world. It was an unnerving but pleasant experience to sit down among friends, without competition and put-downs, not to have to watch out for flying objects, not to be on the alert for nerve-shattering noises, to be in a non-threatening atmosphere. There was obviously something genuine there and it seemed to offer a better way. It also became obvious to me that the gap between the sexes was enormous and that men and women were far from speaking a common language.

### NEW STRUGGLES AND THE RECESSION

In the months ahead there were new struggles. There was the fight to form a women's committee in the union in order to bring women's demands to the fore, to combat sexism among the male workers, and to give women a forum for developing their own outlook, strategy, and leadership. We launched that fight in the fall of 1981, with Mary, a militant woman in our rank-and-file group, in the lead. The old guard, led by the union's national president fought us tooth and nail. The battle extended over a number of months and tumultuous membership meetings, and we eventually lost as the leadership railroaded through its chauvinistic policy. No women's committee was formed. In time, however, the leadership came to support women's rights formally, even though they did little to advance the cause in practice.

In the spring of 1982 the recession finally caught up with us at Westinghouse and there were continuous layoffs in every division. Our bargaining power shrank, everyone was afraid for his or her own job, and the contract became little more than a piece of paper as the company moved aggressively to roll back the clock on our hard-won traditions on seniority rules, health and safety regulations, and so on. Bitterness and frustration were everywhere.

The company went after the women. Their seniority rights were blatantly ignored as they were transferred to "chip and grind" duties —the least skilled, the heaviest, dirtiest, and most unpleasant jobs. The progress the men had made also seemed to vanish. From the first day of the layoff announcements, many rallied to the call of "Get the women out first." Those most hostile to women came back out in the open and campaigned full blast. They found many sympathetic responses on the shop floor: protect the breadwinnerrs and, what's more, no women should be allowed to bump a male since they're not physically capable of doing the jobs anyway. It was the war of the sexes all over again, but far worse now because the situation allowed little leeway. There was some baiting of the women, and the plant became a tension-ridden, hateful place for all workers.

The bosses managed to seize back many of the powers the shop floor had wrenched away from them over the years, and even to create newer and deeper divisions within the workforce. But the recession was not all-powerful. We still managed to win all our battles on health and safety, and the shop floor continued to elect our militant shop stewards.

Some of the women gave in to the inevitable and were laid off despite their seniority. But others fought back and fought well. Some of them were even able to gain the sympathy of the male workers who had at first stood aside or resisted them. In some cases, the men joined in and helped the women retain their jobs.

Obviously, things had changed a great deal amongst the men since the first women began to come into the division. *When the chips were down, many men took their stand with their sisters against the company—despite the recession.*

## THE WORKPLACE AND BEYOND

Women in the labor movement have made gains largely on their own, using their own organized power. But unions were founded to fight for equal treatment for all workers—an injury to one is an injury to all.

The male unionists ought to take on that fight for their sisters' advancement more forcefully and openly battle their foes—the employers and also the chauvinists, harassers, and sexist bullies within our own midst. Sexism is anti-labor and it shouldn't be tolerated, even passively, by the men. Take them on like we take on the squeakers, brown-nosers, and back-stabbers in the shop—opponents of our common struggle.

All this is a fight to aid women, who are the prime victims of sexist structures and behavior. But the fight against sexism is also a fight for men. Sexism is destructive of the labor movement and the workingman's struggle. It has led men to confuse our class interests, to side with the boss time after time, to seek false and illusory solutions to our situation as exploited wage earners, and to escape the injustices of class by lording it over the women.

Sexism instills the ideas and values of the enemy class in our ranks. It ingrains false ideas of manhood and strength. It cultivates individualistic attitudes and competitive behavior when what we need is collective struggle. It deludes men and pushes them into irrational actions. It channels men's anger and rebellion along destructive paths—destructive to themselves as well as to our sisters. This sexist madness is part of how capitalism keeps male workers in line. It's anti-labor and anti-working class. We should so label it and treat it. In doing so, we are fighting for our own liberation, as well as that of our sisters.

That fight goes beyond the workplace. The sexist structures of family and community perpetuate those at work. And the problems are in those structures and those ways of living, not just in men's heads. One of these is the unequal sharing of community responsibilities, particularly the raising of children. Another is authoritarianism. Fear of authority keeps workingmen down. Good unionists have rebelled against the authority of the boss and the society, but they often reassert that authority over their fellow workers. Union office can sometimes become a power trip for male presidents, chief stewards, and staff reps. They want to run the union like an army, become our foremen, and think like patriarchs. This is harmful to the labor movement because it is anti-democratic, restricts participation, and inhibits the development of a self-reliant rank and file, which is the source of real power.

I learned about the errors of authoritarianism from some of my experiences in the shop. Over the years I have seen that it is important for union activists to be noncompetitive with fellow workers, to talk and reason as equals, listen, learn, try to convince, make common cause, tease in a spirit of friendship. It was important not to put down, make fun of others, or threaten and intimidate. Those were the weapons you used against adversaries. We were trying to build a self-confident and open-eyed group of workers, which you can't do by humiliating or bullying or manipulating.

I was taking a leaf from the book of the psycho-sexists when I challenged the masculinity of fellow male workers during the campaign to get women into our department. But I was also taking a leaf from the book of some union leaders, for I was intimidating my fellow workers. I was up against the wall and so I lashed out with the weapons of the union bully boys. I used my position as steward and my resources as a strong personality to frighten the guys, to push them into a position where they behaved the "right" way. It worked, in the short run. But I was disturbed by what had happened and realized that all I was doing was to reinforce the sexism I was trying to combat. I didn't resort to those methods again.

Authoritarianism, intimidation, aggression—these are a basic part of sexism. You can't separate aggression from sexism. Aggressive ways of relating to people are part of what sexism is. To be a male chauvinist is to establish a competitive power relationship to your own people, to seek to dominate your brothers and sisters, to treat *us* as *them*.

You can't combat sexism by reinforcing the fear of authority or by intimidating the men, by becoming the loudest shouter at the male lunch table. The peaceful women's table was stronger because it was collective and noncompetitive. During some of the campaigns at the plant, I saw that management was a lot more frightened of the quiet women than they were of the mouthy men. Force and authority can outlaw discriminatory practices and structures, but sexist attitudes cannot be fought with the weapons of authority. Authoritarianism itself must be undermined.

Labor has to go beyond paper resolutions and do more than place women in top positions. We have to deepen the struggle against sexism where it really counts—on the shop floor and within the locals.

Militant men in the labor movement have to organize themselves and speak out publicly. We need to express an anti-sexist position that reflects men's experiences, speaks in a masculine voice, and develops a language of our own. Such a position would label sexism as antilabor and show how it is harmful to women *and* to male wage earners. This rank-and-file male voice would be distinct from the women's voice but allied to it in a common fight.

Men need to speak to men about sexism. Men need to learn from the women who have been playing a dynamic part in the labor movement, and we must confront on our own the issues the women's movement has raised: equal treatment, union democracy, non-competititve structures, a humanization of the use of power, the relation between community and workplace problems, the family, sexuality, repression, authoritarianism. Men need to debate these issues in our own way, developing our own non-sexist answers.

The experience of women is enriching and strengthening the world of labor in many ways. Men have to recognize and appreciate these contributions. This means recasting our conception of work and labor as something uniquely masculine and accepting and learning from the distinct methods, rhythms, and styles of women assemblers, machinists, miners.

Workingmen share basic common interests with our sisters. When more of us recognize this, define and speak about these interests in our own way, and act in common with women, then we will be able to start moving the mountains that stand in our way.

# NOTES

[1]United Electrical Workers (UE) is a union whose militant rhetoric is rarely matched by its actual behavior. For example, it has passed resolutions at its national conventions favoring the formation of women's committees at the national and local levels, but what is on paper often does not match daily reality. Some leaders have a habit of advocating a position that suits the political needs of the moment rather than consistent principles. These limitations are not peculiar to UE, which is much like the rest of the labor movement, despite its sometimes radical rhetoric. Like most of the labor movement, it has its good and its bad locals, its good and its bad leaders. Like a lot of other unions it has moved toward a better position on "women's" issues, although with a lot of sharp contradictions and see-saws in behavior along the way, given its authoritarian style.

[2]The names of the plant workers in this article are not their real ones.

# The Cult of Masculinity: American Social Character and the Legacy of the Cowboy

## MICHAEL S. KIMMEL

*Doctor, I can't stand anymore being frightened like this over nothing.*
*Bless me with manhood! Make me brave! Make me strong!*

Philip Roth, *Portnoy's Complaint*

Is there a distinctive "American social character,"[2] a unique combination of attitudes, aspirations, and activities that sets the American apart from other nationalities? Is the American a type that can be instantly recognized and categorized? Traditionally, analysts of the American personality have given three sorts of answers in their attempts to define the American social character. One sort of assessment often reads like horoscopes, so vague and blandly noncommittal that anyone could believe them to be true. The adjectives that define this distinctively American character type would also be instantly recognized, I'm afraid, as the "essential" defining features of the Afghani, the Burmese, the Senegalese, the Australian, or even the German personality. For example, one respected social scientist lists fifteen "value orientations" of the American personality, among them: achievement and success, humanitarianism, efficiency and practicality, belief in progress, valuing of material comfort, and a belief in freedom, equality, scientific rationality, nationalism, individualism, and conformity.[3] Political scientist Harold Laski listed an orientation to the future, dynamism, worship of bigness, sense of destiny, fluidity of classes, pioneer spirit, individualism, anti-statism, versatility, empiricism, hard work, and a sense of property among his components of the American "spirit."[4] Max Lerner's sprawling classic, *America as a Civilization* (1957), reads like a catalog of contradictory adjectives intended to capture the extemes of American life. Americans, he claims, are mobile and restless, resilient, and temperamental, "over-organized in some areas and underorganized in others," composed of "vendible" and "author-

235

itarian" personalities. Not only are they "extremely moral" but also habitually "moral breaking"; what's more, they also subscribe to an ethic in which the "reigning moral deity . . . is fun."[5]

If this analytic imprecision is confusing, it is no less so than a second mode of understanding the American social character. In this version of American exceptionalism, the American personality is cast as an indescribably and existentially unique formation. In this depiction, bland platitudes are replaced by soaring superlatives, frequently referring to a mythic, historical, even sacred destiny awaiting fulfillment. "We Americans are the peculiar, chosen people," wrote Herman Melville in 1850, "the Israel of our time." Over a century later, the English observer D.W. Brogan caricatured American exceptionalism when he remarked in *The American Character* that Americans assume that "all modern historical events are either American or unimportant."[6]

A third school of thought is more ambivalent. Some authors are not sure exactly what an American is; they are sure only that he or she is not a European. What makes the American unique is his or her difference from the European. The seemingly unlimited frontier and the absence of a feudal heritage allowed the full flowering of what had only been a tendency in Europe. "America is Europe with all the walls down," noted one astute observer. To Richard Hofstadter, one of the United States' most celebrated historians, U.S. anti-intellectualism is a sharp contrast to the European kind. Europeans theorize and plan, he argued, while Americans act on the basis of their primitive instincts and imagination to advance a new world order based on individual abilities and accomplishments.[7] As Alexis de Tocqueville, that perceptive French aristocrat, observed in the 1830s, the "spirit of the Americans is averse to general ideas; it does not seek theoretical discoveries."[8] If the European thinks, the American acts; the European is careful, precise, elegant, while the American counterpart is reckless, rough, and daring. (Think, for example, of the contrast between James Bond and Dirty Harry.) Geographic limits bind the European to civil law, but the peculiar American relationship to nature—the twin myths of the limitless frontier and of inexhaustible resources—allows us to continue to see the New World as the state of nature, ruled by natural law, unrestrained by the historic obligation to civilization. (This relationship to nature has been said to justify both intervention in world affairs and U.S. isolation.)[9]

Different as these three types of analysis may be, they all use several similar adjectives, which may describe some essential elements of an

American social character, a cultural personality that explains present-day U.S. foreign policy.

Interestingly enough, these common characteristics—violence, aggression, extreme competitiveness, a gnawing insecurity—are also the defining features of compulsive masculinity, a masculinity that must always prove itself and that is always in doubt.

And American violence and aggression, these observers tell us, are distinctly American. For example, the American acts aggressively, not like a bully, seeking a confrontation, but rather in response to provocation. American school children are invariably taught that the United States has "never lost a war and never been the aggressor," which is a remarkable achievement, since the United States has only been invaded twice (in 1812 and 1941) since 1800 but has invaded scores of countries itself. American aggression is peculiar, wrote anthropologist Margaret Mead, because it is "seen as a response rather than as primary behavior." In *And Keep Your Powder Dry* (1944, revised in 1968), Mead explained that ours is an "aggressiveness which can never be shown except when the other fellow starts it . . . which is so unsure of itself that it had to be proved."[10]

Americans, Mead continued, "fight best when other people start pushing us around." As an editorial in the *Chicago Tribune* put it in 1883, "Having been kicked, it is time to kick back, and kick back hard, and keep on kicking back until they are kicked into something like reciprocity." American aggression is usually, in this mythic representation, retaliatory, a response to an apparent injury. And the retaliation is swift, effective, and inevitably disproportionately severe. Once provoked, the United States tends to get carried away by a boundless fury. Not one, but two atomic bombs were thought necessary and suitable retaliation against an already weakened enemy.

At the individual behavioral level, is it any wonder that the United States leads all modern industrial democracies in rapes, aggravated assaults, homicides, and robberies, and ranks among the highest in group violence and assassination? The National Commission on the Causes and Prevention of Violence suggested that "proving masculinity may require frequent rehearsals of toughness, the exploitation of women, and quick, aggressive responses." Such an analysis raises a most important issue, specifically that American aggression and violence conform to this compulsive masculinity, a socially constructed gender identity that is manifest both in individual behavior and in foreign and domestic policies. It is the central argument of this article that the aggregate compulsive masculinity in the United

States makes it a dangerous country in the modern world.

In the rest of this article I will trace the development of the cult of masculinity among U.S. political leaders through the course of U.S. history, indicating several of the forces that gave rise to it. Then I shall discuss the cult of masculinity in recent years and suggest a few reasons why this construct, both as a model for individual leaders and as a national posture, is beginning to break down, even at the moment it appears to be so vigorously reasserted. But first, let's look briefly at the constituent elements of masculinity, and observe how it so easily becomes a cult of excessive masculinity.

## U.S. HISTORY AS A TEST OF MANHOOD

The psychologist Robert Brannon has identified four components of the dominant traditional male sex role in the rules that define how a man is supposed to behave.[11] The first rule, "no sissy stuff," suggests that a stigma is attached to any behavior that appears even vaguely feminine. The second rule, "be a big wheel," says that success and status are vital elements of masculinity, and that men crave admiration. A man must also "be a sturdy oak," exuding a manly air of toughness, confidence, and self-reliance, so that others may come to rely on him. A final rule admonishes men to "give 'em hell," to evince an aura of aggression, violence, and daring. While this version of masculinity was originally intended to delineate the pressures on individual men to adopt a traditional kind of behavior, even a cursory glance at U.S. history, and the administrations of its political leaders, reveals a marked national preoccupation with masculinity. For the United States has been the archetypal male society, both because traditional masculinity permeates every facet of its political life, and because American men are never certain of our masculinity, never secure in our identity, always restless, eternally anxious, unrelentingly competitive. It's as if only Americans can be "real men."

Nowhere is the dynamic of American masculinity more manifest than in our singular contribution to the world's storehouse of cultural heroes: the cowboy. It was the United States that gave the world the cowboy legend, and Americans continue to see him as the embodiment of the American spirit. Even if the rest of the world finds him somewhat poignantly anachronistic, the United States has been trying to live up to the cowboy ideal ever since he appeared on the mythical historical stage.

Ideally, the cowboy is fierce and brave, willing to venture into unknown territory and tame it for its less-than-masculine inhabitants. As soon as the environment is subdued though, he must move on, unconstrained by the demands of civilized life, unhampered by clinging women and whining children. The cowboy is a man of impeccable ethics, whose faith in natural law and natural right is eclipsed only by the astonishing fury with which he demands adherence to them. He moves in a world of men, in which daring, bravery, and skill are constantly tested. He lives by his physical strength and rational calculation; his compassion is social and generalized, but he forms no lasting emotional bonds with any single person. The cowboy therefore lives alone—on the range, in the woods, settling the west. Like the United States' view of itself as the lone voice of reason in a hostile sea, the cowboy's mission was to reassert natural law against those forces that would destroy it (monarchy and aristocracy in the nineteenth century and communism in the twentieth, each of which is considered a foreign ideology, imported from Europe).

The American-as-cowboy theme resonates through the history of the United States. The pioneers and explorers of the early nineteenth century—Daniel Boone, Davey Crockett, Kit Carson—remain some of the nation's most potent cultural heroes, blazing the trail westward. The virgin land of the American west "gave America its identity," writes one commentator; the frontier was the place where manhood was tested, where, locked in a life or death struggle against the natural elements and against other men, a man discovered if he truly was a real man.[12]

If we see the cowboy as the embodiment of the American identity, Americans expect no less from their contemporary leaders, from the men they elect as the personification of American aspirations. Almost every presidential administration has been marked by a concern for masculinity; at times this is muted by a relative security, while at other times a convulsively bellicose masculinity becomes the defining feature of the administration. No American president better has expressed this compulsive masculine style than Andrew Jackson—a "man of violent character and middling capacities" according to Tocqueville—who carved out a distinctly American identity against both the effete "European" banks of the eastern establishment and the frighteningly "primitive" native American population.

Jackson's Indian policies illustrate well the tragic consequences of compulsive masculinity as a political style, particularly in combination with the needs of an expanding capitalist economy. By dispossessing the Indians of their land through a strategy of "internal colonialism" and genocide, Americans began to fulfill their destiny as possessors, a destiny that resounded through the nineteenth and twentieth centuries in countless imperialist adventures and reverberates today in Central America, the Middle East, and Southeast Asia. In *Fathers and Children* (1975), a brilliant psychoanalytically informed cultural history of Jacksonian America, political scientist Michael Rogin suggests that while the black man represented a "sexual Oedipal threat to the white man," the Indian represented a pre-Oedipal aggressive threat to the mother-child relationship." Such aggression (whether real or imagined) was sufficient provocation for Jackson and his new-born country, whose response was to reassert the authority of the Great White Father against his "red children." Thus Jackson said to three Florida Indian chiefs that they had listened to bad counsel, which

> compelled your Father the President to send his white children to chastise and subdue you, and thereby give peace to his children both red and white . . . . I give to you a plain, straight talk, and do not speak with a forked tongue. It is necessary that you be brought together, either within the bounds of your old Nation, or at some point, where your Father the President may be enabled to extend to you his fatherly care and assistance.[13]

The Indians were to be "resettled," forcibly removed from their traditional homelands, and placed on reservations (not unlike the relocation camps for Japanese Americans during the Second World War and the "strategic hamlets" of the Vietnam War), where they would be protected from the excesses of less enlightened whites. "Like a kind father," explained Jackson's military aide, "the President says to you, there are lands enough for both his white and his red children. His white children are strong, and might exterminate his red, but he will not permit them. He will preserve his red children."[14]

The consequences of this forced resettlement onto reservations, a profound infantilization of the subject population, had far-reaching consequences for native American identity. For the white Americans,the consequences were different. "By killing Indians whites grounded their growing up in a securely achieved manhood, and securely possessed their land."[15] Masculinity became linked to the subjugation of other people and the secure appropriation of their land.

POST-BELLUM FLEXING

Masculinity in the United States is certain only in its uncertainty; its stability and sense of well-being depend on a frantic drive to control its environment. And no sooner did this identity establish itself in the mid-nineteenth century than the walls of the male establishment began to crack. The bloody Civil War, an orgy of fratricide, left a significant legacy to the American self-image. For one thing, wartime industrialization contributed to a dramatic reshaping of the nature of work in American society. The independent artisan, the autonomous small farmer, the small shopkeeper was everywhere disappearing— before the Civil War, 88 per cent of American men were farmers or self-employed businessmen—replaced by an industrial working class that was tuned to the demands of the assembly line, and that held less and less control over its labors or its fruits. The organization of the Knights of Labor and the Populist Movement tried to stop this massive proletarianization, but in the end, like their European counterparts, American workers lost their struggle to retain the integrity of their work. Rapid industrialization also exacerbated the separation of work and home and extended the period of childhood socialization, contributing to what many observers labeled a "feminization" of American life.[16] Women, as mothers, public school teachers, and Sunday school teachers were thought to be softening the American character and replacing heroic male virtues of valor and honor with a generous compassion and emotional expressiveness. As William James put it, "There is no more contemptible type of human character than that of the nervous sentimentalist and dreamer, who spends his life in a weltering sea of sensibility and emotion, but who never does a concrete manly deed."[17] Finally, the fronter itself began to close, forcing America back onto itself. "For nearly three centuries," wrote Frederick Jackson Turner in 1896, "the dominant fact in American life has been expansion. And now the frontier is gone, and with its going has closed the first period of American history."

To counteract the effects of the closing of the frontier and the loss of patriarchal control over home and workplace, the twenty years preceding the entry of the United States into the First World War witnessed a striking resurgence of concern about masculinity. Writers extolled martial virtues and the heroic individual squaring off against faceless bureaucrats, and celebrated the charisma of the warrior, the willingness to die for what is natural and real. "The greatest danger that a long period of profound peace offers to a nation is that of creating effeminate tendencies in young men," noted one author in 1898. Psychologist Theodore Roszack observes that the years leading up to 1914 read "like one long drunken stag party where boys from every walk of life and ideological persuasion goad one another on to ever more bizarre professions of toughness, daring, and counterphobic mania—until at last the boasting turns suicidal and these would-be supermen plunge the whole Western society into the blood bath of world war.[18] Imperialist adventures took on qualities of national purification; military madness offered moral regeneration through the creation of an overseas empire. "Every argument that can be made for the Filipinos could be made for the Apaches," argued Theodore Roosevelt against those who cautioned restraint in the Philippines. Here, then, was the new frontier.

To sabotage the feminization of American culture meant, of course, a recharged opposition to women's suffrage, a cert. in subterfuge of American male values. "The American Republic stands before the world as the supreme expression of masculine force," proclaimed the Illinois Asociation Opposed to Women's Suffrage in 1910. The nation had grown soft and lazy, and America would soon lose its dominance in world affairs if its young boys did not metamorphose into vigorous, virile men. A spate of books of advice appeared for young men to guide their development, sabotage women's influence, and urge the adoption of traditional masculinity. Senator Albert Beveridge of Indiana's *Young Man and the World* (1906) counseled boys to "avoid books, in fact avoid all artificial learning, for the forefathers put America on the right path by learning from completely natural experience."[19]

It is interesting that, to counter these arguments about feminization, many early feminists and suffragists argued that the cult of masculinity was the true threat to the American way of life. Alice Duer Miller's amusing but effective rejoinder to those who would exclude women from public affairs has a contemporary ring, but was written in 1915. In "Why We Oppose Votes for Men"[20] she writes

1. Because Man's place is in the army.

2. Because no really manly man wants to settle any question otherwise than by fighting about it.

3. Because if men should adopt peaceable methods women will no longer look up to them.

4. Because men will lose their charm if they step out of their natural sphere and interest themselves in other matters than feats of arms, uniforms and drums.

5. Because men are too emotional to vote. Their conduct at baseball games and political conventions shows this, while their innate tendency to appeal to force renders them particularly unfit for the task of government.

Perhaps the most revealing event in the drive to counter the forces of feminization and maintain traditional manhood was the founding of the Boy Scouts of America in 1910. The Boy Scouts celebrated a masculinity tested against, and proved, in the world of nature and other men, far from the restraints of home, hearth, school, and church. The Boy Scouts stressed chivalry, courage, honor, activity, and thoughtfulness; Theodore Roosevelt claimed that "all daring and courage, all iron endurance of misfortune make for a finer and nobler type of manhood." "Spectatoritis," wrote E.T. Seton in *The Boy Scouts of America* (1910) had turned "robust, manly, self-reliant boyhood into a lot of flat-chested cigarette smokers with shaky nerves and doubtful vitality."[21] The Boy Scouts provided an institutional sphere for the validation of masculinity that had been previously generated by the flow of daily social life and affirmed in one's work. As one official Boy Scout manual put it in 1914,

> The Wilderness is gone, the Buckskin Man is gone, the painted Indian has hit the trail over the Great Divide, the hardships and privations of pioneer life which did so much to develop sterling manhood are now but a legend in history, and we must depend upon the Boy Scout movement to produce the MEN of the future.[22]

As no one else before him, President Theodore Roosevelt epitomized these masculine virtues, and he was heralded as the most manly of American presidents. His triumph over his frail body (he was dangerously asthmatic as a child) and his transformation into a robust, vigorous physical presence served as a template for the re-vitalized American social character in the twentieth century. Roosevelt's foreign policy was militaristic and expansionist; the Roosevelt corollary to the Monroe Doctrine extended the frontier once again, in the guise of "manifest destiny" to include the entire western hemisphere. "The nation that has trained itself to a cancer of un-warlike and isolated ease is bound, in the end, to go down before other nations who have not lost the manly and adventurous virtues," he argued. Or again: "There is no place in the world for nations who have become enervated by soft and easy life, or who have lost their fiber of vigorous hardiness and masculinity." A newspaper editor from Kansas praised Roosevelt's masculinity—his "hard muscled frame" and his "crackling voice"—as a model for Americans.[23]

## ROUGH RIDING OFF TO WORLD WAR

Teddy Roosevelt and his band of Rough Riders may have symbolized a hyper-masculine style in America, but he was surely not alone. All across Europe, turn-of-the-century leaders symbolically flexed their muscles and prepared themselves for the ultimate test of their virility. Insecure masculinity is not uniquely American, but rather emerges in the nineteenth century as the bourgeoisie ascends to national political dominance. According to the French historian and critic Michel Foucault, it is the bourgeois preoccupation with order and control and with an interminable ordering and disciplining of the natural and social environment that defines the era of bourgeois hegemony. In this regard, the United States is not unique, but presents perhaps the least adulterated case of the pathological insecurity of the bourgeois man about his own masculinity. The reassertion of manhood was the dominant theme of the political rhetoric of the entire era. U.S. general Homer Lea put it that "manhood marks the height of physical vigor among mankind, so the militant successes of a nation mark the zenith of its physical greatness."[24] Patrick Pearse, the Irish revolutionary poet, believed that bloodshed "is a cleansing and sanctifying thing and the nation which regards it as a final horror has lost its manhood."[25] Or, perhaps most strikingly, Spanish political philosopher Juan Donoso-Cortes, who claimed that "when a nation shows a civilized horror of war, it receives directly the punishment of its mistake. God changes its sex, despoils it of its common mark of virility, changes it into a feminine nation, and sends conquerers to ravish it of its honor."[26]

Every American generation since 1840 had fought in a war, and the generation of 1914 carried the additional burden of a masculinity-in-question, challenged by cultural softness, leisure, feminization, and a decade of peace. There was a lot on the line for America as a virile nation and enormous pressures on individual soldiers to prove themselves in battle, to emerge as a man among men. When poet Joyce Kilmer was killed in battle, one magazine offered this eulogy: "Kilmer was young, only 32, and the scholarly type of man. One did not think of him as a warrior. And yet from the time we entered the war he could think of but one thing—that he must, with his own hands, strike a blow at the Hun. He was a man."[27] And such tests of manliness were not limited to the U.S. infantry; businessmen and entrepreneurs also embraced the cowboy myth and yearned to outwit the competition and emerge as men among men. Recent biographies of robber barons such as John D. Rockefeller, Andrew Carnegie, Andrew Mellon, Henry Ford, and Leland Stanford reveal a startlingly common preoccupation with masculinity, in which their supremacy was proved daily on the corporate battlefield.[28]

If Teddy Roosevelt had been America's idealized version of a "real man" when the nation entered the First World War, by the war's end the country had discovered a new style of man and a new masculinity.

Woodrow Wilson was, in many ways, Roosevelt's antithesis. Roosevelt harked back to Andrew Jackson, but Wilson was reminiscent of idealistic visionaries like Abraham Lincoln and Thomas Jefferson. Whereas Roosevelt was a man of action, vigorous and impulsive, Wilson was thoughtful and contemplative, rational, paternal, and intellectual. Roosevelt was the heroic patriarch, always "Old Rough and Ready"; Wilson was the meditative fatherly executive, who always listened to others' problems.

Yet both conformed to the four elements of the male role: they were "sturdy oaks" and "big wheels," they were not "sissies" and they "gave 'em hell." Each combined those elements in a somewhat different way, and both were vigorous reformers and among the most important supporters of American progressivism in the years after the war. Both believed that their domestic and foreign policies were expressions of their masculinity and that reformism at home and militarism abroad were the most consistent strategies for the continued assertion of American masculinity. One author recently argued that many of the most prominent progressives were impelled to political reform as a compensation for feelings of inadequate masculinity. Even if the "cowboy-president" now shared center stage in the American psyche with the "professor-president," compulsive masculinity was never written out of America's cultural drama.

The Japanese attack on Pearl Harbor in 1941 again inspired a new generation of American men to test their masculinity on the fields of battle. As always, Americans went into war armed with a moral imperative, believing that they alone carried the moral burden of the fate of the earth. This mythic legacy is so powerful that almost fifty years after Pearl Harbor youngsters in the United States continue to play American GI against German and Japanese.

POST-WAR COWBOYS

Since the end of the Second World War, the cult of masculinity in American politics has remained a dominant theme. The Cold War and the "race for space" introduced an intractable national competitiveness, so that a contest over whether the Soviet Union or the United States is the "better" society is indelibly etched into the national consciousness. Interestingly enough, space exploration, diplomatic negotiations, and even international hockey games have taken their place alongside the battlefield as the testing ground of an insecure and compulsive masculinity. And lucky for us that they have, too, for the nuclear stakes are too high for men who need to prove their manhood at every turn. Nonetheless, the exaggerated competitiveness, the terror of appearing soft and weak, has marked the administration of each post-war president. John F. Kennedy, who proclaimed his administration as "The New Frontier," was possessed, according to biographer Joe McCarthy, by a "keyed up, almost compulsive competitiveness."[29] And Richard Nixon was chronically terrified of appearing to be "soft" on communism or on anything else. Bruce Mazlish, author of the psychoanalytic study *In Search of Nixon,* wrote that Nixon was "afraid of being acted upon, of being inactive, of being soft, of being thought impotent, of being dependent on anyone else."[30]

Frequently, a president's machismo is expressed in opposition to Congress, whose incapacity for resolute action stems, the presidents suggest, from their immediate dependence on their constituents and their ultimate less-than-total manhood. Thus Barry Goldwater promised that Nixon's impressive resolve would overcome the "weak-kneed, jelly-backed attitude" of some members of the Congress on the Vietnam war, and in 1972 Gerald Ford argued that the Congressional vote on the SuperSonic Transport, a questionably efficient and unquestionably overpriced airplane would determine whether each Congressman was "a man or a mouse."

In many ways, the post-war era, and especially the 1980s, resembles the turn of the century, in which similar economic and social changes have structured individual men's struggles and America's national struggle, to appear heroic and masculine. The closing of the frontier is today evidenced by the rising tide of struggles for national liberation and the promise of decolonization in the Third World. The dramatic transformation of the nature of work in the past two decades finds even the assembly line worker threatened by Third World workers on the one hand and by computers and robots in an increasingly service economy on the other. And it is widely believed that American culture has entered a new era of feminization, opposition to military adventures in Central America, a deepening concern for the devastation of the environment, the impressive gains registered by the women's movement and the gay movement in challenging traditional sexual scripts, and a growing trend toward a surface androgyny. (This movement toward androgyny was more marked in the 1960s when long hair, love beads, sandals, and bell-bottoms adorned a counter-culture of men dedicated to abandoning traditional masculinity; today it is more evident in the growing trend of "cross dressing.") And, as at the turn of the century, there is a flood of advice about behavior for both men and women.

Among America's political leaders, the cult of masculinity has found no better expression in recent years than in Lyndon Johnson and Ronald Reagan. (As a liberal Democrat and conservative Republican respectively, Johnson and Reagan demonstrate that compulsive masculinity knows no one political party.) Johnson was so deeply insecure about it that his political rhetoric resonated with metaphors of aggressive masculinity; affairs of state appeared to be conducted as much with his genitals as with political genius. There was a lot at stake for Johnson, as David Halberstam noted in his monumental study, *The Best and the Brightest:*

> He has always been haunted by the idea that he would be judged as being insufficiently manly for the job, that he would lack courage at a crucial moment. More than a little insecure himself, he wanted very much to be seen as a man; it was a conscious thing . . . . [H]e wanted the respect of men who were tough, real men, and they would turn out to be the hawks. He had unconsciously divided people around him between men and boys. Men were activists, doers, who conquered business empires, who acted instead of talked, who made it in the world of other men and had the respect of other men. Boys were the talkers and the writers and the intellectuals, who sat around thinking and criticizing and doubting instead of doing.[31]

Johnson's terror of an insufficient masculinity, especially that he would be seen as less of a man than John Kennedy, impelled him to escalate the war in Vietnam. When opposed, by enemies real or imagined, Johnson attacked their manhood. When informed that one member of his administration was becoming a dove on Vietnam, Johnson retorted, "Hell, he has to squat to piss." And as he celebrated the bombings of North Vietnam, Johnson declared proudly, "I didn't just screw Ho Chi Minh. I cut his pecker off."[32]

And just as Teddy Roosevelt rode the rising tide of recharged vitality from San Juan Hill to the White House, so did Ronald Reagan, riding in from his western ranch, hitch his political fortunes to the cult of compulsive masculinity. Reagan capitalized on Carter's "failure of will" in the botched invasion of Iran, and his alleged softness on domestic issues such as civil rights and environmental issues. Reagan sits tall in the saddle, riding roughly over the environment, Central America, Grenada, toward the gunfight at the nuclear arsenal, the ultimate test of the modern cowboy's mettle. The quickest gun in the west is now the fastest finger to the button of nuclear annihilation. President Reagan is the country's most obvious cowboy-president.[33]

And he may also be one of our last. The limitations of the cult of masculinity in American politics are slowly being revealed. A growing "gender gap," a difference in the political attitudes and preferences between men and women, threatens the unfettered continuation of macho politics. During the invasion of Grenada, the *New York Times* reported, the gap between male and female support for Reagan reached 20 per cent, the most significant difference on record in U.S. political history. The conservative political agenda, long linked to the expression of manhood through mercilessly tough foreign policies and equally compassionless domestic strategies, has also shown signs of shifting away from cowboy euphoria. The cowboy swagger of the former Secretary of the Interior James Watt as he attempted to sell or lease some of the country's most valuable land was too much even for the laissez-faire, free-drilling right wing. Even conservatives have counseled against the invasion of Central America, and Reagan was urged to withdraw from Lebanon. Across Europe, demonstrations against America's apocalyptic posturing with nuclear weapons have cast further doubts on the suitability of the cowboy as a policy maker for the 1980s.

The disappearance of the cowboy as the model of American masculinity will be a gain, not a loss. His disappearance as an individual hero, a template for individual role-modeling, may help free U.S. men from the constraints of a compulsively competitive masculinity and create new options for men as nurturing fathers, expressive husbands and lovers, and generous, sympathetic friends. Similarly, the decline of the cowboy ethic in American political life may finally permit the United States to cease proving its masculinity through every policy and every act of state. By giving up the insecure quest for macho heroism, the United States might become at last a compassionate democracy, concerned with human dignity and justice, which would allow it to become finally a truly heroic nation.

## NOTES

An earlier version of this article was published as "Der Männlichkeitskult: Amerikanischer Sozialcharakter und das Vermächtnis des Cowboys" in Andreas Guha and Sven Papke, eds., *Amerika: Der Riskante Partner* (Bonn: Athenäum, 1984). I am grateful to Bob and Joann Brannon, Michael Kaufman, Marty Oppenheimer, and Joseph Pleck for critical comments and support through various drafts.

[1]Philip Roth, *Portnoy's Complaint* (New York: Random, 1969).

[2]Although I continue to use the word "American" in several places throughout this essay, I have tried to limit its use to those places in which I join the discourse on the "American personality" or the "American character." But even there, I do not use the term to refer to all the Americas, but rather to the United States in particular. In those places where I am not engaged in the discourse about the American personality, I have tried to use the more accurate (if more cumbersome) specific term "United States" or "U.S."

[3]Robin M. Williams, *American Society* (New York: Alfred Knopf, 1951).

[4]Harold Laski, *The American Democracy* (New York: Viking, 1948).

[5]Max Lerner, *America as a Civilization* (New York: Alfred Knopf, 1957), 62, 550, 655, 675.

[6]D.W. Brogan, *The American Character* (New York: Vintage, 1954), 176.

[7]Richard Hofstadter, *The Paranoid Style in American Politics* (New York: Basic Books, 1965).

[8]Alexis de Tocqueville, *Democracy in America,* 2 vols. (New York: Doubleday, 1974), vol. 1, 326.

[9]Lerner, *op. cit.,* 920.

[10]Margaret Mead, *And Keep Your Powder Dry* (New York: William Morrow, 1965), 151, 157.

[11]Deborah David and Robert Brannon, "The Male Sex Role," in David and Brannon, eds., *The Forty-Nine Percent Majority* (Reading: Addison-Wesley, 1976), 12.

[12]It is curious that the United States does not evince a concept of "Motherland" in the same way as other advanced capitalist nations do. Perhaps the westward expansion was cast in such terms, as "taming" and "subduing," that the protection afforded an archetypal mother was replaced by the violent subjugation of a wild territory, an errant child. Michael Kaufman suggested to me that part of the answer lies in the patriarchal, yet not traditionally paternal, nature of the U.S. state (as opposed to individual politicians), again, perhaps, a father of fury and not a father of compassion.

[13]Michael Rogin, *Fathers and Children* (New York: Vintage, 1975), 79, 199.

[14]*Ibid.*

[15]*Ibid,* 125.

[16]Ann Douglas, *The Feminization of American Culture* (New York: Alfred Knopf, 1977).

[17]Cited by Robert Bellah *et al., Habits of the Heart* (Berkeley: University of California Press, 1985), 120.

[18]Theodore Roszak, "The Hard and the Soft: The Force of Feminism in Modern Times," in T. and B. Roszak, eds., *Masculine/Feminine* (New York: Harper and Row, 1969), 92.

[19]Albert Beveridge, *The Young Man and the World* (New York: Appleton, 1906).

[20]Reprinted in David and Brannon, *op. cit.,* 215.

[21]Ernest T. Seton, *The Boy Scouts of America* (New York: Doubleday, 1910), xi, quoted in Jeffrey Hantover, "The Boy Scouts and the Validation of Masculinity," in E.H. Pleck and J.H. Pleck, *The American Man* (Englewood Cliffs: Prentice-Hall, 1980), 294.

[22]D.C. Beard, *Boy Scouts of America* (1914), 109, cited by Jeffrey Hantover, *op. cit.,* 293.

[23]Quoted by Joe Dubbert, "Progressivism and the Masculinity Crisis," in Pleck and Pleck, *op. cit.,* 313.

[24]T. Roszak, *op. cit.,* 92.

[25]*Ibid.*

[26]*Ibid.*

[27]Quoted in Peter Filene, "In Time of War," in Pleck and Pleck, *op. cit.,* 324.

[28]*Cf.* Philip Slater, *Wealth Addiction* (New York: E.P. Dutton, 1980).

[29]Joe McCarthy, *The Remarkable Kennedys* (New York: Dial, 1960), 30, quoted in Mark Fasteau, "Vietnam and the Cult of Toughness in Foreign Policy," in Pleck and Pleck, *op. cit.,* 385.

[30]Bruce Mazlish, *In Search of Nixon* (New York: Basic, 1972), 116.

[31]David Halberstam, *The Best and the Brightest* (New York: Random House, 1972), 531, quoted by M. Fasteau, *op. cit.,* 394-5.

[32]*Ibid.,* 396.

[33]President Reagan may be a "cowboy president" in his foreign policy posturing, especially vis-à-vis the mythic Communist monolith that stretches from Central America to Africa to the Soviet Union. But his domestic policies—while no less compulsively masculine and compassionless— are cast in a "Father Knows Best" kind of paternalism that, I believe, softens their impact and lends an air of kindliness to rather systematically unkind domestic policies. This "successful" blend of patriarchy and paternalism—a father of fury *and* a father of compassion—might be the key to Reagan's popularity.

# Sports and Masculinity

## BRUCE KIDD

"Ideology is like B.O.," a wag once said. "You never smell your own." That's certainly true for men in sports. Most of us grew up playing sports, dreaming about starring in them, and making lifelong friends through them. Many of us still play them as adults, and we follow them endlessly, admiring and analyzing the performances of our favorites, discussing them with friends and workmates in the daily rituals of coffee and the pub, scheduling our lives around the calendar of the major sports events. Some of us actively encourage our children in them, driving them to the rink or park, helping with coaching and officiating. Yet men have rarely subjected our engagement in sports to the systematic questioning we focus on work, life and love, and other forms of cultural expression—literature and the visual and performing arts. Because they are so engrossing and so familiar, we assume that they have always been played, and that they have been unaffected by history or politics. Even when an Olympic boycott forces us to admit some connection between the structures and conflicts of a society and its sports, our personal experience leads us to protest that the activity itself is innocent of partisanship or prejudice and beneficial to all. Yet an outpouring of feminist scholarship now compels us to revise the popular image and explore the ways in which men have created sports to celebrate and buttress patriarchal (and class) power. Such an examination is not without its terrors, for it requires us to question radically something that many of us have found to be joyous and validating. But it is essential if we are to understand fully what it means "to be a man" and to promote human liberation.

The purpose of this article is to contribute to this necessary analysis by synthesizing the revisionist scholarship and then discussing its implications for men. I will argue that the games we play were created by males for males without taking the needs and experiences of females into account in any way. I will also argue that rather than being an "innocent" pastime, modern sports reinforce the sexual division of labor, thereby perpetuating the great inequality between the sexes and contributing to the exploitation and repression of both males and females. I do not advocate the abolition of sports, for they can strengthen people of both sexes in beneficial, exhilarating ways. But I will contend that they should be transformed and, to this end, I will suggest some practical steps.

## THE "NATURALNESS" OF SPORTS

My starting point is the insight of social history that sports as we know them today are not the universal, transhistorical physical activity they are commonly thought to be, played in much the same way by all peoples in all periods of human history. They are, rather, a group of activities developed under the specific social conditions of rapidly industrializing nineteenth-century Britain and spread to the rest of the world through emigration, emulation, and imperialism. Although modern sports are popularly equated to the athletic events of the ancient Olympic Games, scholars now argue that the differences between the Olympic contests of antiquity and those of our own era significantly outweigh the similarities and that we must seek to understand each of these competitions in its own terms.[1]

The classical games also celebrated class and patriarchal power, but few of us would have recognized in them what we call sport. By modern standards, they were extremely violent. The combative events, which were the most popular spectacles, were conducted with little regard for safety or fairness. There were no weight categories to equalize strength and size, no rounds, and no ring. Bouts were essentially fights to the finish, which is not surprising when you consider that these competitions began as preparations for war. Victory alone brought glory; defeat brought undying shame. Although the Greeks had the technology to measure records in the running, jumping, and throwing events, they rarely did so: performance for itself—pursuing the personal best despite one's placing—was meaningless to them. In fact, champions tried to intimidate their opponents so that they would withdraw and the victor could boast that he had won without having to compete. There were no team events, because competitors did not want to share the glory of victory. No competitor would have congratulated an opponent for a fairly fought or outstanding triumph. Today's handshake would have seemed an act of cowardice to them.[2] Nor were those fiercely competitive games common to all cultures living along the Mediterranean in that period. In fact, anthropologists have established that only warlike peoples have used their leisure for combative events.[3]

SPORTS AS "MALE PRACTICE"

Armed with this insight about the social specificity of the various forms of physical activity, we can begin to take a closer look at our own. Pierre de Coubertin did not revive the Olympics, as he liked to claim: he appropriated and recast the symbols of the ancient games for his own purpose, which was to combat the decadence and militarism of *fin-de-siècle* Europe by inculcating in young men the qualities he admired in English rugby and cricket.[4] These sports had their origins in the rural folk games of the late middle ages. In the mid-to late nineteenth century, they were fashioned into the first modern sports—characterized by standard rules, a bureaucratic structure, the overemphasis on setting records and the concept of fair play—by middle- and upper-class males in the increasingly bourgeois institutions of the public school, the university, and the private club.[5] Innovators, organizers, and creative publicists like Coubertin, consciously regarded sports as educational, preparing boys and young men for careers in business, government, colonial administration, and the military by instilling physical and mental toughness, obedience to authority, and loyalty to the "team."[6] When working-class males began to take them up too, some groups refused to accommodate them: at the Royal Henley Regatta, for example, working-class oarsmen were excluded by definition until 1933.[7] Most groups, however, eventually adopted the strategy of "rational recreation," incorporating workers as players and spectators, under strict middle-class leadership, as a means of fostering respect for the established order and reducing class tensions.[8] In the sports contested in Coubertin's Olympics, the tactic most frequently employed to regulate class relations was the amateur code. As the sociologist Richard Gruneau has written, sports "mobilize middle class bias" to this day.[9]

Education or socialization through sport was consciously understood to be "masculinizing." At the outset of Thomas Hughes's *Tom Brown's Schooldays,* the romanticization of the all-male Rugby School under Thomas Arnold, Squire Brown ponders what advice to give his son who is departing for Rugby:

Shall I tell him to mind his work, and say he's sent to school to make himself a good scholar? Well, but he isn't sent to school for that—at any rate, not for that mainly. I don't care a straw for Greek particles, or the digamma; no more does his mother. What is he sent to school for? Well, partly because he wanted so to go. If he'll only turn out a brave, helpful, truthtelling Englishman, and a gentleman, and a Christian, that's all I want.[10]

Then in the course of six years of rugby, cricket, cross-country running, and impromptu fist fighting, young Brown acquires courage and stamina, ingenuity, close friendships, and leadership, attributes traditionally associated with maleness by the dominant class. Hughes's bestseller persuaded schoolmasters and youth leaders throughout the English-speaking world to encourage sports as a "toughener" for their male charges and inspired Coubertin to develop the ideology of the modern Olympics. Working-class men also imbued sports with notions of masculinity.[11] The most popular nineteenth-century games and contests—football, hockey, lacrosse, track and field, and boxing—were termed "the manly sports." Although they have now lost the epithet, they continue to be encouraged for the same reason.

To be sure, there have been differences in the values emphasized by sports and in the approaches different participants may take to a single sport. Soccer and rugby have always encouraged more spontaneous creativity than North American football. The Montreal Canadiens have never practiced the "beat-'em-in-the-alley" tactics of their traditional rivals, the Toronto Maple Leafs. These differences should be read in part as contributions to a continuing debate about which aspects of masculinity are most attractive. When Charles Dickens championed boxing in the pages of *The Pickwick Papers* against the contemporary prohibition, he was not endorsing brutality, but a more scientific, humane, and democratic method for men to settle their disputes than the duel.[12] When Wayne Gretsky skated away from a fight in a playoff game several years ago, he made it clear he was rejecting the dominant code of "masculinity" in North American hockey—which emphasizes defending your "honor" by dropping your stick and gloves to fight—in favor of the intelligence of staying out of the penalty box.[13] The frequent vehemence of these debates only serves to underline the importance of sports as signifiers of "masculinity."

## SPORTS AS MALE PRESERVES

The men who developed and promoted sports in the nineteenth and twentieth centuries were careful to ensure that only males were masculinized in this way. They kept sports as male preserves by actively discouraging females from participating. They denied them adequate facilities and programs, ridiculed their attempts, and threatened them with the specter of ill health and "race suicide." Male doctors and physical educators argued that humans had only a finite quantity of energy, which in the case of women was needed for reproduction, an energy drain "which would make the stroke oar of the University crew falter." If women used up their energy in vigorous athletic activity, went the argument, they would not only be undermining their own health, but the future of the white race. Working-class men generally shared these prejudices and contributed to the exclusionary practices. Thus sports helped to strengthen and extend male bonds between classes. Many girls and women were also deterred from taking part in sports by economic and social conditions—long hours of domestic labor, differential and generally less adequate diets, and restrictive dress.[14]

Women persisted, however. During the 1920s and 1970s especially, girls and women engaged in competitive sports in growing numbers. But males have continued to exclude them from their own games and contests, requiring them to play on women's teams with inferior resources.[15] Despite the examples from agriculture, industry, and sports of women performing arduous "men's tasks," many persist in the belief that a distinct female biology prevents women from competing in the male realm. (The argument falsely assumes that all men are the same in size, strength, and fitness, and that all women are uniformly inferior. In the reality many so blithely ignore, there is a tremendous range in male and female size, strength, fitness, and so on. For most of the population, including trained athletes, those ranges overlap.)[16] Organizers have also tried to confine females to those sports believed to enhance traditional "femininity," such as swimming, tennis, and gymnastics, and to devise "girls' rules" to discourage the ambitious and aggressive play expected of boys and men.[17] Women athletes have also faced inordinate pressure to conform to the heterosexual expectations of most men.[18]

SPORTS AS PATRIARCHAL IDEOLOGY

One legacy of this pattern of development is the well-known inequalities that continue to plague females seeking sporting opportunities and careers. In North America, despite a decade of "progress," males still have more than twice the opportunities and public resources available for sport. There is little evidence that the men who control sport are genuinely committed to redressing the balance. In the Olympic Games, there are still more than twice as many events for men as for women.[19] But if we were to conclude that the problem is simply one of allocation, we would be missing the most important insight of the feminist critique. The effect of sports is also to perpetuate patriarchy by reinforcing the sexual division of labor. By giving males exciting opportunities, preaching that the qualities they learn from them are "masculine," and preventing girls and women from learning in the same situations, sports confirm the prejudice that males are a breed apart. By encouraging us to spend our most creative and engrossing moments as children and our favorite forms of recreation as adults in the company of other males, they condition us to trust each other much more than women. By publicly celebrating the dramatic achievements of the best males, while marginalizing females as cheerleaders and spectators, they validate the male claim to the most important positions in society. Abby Hoffman, a four-time Canadian Olympian and now Director-General of Sport Canada, has written:

> The overall place of women in the labor force is in the lower-paying and sedentary occupations. There are of course many reasons for this, but certainly arguments about the physical inferiority of women learned and repeated through sport help buttress a system where women become stenographers, typists, retail salespersons, telephone operators, etc., and men become truck drivers, carpenters, labourers, construction workers, and workers in a host of manual trades which involve a modicum of physical capacity.[20]

Sports contribute to the underdevelopment of the female majority of the population and the undervaluing of those traditionally "feminine" skills of nurturing and emotional maintenance essential to human survival and growth.

I believe these relationships are understood by sportsmen as well. In nineteenth-century Canada and the United States, men introduced sports to public-school boys and the adolescent members of organizations such as the YMCA to combat the feminization of teaching.[21] British sociologists Kevin Sheard and Eric Dunning have suggested a direct relationship between the development of the boorish, sexist subculture of rugby—the public moonings, songs of male sexual conquest of women, and exaggerated drinking—and first-wave feminism:

> The historical conjuncture represented by the simultaneous rise of rugby football and the suffragette movement within the upper and middle classes may have been of some significance with respect to the emergence of the specific pattern of socially tolerated taboo breaking. For women were increasingly becoming a threat to men, and men responded by developing

rugby football as a male preserve in which they could bolster up their threatened masculinity and at the same time mock, objectify, and vilify women, the principal source of the threat.[22]

We are witnessing a similar conjuncture today. In Toronto, where there is a strong women's movement, the city fathers have just given final approval to a new domed stadium, to be built on prime public land and subsidized by municipal and provincial grants. The architect calls it "a secular cathedral." I suggest it be called the Men's Cultural Center. It is being developed by an almost exclusively male board of a provincial crown corporation. Its primary tenants will be the local franchises of the commercial baseball and football cartels, the Blue Jays and the Argonauts, which stage male team games for largely male audiences. The other major beneficiaries will be the public and private media corporations, which sell the predominantly male audiences to the sponsoring advertisers.[23] There is no doubt the stadium is popular, among both men and women. It will be a great improvement over the existing stadium, increasing the pleasure derived from watching gifted athletes. But at the ideological level, especially in the absence of comparable opportunities for female athletes, coaches, managers, and sports impresarios, it will celebrate male privilege, displaying male prowess while leaving the gendered nature of sport unchallenged. Women as well as men are capable of difficult, dramatic, and pleasing feats of grace, agility, strength, and teamwork, but we will never know this from this stadium. They will be either rendered invisible or exploited as sex objects (cheerleaders) along the sidelines. Males who identify with the athletes on the field are also basking in the privilege that sports bring them and in the "symbolic annihilation"[24] of women. If a city were to devote twenty-five acres of prime downtown real estate and at least $85 million of public funds to a stadium in which only Anglo-Saxons could play, there would be howls of protest, but in the matter of sex, most of us take such favoritism for granted. Needless to say, there are other forces at work—in Toronto's case, the deal was initiated by land developers and the holding company of the brewery that owns the baseball team—but it is more than a coincidence that during the period of second-wave feminism, male political leaders and business and media executives have worked hard to place the male-only sports on a more commodious and visible stage, while women's crisis centers go underfunded. The stadium will even look like a Men's Cultural Center. Standing at the foot of the world's tallest freestanding telecommunications tower, it will be a gigantic Klaes Oldenberg-like sculpture of the male genitals.

MEN'S FEARS

The Australian social biologist Ken Dyer has shown that women's records in the measurable sports like track and field and swimming are now being broken significantly faster than men's records in the same events and has concluded that lack of opportunity—not biology—is the primary reason why female performances have always lagged behind those of males. Projecting his findings into the future, he suggests that if opportunities for women can be equalized, in most sports the best females will eventually be able to compete on a par with the best males.[25] Imagine a woman winning the open 100 metres at the Olympics or playing in the National Hockey League! Performances once considered impossible are now common in virtually every sport, but most men balk at Dyer's suggestion. It's not only that they don't believe it could happen, but it frightens them. They fear that the character of sport would change if women played with men. "You have to play softer with women," a softball official testified to the Ontario Human Rights Commission to explain why he felt integrated competition, even when the female players had been chosen for their ability, would reduce the satisfaction for males.[26] But although it is unspoken, I believe they also fear the profound social and psychological changes that might result if women were understood to be fully competent in the special domain of men. At present in Ontario, the 500,000-male-strong Ontario Hockey Association has refused to allow a thirteen-year-old girl to play on one of its teams, although she won a place on the team in a competitive tryout. The OHA has gone to court three times in an effort to stop her, and it continues to block her participation while the matter will be heard one more time by the Ontario Human Rights Commission.[27] Is one thirteen-year-old female player, or even two hundred female players, going to topple the male hockey leadership, or drastically alter the values of this century-old sport? Hardly. There must be something deeper.

In part, what they fear is the disorientation of the male psyche. As Nancy Chodorow has argued in *The Reproduction of Mothering*,[28] boys develop their identity by differentiating themselves from their mothers. Since most child rearing has been done by women, the primary interaction for young males has been with women, with the result that they have great difficulty in identifying with their fathers. So, Chodorow says, in developing a "masculine" identity, males are essentially learning to differentiate themselves from their mothers and from women in general. They rehearse and strengthen this "positional" masculinity in activities that accentuate male-female differences and stigmatize those characteristics generally associated with women. Although Chodorow does not discuss sports, it is clear that they were developed—and serve—that very purpose in the industrial capitalist societies with which we are most familiar. It was certainly my experience growing up in Toronto in the 1940s and 1950s. I played sports endlessly as a child. I gobbled up the rules, skills, strategies, and lore, none of which seemed to interest my mother, her friends, or the girls of my own age on the street. Certainly we rarely included them. I also learned to accept (rather than question) physical pain, to deny anxiety and anger, and to be aggressive in ways that were clearly valued as "manly." I realize now that I gained an enormous sense of my own power when I could respond to challenges in this way, for it meant I was not "like a girl." In fact, sometimes I teased my mother and sister to tears to confirm that I had succeeded in being different from them. Yet it shows how shaky such positional identity can be, because when I put myself into the emotional state I remember from that period, I realize that I would have been devastated if a girl had played on any of the teams I was so proud to belong to. It would have proclaimed to the world that I was inadequate. At the deepest psychological levels, the blurring of sex roles undermines not only the male-privileging sexual division of labor, but the very process by which males raised within sexually segregated sports have gained personal confidence and social validation.

There are other possible disruptions as well. Men also fear the loss of traditional nurturing that might result if women learned through sports (and other predominantly male activities) to be as hard and unyielding as males. This helps explain why so many men are still determined to keep sports a male sanctuary, why in the quintessentially masculine sport of boxing many jurisdictions still prohibit women from competing at all, even against other women. It also helps us understand the psychological weight of the pressures on female athletes to be "feminine." To be sure, many women share these fears and support the status quo. As Dorothy Dinnerstein points out, males and females actively collaborate to maintain the existing gender arrangements: "nostalgia for the familiar is a feeling that has . . . been mobilized in opposition to social change."[29] But the price of such collaboration is high.

A MEN'S PROBLEM

Most observers consider the inequalities and power dynamics I have described to be a "women's problem," but I would argue that the patriarchal nature of modern sports has harmed men, too. By encouraging and reinforcing a positional identity, sports have led us to limit our options as humans, to deny feelings and to disparage—and therefore not to learn—the interpersonal skills associated with females. By teaching us a form of strength and assertiveness disconnected from emotional understanding and the skills of emotional support, they have encouraged us to ignore our own inner feelings and those of others. Through sports, men learn to cooperate with, care for, and love other men, in a myriad of rewarding ways, but they rarely learn to be intimate with each other or emotionally honest. On the contrary, the only way many of us express fondness for other men is by teasing or mock fighting (the private version of what has become a public form of tribute—the roast). As other authors in this volume point out, anything more openly affectionate would be suspect.

Chodorow and Dinnerstein argue that the development of positional identity has also contributed to the process by which males value abstract achievement—which in sport has meant victory and records. Because they elevate external goals over intrinsic ones, sports have encouraged those who become athletes to treat their bodies as instruments and to submit to physical and psychological injury and to inflict it on others. The active repression of pain is an everyday part of the sports world: "no pain, no gain" is a common slogan, but it has ruined the careers of countless athletes and left many permanently crippled. There are also psychological scars: the constant emphasis on external goals such as winning and being chosen for an international team is highly pathological and leaves many forever stunted and unable to define their own goals. At the same time, sports label those who cannot meet the ever higher standards of performance expected of athletes as "failures."[30]

I am particularly concerned about the effect of sports on our relations with other men. The Australian sociologist Bob Connell suggests that sports instruct men in two aspects of power: the development of force ("the irresistible occupation of space") and skill ("the ability to operate on the objects within that space, including other humans").[31] The rules of football (all codes), basketball, boxing, hockey, and other sports where territorial control is important almost literally conform to this definition. They encourage athletes to treat each other as enemies to be intimidated and brutalized, when in reality they are co-players without whom the rewards of playing cannot be obtained. This is the other side of "that sweet spot in time," or "walking tall," the exhilaration of doing it right in sport. Thomas Tutko, the noted American sports psychologist, likes to say that "to be a champion, you have to be the meanest Son-of-a-Bitch in the valley."[32] Certainly I felt this when I was a successful middle-distance runner. I developed the sense that I owned every race, and I instinctively resented—without ever really thinking about it—any attempt by other runners to try for the lead. "How dare they!" I'd hear my inner self say, as I surged to beat back their challenge. I also revelled in the psychological warfare that is endemic in sports and loved to probe a competitor's personality and to devise tactics to intimidate him. But as productive as aggressiveness and competitiveness were when it came to winning races, they are enormous barriers to the development and maintenance of close relationships. I've spent the past twenty years trying to bring them under control. Other athletes I know say the same.

## TOWARD MORE HUMANE SPORTING PRACTICES

There are no magic solutions to the problems I have described. They are deeply rooted in long-established patterns of child rearing and human interaction and are perpetuated by powerful economic and political interests. We cannot dismiss or abolish sports, as some on the left have suggested, nor should we want to. They can help all humans acquire self-mastery in pleasurable, healthy and popular skills and rituals. Such opportunities are particularly important in societies like our own where work is more and more automated and alienating. Sports can also provide easily understood popular dramas in ways that strengthen the sense of community and confirm some of the most widely shared human values. Hockey may be a puberty rite for Canadian boys, but it is also a celebration of the creativity, energy, and elan of the human spirit in the depths of winter, the season of death. The contradictions of modern sports can sometimes undermine the very privilege they enshrine. In their claim to be democratic, sports organizations provide the arguments—though less frequently opportunities—for the disadvantaged to demonstrate their right to a better future. In the Olympic Games, for example, the universalist aspirations of the ruling International Olympic Committee (IOC) have paved the way for athletes from the poorest and smallest national communities to compete, even when they have had little chance at medals. In turn, the overwhelming presence of the Third World nations—there are now 161 national Olympic committees—has persuaded the elitist IOC, which is dominated by Western European countries, to support the international struggle against apartheid and racism and to begin a program of technical assistance to the have-not nations.

The liberation of sports from patriarchal (and class and Western) structures of domination will be a long and complex process. It will have to be undertaken in conjunction with similar efforts in other areas of everyday life. The outcome—how humans will play sports in a more egalitarian, less oppressive age—will largely depend upon those broader struggles, because as we have seen, forms of physical activity, including sport, are determined by history. But that should not dissuade us.

We can start by actively questioning the pervasive masculinist bias in the sports world. The language is rife with words that unconsciously reinforce the male preserve: "jock," the popular term for athlete; "tomboy" to describe any bright, active girl who likes physical activity and is good at sports; "suck" and "sissy" to condemn anyone who betrays anxiety or fear—all remind us that sports were designed to harden males. We should challenge those words the way the civil rights movement did with "nigger" and "boy" and the women's movement has done with "mankind" and "girl". We need to develop substitutes (such as "athlete" for "jock") and then campaign to remove the offending terms from use. In some cases, it will be necessary to change the practices as well. Although we will always admire physical courage, we do ourselves a disservice if we continue uncritically to condemn the expression of pain and uneasiness that is usually associated with being a "sissy."

We should challenge the gross sexism of that inner sanctuary of patriarchy, the locker and shower room. Allen Sack, an American sociologist who played on the 1966 Notre Dame championship football team, has said that in many ways football is a training ground for rape. In the game, players learn to control the field and to dominate other players, and in the dressing room they endlessly fantasize and celebrate the male sexual conquest of women.[33] It takes a different kind of courage to contest the explicit, omnipresent misogyny of the locker room. Much of what is said is often exuberantly rich in humor. Yet it contributes to our own repression, as well as to the exploitation of women. If you contest it, you'll get anger and denial—"it's just a joke; I'm not a chauvinist!"—but it does cause a person to reconsider.

We can also help to redefine the rules and values of sports to make them more inviting to everybody. Physical educators, coaches, and community groups of both sexes have amended rules to make games safer and more genuinely educational. In Canada, parents, players, teachers, and government leaders have contributed to the effort to eliminate the gratuitous violence of ice hockey. In my neighborhood, a community softball league, to reduce collisions between players, has added a second first base (immediately adjacent to the original base, but in foul territory) and has eliminated the necessity of tagging the runner at home. These changes often require tradeoffs—I was sorry to see the softballers discourage the slide—but by doing so they subtly reduced the premium on physical dominance. (When I was nine, I was taught to throw a cross-body block at second, third, and home. "There's $10 on every bag," our coach would tell us, "and if you don't get it, he will.") These experiments, expecially when they result from open discussion about the purpose of sports, should be encouraged. To opponents who appeal to "tradition," we can point out that the rules of games have been continually changed for other reasons, so why not to make them more humane?

We should also struggle to change the tendency to see sports as battles. Competitions are viewed as zero-sum contests, and athletes are encouraged to treat each other as enemies. Military metaphors abound: quarterbacks "throw the long bomb"; teams "whip," "punish," "roll over," and "savage" each other. This imagery is hardly coincidental: in many societies competitive physical activity has been closely associated with military training. But instead, I suggest we consider sports to be glorious improvisations, dialectical play, or collective theatre where athletes are part antagonist, part partner. We can still applaud the winner, but not at the expense of other members of the cast. Such alternative descriptions fit the private experiences of many athletes. I realize now that while I defined them as combats, some of my best races came when other runners "helped with the work" of pace-setting, and challenged me with novel tactics. In the most intrinsically rewarding races, this reciprocal process of "let me lead the way" went on and on and invariably all of us were urged on to outstanding performances. Many other athletes have made the same point. Bill Russell of the Boston Celtics, one of the greatest basketball players of all time, has written:

> Every so often a Celtic game would heat up so that it became more than a physical or even a mental game, and would be magical. That feeling is difficult to describe, and I certainly never talked about it when I was playing. When it happened I could feel my play rise to a new level. That feeling would surround not only me, and the other Celtics, but also the players on the other team, and even the referees. To me, the key was that *both* teams had to be playing at their peaks, and they had to be competitive. The Celtics could not do it alone. . . .

Sometimes the feeling would last all the way to the end of the game, and when that happened I never cared who won. I can honestly say that those few times were the only ones when I did *not* care. I don't mean that I was a good sport about it—I did not care who had won. If we lost, I'd still be as free as a sky hawk. But I had to keep quiet about it.[34]

If confident champions have "to keep quiet," what about the less gifted? We should strive to help all athletes understand their experiences this way.

There are powerful forces that structure games as contests and fuel the tremendous exhilaration of triumph. In North America, the mass media and governments have monopolized the interpretation of athletic performance, and the participants' voice has been distorted, if not silenced. But other cultural performers—painters, dancers, actors, film makers—and their audiences have begun to contest the corporate media's interpretation of their work, and sportspersons could well learn from their example. A sports culture that de-emphasized winning in favor of exploring artistry and skill and the creative interaction of "rival" athletes would be much less repressive.

Finally, we should actively support those feminists who are struggling to combat sexism and inequality in sports. In this, we should take our lead from advocacy groups, like the Canadian Association for the Advancement of Women and Sport (the "and Sport" rather than "in Sport" was a conscious recognition that it will not be enough just to increase the number of opportunities), that represent females on the front lines of these issues and have developed strategies and tactics from the experience. Here, too, the most useful work we can do will be with men. It will be necessary to assure males who resist integration on the basis of ability that we are strong enough to survive an "invasion" of outstanding female athletes. We can help defend affirmative action and hiring programs planned to help sports women overcome the historic inequalities they face; we can support protections for the existing all-female programs and the scarce resources and opportunities they enjoy. The most difficult task will be to persuade other men that sex-divided sports are not only a "women's problem," but in dialectical interaction, harm us as well. Once that is understood, the essential redesigning of sports can really begin.

## NOTES

An earlier version of this article appears in the *Queen's Quarterly* 94, no. 1 (sprin

[1]Norbert Elias, "The Genesis of Sport as a Sociological Problem," in Eric Du
*Sociology of Sport* (Toronto: University of Toronto, 1972), 85-115.

[2]M.I. Finlay and H.W. Pleket, *The Olympic Games: The First Thousand Years* (London: Chatto and Windus, 1976) and David Young, *The Myth of Greek Amateur Athletics* (Chicago: Ares, 1985).

[3]R.G. Sipes, "War, sports, and aggression," *American Anthropoligist* 75 (1973): 64-86.

[4]John MacAloon, *This Great Symbol: Pierre de Coubertin and the Origins of the Modern Olympic Games* (Chicago: University of Chicago, 1981).

[5]Hugh Cunningham, *Leisure in the Industrial Revolution* (London: Croom Helm, 1980); Eric Dunning and Kevin Sheard, *Barbarians, Gentlemen and Players* (New York: New York University, 1979); and Allen Guttman, *From Ritual to Record* (New York: Columbia, 1978).

[6]J.A. Mangan, *Athleticism in the Victorian and Edwardian Public School* (Cambridge: Cambridge University Press, 1981).

[7]Lincoln Allison, "Batsman and Bowler: the Key Relationship of Victorian England," *Journal of Sport History* 7, no. 2 (1980): 5-20.

[8]Peter Bailey, *Leisure and Class in Victorian England* (Toronto: University of Toronto, 1978) and Morris Mott, "One Solution to the Urban Crisis: Manly Sports and Winnipeggers, 1900-1914," *Urban History Review* 12, no. 2 (1983): 57-70.

[9]Richard Gruneau, *Class, Sports and Social Development* (Amherst: University of Massachusetts, 1983), 91-135.

[10]Thomas Hughes, *Tom Brown's Schooldays* (London: Macmillan, 1979), 60-1; first published in 1867.

[11]See, for example, Bryan Palmer, *A Culture in Conflict* (Montreal and Kingston: McGill-Queen's University Press, 1979), 35-70.

[12]James Marlow, "Popular Culture, Pugilism, and Pickwick," *Journal of Popular Culture* 15, no. 4 (1982).

[13]Bruce Kidd, "Skating away from a fight: Canadian sport, culture, and personal responsibility," in William Baker and James Rog, eds., *Sports and the Humanities* (Orono: University of Maine at Orono, 1983), 41-54.

[14]Paul Atkinson, "Fitness, Feminism, and Schooling," in Sara Delamont and Lorna Duffin, eds., *The Nineteenth Century Woman: Her Physical and Cultural World* (London: Croom Helm, 1978) and Helen Lenskyj, *Out of Bounds: Women, Sports, and Sexuality* (Toronto: Women's Press, 1986). The quotation is from London medical professor Henry Maudsley, quoted by Atkinson, p. 103.

[15]Ann M. Hall and Dorothy Richardson, *Fair Ball* (Ottawa: Canadian Advisory Council on the Status of Women, 1982) and Mary Boutilier and Lucinda San Giovanni, *The Sporting Woman* (Champagne, Ill.: Human Kinetics, 1983).

[16]Ruth Hubbard, Mary Sue Henifin, and Barbara Fried, *Biological Woman: The Convenient Myth* (Cambridge: Schenkman, 1982) and Lynda Birke, *Women, Feminism and Biology* (Brighton: Harvester, 1986).

[17]Many women contributed to the development of "girls' rules." Paul Atkinson, Helen Lenskyj, and others have argued that in part this was a tactically necessary defense against male control of women's institutions, that without them girls and women would not have been allowed to play at all, and that they were a creative attempt to avoid some of the most brutalizing features of male sport. Nevertheless, they confined most females interested in sports to a ghetto of inequality and left the existing stereotypes about female frailty unchallenged.

[18]Dorothy Kidd, "Getting Physical: Compulsory Heterosexuality in Sport" *Canadian Woman Studies 4*, no. 3 (1983): 62-5.

[19]See for example John Sopinka, *Can I Play? Report of the Task Force on Equality in Athletics* (Toronto: Ontario Ministry of Labour 1983 and 1984) vols. 1 and 2. The Canadian sports minister Otto Jelinek, has admitted that despite a twelve-year federal effort to increase women's opportunities, very little change has occurred. "My belief is that there hasn't been a commitment to promote the women's program," he said. See "Ottawa aiming to get more girls involved in sport," the *Globe and Mail*, 7 Oct. 1986.

[20]Abby Hoffman, "Towards Equality for Women in Sport—a Canadian Perspective," *Momentum* 4, no. 2 (1979): 3.

[21]Joseph Kett, *Rites of Passage* (New York: Basic, 1977); Leila Mitchell McKee, " 'Nature's medicine': the physical education and outdoor recreation programs in Toronto volunteer youth

groups," in Bruce Kidd, ed., *Proceedings of the 5th Canadian Symposium on the History of Sport and Physical Education* (Toronto: School of Physical and Health Education, 1982), 128-39; and David MacLeod, *Building Character in the American Boy* (Madison: University of Wisconsin, 1983).

22Kevin Sheard and Eric Dunning, "The Rugby Football Club as a Male Preserve," *International Review of Sports Sociology* 3-4 (1973): 12.

23Sut Jhally, "The Spectacle of Accumulation: Material and Cultural Factors in the Evolution of the Sports/Media Complex," *The Insurgent Sociologist* 12, no. 3 (1984): 41-57.

24Boutilier and San Giovanni, *The Sporting Woman,* 185-218.

25K.F. Dyer, *Challenging the Men* (New York: University of Queensland, 1982). For a critical feminist review, see Cathy Bray, *Canadian Woman Studies 4,* no. 3 (1983): 92-3.

26*Re Ontario Softball Association and Bannerman* (1978), 21 O.R. (2d) 395 (H.C.J.—Div. Ct.).

27The player, Justine Blainey, was successful in having the Ontario Court of Appeal declare that section 19(2) of the Ontario Human Rights Code, which had allowed sports bodies to discriminate on the basis of sex, was in violation of the Charter of Rights and Freedoms and therefore invalid. But the court would not declare that the OHA's refusal to allow Blainey to play was a violation of the code as amended by that decision. Blainey is therefore seeking such a ruling from the OHRC. See Bruce Kidd "Ontario legalizes discrimination," *Canadian Woman Studies* 4, no. 3 (1984): 41-3 and Justine Blainey v. Ontario Hockey Association and Ontario Human Rights Commission, 17 April 1986, unreported (Ont. C.A. # 630/85).

28Chodorow *The Reproduction of Mothering* (Berkeley: University of California, 1978).

29Dinnerstein *The Mermaid and the Minotaur* (New York: Harper, 1976), 229.

30Dorcus Susan Butt, *Psychology of Sport* (Toronto: Van Nostrand Reinhold, 1976) and Terry Orlick and Cal Botterill, *Every Kid Can Win* (Chicago: Nelson Hall, 1974).

31R.W. Connell, "Men's Bodies," in *Which way is up?* (Sydney: George Allen and Unwin 1983), 18.

32Thomas A. Tutko and H. Bruns, *Winning is everything and other American myths* (New York: Macmillan, 1976).

33Quoted by Varda Burstyn, "Play, Performance and Power—the Men," CBC Radio "Ideas," 2 Oct. 1986. The script is available from CBC Transcripts.

34Bill Russell and Taylor Branch, *Second Wind: The Memories of an Opinionated Man* (New York: Random House, 1979).

# Raging Bull: The Homosexual Subtext in Film

ROBIN WOOD

It has been asked why Martin Scorsese should have wanted to make a film about so unattractive, unpleasant, and limited a character as boxer Jake La Motta, as he is created by Scorsese and Robert DeNiro. Indeed, *Raging Bull* seems a particularly difficult *kind* of film to criticize. The acting style favored by the director and lead actor—derived from the Actors' Studio and from the Method school, with its emphasis on spontaneity, improvisation, and behaviorism—tends to deflect the viewer's attention from the structure and the kinds of meaning generated by it and to focus attention upon the acting and character study. Thus critic Andrew Sarris can complain of Scorsese's lack of a sense of structure (meaning, presumably, that his films do not have the "well-made" scenario of classical Hollywood) and see *Raging Bull* only as a number of extraordinary moments strung together.[1]

The meaning the film at first appears to offer—La Motta's progress toward some kind of partial understanding, acceptance, or grace—seems insufficient to justify the project. After all, the film is extremely vague about the nature of this grace or how it has been achieved. Any suggestion of that kind is thoroughly outweighed by the sense the film conveys of pointless and unredeemed pain—both the pain La Motta experiences and the pain he inflicts. If this overwhelming sense of pointless pain leads the audience to question the institutions of masculinity and obsessive heterosexuality, it is because of the impact of the film on the viewer and not because of the progress of La Motta toward a state of grace and understanding. The difficulty of escaping the power of these institutions is made brutally clear as the boxer bashes his way incoherently from beginning to end.

If one rejects the film's invitation to understand it as a movement toward salvation, one must accept the invitation to read it centrally as a character study (though "case history" might be the more felicitous term). The film's fragmented structure can be attributed to La Motta's own incoherence, to Scorsese's fascination with that incoherence, and to the violence that is the product of that incoherence. That audiences are also fascinated by La Motta, not merely appalled, testifies to the representativeness that the film's apparent concentration on a singular individual seems to deny. If we can make sense of La Motta we shall make sense of the film's structure and, simultaneously, be in a position to explain the fascination that La Motta and the film hold for us.

Seeking a way into the film, we may begin with the montage sequence that intercuts La Motta's home movies with a series of his fights. That sequence is highlighted in two ways: first it is a very unusual kind of sequence, virtually unclassifiable within the cinematic categories of Metz's "Grande Syntagmatique."[2] Second, it is marked by the only intrusion into the film of colour (aside from the opening credits). The intercutting suggests that there is an intimate relationship between two seemingly disparate aspects of La Motta's life, that the fights are somehow necessary to the construction of "domestic happiness" that is the raison d'être of the home movies. By this point (about a third of the way through), the film has definitively established black-and-white as its "reality"; conversely, then, the color signifies illusion. This *illusion* of domestic happiness is presented clearly as Jake's construction: he "directs" the movies, he brings gifts to his wife, Vickie, he drops her into the swimming pool, and so on. At the same time, the fights are given an illusory quality of another order by the use of technical devices such as stills and slow motion: black-and-white reality becomes a dream.

Jake's exclusion from a lived reality is dramatized particularly in his relationship with women, which is characterized by an inability to respond to them as persons. It is one of the film's finest achievements, given the extent to which it is centered on Jake's consciousness, to convey to the audience (through the performance of Cathy Moriarty as Vickie, but also through the very small role of Jake's first wife) a female response that is shown simultaneously to be beyond Jake's comprehension. For Jake, Vickie is from first to last an object without independent existence. The film associates her repeatedly with swimming pools—the tenement pool where Jake first sees her, the pool of the home movies, the pool of their Miami home—and with the Lana Turner image—the most plastic and constructed of all the Hollywood star images: she is first shown posed by the pool in 1941, the release year of *Honky Tonk, Johnny Eager, Ziegfeld Girl,* and *Dr. Jekyll and Mr. Hyde*—the year of Turner's rise to the position of major star and glamor-symbol. The image is completed in the 1946 home movies (release year of *The Postman Always Rings Twice*) by Vickie's adoption of the famous white turban and sunsuit. Vickie is shown to be an accomplice in her own objectification and yet to have an existence outside it. In the course of the film Jake undergoes striking physical transformations, which were made much of in the publicity surrounding DeNiro, while Vickie remains unchanged, as Jake's object, construction, and possession. Specifically, Jake can't relate to mature women or to women who demand recognition as autonomous beings (see the casting-off of the first wife). A scene in his Miami nightclub contrasts his flirtations with the teenage girls, who "prove" they're not under age by kissing him, with his animosity toward mature women. As he kisses the state attorney's wife he upsets a drink all over her.

The film counterpoints two forms of violence: violence against women and violence against men, the latter subdivided between the socially licensed violence in the ring and the socially proscribed "spontaneous" violence in public and private. While the motivations for these different manifestations of violence may seem quite distinct—Jake's pursuit of a boxing career, his jealousy of Vickie—I think a true understanding of the film depends on grasping the relationship between them.[3] The film suggests quite clearly that there is a connection: on two occasions, Jake's fears of being overweight, that is, of not being allowed to fight a man in the ring, are closely linked to another explosion of paranoid jealousy and potential or actual violence toward Vickie. Through a repeated motif the film also connects phallus and fist: Jake douses his cock with cold water to prevent himself reaching orgasm, and in a subsequent moment marked by a close-up he plunges his fist into an ice bucket to cool it after a fight. It is important to notice that the violence, though centered on Jake, is by no means exclusive to him but is generalized as a characteristic of the society, the product of its construction of sexual difference. By "the society," I mean something much wider than the specific Italian-American subculture within which the film is set. Furthermore, both forms of violence can be interpreted as Jake's defenses against the return of his repressed homosexuality.

## FREUD (AND SCORSESE) ON PARANOIA AND REPRESSED HOMOSEXUALITY

As a conclusion to his well-known analysis of the Schreber case, Freud offers a general statement about paranoia and the principal forms of paranoid delusion that seems as relevant to the Jake La Motta of *Raging Bull* as to Dr. Schreber:

> We are ... driven by experience to attribute to the homosexual wish-phantasy an intimate (perhaps an invariable) relation to this particular form of disease. Distrusting my own experience on the subject, I have during the last few years joined with my friends C.G. Jung ... and S. Ferenczi ... in investigating upon this single point a number of cases of paranoid disorder which have come under observation. The patients whose histories provided the material for this inquiry included both men and women, and varied in race, occupation, and social standing. Yet we were astonished to find that in all of these cases a defense against a homosexual wish was clearly recognizable at the very center of the conflict which underlay the disease, and that it was in an attempt to master an unconsciously reinforced current of homosexuality that they had all of them come to grief.[4]

Since, four pages later, Freud remarks in a casual aside that "a similar disposition would have to be assigned to patients suffering from ... schizophrenia,"[5] we can see that he had come close to positing repressed homosexuality as a major source of mental illness. It is important to note that Freud says the problem is not the homosexuality or bisexuality itself, but the attempts to repress these wishes.

We can now consider the La Motta of *Raging Bull* in relation to the four forms of paranoia referred to by Freud. "The familiar principal forms of paranoia can all be represented as contradictions of the single proposition: '*I* (as man) *love him* (a man).' " Of the four forms listed by Freud, no fewer than three apply strikingly to *Raging Bull*. To express these forms Freud uses simple phrases of contradiction to express a constellation of unconscious thoughts:

1. "I do not *love* him—I *hate* him." According to Freud, this usually requires the justification of delusions of persecution, as the hatred must be felt to be morally and rationally motivated ("I hate him because he persecutes me"). But it is precisely Jake's profession that renders such a cover superfluous: as a boxer, he is licensed to express his animosity against male bodies directly and in public before an approving audience. Two points need to be made here that lead in somewhat opposite directions. First, Jake is presented as an exceptional case, a boxer noted, not for his skill, grace, and agility, but for obsessive ferocity and excess. This of course confirms the Freudian diagnosis of La Motta as an individual "case," but it may distract us from the more general implications of boxing as a social institution. Secondly, we should not lose sight of these wider issues, though it is beyond the scope of the present article to pursue them: I mean the cultural significance of boxing itself as licensed and ritualized violence in which one man attempts to smash the near-naked body of

another for the satisfaction of a predominantly male, mass audience. It would be interesting to discover whether there is any significant correlation between an enthusiasm for boxing and homophobia.

2. The least relevant of Freud's categories is what one might call the Don Juan syndrome: homosexuality is denied by means of obsessive pursuit of women ("I don't love men—I love women"). It is not presented as a prominent symptom of the La Motta case history, though strong traces of it manifest themselves in the latter part of the film, in Jake's need to be admired by women (especially attractive young women) in his nightclub at the expense of Vickie and the domestic "happiness" constructed in the home movies. Three points are germane: (a) It is clearly essential that this take place in public. The motive behind this behavior is to preserve Jake's image as a man both attractive to and attracted by women, rather than to obtain any actual erotic satisfaction. (b) The form the syndrome finally takes is Jake's trick with the champagne glasses of constructing a phallus, in public, before the admiring gaze of women. (We discover subsequently that it is during this action that Vickie is preparing finally to leave him.) (c) The syndrome manifests itself only after Jake has been denied his real erotic satisfaction of pummelling men in the ring. The public display of "I don't love men—I hate them" gives way to the public display of "I don't love men—I love women (and they love me)."

3. Another of Freud's categories contains his explanation of the close connection between paranoia and megalomania: the ultimate denial. "I don't love at all" has as its corollary "I love only myself." Thus megalomania is "a sexual overestimation [or overvaluation] of the ego." The relevance of this to La Motta is obvious.

4. I have left to last what is actually the third of Freud's categories of contradiction in the discussion of paranoia because, in relation to *Raging Bull,* it is the most resonant of all. This is the form of "sexual delusions of jealousy." We should not let ourselves be diverted from its implications by Freud's association of it with alcohol, which is clearly inessential. He writes:

> It is not infrequently disappointment over a woman that drives a man to drink—which means, as a rule, that he resorts to the public-house and to the company of men, who afford him the emotional satisfaction which he has failed to get from his wife at home. If now these men become the objects of a strong libidinal cathexis in his unconscious, he will ward it off with the third kind of contradiction: "It is not *I* who love the man—*she* loves him" and he suspects the woman in relation to all the men whom he himself is tempted to love.[6]

We can examine one manifestation of this last form of paranoia in the "Pelham, 1947" section of the film—the series of scenes that culminates in the fight with Janiro. The structure is as follows: (a) A domestic scene (Jake's family, his brother Joey's family) that links Jake's anxiety about his weight to his anxiety about Vickie. (b) The Copacabana scene: Vickie is invited to another table (presided over by Tommy, the godfather figure) and is kissed by other men. This is followed by Jake's obsessive questioning and distrust. He accepts the invitation to join the other men, and the conversation shifts to Janiro's physical beauty. Jake remarks, as a joke, "I don't know whether to fuck him or fight him." (c) At home, Jake awakens Vickie and resumes the interrogation about other men, finally attributing remarks about Janiro's beauty to her. "I don't even know what he looks like," she replies. (d) The fight: Jake deliberately destroys Janiro's face, with a smile of complicity at Vickie. He has effectively destroyed the threat Janiro posed, not by being attractive to Vickie, but by being attractive to himself.

This is perhaps the most obvious instance in the film of the kind of internal logic that it is my purpose to trace, but it is certainly not the only one. Near the beginning of the film, we are shown Jake's apparently irrational (and never adequately explained) hatred of Salvy, who is both a friend of Jake's brother Joey and, because of his Mafia connections, a potential booster of Jake's professional advancement. Salvy is with Vickie when Jake sees her for the first time at the tenement pool and immediately becomes fixated on her as an object. What the film dramatizes here is, very precisely, the relationship between "I don't love him—I *hate* him" and "I don't love him—I love *her*." This represents the possibility of movement from one of the forms of paranoia to another. Subsequently, Salvy is recruited into the ever-growing ranks of men Jake believes Vickie to have had sexual relations with.

We must briefly consider one possible objection to this reading of La Motta (and of the film): apart from Janiro, with his disturbing physical beauty, and Salvy, with his florid good looks, the two men who precipitate Jake's outbursts of paranoid jealousy are the sexually unattractive old godfather, Tommy, and Jake's own brother, Joey. Here we may have the film's most remarkable insight and the one that will be hardest to accept: it is precisely here that the parallels between the film and Freud's analysis of the Schreber case are most fascinating. Freud maintains that Schreber's original love objects (for whom all later men were stand-ins) must have been his own father and brother. Tommy patently functions in the film as the father figure;

Joey is Jake's actual brother. The film's insights are closely in line with Freud's insistence that erotic impulses take as their first objects the members of the immediate family circle. (One might note here the closeness of Italian-American family relationships, without attempting to restrict the film's implications to any specific milieu.) What provokes the ultimate, cataclysmic explosion of Jake's paranoid fantasy is Vickie's defiant, sarcastic assertion that she sucked Joey's cock.

### FROM BEGINNING TO END: IMPASSE AND A DUBIOUS EMBRACE

Despite the frequent complaint that Scorsese lacks a sense of structure, *Raging Bull* conforms to the familiar cinematic formula of "the end answers the beginning." But the symmetry and conclusion do not necessarily entail a restoration of patriarchal order. Rather, their function may be to mark precisely the point the narrative has reached by returning our memories to its starting point. We can single out two points of reference.

Near the beginning, during the violent row between Jake and his first wife, an unseen neighbor shouts that they are "animals" (consider also the film's title and Jake's predilection for dressing in animal skins for his entries into the ring). This scene is followed immediately by the scene with Joey in which, shortly after Joey has asked why Jake can't stand Salvy, Jake demands that his brother punch him in the face. These moments are "answered" by the prison sequence near the end where Jake, in the extremest instance of self-punishment, repeatedly beats his head against the wall of his cell after asserting, "I'm not an animal." It is also answered by the scene in the garage to which he follows Joey, repeatedly embracing him and kissing him. (The moment can be read as an ironic inversion of the notion of the kiss as a privileged climactic moment of classical cinema, epitomizing the formation of the heterosexual couple.)

We may also adduce here the moment at the beginning when Jake and Joey leave for the nightclub and Jake's wife screams after him, "Fucking queer." The prison and garage scenes, in fact, answer all these moments from the beginning: if Jake behaves like an "animal" (violently toward men and women) it is because he is blocked from loving either. His insistence that Joey punch him in the face is answered by the embrace. The self-punishment motif, in relation to Joey, is not only taken up symmetrically at the end: it is also treated very thoroughly earlier, in the climactic fight with Robinson, the point of Jake's retirement from the ring, which immediately follows his failure to apologize to Joey on the phone—the fight in which Jake allows himself to be beaten to a pulp, scarcely retaliating, but saving face by not being knocked down.

This is one instance in the film where screen time takes precedence over narrative chronology. We don't know how much time has elapsed between the abortive phone call to his brother and the Robinson fight, but Scorsese's montage has the latter directly follow the former, obeying the inner logic of psychological movement.

We have to confront the puzzle of the film's end, which is a more drastic use of the same license. The film begins and ends with Jake in 1964, fat, middle-aged, alone in his dressing room, practicing his nightclub act. At the beginning of the film he is inarticulate, thoroughly incompetent, unable to master his lines, a potential laughingstock. At the end, he has mastered himself and his material (the *On the Waterfront* speech of Brando to Steiger in the taxi) sufficiently to maintain his dignity. The intriguing problem here is of chronology. The film ends as it begins, in Jake's dressing room. But is it the same night?—the film doesn't tell us. Why is Jake incompetent at the start, adequate at the end?—the film doesn't tell us. One is forced to posit two chronologies at work—the narrative chronology (within which Jake's transformation makes no sense) and the actual movement of the film, in which the final scene directly follows the garage scene and the embrace. The film specifies a six-year gap between the garage scene and embrace and the final scene; the editing has one follow on from the other, as if its logical consequence. It is as if Scorsese wished simultaneously to assert and deny that the embrace was what made it possible for Jake to go through with his act—a speech, after all, about one brother's unsatisfied emotional dependence upon another ("I could have been a contender . . .").

The narrative of *Raging Bull,* then, has its own inner logic, its own internal correspondence and interrelationships. Far from being a rambling and structureless stringing together of "moments" or a "mere" character study, it is among the major cinematic statements of our age: a work that single-mindedly chronicles the disastrous consequences, for men and women alike, of the repression of constitutional bisexuality within our culture.

BISEXUALITY AND THE HOMOSEXUAL SUBTEXT OF RAGING BULL

The final point of this discussion, but really the starting point of the analysis, relates to Freud's important "discovery" of constitutional bisexuality. Freud himself was reluctant to pursue the implications of this discovery but, to his own evident surprise and discomfiture, found that in all the cases he analyzed, he discovered the traces of repressed homosexuality; and this revelation chimed with his investigations into the sexuality of children, the existence in infants and children of all those erotic impulses that our adult world of patriarchal "normality" labels "perversions."[7]

It is no surprise that Freud, himself an eminent turn-of-the-century patriarch with his own stake in that "normality," was incapable of pursuing the revolutionary implications of his discovery: he could only fall back lamely on the ideological assumption, which he never questioned or scrutinized, that the process of repression and the progress toward and into "normality" was both desirable and inevitable, despite his clear awareness that that very "normality" was characterized by misery, frustration, and neurosis.

What is repressed is never, of course, annihilated: it will always strive to return, in disguised forms, in dreams, or as neurotic symptoms. If Freud was correct we should expect to find the traces of repressed homosexuality in every film, just as we should expect to find them in every person, usually lurking beneath the surface, occasionally rupturing it, and informing in various ways the human relationships depicted. Hence this attempt to examine those traces in *Raging Bull,* which account for its relentless and almost hysterical intensity. The subtitle of this article comes from Martin Scorsese himself, who told me in a conversation in 1983 that, though he was not aware of it while making the film, he now saw that *Raging Bull* has a "homosexual subtext." But I hope it is clear that I wish my title to refer—at least by implication—far beyond the "homosexual subtext" of one film or even many. What I have in mind is the homosexual subtext of our culture as a whole.

Perhaps the connection between repressed bisexuality and aggressive, obsessive masculinity has never been posed more starkly and brutally than in *Raging Bull.* The film stands not only as a testimony and a warning but as an appeal for the emergence of a new psychosexual and social order.

BEYOND HOMOPHOBIC MASCULINITY

One evening in 1981 I was having a drink with a group of male students in a pub at York University. It was shortly after the police raids on Toronto's gay baths, and the city had already witnessed a series of vociferous and much-publicized rallies and protest marches. My students—good liberals all, with the very best intentions—were lamenting the political apathy of their generation. One of them, the most articulate, regretted that there was no longer a Spanish Civil War to serve as a rallying point for left-wing consciousness. I suggested that there was at least a partial equivalent right here on their doorstep in the gay rights movement. They looked surprised, but nodded sympathetically. "But," said their spokesperson, "we're not gay." "Oh," I replied, "are you Spanish?"

The incident, trivial in itself, has widespread and profoundly depressing implications. It testifies to the strength and recalcitrance of the barriers that exist between even the most liberal heterosexual men and their gay brothers: one can imagine dying in a just war, but to participate in a gay protest march is unthinkable (to what conclusions might one's friends leap?). Our society now recognizes and seems ready to condemn homophobia in its grosser and more public expressions such as "queer bashing." But my anecdote suggests that homophobia is far subtler and more pervasive than has generally been perceived, one of its subtlest manifestations being the fear of being mistaken for gay, which implies that being gay is something to be ashamed of.

The phenomenon of homophobia has no rational explanation: why should anyone fear and hate a social group because of its sexual orientation? In order to explain it I have drawn on psychoanalysis, with its insights into unconscious motivation, in particular the notion of innate bisexuality. The repression of the homosexual side of one's bisexuality is crucial to the social construction of masculinity, but because what is repressed lives on, perhaps deeply buried, it can be experienced as a constant threat. What the homophobe hates is his own precariously repressed homosexuality, which he disowns and projects onto others so that he can denounce, ridicule, and violently repudiate it. For the sexually secure student who longed for a new Spanish Civil War, to give vent to open hostility to gays would have been quite alien. Yet even he was sufficiently threatened to be unable, even in his imagination, to bridge the gulf that our culture maintains in order to perpetuate its established gender roles: for him too gays must remain "the Other" with whom brotherly or comradely solidarity was unthinkable. Homophobia is one of the most unfortunate effects of the social construction of masculinity. Without eliminating it one cannot hope to change that social construction.

# NOTES

This is substantially revised version of "The Homosexual Subtext in Film: Raging Bull" that appeared in *Hollywood from Vietnam to Reagan* (New York: Columbia University Press, 1985).

[1] Andrew Sarris has made this point about Scorsese's films several times, including in the *Village Voice*.

[2] It combines certain defining characteristics of Metz's categories, the bracket syntagma, the alternating syntagma, and the episodic sequence. See Metz, *Film Language* (New York: Oxford University Press, 1974), chap. 5.

[3] The relationship between different manifestations of violence is the subject of Michael Kaufman's article "The Construction of Masculinity" elsewhere in this volume.

[4] Sigmund Freud, "From the History of an Infantile Neurosis" (1918), in *Three Case Histories* (New York, Collier, 1963) 162.

[5] *Ibid.*, 165-8.

[6] *Ibid.*

[7] On Freud's theory of constitutional bisexuality and its repressions see, for example, S. Freud, "Three Essays on the Theory of Sexuality (1905). Also see the extensive discussion in Gad Horowitz, *Repression* (Toronto, University of Toronto Press, 1977), especially chap. 4, and "Male Sexuality: Towards a Theory" by Horowitz and Kaufman elsewhere in this volume.

# From Voyeur to Narcissist: Imaging Men in Contemporary Advertising

## ANDREW WERNICK

Advertising messages greet us at every turn. An indispensable ingredient of the media fare we depend on for entertainment, information, and general social cues, their effects are hard to gauge but certainly go beyond the economic function that is their prime reason for being. By continually tapping into our dreams and identities and by integrally linking products to the wider circulation of signs,[1] advertising has also developed, and as an outgrowth of salesmanship itself, into a major cultural force.[2]

It is a force moreover that, even though often criticized, meets with little real opposition—partly because ads are mostly received at home, partly because we have learned to screen them out, and partly because their euphoric vision of affluence has genuinely come to hold sway. Our adaptation to advertising has been aided, in any case, by its adaptation to us. In pitching to the mass, advertisers have had to pitch to the norm; and as conventions, clichés, and popular iconography have changed, promotional strategies have changed too. Only at times of general social upheaval, then, is advertising as a total institution likely to come under sustained attack. And when that happens, as it did in the late sixties, the assault is likely to be mounted by those with the least investment in consumerhood and its ways: the excluded minorities and the transitional young.

Even in quieter times, though, the language and imagery of advertising can still provoke controversy if some aspect of the value consensus to which it makes appeal (and, in turn, reinforces) begins to break down. Since the 1950s this has manifestly been the case with respect to sex and gender, and perhaps no aspect of social life has given advertisers greater trouble. The modern women's movement virtually cut its teeth in an attack on the "feminine mystique" propagated by commercial media during the postwar boom,[3] and such criticism has been a leitmotif of feminist agitation in North America and elsewhere ever since. Betty Friedan's opening salvos were directed against the stereotyping of women as glamorized mothers and housewives. In a subsequent phase, which began with the celebrated trashing of the 1968 Miss World contest, attention shifted to sexual objectification, particularly to the widespread use by advertisers of photographed women as decorative symbols of desire. This concern, in turn, paved the way for the more recent movement against sexist visual porn.

Neither in actuality nor at the level of cultural representation has male dominance disappeared. But these campaigns, combined with the large-scale entry of women into the work force that gave them such currency, have to some extent led advertisers to modify their use of images. What is more important, perhaps, they have also helped foster a wider awareness of how the commercial media help to maintain an entrenched gender hierarchy. At the most sophisticated level, studies like Judith Williamson's *Decoding Advertising*[4] and Erving Goffman's *Gender Advertisements*[5] have developed linguistic arguments to show how sexism in ads is not just incidental but is a systematic effect of the larger (masculinist) gender code that advertisers are obliged by the conventionalist practices of their craft to employ.

For all the strength of the feminist critique, however, our understanding of how advertising shapes and transmits gender ideology will remain incomplete so long as the question is pursued solely from the side of—and in terms of—representations of women. To round out the picture it is also important to consider how modern advertising depicts and addresses men. For men themselves, indeed, this question has become quite timely. For the sexual shake-up of the sixties and seventies has not only put in question prevailing notions of masculinity: it has also changed the relation of men to advertising itself.

Over the past thirty years, to begin with, men have become significantly more involved in "private" mass consumption. This trend has counterpointed the much more commented upon entry of women into the work force and to some degree has followed from it. Even if men have been slow to adapt, the acquisition by women of outside roles has forced them to take greater responsibility for some domestic chores. In addition, the growth in the number of students, the rise in the age at first marriage, the increase in divorce rates, and the open emergence of gay households have enlarged the category of men who, from the standpoint of day-to-day consumption, effectively live apart from women. Advertisers for everything from toothpaste and tissues to light bulbs and pasta have thus increasingly had to take into account that men as well as women are potential buyers of their product, and so must be treated as part of the "you" they address.[6]

But that is not all. Beyond the general extension of consumer status to men, there has been an extension in the range of commodities aimed especially at them. In the fifties, a list of such goods would have included cars, beer and booze, certain brands of cigarettes, hobby gear, and life insurance. Since then we have seen an ever-expanding array of male-oriented leisure goods (including pornography), a steady drive to incorporate male clothing into fashion, and mounting efforts to sell men all manner of personal-care products, from tooth-paste and bath oil to hair dye and makeup. Men as private persons, in short, have been targeted for economic development and are begin-ning to undergo, seventy years after women went through something similar, a process of intensive consumerization. For men to become more critically aware of how ads are beginning to encode their sex is for men to become more aware of what their enhanced role as consumers culturally implies.

But what makes the advertising side of this process doubly interest-ing is that at the same time as advertisers have become more inter-ested in speaking to men, the definition of masculinity has itself become confused. To some degree this has been a disruptive result of consumerization itself. The promotion of fragrance to straight men, for example, involves a break with the formula that men hunt, women attract—not to mention the overcoming of homophobic re-sistance. But, independently of this, male gender identity has also been shaken by that more general sex-gender upheaval associated, most dramatically, with the rise of the women's movement. Men still predominate within the public sphere, but they have lost their auto-matic privilege; men still earn more than women, but they are no longer defined as the breadwinners; heterosexuality is still the norm, but homosexuality, in the jargon of the market, is becoming "an acceptable lifestyle." All in all, the puritan-patriarchal complex, re-stored to official favor in the corporatist heyday of the Cold War, has lost its self-certainty, all its assumptions about male-female relations, sexuality, and the family hotly contested in debates that have come to divide the sexes among themselves as well as from one another. In such flux the Reaganite call for a return to traditional gender values is evidently only one of the options. What, indeed, does it mean these days to be male?

Not only men but advertisers have to answer that question. They must do so, moreover, in a manner that recognizes the full spectrum of sex-gender interests and orientations currently represented in the market. As we slide, ambiguously, toward a world of greater gender equality, the second issue that the treatment of men in advertising raises for men themselves, then, is not just how such treatment reflects values which resist that change; but also how advertising, in its compromising and consumerist way, is beginning to adapt—and, in adapting, is helping to redefine the norm for masculinity itself.

In this regard, even a cursory glance at what has happened to advertising since the mid-fifties reveals significant, if contradictory, shifts. Patriarchal values have certainly endured. Business, Science, and the Military, for example, continue to be represented as so many forms and aspects of masculine power. But the sexual turmoil of the sixties and seventies has also left its mark, and not just in such pseudo-liberated female images as Revlon's Charlie-the-independent-career-lady. For it has also provided advertisers with such divergent models of male identity as those arising, on the one hand, from the macho-playboy protest against "momism" traced by Barbara Ehrenreich (in *Hearts of Men*)[7] and, on the other, from gender-bending pop stars and the coming out of gays. Moreover, patriarchal symbolism has also been weakened by a tendency that points in the long run to its dissolution altogether. In certain limited respects, that is, advertisers are beginning to treat male and female, for all their marked differences, as formally interchangeable terms.[8]

Measured against the family and gender system that prevailed during the Eisenhower years, there are, in fact, three ways in which the imaging of men in more recent ads has softened in that direction. These concern, respectively, men's depicted relation to their social milieu, to the world of things, and to sexuality. While changes in one area of representation have doubtless interacted with changes in others, before we try to assess the modified masculinity they have combined to effect, let us first disentangle the levels and note the changes to male imagery that have been associated with each.

Consider, first, what has happened to the way men are socially portrayed. In the ads of the fifties, the well-nigh universal touchstone for defining roles and identities was the family. Not just any family, of course, but the nuclear, role-divided (he works, she nurtures), two-to-three-children, middle-class ideal—with advertiser attention fixed firmly on the nest-building couple at its purchasing center. Male, no less than female consumers, were automatically presumed to belong to such a structure and were rarely presented outside its framework. Shirt wearers, pipe smokers, television buyers, car drivers (invariably male) all appear as so many hubbies, dads, and career-striving providers. The automobile itself was promoted as a family vehicle: with the woman in the passenger seat and the kids in the back, a virtual emblem indeed of the domestic set-up for which it was designed. The further back we go, the clearer this pattern becomes. A general trade promotion in the October 1950 issue of *Colliers* advises its readers, "If he comes home 'under pressure' give him tea." From the same issue another ad has a cutesy baby saying, "I should say not! My Dad would never smoke anything but Marlborough."

If there was a counter-trend it was in the sometimes wildly romantic imagery used by women's fashions ads, particularly for cosmetics. The fantasy male (usually unshown) waiting to dance attendance on the wearer of Givenchy or Charles-of-the-Ritz could be her actual or, more likely, her prospective husband. But he could also be her extramarital lover; and in this exotic stranger (Prince Charming? Don Juan?) there is more than a shadow of the bad man who, like the bad woman, has always been an important element of Western sexual mythology. Such a figure, grafted onto movie-derived images of male sexual independence, increasingly came to appear also in ads aimed at men. In its anodyne version we got "the bold look" touted by Camp socks in the late forties; more rakishly came the trench-coated Bogart type used by later Marlborough ads and the black eye-patch of Hathaway.

Still, the romance complex was the official basis for marriage (and, de-sentimentalized, still is), and even its disruptive side was neutralized in such ads by a certain blandness: for all his shady intensity, the Marlborough man has clean-cut features and may just be phoning his wife. Besides, until at least the late fifties, these anti-Dagwood poses jostled side by side with images of unabashed familism. A 1957 bathrobe ad shows an awkward-looking (because virile) father holding an infant, while an off-stage voice reminds him, "It's your turn to bath the baby tonight, darling." Daddy's wry smile may express humor, but there is certainly no trace here of protest or refusal.

By contrast, while the family has made something of a comeback in the eighties the trend in more recent advertising has been firmly away from depicting men in family roles. In the mid-July 1986 issue of *Time,* for example, of the eight male figures shown (in thirteen full-page ads), only one gives any sign of family ties; and even here, in an ad for diamond rings, the man himself is not directly shown. The comparable figures for July 1971, at the height of sex-gender turmoil, were twelve and five; and for July 1956, twelve and ten. Similar calculations for other consumer magazines, from *Cosmopolitan* to *Sports Illustrated,* would show the same tendency—to such an extent that, except in explicitly family-oriented publications, it has become unusual today for display ads even to mention the family status of the individuals they depict.

In the majority of cases (where humans are used at all) the need for such information is in any case reduced because the people shown are shown alone. Combined with close-ups and truncated shots, this pictorial simplification is partly just a device to avoid clutter. But it also permits ambiguity, letting the consumers place themselves in an ad from a whole variety of positions, in keeping with whatever roles and arrangements they may actually live. In two respects, moreover, the absence of ties has come to be presented, particularly for men, as a distinct and desirable condition in itself. In the transitional sense, first, of the not-yet-married, "singles" have emerged not just as a commercially important demographic category (the product of prolonged middle-class schooling) but as a sign, when placed in a suitably affluent setting, of general upward mobility. Hence that great cliché of current promotion, the single young exec, eternally in his early thirties and dressed for success—a figure that has evidently replaced the older, married, and more established business type in the Good Life imagery held out before aspiring men. Some ads, like Camel's long-running "one of a kind" series, go even further, crossing the lone man theme with frontier myths of rugged individualism to produce visions of total male self-sufficiency. Rendered in this more absolute way, the single state is converted into an existential imperative and then equated, in all its antisocial glory, with masculinity itself.

Even where men are shown with others, the family frame is generally absent. The commonest group, to be sure, is the male-female couple, which represents not just the hint of a new unit but the family itself stripped down to its ideologically central ingredient. However, couples are usually shown in motion, at the point of becoming involved, with commitment not yet settled and the marital context, if any, left vague. Other configurations, from the male-male twosome (rare, but no longer unheard of), to the three-plus male peer group, and various combinations of the above, are still further removed from the family; and indeed the cosy aggregation in which they culminate, the mixed group of age peers, comes itself to assume one of the sidelined family's main roles: providing personal identity with its primary social support. This elevation of the peer group has been particularly evident in ads, like those for drinks, that push their product as symbols of a wider social belonging. In the most youthful and expansive versions of this theme—one thinks of Coke and Pepsi--solidarity with a whole generation is invoked. In a more adult and careerist mode the emphasis is on interpersonal support: "Smirnoff," says the text over a bar full of affluent age peers, "means friends."

Whatever the similarities, the peer groups thus depicted are quite different from kin, having only one generation and, indeed, no fixed positions or essential members. Like the empty landscapes of Man-the-Adventurer ads, such groups present themselves above all as a kind of medium, an ego-site, within which the consuming subject is free to roam at will. And this is just the point: the displacement of males with respect to the family in contemporary advertising has had as its reverse side the rise of a sign system that highlights the fluidity of social bonding and associates the pleasures of consumption with the sexual, status, or existential rewards to be obtained from exercising freedom in that setting. Desire itself is defined as an attribute of detachment; and male sociosexual success is characterized in terms of either the status of the female(s) drawn into his orbit or by what (from his appearance) we can assume he has renounced in that regard by splendidly isolating himself from the contest.

A second set of changes has concerned the more general construction of masculinity as a symbolic term. At the level of social representation, as we have seen, patriarchal codings have been weakened by the disappearance of images depicting the literal family. But at the cosmological level there has also been a disappearance of what one might call the metaphorical family: that parallel set of father-dominant relations that advertising has conventionally projected—through gender-coded goods, nature, and production onto its pictures of the material world.

As many commentators have pointed out,[9] such a myth complex in one form or another has helped to sustain and legitimize the West's industrial drive since at least the Renaissance. Combining archaic patriarchal symbols with a newer worship of the laboring subject, its central motifs were classically embodied in updated versions of Prometheus and Adam. Through the former, progress based on science was depicted as the heroic strivings of a demigod. Through the latter, industrial Man was made lord of the earth.

Linked to this whole androcentric amalgam, moreoever, has been a powerful sexual phantasm—warrior man subjugating woman nature—which renders capitalist technology as an extension of the male organ and its penetrations of the environment as a series of sexual acts. Nature, in this primal scene, is the dominated bride and we ourselves, arms outstretched to receive the gifts of life from above, the grateful children. But we are not the only progeny, for consumer goods are also products of the union of nature and technology; and, unconsciously, at least, the consumption of those goods—sibs eating sibs, as it were—can even be regarded as a kind of incestuous sacrifice designed to keep the father-god of production happy and alive.

Fueled by urban redevelopment, an electronics boom, and the arms race, the fifties was a period of heady technological optimism. It was also, with soldiers returned to the domestic fold and traditional gender lines restored, a period of renewed family-centeredness. Thus the whole value structure of what one might call patriarchal techno-worship was strongly reinforced, and in the advertising of the time its themes and images were very much to the fore.

At the symbolic summit was technological Man himself, represented most clearly in a recurrent image best described as "the hand of God." Union Carbide based a whole campaign on this theme. In one such ad the hand—huge, male, reaching from the clouds—offers titanium, in another hydrocarbons, in another whole fighter squadrons built from the minerals plucked Superman-style from the mountains nearby. A 1955 promotion for Morgan Guaranty Trust uses the same device. Here the hook is air conditioning, a breakthrough made possible (according to the small print) by the money put up by Morgan. "At the touch of a finger," boasts the headline, "man-made climate that's better than nature's." To illustrate which, a strong but gentle male hand stretches horizontally across the page. Above, a fierce storm is raging. Below, bathed in a light that seems to be emanating from the hand itself, Mum (sewing), Dad (smoking), and little girl (playing) luxuriate in the warmth of their domestic circle. In the background, female office clerks work happily away, equally oblivious to the storm from which the new technology now delivers them. The hand is evidently divine, but its connection with more earthly powers is not concealed. Just visible where the arm enters the page is a hint of immaculate black sleeve and white cuff, indicating that the Big Guy is corporate and really just an extension of the Board.

Such ads move back and forth, in fact, between emphasizing the fatherly qualities of "technology" *per se* and those of the business enterprise that controls it. Rendering the latter in paternal terms was not itself, perhaps, particularly new; but until the fifties consumers (as opposed to workers) had never been so explicitly portrayed as dependents in that family sense. With respect to the analogy with marital dependence, a 1957 ad for New England Life shows a pipe-smoking husband, somewhere in his thirties, confidently watching his wife through a window as she gathers flowers in the garden. "A better life for her," says the text, implying not just that she is to him as he is to the insurance company, but also that the larger protection offered by the company is indispensable if he himself is to play his own protective role. An even more direct example, but on the parental side, is provided by a 1954 Texas and Pacific Railway ad. This shows a little girl holding the hand of a doll that looks exactly like her, while both stare reverently into the sunset. Over an unctuous credo linking freedom to capitalism to the American Founding Fathers hovers the operative word that ties it, us, and the figures in the picture all together: Faith.

The sexual, that is, phallocentric, aspect of this patriarchal cosmology was also much in evidence. Indeed, with space exploration as its most spectacular external embodiment, and car design as its main expression in the consumer sphere, the phallic character of modern technological striving was almost obsessively emphasized in the promotion of the period. The sleek, thrusting, venturesome profile of rocket ships was a particularly common motif, both as the product (in defense industry ads) and as an incidental sign of futuristic progress used to promote everything from cars and tires to railway travel and kitchenware. Even such "low tech" artifacts as fountain pens were depicted in this fashion. One from 1956 shows a porthole shot of a lunar landscape, dominated by a smooth launchfield, with various space vehicles dotted about. Front and center, pointing vertically to the stars, stands a huge red and gold Parker '61' fountain pen: a bizarre image that combines the erect quill of print man with the projectile being readied in the electric age to shoot him into space.

Not surprisingly, the Nature depicted as corresponding to this triumphant masculine reverie was passive, subordinate, and unthreatening. Nature in the raw—the nature we are part of and that can destroy us—was as absent from the promotional picture as female rage was from the pages of *Playboy*. Even when the forces of chaos were acknowledged, which was rare, they were kept firmly outside the gates. Nor, of course, do fifties ads show us the messy (and implicitly sexual) activity of subjugation and appropriation itself. The action is always over, with Nature already "cooked": and cooked indeed to look like Nature in precisely this compliant, that is, verdant, tranquil, and orderly sense. Here, as elsewhere, promotion and the symbolism of everyday life came to intersect. The postwar dream of the suburbs had as one of its definitive elements the tamed wilderness in every backyard. Some ads, especially for household durables, simply played this figure back through window shots of neatly trimmed lawns. Others projected it onto the larger canvas of the Great Outdoors. When placed in leisure contexts (for example in a 1954 Canada=fishing ad for Dominion Ten Whiskey), such landscapes could even acquire some Siren-like power of their own. But for the most part feminized Nature knew her place: to provide the raw materials or the picturesque backdrop for the world of private plenty that Promethean Man was proudly ushering in.

Today such images seem inflated to the point of parody. It is not that capitalism, male dominance, and ecologically insensitive forms of industrial development have gone away; but rather that the cultural upheavals, economic dislocations and technological implosion[10] of the past two decades have created social upheaval and darkened the celebratory mood.

Advertisers, of necessity, have tacked with these winds. Overall the corporate father-god has been scaled down, where not effaced. His former pretensions have even become the butt of the occasional joke. ("Marriages," declares a 1979 Hilton ad over a breathtaking cloudscape, "are made in heaven—why not hold the reception here?") The phallic styling of consumer goods has similarly gone out of vogue, and its main vehicle, rocketry, has virtually disappeared. Power-between-the-legs appeal is still important, of course, to the marketing of speed machines like outboards, motorbikes, and snowmobiles. But the new signage of technological progress, which is derived from computers and video screens, stresses operation over motion, not the body of the contraption but its control-panel face.

Cars themselves, as a mixture of both modes, have always been ambiguously gendered in this regard. But the rise of electronic, communication-related goods has confounded still further the identification of technology with masculinity in the depiction of such products—and to the point where their associated gender has become virtually indeterminate. Thus, while stereos promise power and wars are fought by keyboard, home-entertainment equipment, including computers, presents itself as user-friendly and is often shaped along soft feminine lines. Even here, moreover, there is scope for variation. IBM PC's, for example, as befits their male business market, are straight, functional, and angular; Apples, by contrast, which according to trade lore, were originally designed for women, are cutesy, cuddly, and round.

The partial decoupling of phallic and frontier masculinity from symbols of technological progress reflects more, it should be said, than just a shift in product design; and more, indeed, than the combination of this with the way in which the patriarchy of an older industrialism has itself come under seige. Reinforced by the development of the wired home, it symptomizes too, a flight to the private that has issued from a loss of confidence in the whole industrial project. Resource limits, external effects, and global poverty all press in. Indeed, together with terrorism, crime, and the threat of war, these difficulties have been woven together into a composite picture of gathering doom by the very media to which we turn for solace.

This darker mood, and the very real stress of urban living, have led to a marked elevation of the nature-as-escape motif that was purely secondary before. Cars in contemporary ads are almost never shown in city streets, and often not on roads at all. Instead, they stand in fields, by the sea, or on the surface of the moon. In these and countless similar ads for liquor, tobacco, fashion, and food, tranquilizing pictures of earth, sky, and water have become commonplace as ways to depict Nature as the ultimate balm: the redeeming maternal opposite, in effect, of city, industry, and Man. The Great Mother, it seems, just as we are staving in her planetary face, is staging an ironic return as a mirage projected from progress gone wrong.

In the end, as a result of all these shifts and reversals, the masculinist complex has not only begun to fade: it has given way to a contradictory mélange in which the wider meaning of gender within the advertising cosmos cannot with any consistency be pinned down at all. If male and female are still tied to one another as complementary poles, the assignment of gender to particular forces, institutions, and product types has become much less fixed. The whole system has become freer to float. Ads in consequence have begun to take a more circumscribed, and even abstract, approach to gender coding. Some products, like expensive watches, are designed from the start to be displayed in matching pairs—a minimalist binary of his and hers that reduces male and female to marks (color, shape, size, etc.) of a purely external difference. In other cases these reduced and free-floating symbols have become a topic for humor. A 1985 car stereo ad juxtaposes a sporty red car and the black, powerful stereo itself. The first is named "beauty," the second "the beast." While the ad uses conventional young-buck imagery, it is also tongue-in-cheek; and at that level its aim is to flatter the consumer not so much sexually as intellectually—as a person smart and contemporary enough to appreciate the wit.

The displacement of men in ads from fixed family roles and the wider retreat of masculinity as an ideologically fixed term have been complemented, finally, by a parallel loosening of masculinity as a sexual construct. Here, an even more basic aspect of the old patriarchal code has begun to come unstuck, putting in question not just the traditional model of male identity, but the very polarity between the sexes that has hitherto defined gender as codable at all. At the risk

of oversimplifying what has evidently been a complex and contradictory development, a comparison between two ads, one from the mid-
fifties, one from twenty years later, may serve to illustrate at least the
general direction of this change.

The first, for Kayser stockings, appeared in the May 1959 issue of
the *New Yorker*. It is dominated by two vertically separated panels.
The smaller one on the left shows the front of a man's face, bisected
vertically through the nose. He is looking directly to his right, and his
features seem to twinkle, with a barely suppressed whoop of amaze-
ment, approval, and delight.

As we follow the man's gaze across the page the object of all this
admiration comes into view. In the right-hand panel our eye is
caught, as is his, by a magnificent pair of female legs. Further still to
the right, the picture is completed by a floral logo, the word "Kayser"
and, in tiny letters, the word that finally tells us what is actually for
sale: "hosiery." The legs themselves, to which our eyes and his
continuously return, are like Greek pillars: statuesque, dazzling and
gently curved. Incongruously (if unintentionally so), they are supported by the daintiest of spike heels, with one foot raised slightly
from the ground.

The awkward shoes and submissive posture ill suit this woman for
fight or flight. Equally constricting is the tight skirt whose hemline is
just apparent at the top of the frame. By all these signs she expresses
her helplessness in the social jungle, and her need for a protector. At
the same time they are gestures of self-display; to emphasize which
the covetous male eye is shown level with the woman's calves, as if
she is standing on a raised platform—a pedestal no less—expressly to
be admired. And so the circle is complete: his gaze and her legs, the
passive activity of the former complemented perfectly by the active
passivity of the latter. Nor, according to the summarizing caption
below, is there any other way for desire to flow. As the prescriptive
caption at the foot of the page pointedly puts it: "You" (Kayser
wearer, woman) "owe it" (the allure of self-display) "to your audience" (men).

There is nothing surprising, of course, in nylon manufacturers
playing on the fetishization of female legs. The ad is remarkable only
for the clarity with which this promotional point, and the gender
myth to which it is tied, are pushed. The terms at the left and center,
focusing on the legs themselves, gather together to provide a meaning
for the brand name posted on the right. The result is a set of identities:
Kayser equals hosiery equals Woman's legs (the kind that attract

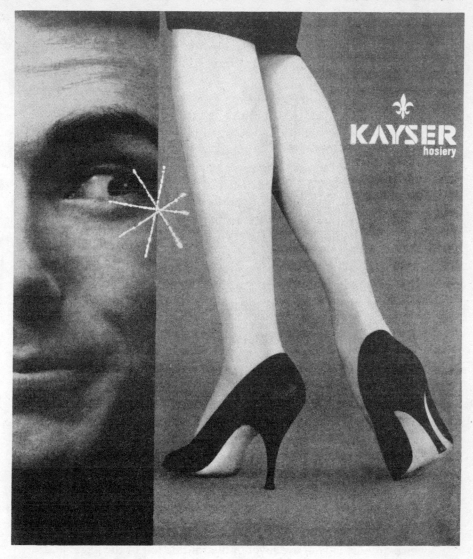

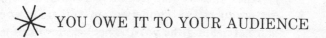 YOU OWE IT TO YOUR AUDIENCE

Men); all of which is to be identified as the magical essence of femininity itself.

But the myth is not only about women. The syllogism is emphasized, indeed its logic commanded, by the male gaze that is the ad's principal visual thread. And this connection is further underlined by the placement of a small star at the eye's lower right-hand corner, a theme that is echoed in the logo on top of the Y and S of "Kayser," and again in the asterisk that draws us to the caption underneath. At once a further set of equivalences are implied: Kaysers, like women's legs, like Woman herself are all as one with the star, at once erotic and romantic, that burns in Man's eye. And, conversely, Man himself is equated with that same star, but this time as the subject, not the object, of its light. In defining femininity, in other words, the ad defines masculinity too. If Woman exists sexually only in Man's eye, Man himself only exists in the (Woman-watching) exercise of that same organ.

The second ad, for Braggi aftershave, appeared in the September 1975 issue of *Penthouse.* One scene dominates the page. Awash with yellow and amber light, it shows the inside of a bathroom, cut off on the left and framed by an open folding door on the right. On the counter to the right of the vanity—pink and shiny, pipes showing— sits an elegant woman wearing a kimono bathrobe, slippers, earrings, and (we guess) nothing else. Without a flicker of emotion she looks straight into our eyes, her line of sight just a fraction higher than our own. To her left, occupying the whole vertical plane, is a naked man. Lean, muscular, dark-haired, tanned, he stands intently before a mirror, in whose reflection (which he is watching too) we can see that he is shaving. The whiteness of the reflected cream we see on his face —on a line between the couple's actual two heads—is picked up by the whiteness of the bath towel draped around his neck. And from the towel itself our eye descends down his back: drawn visually, if not erotically, by the lighter shade of skin on his buttocks (small and neat) which are virtually at eye level in the middle left of the page.

At the bottom right is a smaller rectangle, within which, against a jet-black background, a male right hand is gently holding a bottle of the product. The hand is clean and manicured and wears a gold bracelet around the wrist. The product itself is a transparent elixir within a fist-sized straight-edged glass bottle, whose color (aside from the black top and black and gold label), derives from all the flesh tones it reflects. And in dazzling white letters, directly above the hand and its prize, is the caption wherein both the brand name and its meaning

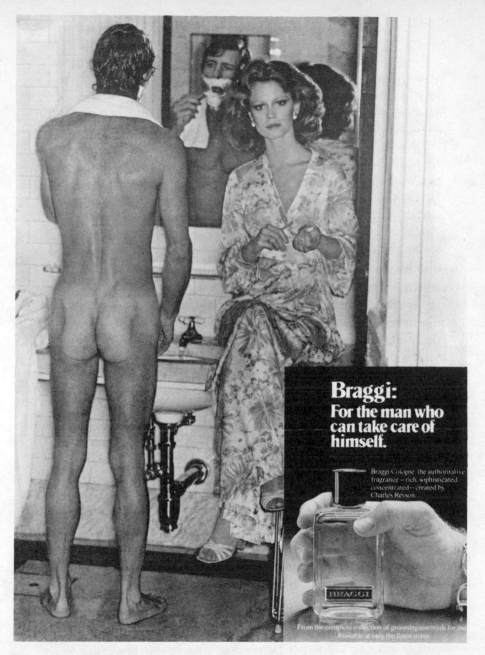

Braggi:
For the man who
can take care of
himself.

Braggi Cologne: the authoritative
fragrance – rich, sophisticated,
concentrated – created by
Charles Revson.

From the complete collection of grooming essentials for men.
Available at only the finest stores.

are tersely spelled out: "Braggi: for the man who can take care of himself."

The sexual codings embedded here are more complex than in the other ad, but they are equally legible and the contrast is certainly clear. In the smaller box, Braggi is the aroused penis of the auto-erotic male. Paralleling this, but more figuratively, Braggi (a fragrance welded onto the act of shaving) in the main picture is the medium that transforms this daily grooming ritual into a fully self-indulgent act.

Again, the pitch is unremarkable, given the kind of product being advertised. It runs exactly parallel, indeed, to a multitude of ads for similar products aimed at women. But this is exactly what is so striking, since narcissism has long been encouraged in women, as the gender defined as the object of a look. To depict men as narcissists, on the other hand, runs altogether counter to a code that has traditionally defined men as the ones who do the looking. In that context, moreover, the ad's treatment of narcissism is especially norm-breaking; for the homo-erotic desire that is always implicit in taking oneself as a sexual object, and which conventional masculinity is largely constituted as a reaction against, is here fully exposed. And not only in a way designed to appeal to gays (though they are doubtless one of the target markets). For as our attention strays to inspect the man's fair ass, it is constantly interrupted by the eyes of the woman, who is herself always looking on. Those eyes at once judge and condone. But above all they also provide a crucial heterosexual cover, both for him and for us. What more is happening, after all, than just that a man is shaving after he and his girlfriend have spent a pleasurable night together in bed?

Between the first ad and the second there is evidently a reversal of terms. If, in the former, Man is defined as the one who gazes at Woman, in the second it is he who is the object of such a look. And in switching roles, he himself, as the one admired, is redefined (like the female nude with mirror of classical erotic art)[11] as the being naturally in love with an image of himself.

It would be misleading to suggest, of course, that the kind of active, outwardly directed version of male sexuality presented by the Kayser ad has now been replaced across the board by the passively narcissistic version presented by the one for Braggi. The latter may reflect a trend; but, as the casual scrutiny of any current women's fashion magazine would show, it is not the only one. In general, what we now have, in fact, is a heterogeneous picture in which both constructions of masculinity (and, by implication, femininity) have come to co-exist. The aftershave example itself, replete with *Pent-*

*house* fantasies of the bachelor pad, at once bespeaks the old gender code and breaks from it. What the contrast does make clear, though, is that the monopoly of the older code has been broken; and that as a result promotional images are becoming flexible enough to allow men and women to appear, with increasingly equal plausibility, at either end of the objectified–objectifying sexual scale.

In extreme cases, particularly in ads aimed at both sexes, such male-female interchangeability is emphasized for its own sake. And in the androgynous imagery that often results, even the sexual orientation of the figures depicted may then be left up in the air. A 1985 ad for Lee jeans shows two males and one female draped around a bicycle, all wearing the hip-hugging product, each in physical and visual contact with the other two. Like the demure orgies shown in Calvin Klein's famous Obsession campaign, the sexual meaning of the scene is completely ambiguous. The reading it permits is male as well as female, gay as well as straight; beyond which, indeed, can be discerned yet a fifth possibility—bisexual and of indeterminate gender—which synthesizes the others by emphasizing the very principle of gender equivalence that keeps them all in play.

With regard to promotional depictions of male sexuality, as with those of men's family role and with those of masculinity as a wider symbolic term, the same overall point can thus be made: what advertising has been increasingly showing, reflecting, and insisting upon is that male and female, for all their traditional differences, are to be conceived of as fluid, labile categories that occupy, in the last analysis, equivalent if not identical places in the world.

Now at first blush, any trend toward sexual equality, or toward an ideology of sexual equality, ought to be welcomed as a step toward human liberation. However, it is a lazy liberalism that univocally identifies progress with the leveling effects of the market. The equivalence values arising in patriarchy's stead have themselves been bound up with the intensified consumerization of our sex. Consequently, there is no warrant for progressive men—or women[12]—to regard this whole development as anything more than a very mixed blessing. Indeed, to formulate even the glimmerings of an adequate response, three of its regressive implications particularly need to be faced.

The first, and most obvious, is that in gender, as in class, the official ascendancy of equality as a value, particularly where embodied in socially real-seeming representations, masks the inequities that still really prevail. It is one thing for men and women to look and behave more nearly the same in the unencumbered leisure situations shown in ads; it is quite another for their economic, cultural, and political power to have actually become equal.

The second concerns the significance of what has been occurring on the plane of promotional imagery itself. The detachment of masculinity from fixed cosmological, sexual, and family roles has in effect transformed it and other sex-gender terms into what structural linguists would call floating signifiers, free within any given promotional context to swirl around and substitute for one another at will. Artists may find in this vortex of signs a new experience of the sublime.[13] The commercial realities that predominate, however, give it a much duller and more alienating edge. Like color, setting, and decor, sex and gender have become mere predicates of the commodities to which they are linked, and the choice of any particular set is determined by the marketing context those commodities have to face. In this way, male and female, masculine and feminine, men and women, have joined with other aspects of life and society to become the mere stuff of cultural coinage, artificially stamped, and, above all, without organic connection to the life processes that such images purport to reflect and express.[14]

The third problem is social and concerns the relation of all this traffic in persons-as-signs to corresponding developments in everyday life. For men to be depicted as women's equivalents is not solely a promotional mirage. It replicates, and also naturalizes, precisely what has happened to the ascribed place of men and women in sociosexual relations at large. The growing equality in this sphere has partly been a function of the way in which men and women, despite continuing disparities in wealth and income, have come to occupy more similar socioeconomic roles, particularly (from an advertising perspective) as consumers. Investigations of this process (women entering the work force, men entering domesticity) have tended to focus on its ambiguous implications for "actual" equality. But there is a personal and family side that needs to be examined as well. In effect, as work and leisure have become more desegregated and sexist barriers to meeting and mating have begun to crumble, the primordial asymmetry within the social relations market between males (seeking) and females (sought) has begun to disappear. And with this shift, which equalizing trends in the imagery of promotional culture have helped to legitimize, the culminating phase has been reached in that broader transformation of kinship noted by Lévi-Strauss: from a "restricted" system, where mate selection is closely prescribed, to an ultra-open one of "generalized exchange."[15]

In the abstract, of course, there is nothing wrong with this. Indeed, no friend of freedom would wish to retard it, let alone if it meant going back to more rigid sexual and family controls. But, for all its liberating potential, the expanded circulation that men, like women, are now obliged to enter into if they are to find suitable mates, companions, and friends, is hemmed in, and even deformed, by its socioeconomic setting. Interpersonal exchange may be competitive, but it is certainly not free. Besides the persistence of inequalities between the sexes themselves, class differences and the status hierarchies based on them crucially mediate the search for personal satisfaction and ties, so that the whole process becomes (or remains) deeply enmeshed in the more general scramble for wealth, power, and status. In such a context, whether at school, work, prayer, or play, who you are is always, at least partly, a function of who you are with; just as, in an age of equivalence, the status of such significant others is also affected by yours.

Given the increasing extent to which men's and women's places in this dynamic have come to converge, it is clear that the recent rise of fashion magazines like *Gentleman's Quarterly* has been aided by the growth of demand from below. But consumerization, here, is not just a matter of attending to products: what the glossy pages of every current male-oriented consumer magazine make clear is that the more intensively men have entered into competitive circulation, the more they have become, like women before them, analogous to consumer goods themselves.

It is from just this angle that the narcissism played on so explicitly in ads like the one for Braggi is most troubling. The equalization that men are becoming subjected to in the sphere of consumption is not in the least the equality we might dream of, the equality of free and self-determining beings in free and self-determining association with one another. It is the equality, rather, of self-absorbed yet emotionally anxious personalities for sale. With the makeup mirror dangled invitingly before them, men, like women, are encouraged to focus their energies not on realizing themselves as self-activating subjects, but on maximizing their value as tokens of exchange. Beyond lamenting this, the practical conclusion may be drawn that if gender equality is to mean real freedom—though individual psychology is hardly the place to begin—we will have to learn to do without the mirror that bids fair to hold both sexes in its thrall. The outcome, though anticonsumerist, need not be ascetic: live music, as the American Federation of Musicians puts it, is best.

# NOTES

[1]The modern examination of cultural symbolism in terms of a focus on signs, i.e., units of represented meaning, derives from the work of the Swiss linguist, Ferdinand de Saussure, who sought to develop a new branch of knowledge, semiology, defined as the general science of signs.

[2]A good account of the rise of advertising and its dual economic and cultural role is provided by S. Ewen, *Captains of Consciousness,* (New York: McGraw-Hill, 1976). The most complete current examination of advertising as a form of social communication is to be found in W. Leiss, S. Kline and S. Jhally, *Social Communication in Advertising* (New York and London: Methuen, 1986). For a discussion of the middle-of-the-road effect see G. Murdoch and P. Golding, "Capitalism, Communication and Class Relations," in J. Curran, M. Gurevitch and J. Woollacott, eds., *Mass Communications and Society* (London: Edward Arnold, 1977), 40; and the author's "Advertising and ideology: an interpretive framework," *Theorty, Culture and Society* 2 (no. 1).

[3]B. Friedan, *The Feminine Mystique* (New York: Norton, 1963).

[4]J. Williamson, *Decoding Advertising* (London: Marion Boyars, 1978).

[5]E. Goffman, *Gender Advertising* (New York: Harper, 1979).

[6]The following report indicates the trend:

Researchers are beginning to urge advertisers to segment the estimated 500,000 males in Canada and nine million males in the United States who live alone and are worthy targets of home-care products, according to Baker Lovick Ltd. of Toronto.

"They point to the vast numbers of men who live alone—or at least without a female helpmate—and take care and some pride in their cooking, shopping, cleaning and even laundry. The agency reports the segment is in the 30 to 65 age range and would include potential buyers of microwave ovens, frozen foods and drip-dry shirts.

"Whatever the reasons, they live alone and like it. The research reports there are subtle suggestions that advertisers should show men in a more favorable light so far as laundry is concerned and take it easy on such appeals as 'detergents for your finest washables' while showing lacy lingerie." Toronto *Globe and Mail,* 9 Jan. 1985.

[7]B. Ehrenreich, *Hearts of Men: American Dreams and the Flight from Commitment* (Garden City: Doubleday, 1983).

[8]Early, but still relevant, explorations of social exchange and the forms it takes under market conditions are to be found in M. Mauss, "Essai sur le don: Forme et raison de l'échange dans les sociétés achaïques," *Année Sociologique* 1(1925), as well as in many of the writings of Thorstein Veblen. The cultural implications of mass-media symbols being drawn into this process are trenchantly examined by the contemporary French social critic Jean Baudrillard, especially in *Towards a Critique of the Political Economy of the Sign,* trans. C. Levin and A. Younger (St. Louis: Telos Press, 1984).

[9]The idea was a staple of critical theory between the wars, particularly as exemplified in the work of the Frankfurt School. The *locus classicus* is T. Adorno and H. Horkheimer, *Dialectic of Enlightenment* (New York: Herder and Herder, 1972).

[10]For the idea that technological progress in the age of electronics and computers has started to reverse the explosive and expansionary effect of an earlier form of industrialization based on the machine, see M. McLuhan, *Understanding Media: The Extensions of Man* (New York: McGraw-Hill, 1964), ch. 33.

[11]See J. Berger, *Ways of Seeing* (Harmondsworth: Penguin, 1972), especially the chapter on the history of the nude.

[12]For a feminist critique of the kind of abstract gender equality promoted in liberal thought and market-driven practice, see J. Mitchell, "Women and Equality," in J. Mitchell and A. Oakley, *The Rights and Wrongs of Women* (Harmondsworth: Penguin, 1976), and H. J. Maroney, "Embracing Motherhood: New Feminist Theory," in M. Kroker, A. Kroker, P. McCallum and M. Verthuy, eds., *Feminism Now* (Montreal: New World Perspectives, 1985).

[13]For a general, experientially oriented discussion of modernity in these terms, see M. Berman, *All That is Solid Melts into Air* (New York: Simon and Schuster, 1982) as well as a critical exchange

about Berman's pro-modernity argument in *New Left Review* 144. For a linking of postmodernist aesthetics to the romantic notion of the sublime, see F. Jamieson, "Postmodernism, or The Cultural Logic of Capital," *New Left Review* 146. A shorter version of this paper is also to be found in H. Foster, ed., *The Anti-Aesthetic: Essays on Postmodern Culture* (New York: Bay Press, 1984).

[14]For a critique of modern mass media in these terms see J. Baudrillard, *op. cit.,* especially the essay "Requiem for the Media."

[15]*Q.v.* C. Lévi-Strauss, *The Elementary Structures of Kinship* (Boston: Beacon, 1969).

# Constructing Our Future: Men, Women, and Feminist Utopian Fiction

## PETER FITTING

It is one thing to analyze the form and nature of patriarchal society, as many feminist thinkers have done, and to struggle against the institutions and practices of such a society, as a growing number of women and men are doing. But it is another thing altogether to imagine, through works of fiction, future worlds stripped of hierarchical and oppressive relationships and behavior. Or is it really another thing? Perhaps these attempts are important because, rather than assenting to the dominant view that there are no acceptable alternatives to the present system, they challenge attitudes of resignation and defeat; they eloquently proclaim that we do have the possibility of constructing a future of our own choosing.

Over the last decade there has been a revival in literary attempts to imagine societies based on new social and sexual relationships, particularly within the existing popular genres of fantasy and science fiction.[1] These works help us imagine qualitatively different societies, ones without sexual exploitation and domination. They allow us to catch sight of something we lose in the midst of our day-to-day lives. These alternative visions are also important because they reach beyond the restricted public of the converted and speak to an audience that often discounts the possibility of alternatives to the fundamental insufficiency of the present. And they seem particularly important to men for the simple reason that in many of these utopian visions men are partially or totally excluded. But in effect it is not men who have been excluded from these visions; it is traditional masculine values and roles.

This article will outline some of these recent works particularly insofar as they portray non-hierarchical and non-oppressive social and sexual relationships. I am interested both in the content of these utopias—the social and sexual relations they depict—and in their effectiveness in awakening and giving shape to hopes for emancipation. It is pertinent to acknowledge that I occupy a position of privilege along the several axes of power addressed in these novels: that of a white, heterosexual male with a relatively privileged economic situation. Nonetheless, these visions of human societies freed from class exploitation and sexual oppression also speak to me, intellectually and emotionally. As a man writing about feminist utopias, my interest is not to preempt or neutralize the force of the feminist critique but rather to join in a struggle to transform the existing society.

To represent the range and features of the recent revival of utopian writing under the impact of feminism, I have chosen to discuss seven novels: four that are usually considered the basic texts of the utopian revival of the 1970s—Samuel Delany's *Triton* (1976), Ursula K. Le Guin's *The Dispossessed* (1974), Marge Piercy's *Woman on the Edge of Time* (1976), and Joanna Russ's *The Female Man* (1975)—along with a more traditional utopia of the same period, Ernest Callenbach's *Ecotopia* (1975), as well as Suzy McKee Charnas's "science fantasy" *Motherlines* (1978) and Sally Gearhart's *The Wanderground* (1979).[2]

## CHARACTERISTICS OF RECENT UTOPIAN WRITINGS

Science fiction and fantasy are popular fictional genres that have traditionally been characterized by their sexism and their stereotyping of male and female characters.[3] But in the hands of a new generation of writers, the potential of these forms to describe other worlds and societies—in opposition to the dominant realism of mainstream popular fiction—has been richly developed. The utopian writing I will look at is both critical and constructive. Each novel grows out of the feminist critique of the ideological, psychological, social, and economic forms of gender division and their links with the exploitive and oppressive structures of capitalism. And each novel constructs an alternative society based on egalitarian social and sexual relations.

Although these recent writings have similarities with some early utopias (such as economic and political reorganization emphasizing communitarian goals), they stress changed social and sexual relationships. The focus of the books is not macro-social structures, which are left in the background, but the forms and textures of everyday life. There has been a shift away from the older, systematic, planned utopias toward more open and ambiguous societies. Unlike traditional utopian fiction, which often presented a society as uniform and unchanging, these newer works depict societies that are in process, are straining to come into being, and are open to change. These strains are presented through the lives of the characters, who represent the doubts and the tensions of the new worlds. As a result, whereas older utopian fiction was often a kind of guided tour, recent writings have tried to involve the reader in the thoughts and feelings of characters who are involved in the daily struggle to build a world of human freedom and self-fulfillment.

This emphasis on daily life is an application of the feminist slogan "the personal is political" and a recognition that the purpose of any social transformation is to produce genuine changes in our daily lives. Consequently these novels address such personal issues as living arrangements and sexuality (they are opposed to the nuclear family and the norms of heterosexuality and procreative sexuality), and more generally present a critique of the ideological, psychological, and economic structures of gender division in the world today. In calling attention to the centrality of the everyday, these works attempt to imagine societies in which all forms of human behavior are valued. Gone are the dichotomies that now shape our lives—work vs. play, intellectual vs. manual labor, creative vs. non-creative, home vs. workplace, productive vs. non-productive work.

The valuing of all forms of human activity begins with a fundamental transformation of work itself, from an "obligation enforced by poverty and external goals" to more rewarding and largely self-determined activities.[4] The ability to choose work according to individual inclinations marks the end of the sexual division of labor in these novels. Moreover, to ensure that people can vary their tasks with their ability and inclination, and to balance those inclinations with the needs of society, these novels propose a variety of work-posting schemes. Disagreeable work is shared more equitably, or in some cases reduced through technology, and in all these worlds there is a reduction in the socially necessary labor each individual must perform.

Although socialists have usually considered the workplace as the primary site of social struggle, this is not the case in these novels. The texts go beyond economic exploitation to show that alienation and domination are embedded in the patriarchal structures of everyday existence—structures that would not of themselves disappear following the collectivization of the means of production. As we shall see, these works develop new social forms based on equality of the sexes and on alternative forms of habitation patterns, love relationships, and parenthood. Women are in full control of their reproductive functions and diverse forms of sexual expression, most particularly of homosexuality, are accepted.[5]

Finally, the emphasis on everyday life extends to the biosphere as well. These works all reject the commitment in most earlier utopias to growth and the domination of nature. In varying ways and to varying degrees, they espouse the development of an integrative and non-exploitive attitude toward nature. In the attention given to everyday life, then, these works blend the practical description of new social and human relations with the vision of an alternative society and with the images of an emancipated human nature in which play-fulness, spontaneity, creativity, and eroticism are no longer subju-gated by the demands of economic, social, and political control.

### Societies without Men

Three of these books—Charnas's *Motherlines*, Gearhart's *Wan-derground*, and Russ's *The Female Man*—portray societies without men. The societies of the first two depict all-woman societies on the margins of a collapsing patriarchal and industrial society. *The Wan-derground* juxtaposes the "natural" lives of the Hill Women in the countryside with a repressive patriarchy of the cities. The emphasis is on the new rituals and changed lives of the Hill Women, although there is a fragile relationship with a few sympathetic men (the "gen-tles") in the cities. The new values and rituals are based on a belief in a specifically female nature connected (as in Charlotte Perkins Gilman's classic feminist utopia *Herland* of 1915) to motherhood and a close identification with the body of the Earth. The Hill Women reproduce spontaneously, without men and without recourse to the technology that characterizes reproduction in the novels of Charnas and Russ. There is also a deemphasis on sexuality.

Charnas's *Motherlines* describes the tribal society of the Riding Women and the precarious relationship with the "free fems"—women who have escaped the brutally repressive societies of the cities. The Riding Women live a nomadic existence, full of energy and a fierce love of life. Whereas in *Wanderground* female nature is equated with a peaceable nature at large, the women in *Motherlines* lead hard and joyful lives that include games, duels, and feuds.

Joanna Russ's *The Female Man* is a remarkable and controversial novel that has often been dismissed because of its polemical aspects and unconventional form. The novel superimposes four versions or "other selves" of the narrator—a 1950s woman desperately trying to meet social expectations, the "female man" of the title who has understood and rejected patriarchal conventions, and two visitors from the future. One visitor, Janet, is from nine hundred years in the future, where, after a plague has killed all the men, the women have learned to fend for themselves and in the process have developed a more human, satisfying, and nurturing world. However, as we learn late in the novel, Janet's story of a plague is itself a myth. As the visitor from the more immediate future tells us, the world without men was a consequence of a war of the sexes. She tells Janet that a "thousand years of peace and love" have been nourished "on the bones of the men we have slain."[6]

Russ's pastoral Earth of the future bears some resemblance to the much smaller societies of Charnas and Gearhart. There are no true cities left, and life is organized cooperatively around families of women. However, although there is harmony with nature, in Russ's book there is also a deep reliance on technology, which includes not only reproductive technology, but also time travel, and mining colonies in space. Rather than the spiritual focus of Gearhart's *Wanderground,* there is a strong emphasis on "appropriate" technology and the practical education of young girls.

It is not surprising that, in the attempt to imagine a world beyond male domination, some women would resolve the problem by developing one without men at all. Writing about the genesis of *Motherlines,* Suzy Charnas explains that "the decision to exclude men was not dispassionate and political. I tried to write them in [but] no matter what I wrote, men would not fit. Every scene they entered went dead." But rather than assume that the exclusion of men eliminates the utopian force of these novels or their usefulness in helping men to develop new attitudes and roles, I will argue the contrary: that in the imagined patterns of social interaction and behavior, the male reader can glimpse a society in which present-day gender roles and the sexual division of labor have finally disappeared. The biological distinction between sexual difference and the social construction of gender—the process that makes "men" and "women" out of male and female persons—is crucial. As Charnas comments, once she realized that there would be no men in her novel she discovered that

With the spectrum of human behavior in my story no longer split into male roles (everything active, intelligent, brave and muscular) and female roles (everything passive, intuitive, shrinking, and soft), my emerging women had access to the entire range of human behavior. They acted new roles appropriate to social relationships among a society of equals which allowed them to behave simply as human beings.[7]

## Androgynous Utopias

The other four novels present what some critics have called "androgynous" utopias. In contradistinction to the older utopias, which usually left existing gender roles in place, these new societies are made up of men and women living together in altered social and sexual relations in which there are no longer any distinctions or hierarchy based on sex.[8]

Callenbach's *Ecotopia* is an explicitly utopian novel written outside the conventions of science fiction and fantasy. It is set in the year 2000, twenty years after northern California, Oregon, and Washington have seceded from the United States to set up a cooperative, ecological, feminist society. It is a traditional utopian novel insofar as it presents the new society through the eyes of an outsider who gradually becomes convinced of its beauty and insofar as it pays considerable attention to economic and political organization.

Marge Piercy's *Woman on the Edge of Time* concerns Connie, a poor Hispanic-American woman who is unjustly confined to a mental hospital in New York City and who is telepathically contacted from the future, a future she is then able to visit in the same way. A hundred and fifty years in the future the people of Earth live in an interlocking network of self-sufficient regions in which communitarian, ecological, and feminist ideals prevail. This future has emerged out of a struggle against multinational capital; it is a future still threatened by the remnants of the old order. The central character comes to appreciate the relation between her own situation and the struggle to create the utopian future and to preserve it against its enemies. Connie isn't saved by a happy ending, for she must live in the present. But, so the novel tells us, if we begin to fight, we may yet win the battle for the future.

Samuel Delany's *Triton* is also set some 150 years in the future in an enclosed city on a moon of Neptune. There is a minimal plot as we follow a character who, despite the freedom and economic guarantees of his society, is unhappy and whose distress questions the assumption of universal happiness portrayed in earlier utopias:

> Somewhere, in your sector or in mine, in this unit or in that one, there it is: pleasure, community, respect—all you have to do is know the kind, and how much of it, and to what extent you want it. . . . But what happens to those of us who *don't* know? What happens to those of us who have problems and don't know *why* we have the problems we do? . . . Well, what about the ones of us who only know what we *don't* like?[9]

Finally, even more than the others, Le Guin's *The Dispossessed* has reached a wide audience. Two worlds are juxtaposed, an older world that caricatures our own major socioeconomic systems, and its moon where people have emigrated to set up a model society but where hierarchy and privilege are once again emerging. By counterpoising an abusive and exploitive capitalist patriarchy with the increasing bureaucratization of the utopian experiment, the author questions the validity of that experiment itself, but the doubts of her main character are overcome in his renewed commitment to the "permanent revolution" of the new society. That the new society "had fallen short of the ideal did not, in his eyes, lessen his responsibility to it."[10]

## Differences and Similarities of Vision

Although each work begins from the conviction that sexual oppression and limits on human potential in our society will only end with a profound transformation of society, and although each work shares collective ideals, there are many differences between the societies envisaged.

There are differences between the all-women societies of Russ's *Female Man* and Charnas's *Motherlines* (where there are no men at all) and Gearhart's *Wanderground* (where men have been assigned specific and separate roles, either as antagonists or as ones who have renounced masculine ways as well as all sexual activity—the "gentles"). Paradoxically it is easier for the male reader to imagine new roles and patterns of behavior for men based on the former two books than on the latter. In the former two, the absence of men serves as a warning, and the lives and activities of women as models for all humans in a society beyond sexual hierarchy and gender. Gearhart's *Wanderground,* on the other hand, is based on the argument that there is a fundamental and essential difference between men and women: even the "gentles" cannot be trusted.[11]

There are also some differences in the degree of social homogeneity. It is very high in the small and tightly knit society in *The Wanderground,* where the Hill Women are united in a oneness with nature that is said to be specific to women; men, on the other hand, are considered to be innately violent. Other worlds are more heterogeneous, particularly those in *Ecotopia, The Female Man,* and *Triton,* where there are certain shared minimal goals but no unitary, all-embracing world-view, which typified earlier utopias. Each novel portrays societies in process, struggling to come into being or fighting to survive.

Language itself is an issue in these books. One of the recurrent themes of recent feminist analysis has been the recognition that the form of discourse is socially produced and contributes to the maintenance of the status quo. Thus a concern with the generic term *man,* for instance, the implicit equation of "people" with "male people," and the representation of women "as a secondary sex, differentiated from an implied male norm."[12]

There is also a common preoccupation with egalitarian behavior and social interaction that stresses new forms of democracy, including consensual decision making (particularly in the novels by women). This is perhaps nowhere clearer than in the scenes in most of these novels of public debate on issues involving the communities as a whole. There are alternatives to existing forms of decision making in which issues have traditionally been decided, at best, on the basis of verbal skill, parliamentary maneuver, and simple majority votes and, at worst, by autocracy and dictatorship.

The emphasis on the personal and the everyday in these novels is most apparent in their attention to the basic living unit, to the question of gender, to the division of labor, and to sexuality itself.

## Alternatives to the Nuclear Family

All of these novels recognize that the nuclear family is the basic unit for the maintenance and reproduction of patriarchal social relations in our time. There are, accordingly, a variety of collective and communal alternatives presented. The underlying social unit in *Motherlines, Woman on the Edge of Time,* and *The Female Man* is an extended family which is not necessarily based on kinship, while the more urban societies of *Ecotopia* and *Triton* include variations on the extended family as well as cooperatives and communes where people live more or less collectively depending on individual inclination, but without the equivalent of our private, single-family housing. Child rearing becomes a more collective enterprise, whether in the extended families, where there are usually more than two parents (in *Motherlines* and *Woman on the Edge of Time*), or in the community at large, particularly in *Wanderground* and *The Female Man.* To break further the hold of the nuclear family and its place in the institution of private property, children after the age of three or four are quite independent, whether as part of the larger community, or as a group of peers, as in the "child-packs" of *Motherlines* and *The Female Man.* Thus, in the organization of space itself, through the disappearance of the single-family dwelling, to the patterns of sleeping, loving, eating, and parenting, the nuclear family has been dismantled. Most of these novels show us new forms of intimate personal relationships and interaction centered on collective ideals and goals, although *Triton* and *Ecotopia* do offer a wide range of living arrangements and *The Dispossessed* hesitates between the collective impersonality of dormitories and the very strong heterosexual bonding of the main character and the women he loves.

## Sex and Gender

The second transformation depends on breaking the link between one's sex and certain kinds of behavior and abilities. Thus the novels challenge sexual stereotyping, the sexual division of labor, and in some cases the link between biological sex and social gender itself.

As early as the 1960s, science fiction was questioning the link between sex and gender, as seen in Theodore Sturgeon's *Venus Plus X* (1960) and in Ursula K. Le Guin's *The Left Hand of Darkness* (1969), which feature societies in which each individual is both male and female. The utopian features of Sturgeon's *Venus* are undermined because the combination of both male and female sexual organs in each individual is the product of surgery performed on children. Although the need for such surgery may be shocking in itself, the novel's questioning of the linkage of sex and gender is negated by the concealment of that surgery. As in the social construction of gender, human intervention is again misrepresented as a natural development.

Le Guin attempts to correct such problems when, in *The Left Hand of Darkness,* the "ambisexuality" of the Gethenians is the product of an experiment in genetic manipulation in the distant past that has now been forgotten, a change which, unlike the surgery in *Venus Plus X,* does not have to be repeated but is transmitted genetically. The relationship between sex and gender is questioned in several ways, such as in the report of a visitor to the planet:

> When you meet a Gethenian you cannot and must not do what a bisexual naturally does, which is to cast him [*sic*] in the role of Man or Woman, while adopting toward him a corresponding role dependent on your expectations of the patterned or possible interactions between persons of the same or opposite sex. Our entire pattern of socio-sexual interaction is nonexistent here. They cannot play that game. They do not see one another as men or women. This is almost impossible for our imagination to accept. What is the first question we ask about a newborn baby?[13]

But these two novels of the 1960s do not propose workable or practical (or even "utopian") solutions to the patriarchal hierarchization of people according to biological sex. They reflect instead a first step in the recognition of the problem and begin to question the naturalness of gender. The novels examined in this article go one step further and recognize that gender is socially produced. Thus it is no longer necessary to imagine a society in which everyone is physically both male and female. Instead they challenge the belief that different abilities, aptitudes, and psychological characteristics are *essentially* determined by biological differences. The one exception is Gearhart's *Wanderground,* which argues for specifically male and female natures.

These works envisage a range of solutions to questions of the sexual division of labor. Only in *Wanderground* are the possibilities for the Hill Women particularly limited because their activities are derived from a belief in a female specificity: mothering, nurturing, sharing, and a communion with nature.

In Russ's distant future in *The Female Man,* women are offered a full range of work activities, many of which involve technology and the operation of machinery. Work is not in itself necessarily satisfying, but the work week has been greatly reduced, leaving time for enjoyment in other ways. Motherhood is treasured, particularly because mothers are released from other work for several years.[14]

Following the radical feminist arguments of Shulamith Firestone in *The Dialectic of Sex* (1970), the utopia in Marge Piercy's *Woman on the Edge of Time* goes furthest in rejecting the sexual division of labor by using technology to liberate women from motherhood itself. After breaking the hierarchies of the old society, women gave up "the only power we ever had, in return for more power for everyone. The original production: the power to give birth. 'Cause as long as we were biologically enchained, we'd never be equal. And males would never be humanized to be loving and tender. So we all became mothers."[15] Of course this approach still assumes a link between biology and destiny, an assumption that is now held by only a minority of feminists. On the other hand, in this book male-female social and psychological differences are produced by the social function of reproduction, and not by innate biological differences.[16]

*Beyond Oppression and Stereotypes*

All these books, with the exception of *Wanderground,* challenge the linkage of biological sex with behavior. In *Motherlines,* however, women's activities are limited by material conditions, and some stereotypes remain in the two novels by men and in Le Guin's *The Dispossessed.* As a result it is *The Female Man* and *Woman on the Edge of Time* that offer women a full range of choices and only the latter that concretely offers this full range to men. In all but *Wanderground* men's behavior is attributed to specifically social causes.

The two novels by men do not adequately address women's experience of oppression, an issue that is central in *Woman* and in *Wanderground,* where women collectively remember the past. Several of the novels provide critiques (or caricatures) of contemporary patriarchy. The most unrelenting critique is in the present-day society of *Woman on the Edge of Time,* where the family is the locus of oppression: the central character is committed to a mental hospital by her niece's pimp (thus setting up a symbolic link between women's oppression and economic exploitation), and it is her brother who refuses to sign the papers to have her released.

By women's experience of oppression I mean the experiences of women in our society in which they are defined as wives and mothers within the family and as sexual objects outside. The dichotomy of wife and mother versus sex object is but half of a dialectic that renders men the masters, oppressors, and sexual initiators. In describing their experience of oppression, many women speak of the many forms of socially sanctioned violence. Imagination or willpower cannot suffice to change these conditions of domination—a situation in which there are rewards for those who reproduce the status quo and penalties for those who challenge it. What is required are alternatives based on a sensitivity to the present. In the context of these novels, this sensitivity might begin with the author's choice of sexual identity for the central character or, in another way, through the admission that sex and gender can still be problematic in the new society. For it is a mistake to assume that with the disappearance of patriarchal structures, "natural" patterns of sexual and social behavior will emerge spontaneously. Human consciousness, identity, and sexual desire are developed from a network of psychological and social influences that overlie and shape the instinctual and biological drives. Consequently, the imagining of an alternative future must also address the question of how to develop collectively the consciousness and identities of men and women as much as it must consider the larger social and economic structures that would make such people possible. This is not, however, to promote the manipulative behaviorist techniques of a B.F. Skinner (as in his "utopia" *Walden Two*) or of Aldous Huxley's anti-utopian *Brave New World.* Rather this is to recognize not only that sexism and heterosexism are produced and reinforced by the larger patriarchal structures that constitute our society but that they are also embedded in our own identities and unconscious patterns of behavior. And these patterns—for instance, how men relate to women—will not automatically change with the legal abolition of patriarchy. Some of these writers show their sensitivity to these questions in two complementary ways: first, by juxtaposing the old ways with the new, in a manner that makes clear that, in the present, gender is produced socially, and secondly, by creating obstacles to the main character's search for identity and meaning in a new society to remind us that the new roles and behavior will not emerge without a struggle.

'The contrasts in the treatment of this process of change are seen most strongly between *Ecotopia* and *Woman on the Edge of Time.* The former features a successful reporter from the old society who, in the fashion of much traditional utopian literature, falls in love with a woman of the new society. The reporter's discovery that male and female roles have changed and his acceptance of the new society are relatively painless. Indeed, his own sexuality and identity are reinforced by his experience of change and difference, which lead to immediately enhanced sexual experiences. On the other hand, Connie, the central character of *Woman,* is at the opposite end of the social spectrum. For her the changed sexual roles and identities of the future are deeply troubling; there is no easy transition. Connie's decision to fight back in the present results from her gradual recognition of the benefits of this alternative society for human emancipation and development, and from the related understanding of the place of the interconnected determinants of sex and class in her oppression in the present.

The inherent difficulties of a process of change are highlighted in *The Dispossessed,* but here the focus is less on the changed sexual relations and more on the resurgence of hierarchy and privilege. The utopian ideal is defined primarily through the opposition between private property and the apparatuses of the state on the one hand, and communitarian and cooperative principles on the other. Existing sexual relations of domination and subordination have apparently disappeared, but the central character, a man who is the more active and important half of a monogamous heterosexual couple, can hardly be taken as the model for other forms of personal and sexual relationships.[17]

Gender and sexual identity are the source of severe problems in Delany's *Triton,* where the unhappy hero eventually thinks he would be happier as a woman—and indeed he decides to become one. This occurs even though the tensions that patriarchy induces in many people in our society—specifically the conflicts between one's biological sex and the identity and conduct expected of that person—are much reduced in the extremely diverse, libertarian society of *Triton.* Although the technological means to change both one's sex and one's sexual orientation are available, neither his social background nor the central character's actual sex-change operation are enough to resolve his-her unhappiness. But this situation does force the reader at least to consider the relationship between sex and gender in an emancipated society, while suggesting that identity and satisfaction will not arise spontaneously even in a "utopia."

In most of these novels, then, the central character's own personal struggle includes the attempt to create an identity that is not bound to the traditional sex-linked roles in our society. Even in *Wanderground,* where there is no single hero and where there is a strong belief in women's specificity, the community of women has set out very consciously to develop new rituals that affirm both the individual's identity as a woman and as part of a collectivity. Indeed, the women-centered practices of the Hill Women do not spring up spontaneously, but have to be developed and taught. Moreover, the behavior of the women in our own society, insofar as it conforms to stereotypes, is also examined critically, particularly in the novels by women. But even in the glimpse of the submission and domination of city women in *Wanderground,* the Hill Women remind themselves, "What we are not, we each could be, and every woman is myself."[18] These sisterly critiques of the stereotyped behavior of some women call attention to the gendering process and to the violence used to enforce it, which like the patterned behavior of men, must be challenged for a society of human freedom to emerge.

*Sexuality*

Femininism has made us aware that sexuality—like gender identity—is not simply natural, but the social channeling and control of biological drives. More specifically, patriarchy has defined female sexuality almost exclusively in terms of procreation and in relation to male sexuality and male desire. The feminist challenge to male power has produced demands for an end to all forms of oppression and for women's autonomy, including control of their bodies and of their fertility, and the right to their own sexual pleasure. This means, first of all, an end to sexual harassment and coercion, but it implies as well a questioning of such patriarchal concepts as "monogamy," "promiscuity," and the dichotomy between "heterosexuality" and "homosexuality." This change involves a recognition of the fundamental validity and importance of varying forms of sexual expression and pleasure.

These works differ in their recognition of the problematic nature of the sexuality and sexual expression. *Wanderground* doesn't really mention sex at all, whereas the difficulties and doubts that surround sexuality, even in a society without a sexual hierarchy, are the central issue of Delany's *Triton.* In this society, as one character points out, humans are divided into "forty or fifty basic sexes, falling loosely into nine categories, four homophilic. . . . Homophilic means no matter who or what you like to screw, you prefer to live and have friends primarily from your own sex. The other five are heterophilic."[19]

Most of these novels portray the dual nature of sexuality—as a source of joy and pleasure on the one hand and, on the other, as a source of doubt and anxiety. The concepts of "monogamy" and "promiscuity" have lost their meaning in the extended families depicted in the novels of Charnas (*Motherlines*), Piercy (*Woman on the Edge of Time*), and Russ (*Female Man*), where sexuality and sexual pleasure are represented as joyful and strengthening facets of everyday life, although more traditional couples are part of the worlds of Callenbach (*Ecotopia*) and Le Guin. Delany's novel goes furthest in its call for a tolerance of sexual differences. Homosexuality is not only accepted in all of these societies, but in most cases is also revealed as a historically determined concept that has become meaningless in the sexually diverse societies of the future.[20]

## The Male Reader

More than just expressing abstract goals to which the reader can give intellectual assent, these seven novels speak to us on an emotional level by evoking the textures and images of the recurrent and repeatedly deferred dream of human community, fulfillment, and satisfaction, a world of human freedom filled with new experiences, pleasures, and discoveries.

The fictional society that speaks most forcefully to my own ideas and dreams is that of *Woman on the Edge of Time,* to some extent because of the uncertainty of the future, and because the issues of race and class are addressed along with that of sex. But the full utopian force of the novel flows from the many scenes of everyday life in a community of the future, scenes that strike a balance between ideas and desires, work and play, freedom and necessity, technology and the natural order, all within a community that is loving, playful, and supportive. My reactions as a reader are summed up in Connie's reaction to the sheer intensity of human relations in the community. People were laughing, arguing, crying, joking, constantly touching and caressing, reminding her of her childhood, "when every emotion seemed to find a physical outlet, when both love and punishment had been expressed directly on her skin."[21]

My principal reservation concerns the growing of embryos outside the womb—which seems an unnecessarily complicated solution to the sexual division of labor. The explanation—"So we all became mothers"—might well be taken as the motto for new roles by men. I would prefer the motto to mean that men will learn to nurture and to assume more fully caring roles rather than that women will be deprived of the experience of childbirth and that one of the great wonders of biology will be denied.

My reservations about this specific solution do not, however, extend to technology in general. Indeed, one of my major reservations concerning Gearhart's *Wanderground* is precisely its rejection of technology in building and maintaining a better society. I much prefer the integrative and more balanced attitudes of *Ecotopia, The Female Man,* and *Woman on the Edge of Time.* My second reservation about *Wanderground* is due to its cultural feminist premise of an essential difference between men and women. As I have already said, by portraying men as inferior and untrustworthy, this novel certainly excludes me as a male reader from any real acceptance of its world. (That this is probably a familiar experience for women readers of popular fiction largely populated by male heroes does not make it acceptable to me.) My reservations fade, however, when the novel creates images of an existence beyond the constraints of time and space in which life in the body is no longer separate from the world as a whole.

Although the nomadic existence of the Riding Women in *Motherlines* is not presented as a model society, it too has strong utopian overtones, particularly in the alternatives to the family and in the strong sense of community. At the same time, even as I was drawn to the energetic lives of these women, I felt reluctant to give myself over to a world so limited to, and dominated by, the rhythms and patterns of the natural order. The range of choices and opportunities seems too restricted: the harsh environment severely limits the flowering of human liberation.

At the other end of the spectrum, the Ecotopian society is one of abundance and variety. But whereas I was caught up in the rhythms and activities of the Riding Women, I was bored by the overly didactic tone of *Ecotopia,* and its guided-tour structure, and disturbed by the central character's conversion to Ecotopian ways primarily by a series of sexual experiences.

The future world of Russ's *Female Man* is also an attractive one.

Yet the utopianism of the novel lies not only in the pastoral beauty of a revitalized Earth, but in its aggressively polemical and unconventional form. This very excess, in which the representational conventions of the naturalistic mode are abandoned, expresses in a very different way a promise for the future. The rejection of the instrumental function of language and of the conventions of the genre through polemical excess undermines the authority of the reality principle and points to a realm of freedom lying beyond the realm of necessity. Unfortunately Russ reintroduces the reality principle through the very harsh measures used to enforce each individual's work obligations to society.

In general, much of the attraction of these imaginary worlds is their ability to suggest a world of meaningful activity in which competitiveness and unsatisfying work on the one hand, and the passive and programmed consumption of "leisure" on the other are replaced by the transformation of work *and* play. There are playful elements in most of these novels, but it is perhaps in the esthetic realm that the "free play of human faculties and desires"[22] can best be seen. (*Triton* presents a wonderful account of an ephemeral artistic form that moves across the boundaries of the senses.)

The utopian qualities of *Triton* flow from its basic material guarantees: anyone can do almost anything. In offering so many possibilities, in contradistinction to the other works, which were more unified around common goals and ideals, *Triton* also takes more chances. In this sense my reservations are due to the very failure arising from this range of choices: Delany chooses a central character who will not take chances and who is not happy.

Turning finally to *The Dispossessed,* I have already made it clear that it is not only the questioning of the utopian project itself that bothers me, but the setting up of a world where the struggle to survive looms so large. This scarcity would seem to have a lot to do with the rise of bureaucratism and hierarchy. Nonetheless, that world is a utopia, and for me its utopianism is most convincing in the hero's words at the end of the novel:

> "We have nothing to give you but your own freedom. We have no law but the single principle of mutual aid between individuals. We have no government but the single principle of free association. We have no states, no nations, no presidents, no premiers, no chiefs, no generals, no bosses, no bankers, no landlords, no wages, no charity, no police, no soldiers, no wars. Nor do we have much else. We are sharers, not owners. We are not prosperous. None of us is rich. None of us is powerful. If [this] is what you want, if it is the future you seek, then I tell you that you must come to it with empty hands."[23]

This has been an overview of some recent fictional attempts to imagine a qualitatively different future based on egalitarian and cooperative principles. It is my contention that there is very often a failure of vision among those of us active in the struggle for social change and an equally debilitating lack of any sense of possible alternatives on the part of those we hope to mobilize for such a transformation. To some degree, because of the very extent of the cutbacks in the social programs of the welfare state and because of the reactions against the feminist challenge to patriarchy, much of to-day's political organizing and struggle seems to be limited to single issues and to a reactive politics of fear. However important such single-issue struggles are (for day care, freedom of choice on abortion, equal pay, and so on), even when successful they are only partial solutions that will not necessarily lead to the social transformation necessary for full human emancipation and fulfillment. And because of the grim reality of the already existing socialist states, many today have accepted the dominant view that there are no alternatives to the present system. Fueled by a feminist politics of hope, these explicitly utopian works of popular fiction contradict and challenge such de-featist attitudes by eloquently proclaiming that we still do have the possibility of constructing a future of our own choosing.

Because these works place the changed lives and experiences of their characters in the foreground as much as they elaborate the structure of an alternative society that would make such new patterns of bchavior and interpersonal relations possible, these works give to me, as a man, an experience, however limited, of what an end to sexual hierarchy and domination would imply for my everyday life. Insofar as domination and exploitation are systemic, our imaginary alternatives often do not go beyond a sense of how we as individuals might change our behavior. In portraying scenes of institutionalized as well as internalized and specific acts of oppression, these novels draw attention to the social construction of gender and to the ways in which the role of individual men in women's oppression is often concealed by the purportedly "natural" institutions and practices of patriarchy. An understanding of the interdependence of larger struc-tures and discrete practices is important, not only in order to imagine the larger social forms that would make new identities and patterns of behavior possible, but expecially because, as men who may have directly or indirectly benefited from or participated in the exercise of men's power, we must realize that these new forms and patterns will not emerge spontaneously with the collectivization of society (as in the traditional socialist model) or even with the "abolition" of patriarchy. Our own identities and unconscious patterns of behavior must be examined and reshaped. This the challenge to men presented by the all-women utopias in which the solution to patriarchy is a society without men.

Contemporary feminist utopian writing has taken a small, but essential first step toward that new future by seeking to imagine full societies in their everyday workings, societies organized, as we have seen, around egalitarian and cooperative principles in which all forms of human activity are given value and in which the material conditions for freedom are available to all on equal terms. By using the existing forms of popular fiction, these writers have broken out of the narrow confines of the already converted audiences to whom many of us speak, and have attempted to imagine an alternative future based on the politics of hope.

## NOTES

[1]This is a substantially revised version of a longer article, "So We All Became Mothers," *Science-Fiction Studies 12* (1985): 156-83. For an interesting introduction to the question of both real and imaginary alternative communities, see the many essays in Rohrlich, Ruby, and Elaine Hoffman Baruch, eds., *Women in Search of Utopia: Mavericks and Mythmakers* (New York: Schocken, 1984). See also Carol Farley Kessler, ed., *Daring to Dream: Utopian Fiction by United States Women, 1836-1919* (Boston: Pandora Press, 1984.) In addition to a selection of utopian stories, this book contains a very useful introduction and an annotated bibliography of 137 book-length utopias by American women through 1980.

[2]All page references in this article are to the following editions: Ernest Callenbach, *Ecotopia* (New York: Bantam, 1982); Suzy McKee Charnas, *Motherlines* (New York: Berkeley, 1979); Samuel Delany, *Triton* (New York: Bantam, 1976); Sally Gearhart, *The Wanderground* (Watertown, Mass.: Persephone Press, 1978); Ursula K. Le Guin, *The Dispossessed* (New York: Avon, 1975); and *The Left Hand of Darkness* (New York: Ace, 1969); Marge Piercy, *Woman on the Edge of Time* (New York: Fawcett Crest Books, 1976); Joanna Russ, *The Female Man* (New York: Bantam, 1975).

[3]See Russ's "*Amor Vincit Foeminam:* The Battle of the Sexes in SF," *SFS* 7 (1980): 2-14.

[4]I have taken many of my ideas about the transformation of work from Herbert Marcuse, *Eros and Civilization* (New York: Vintage, 1955) and from the writing of André Gorz, especially his *Farewell to the Working Class* (Boston: South End, 1982). Consider, for instance, his call for the "abolition of work" in the latter:

> Thus the abolition of work does not mean the abolition of the need for effort, the desire for activity, the pleasure of creation, the need to cooperate with others and be of some use to the community. Instead, the abolition of work simply means the progressive, but never total, suppression of the need to purchase the right to live. (2)

[5]The term *homosexuality* is itself the subject of debate insofar as it connotes, for some feminists, *male* homosexuals (see Adrienne Rich, "Compulsory Heterosexuality and Lesbian Experience," in Ann Snitow, Christine Stansell, and Sharon Thompson, eds., *Powers of Desire: The Politics of Sexuality* (New York: Monthly Review Press, 1983), particularly p. 193. I use the term as a general category which embraces both gay men and lesbians, in contradistinction to the term *heterosexuality*.

[6]Russ, *op. cit.*, 211.

[7]Charnas, "A Woman Appeared," in Marlene S. Barr, ed., *Future Females: A Critical Anthology* (Bowling Green, Ohio: Bowling Green State University Popular Press, 1981), 103-8. For a similar remark on the part of Joanna Russ when asked about the absence of men in *The Female Man,* see the interview published in *Quest* 2 (1975). In her introduction to *Daring to Dream,* Carol Kessler points out that of the fourteen utopias by women published since 1970, half portray all-women societies (18).

[8]Pamela J. Annas, "New Worlds, New Words: Androgny in Feminist Science Fiction," *SFS* 5 (1978): 143-56, quotes Carolyn Heilbrun's definition of "androgyny" as "a condition under which the characteristics of the sexes and the human impulses expressed by men and women are not rigidly assigned. . . . Androgny suggests a spirit of reconciliation between the sexes; it suggests further a full range of experience open to individuals who may, as women, be aggressive, as men, tender." Annas then goes on to argue that "the center of the utopian concern of feminist writers is in modifying sex roles to allow for full human development of each individual person" (146). In her article, she discusses *Venus Plus X, The Female Man,* and the novels of Le Guin and Piercy. In the article mentioned in note 5, Adrienne Rich also addresses one possible and very mistaken assumption which sometimes arises from the term *androgny,* the "assertion that in a world of genuine equality, where men are nonoppressive and nurturing, everyone would be bisexual" (in Snitow *et al.,* 182). There would be a spectrum of sexual choices and identities in a genuine utopian society, of which "bisexuality" would be but one.

[9]Delaney, *op. cit.*, 122.

[10]Le Guin, *op. cit.*, 267.

[11]"I am not scorning any of you or your discovery, she said, 'or even your intent. My mistrust is of a deeper thing.'/Labrys spoke. 'Our maleness.'/Evona nodded" (180). For an extensive critique of "cultural feminism," see Alice Echols, "The New Feminism of Yin and Yang," in Snitow *et al.,* 439-59.

[12]Catherine Belsey, *Critical Practice* (London: Methuen, 1980), 42-3. For a discussion of these issues within the utopian context, see the articles by Barrie, Thorne, Cheris Kramarae, and Nancy Henley, "Imagining a Different World of Talk," and H. Lee Gershuny, "The Linguistic Transformation of Womanhood," both in Rohrlich and Baruch, eds., *Women in Search of Utopia: Mavericks and Mythmakers.* See also Casey Miller and Kate Swift, *The Handbook of Non-Sexist Writing* (New York: Barnes Noble, 1980); Joanna Russ, *How to Suppress Women's Writing* (Austin, Texas: University of Texas Press, 1983).

[13]*Ibid.,* 94.

[14]"Little Whileawayans are to their mothers both sulk and swank, fun and profit, pleasure and contemplation, a show of expressiveness, a slowing-down of life, an opportunity to pursue whatever interests the women have been forced to neglect previously, and the only leisure they have ever had—or will again until old age. A family of thirty persons may have as many as four mother-and-child pairs in the common nursery at one time. Food, cleanliness, and shelter are not the mother's business; Whileawayans say with a straight face that she must be free to attend to the child's 'finer spiritual need.' Then they go off and roar. The truth is they don't want to give up the leisure" (*Female Man,* 49-50).

[15]Piercy, *op. cit.,* 105.

[16]Attitudes within feminism toward motherhood have shifted radically since the 1970s. See, for instance, Adrienne Rich, "*Of Woman Born: Motherhood as Experience and Institution* (1976), and Heather Jon Maroney, "Embracing Motherhood: New Feminist Theory," *Canadian Journal of Political and Social Theory* 9 (1985): 40-64. See also Russ's critique of "technological solutions" to social problems in "SF and Technology and Mystification," *SFS* 5 (1978); 250-60, particularly p. 258—although she is objecting specifically to the surgical solution proposed in *Venus Plus X.*

[17]For a critical development of this point, see Russ's review of *The Dispossessed* in *The Magazine of Fantasy and Science Fiction* (March 1975), 41-4.

[18]Gearhart, *op. cit.,* 63.

[19]Delany, *op. cit.,* 117.

[20]"In this respect gay men and lesbians are well situated to play a special role. Already excluded from families as most of us are, we have had to create, for our survival, networks of support that do not depend on the bonds of blood or the license of the state, but that are freely chosen and nurtured. The building of an 'affectional community' must be as much a part of our political movement as are campaigns for civil rights. In this way we may prefigure the shape of personal relationships in a society grounded in equality and justice rather than exploitation and oppression, a society where autonomy and security do not preclude each other but coexist": John D'Emilio, "Capitalism and Gay Identity," in Snitow *et al.*, *Powers of Desire*, 111.

[21]Piercy, *op. cit.*, 76.

[22]Delany, *op. cit.*, 23.

[23]Le Guin, *op. cit.*, 241.

# Selected Bibliographies
# on Men and Women

There are a large number of bibliographies of women's studies, several on homosexuality, and a small number relating specifically to men. The following are a selection of some of the most recent.

August, Eugene R. *Men's Studies. (A Selected and Annotated Interdisciplinary Bibliography).* Littleton, Colorado: Libraries Unlimited, 1985.

Ballou, Patricia. *Women: A Bibliography of Bibliographies.* Boston: G.K. Hall, 1980.

Bullough, Vern L., W. Dorr Legg, Barrett W. Elcano, and James Kepner. *An Annotated Bibliography of Homosexuality,* 2 vols., New York: Garland, 1976.

Byrne, Pamela R., and Suzanne R. Ontiveros. *Women in the Third World: A Historical Bibliography.* Santa Barbara: ABC-Clio, 1986.

Gilbert, Victor F., and P.S. Tatla. *Women's Studies: A Bibliography of Dissertations, 1870-1982.* New York: B. Blackwell, 1985.

Grady, Kathleen E., Robert Brannon, and Joseph H. Pleck. *The Male Sex Role. A Selected and Annotated Bibliography.* Washington: U.S. Department of Health, Education and Welfare, 1979.

Massachusets Institute of Technology. *Men's Studies Bibliography,* 4th edn., Cambridge, Mass.: MIT Humanities Library, 1979.

McCaghy, M. Dawn. *Sexual Harassment: A Guide to Resources.* Boston: G.K. Hall, 1985.

Mehlman, T. *Annotated Guide to Women's Periodicals in the United States and Canada.* Richmond, Ind.: Earlham College, Women's Programs Office, 1984.

Parker, William. *Homosexuality: A Selected Bibliography.* Metuchen, N.J.: Scarecrow Press, 1971. First supplement, 1970-1975 (1977), second supplement, 1976-1982 (1985).

Remley, Mary L. *Women in Sport: A Guide to Information Sources.* Detroit: Gale Research, 1980.

Sahli, Nancy. *Women and Sexuality in America. A Bibliography.* Boston: G.K. Hall, 1984.

Searing, Susan E. *Introduction to Library Research in Women's Studies.* Boulder, Colorado: Westview Press, 1985.

Stineman, Esther, with C. Loeb. *Women's Studies: A Recommended Core Bibliography.* Littleton, Colorado: Libraries Unlimited, 1979.

Unesco. *Bibliographic Guide to Studies on the Status of Women: Development and Population Trends.* Paris: Bowker/Unipub/Unesco, 1983.

Weinberg, Martin S., and Alan P. Bell, eds. *Homosexuality. An Annotated Bibliography.* New York: Harper and Row, 1972.

Williamson, Jane. *New Feminist Scholarship: A Guide to Bibliographies.* Old Westbury, N.Y.: Feminist Press, 1979.

# Contributors

MICHAEL KAUFMAN teaches social and political sciences at Atkinson College, York University, Toronto and is Deputy Director of the Centre for Research on Latin America and the Caribbean at York University. He has led men's counselling workshops and has participated in various men's groups in Canada and the United States. He is author of *Jamaica Under Manley: Dilemmas of Socialism and Democracy* and lives with his spouse and their young son.

TIM CARRIGAN is a tutor in sociology at Macquarie University in Sydney, Australia. He has done research on the theoretical implications of gay liberation arguments and is working on the history of homosexual subcultures.

BOB CONNELL is a professor of sociology at Macquarie University in Sydney, Australia, and has published a number of books on politics and sociology, including *Making the Difference, Which Way is Up?* and *Society and Sexual Politics.*

RICHARD DALY is a social anthropologist specializing in Iroquoian and West Coast Native peoples. He has worked as a researcher at the Royal Ontario Museum in Toronto and currently does freelance work.

BRIAN EASLEA teaches science studies at the University of Sussex in Brighton, England, and is the author of two books about physics, *Liberation and the Aims of Science* (1973) and *Fathering the Unthinkable* (1983).

PETER FITTING is an associate professor of French at the University of Toronto with a long-time interest in utopian science.

STAN GRAY worked for eleven years at Westinghouse, where he was a shop steward and union health and safety chairman. He is now Director of the Ontario Workers Health Centre, a labor-oriented occupational health facility in Hamilton, Ontario.

GAD HOROWITZ is a professor of political science at the University of Toronto and has a private practise in psychotherapy. He is author of *Repression: Basic and Surplus Repression in Psychoanalytic Theory* and *Canadian Labour in Politics.*

BRUCE KIDD teaches physical education at the University of Toronto. A gold medalist at the 1962 Commonwealth Games and an Olympic participant, he is author of *The Death of Hockey* (with John Macfarlane), *The Political Economy of Sport, Tom Longboat, Athletes' Rights in Canada* (with Mary Eberts), and several books for children.

MICHAEL S. KIMMEL is a sociologist at Rutgers University in New Jersy and is the author of *Absolutism and its Discontents: State and Society in 17th Century France and England* and *Revolution in the Sociological Imagination* (forthcoming). He is writing a book on men's responses to feminism in the United States in the nineteenth and twentieth centuries.

GARY KINSMAN is an activist in the gay liberation and socialist movements in Toronto and is a member of the collective that publishes *Rites*, a magazine for lesbian and gay liberation. He is the author of *The Regulation of Desire*.

SEYMOUR KLEINBERG is the author of *Alienated Affections: Being Gay in America* and teaches at the Brooklyn Center of Long Island University.

JOHN LEE is a researcher in sociology at Macquarie University in Sydney, Australia, and is currently working on the historical development of homosexual subcultures in Australia.

RICHARD LEE is a professor of anthropology at the University of Toronto and is known for his work on the !Kung San of Botswana and other hunting and gathering peoples. His books include *Kalahari Hunter-gatherers, The !Kung San: Men, Women and Work in a Foraging Society,* and *Politics and History in Band Societies* (with Eleanor Leacock).

E. ANTHONY ROTUNDO teaches history and social science at Philips Academy, Andover, Massachusetts, where he shares a job with his wife. He is currently at work on a two-volume history of middle-class manhood in the United States since 1800.

CARMEN SCHIFELLITE has degrees in sociology, biology, and psychology and is finishing his doctorate at the Ontario Institute for Studies in Education at the University of Toronto.

ANDREW WERNICK teaches sociology at Trent University, Peterborough, where he is chair of the Cultural Studies Program and Master of Peter Robinson College. He is a member of the editorial board of the *Canadian Journal of Political and Social Theory* and has published many essays on social theory and mass culture.

ROBIN WOOD teaches film studies at York University and has written numerous books, including *Hitchcock Films* and *Hollywood From Vietnam to Reagan*.